The Vinland Sagas

Original Texts, Translations, and Word Lists

Translated by
Matthew Leigh Embleton

Copyright ©2025 Matthew Leigh Embleton. All rights reserved.

The Vinland Sagas

The Saga of the Greenlanders (*Old Norse*) 4
The Saga of the Greenlanders (*Old Icelandic*) 41
The Saga of Erik the Red (*Old Norse*) 77
The Saga of Erik the Red (*Old Icelandic*) 125
Word List *(Norse to English)* 175
Word List *(English to Norse)* 235

Cover: Old Norse text over an outline of Iceland. Author's design.

The original Old Icelandic and Old Norse texts are in the public domain.
These translations ©2021 Matthew Leigh Embleton
©2025 Matthew Leigh Embleton (This Edition)

Acknowledgments

I have long been fascinated by languages and history, and I am very grateful to the special people in my life who have supported and encouraged me in my work. Thank you for believing in me. You know who you are.

Introduction

The Vínland Sagas (Vínlandingasǫgur) contain two Sagas, The Saga of the Greenlanders (Grœnlendinga Saga), and The Saga of Erik the Red (Eiríks Saga Rauða) which tell the story of the Norse discovery of North America. These stories survived by oral tradition over several centuries before being written down in the 13th Century.

Old Norse is a North Germanic language spoken by inhabitants of Scandinavia from about the 7th to the 15th centuries. Old Icelandic is a variety of Old West Norse that emerged during the Norse settlement of Iceland in the second half of the 9th century.

The meaning of the word 'saga' (plural: 'sǫgur' or 'sögur') translates as 'that which is said', or more widely: a 'saying', 'statement', 'story', 'tale', or 'narrative'.

This book contains:
- The Saga of the Greenlanders (Grœnlendinga Saga) (Old Norse Version)
- The Saga of the Greenlanders (Grœnlendinga Saga) (Old Icelandic Version)
- The Saga of Erik the Red (Eiríks Saga Rauða) (Old Norse Version)
- The Saga of Erik the Red (Eiríks Saga Rauða) (Old Icelandic Version)

The texts are presented in their original Norse, with a literal word-for-word line-by-line translation, and a Modern English translation, all side-by-side. In this way, it is possible to see and feel how the Norse language worked and how it has evolved. Also included is a word list with 3,695 Norse words translated in to English, and 2,262 English words translated into Norse.

This book is designed to be of use and interest to anyone with a passion for the Old Norse or Old Icelandic language, Norse history, or languages and history in general.

The Saga of the Greenlanders (*Old Norse*)

Old Norse	Literal	English
1	1	1
Þorvaldr hét maðr, sonr Ásvalds Úlfssonar, Öxna-Þórissonar.	Thorvald was-called a-man son-of Asvald's Ulfson, Oxna-Thorison.	There was a man named Thorvald, son of Asvald, son of Ulf, son of Oxna-Thorri.
Þorvaldr ok Eiríkr inn rauði, sonr hans, fóru af Jaðri til Íslands fyrir víga sakir.	Thorvald and Erik the Red, son his, travelled from Jaeren to Iceland because-of-a killing conviction.	Thorvald and Erik the Red, his son, travelled from Jaeran to Iceland because of a conviction for a killing.
Þá var víða byggt Ísland.	Then was widely settled Iceland.	Then Iceland was widely settled.
Þeir bjuggu fyrst at Dröngum á Hornströndum.	They lived first at Drangar on Hornstrandir.	They lived first at Drangar in Hornstrandir.
Þar andaðist Þorvaldr.	There died Thorvald.	There Thorvald died.
Eiríkr fekk þá Þjóðhildar, dóttur Jörundar Úlfssonar ok Þorbjargar Knarrarbringu, er þá átti Þorbjörn inn haukdælski.	Erik married then Thjodhild, daughter-of Jorund Ulfson and Thorbjorg Knarrarbringu, who then married Thorbjorn of Haukadal.	Erik then married Thjodhild, daughter of Jorund, son of Ulf, and Thorbjorg Knarrabringu, who then married Thorbjorn of Haukadal.
Réðst Eiríkr þá norðan ok bjó á Eiríksstöðum hjá Vatnshorni.	Went Erik then northwards and lived at Eriksstadir near Vatnshorn.	Erik then went northwards and lived at Eriksstadir near Vantshorn.
Sonr Eiríks ok Þjóðhildar hét Leifr.	Son Erik's and Thjodhild's was-called Leif.	Erik and Thjodhild's son was named Leif.
Enn eftir víg Eyjólfs saurs ok Hólmgöngu-Hrafns var Eiríkr gerr brott ór Haukadal.	But after killing-of Eyolf's the-Foul and Raven-the-Dueller was Erik made away from Haukadal.	But after the killing of Eyolf the Foul and Raven the Dueller, Erik was made to leave Haukadal.
Fór hann vestr til Breiðafjarðar ok bjó í Öxney á Eiríksstöðum.	Travelled he west to Breidafjord and lived at Oxney at Eriksstadir.	He then travelled west to Breidafjord and lived at Oxney in Eriksstadir.
Hann léði Þorgesti á breiðabólstað setstokka ok náði eigi, er hann kallaði til.	He lent Thorgest to upholstery seat-posts and got-not, when he called for them.	He lent Thorgest some upholstery seat posts, and when he asked for them back, he did not get them.

The Vinland Sagas   *The Saga of the Greenlanders (Old Norse)*

Old Norse	Literal	English
Þaðan af gerðust deilur ok bardagar með þeim Þorgesti, sem segir í sögu Eiríks.	From-there of made disputes and battle between them Thorgest, as said in saga Erik's.	From then on there were disputes and battles between him and Thorgest, as told in Erik's Saga.
Styrr Þorgrímsson veitti Eiríki at málum ok Eyjólfr ór Svíney, ok synir Þorbrands ór Álftafirði ok Þorbjörn Vífilsson.	Styrr Thorgrimson supported Erik in case and Eyolf of Sviney, and sons Thorbrand of Alftafjord and Thorbjorn Vifilson.	Styrr Thorgrimson supported Erik in the matter, and Eyolf of Sviney, and Thorbrand's sons of Alftafjord, and Thorbjorn Vifilson.
En Þorgestlingum veittu synir Þórðar gellis ok Þorgeirr ór Hítardal.	But Thorgest's-sons supported sons Thord Howler and Thorgeir of Hitardal.	But Thorgest's sons were supported by Thord Howler, and Thorgeir of Hitardal.
Eiríkr varð sekr á Þórsnessþingi.	Erik was outlawed at-the Thorsnes-assembly.	Erik was outlawed at the Thorsness assembly.
Bjó Eiríkr þá skip sitt til hafs í Eiríksvági.	Prepared Erik then ship his to sea in Eriksvog.	He then prepared his ship to go to sea at Eriksvog.
En er hann var búinn, fylgðu þeir Styrr honum út um eyjar.	And when he was ready, followed they Styrr him out about the-island.	And when he was ready, Styrr followed them about the island.
Eiríkr sagði þeim, at hann ætlaði at leita lands þess, er Gunnbjörn, sonr Úlfs kráku, sá, er hann rak vestr um haf, þá er hann fann Gunnbjarnarsker.	Erik told them, that he intended to search land this, which Gunnbjorn, son-of Ulf Crow, saw, when he-was driven west at sea, when was he found Gunnbjarnarsker.	Erik told them that he intended to search for a land, which Gunnbjorn, son of Ulf Crow, saw when he was driven west at sea, when he found Gunnbjorn's Skerries.
Kveðst hann aftr mundu leita til vina sinna, ef hann fyndi landit.	Said he return would seek to friends his, if he found land.	He said he would return to seek his friends if he found land.
Eiríkr sigldi undan Snæfellsjökli.	Erik sailed from Snaefellsjokli.	Erik sailed from Snaefellsjokli.
Hann fann landit, ok kom útan at því, þar sem hann kallaði Miðjökul.	He found land, and came out of for, there which he call Midjokul.	He found land, and came out therefore, there he called Modjokul.
Sá heitir nú Bláserkr.	This is-called now Blaserkur.	This is now named Blaserkur.
Hann fór þá þaðan suðr með landinu at leita, ef þaðan væri byggjanda landit.	He went then from-there south along land to seek, if there was habitable land.	He travelled south from there along land to see if there was habitable land.

The Vinland Sagas   *The Saga of the Greenlanders (Old Norse)*

Old Norse	Literal	English
Hann var inn fyrsta vetr í Eiríksey, nær miðri inni eystri byggð.	He was the first winter in Eriksey, near-the middle of-the eastern settlement.	The first winter he was at Eriksey, near the middle of the Eastern Settlement.
Um várit eftir fór hann til Eiríksfjarðar ok tók sér þar bústað.	About spring after returned he to Eriksfjord and took he there abode.	After about spring he travelled to Eriksfjord and took he there a dwelling.
Hann fór þat sumar í ina vestri óbyggð ok gaf víða örnefni.	He returned that summer to the western settlement and gave many place-names.	He travelled that summer to the Western Settlement and gave many places names.
Hann var annan vetr í Hólmum við Hvarfsgnípu, en it þriðja sumarit fór allt norðr til Snæfells ok inn í Hrafnsfjörð.	He was second winter at Holm in Hvarfsgnipu, but the third summer went all north to Snaefell and then into Hrafnsfjord.	The second winter he was at Holm in Hvarfsgnipu, but the third summer travelled all the way north to Snaefell and then to Hrafnsfjord.
Þá kvaðst hann kominn fyrir botn Eiríksfjarðar.	Then said he coming for-the bottom-of Eriksfjord.	Then he said he came to the bottom of Eriksfjord.
Hvarf hann þá aftr ok var inn þriðja vetr í Eiríksey fyrir mynni Eiríksfjarðar.	Disappeared he then returned and was the third winter in Eriksey at the-inlet Eriksfjord.	After that he then disappeared and was for the third winter in Eriksey before the inlet Eriksfjord.
Eftir um sumarit fór hann til Íslands ok kom skipi sínu í Breiðafjörð.	After about summer went he to Iceland and came ship his into Breidafjord.	After about summer he travelled to Iceland and his ship came to Breidajord.
Hann kallaði land þat, er hann hafði fundit, Grænland, því at hann kvað þat mundu fýsa menn þangat, ef landit héti vel.	He called land that, which he had found, Greenland, because as he said they would be-attracted people there, if the-land named well.	He called the land which he had found Greenland, because as he said, it would attract people there if it was named well.
Eiríkr var á Íslandi um vetrinn, en um sumarit eftir fór hann at byggja landit.	Erik was in Iceland about winter, but about summer after went he to colonise land.	Erik was in Iceland over winter, but after around summer he travelled to settle the land.
Hann bjó í Brattahlíð í Eiríksfirði.	He dwelt at Brattahlid in Eriksfjord.	He lived at Brattahlid in Eriksfjord.
Svá segja fróðir menn, at á því sama sumri, er Eiríkr rauði fór at byggja Grænland, þá fór hálfr þriði tögr skipa ór Breiðafirði ok Borgarfirði, enn fjórtán kómust út þangat.	So say wise people, that at since same summer, that Erik the-Red went to colonise Greenland, then travelled half-of thirty-and twenty ships from Breidafjord and Borgafjord, but fourteen arrived out there.	So wise men say that after that same summer, Erik the Red travelled to settle Greenland, then half of thirty and twenty ships travelled from Breidafjord and Borgafjord, but fourteen arrived there.

The Vinland Sagas   *The Saga of the Greenlanders (Old Norse)*

Old Norse	Literal	English
Sum rak aftr, en sum týndust.	Some driven back, but some lost.	Some were driven back, but some were lost.
Þat var fimmtán vetrum fyrr en kristni var lögtekin á Íslandi.	This was fifteen winters before that Christianity was law-taken in Iceland.	This was fifteen winters before Christianity became law in Iceland.
Á því sama sumri fór útan Friðrekr biskup ok Þorvaldr Koðránsson.	Then since same summer travelled out Fridrek bishop and Thorvald Kodranson.	After that same summer travelled out Bishop Fridrek and Thorvald Kodranson.
Þessir menn námu land á Grænlandi, er þá fóru út með Eiríki: Herjólfr Herjólfsfjörð, hann bjó á Herjólfsnesi, Ketill Ketilsfjörð, Hrafn Hrafnsfjörð, Sölvi Sölvadal, Helgi Þorbrandsson Álftafjörð, Þorbjörn glóra Siglufjörð, Einarr Einarsfjörð, Hafgrímr Hafgrímsfjörð ok Vatnahverfi, Arnlaugr Arnlaugsfjörð.	These men took land on Greenland, when then travelled out with Erik: Herjolf Herjolfsfjord, he lived at Herjólfsnes, Ketil Ketilsfjord, Hrafn Hrafnsfjord, Sölvi Solvadal, Helgi Thorbrandson Alftafjord, Thorbjorn the-Sensible Siglefjord, Einar Einarsfjord, Hafgrim Hafgrimsfjord and Vatnahverfi, Arnlaug Arnlaugsfjord.	These men took land in Greenland, when they travelled out with Erik: Herjolf took Herjolfsfjord, he lived on Herjolfsnes, Ketil took Ketilsfjord, Hrafn took Hrafnsfjord, Solvi took Solvadal, Helgi Thorbrandson took Alftafjord, Hafgrim took Hafgrimsfjord and Vatnahverfi, and Arnlaug took Arnlaugsfjord.
En sumir fóru til Vestribyggðar.	But some went to Western-Settlement.	But some travelled to the Western Settlement.
2	2	2
Herjólfr var Bárðarson Herjólfssonar.	Herjolf was Bard's-son Herjolf's-son	Herjolf was Bard's son, the son of Herjolf.
Hann var frændi Ingólfs landnámamanns.	He was kinsman Ingolf's land-taking-man.	He was kinsman to Ingolf the land taking man.
Þeim Herjólfi gaf Ingólfr land á milli Vágs ok Reykjaness.	To Herjolf gave Ingolf land in between Vog and Reykjanes.	Ingolf gave to them land between Vogs and Reykjanes.
Herjólfr bjó fyrst á Drepstokki.	Herjolf lived first at Drepstokk.	Herjolf lived first at Drepstokk.
Þorgerðr hét kona hans, en Bjarni sonr þeira ok var inn efniligsti maðr.	Thorgerd was-called wife his, and Bjarni son theirs and was a promising man.	His wife was named Thorgerd and their son Bjarni was a promising man.
Hann fýstist útan þegar á unga aldri.	He desired travel already from young age.	He desired to travel out at a young age.

The Vinland Sagas — The Saga of the Greenlanders (Old Norse)

Old Norse	Literal	English
Varð honum gott bæði til fjár ok mannvirðingar, ok var sinn vetr hvárt, útan lands eða með feðr sínum.	Was he good both to wealth and man-worthiness-(respect) and was he winter either, out-of lands or with father his.	He was good in both wealth and worthiness, and in winter he was either travelling or with his father.
Brátt átti Bjarni skip í förum.	Soon had Bjarni ship to travel.	Soon Bjarni had a ship to travel.
Ok inn síðasta vetr, er hann var í Nóregi, þá brá Herjólfr til Grænlandsferðar með Eiríki ok brá búi sínu.	And the last winter, that he was in Norway, then prepared Herjolf to Greenland-voyage with Erik and prepared farm his.	And the last winter that he was in Norway, then Herjolf prepared for the voyage to Greenland with Erik and prepared his farm.
Með Herjólfi var á skipi suðreyskr maðr, kristinn, sá er orti Hafgerðingadrápu.	With Herjolf was in ship south-islander man, Christian, that who wrote sea-poem.	With Herjolf in his ship was a man from the southern islands, a Christian who wrote a sea poem.
Þar er þetta stef í:	There which this stave in:	There is this stave:
Mínar bið k at munka reyni meinalausan farar beina. Heiðis haldi hárar foldar hallar dróttinn yfir mér stalli.	My bid I that monks tester harmlessly travel assist, heath hold high folds hall master over my altar.	I ask you, monks' tester to assist my travel harmless, holding the heath's high folds hall master over my altar.
Herjólfr bjó á Herjólfsnesi.	Herjolf lived at Herjólfsnes.	Herjolf lived at Herjolfsness.
Hann var inn göfgasti maðr.	He was a respectable man.	He was a respectable man.
Eiríkr rauði bjó í Brattahlíð.	Erik the Red lived-at Brattahlid.	Erik the Red settled at Brattahlid.
Hann var þar með mestri virðingu, ok lutu allir til hans.	He was there with most worthiness, and lent all to him.	He was there given the most respect by all.
Þessi váru börn Eiríks: Leifr, Þorvaldr ok Þorsteinn, en Freydís hét dóttir hans.	These were children Erik's: Leif, Thorvald and Thorstein, but Freydis was-named daughter his.	Erik's children were: Leif, Thorvald, and Thorstein, and his daughter was named Freydis.
Hon var gift þeim manni, er Þorvarðr hét, ok bjuggu þau í Görðum, þar sem nú er biskupsstóll.	She was married to a-man who Thorvald was-named and lived they in Gardar, there where now is bishop's-seat.	She was married to a man named Thorvard, and they lived at Gardar, where the bishop's seat now is.
Hon var svarri mikill, enn Þorvarðr var lítilmenni.	She was haughty very, but Thorvald was little-man.	She was haughty, but Thorvard was not much of a man.

The Vinland Sagas   *The Saga of the Greenlanders (Old Norse)*

Old Norse	Literal	English
Var hon mjök gefin til fjár.	Was she much married to wealth.	She married him very much for this wealth.
Heiðit var fólk á Grænlandi í þann tíma.	Heathen were people in Greenland at this time.	Heathen were the people in Greenland at this time.
Þat sama sumar kom Bjarni skipi sínu á Eyrar, er faðir hans hafði brot siglt um várit.	That same summer came Bjarni ship his to Eyrar where father his had away sailed about spring.	That same summer came Bjarni's ship to Eyrar, where his father had sailed from in the spring.
Þau tíðendi þóttu Bjarna mikil ok vildi eigi bera af skipi sínu.	These tidings thought Bjarni great and willed not unload from ship his.	This news greatly affected Bjarni and he did not want to unload his ship.
Þá spurðu hásetar hans, hvat er hann bærist fyrir, en hann svarar, at hann ætlaði at halda siðvenju sinni ok þiggja at föður sínum vetrvist, "ok vil ek halda skipinu til Grænlands, ef þér vilið mér fylgð veita".	Then asked crew he what was he bearing for but he answered that he intended that to hold custom his and receive by father his winter "and will I hold ship to Greenland if you will me follow lead".	His crew asked him what he wanted to do but he answered that he wanted to keep his custom of spending the winter with his father "and I want sail to Greenland if you will follow me".
Allir kváðust hans ráðum fylgja vilja.	All said his counsel follow would.	All of them said the would follow his counsel.
Þá mælti Bjarni: "Óvitrlig mun þykkja vár ferð, þar sem engi vár hefir komit í Grænlandshaf".	Then said Bjarni: "Unwisely will seem our voyage there since none been have come to Greenland-sea".	Then Bjarni said: "Our voyage will look unwise, since none of us have sailed the Greenland sea".
Enn þó halda þeir nú í haf, þegar þeir váru búnir, ok sigldu þrjá daga, þar til er landit var vatnat, en þá tók af byrina ok lagði á norrænur ok þokur, ok vissu þeir eigi, hvert at þeir fóru, ok skipti þat mörgum dægrum.	But though held they now to sea when they were ready and sailed three days there until was land was water-taken but then took of fair-wind and lay on north-wind and fog and knew they not where that they travelled and time that many days.	But they set sail once they were ready and sailed for three days, until the land disappeared below the horizon, but then the fair wind dropped, and they were met with winds from the north and fog, and they did not know where they were travelling for many days.

The Vinland Sagas   *The Saga of the Greenlanders (Old Norse)*

Old Norse	Literal	English
Eftir þat sá þeir sól ok máttu þá deila ættir, vinda nú segl ok sigla þetta dægr, áðr þeir sá land, ok ræddu um með sér, hvat landi þetta mun vera, en Bjarni kveðst hyggja, at þat mundi eigi Grænland.	After that saw they the-sun and could then share direction, wind now sails and sailed this day before they saw land and discussed among with them what land that could be but Bjarni said thought it that could not-be Greenland.	After that they saw the sun and took their bearings, they hoisted their sails and sailed for the rest of the day before they saw land, and they discussed among themselves what land it could be, but Bjarni said that it could not be Greenland.
Þeir spyrja, hvárt hann vill sigla at þessu landi eðr eigi.	They asked whether he wished sail to this land or not.	They asked whether he wished to sail close to the land or not.
Hann svarar: "Þat er mitt ráð at sigla í nánd við landit".	"It is my advice to sail to close with land".	"I advise that we sail close to the land".
Ok svá gera þeir ok sá þat brátt, at landit var ófjöllótt ok skógi vaxit, ok smár hæðir á landinu, ok létu landit á bakborða ok létu skaut horfa á land.	And so did they and saw that soon that land was without-mountains and forests grown and small heights on land and left land on port-side and let stern turn on land.	And so they did, and saw that the land was not mountainous, but did have small hills and was covered with forests, so keeping land on their port side, they turned their sail-end landwards and angled away from the shore.
Síðan sigla þeir tvau dægr, áðr þeir sá land annat.	Afterwards sailed they two days before they saw land another.	Then they sailed for two days before they saw any more land.
Þeir spyrja, hvárt Bjarni ætlaði þat enn Grænland.	They asked if Bjarni supposed this was Greenland.	They asked Bjarni if he thought this land was Greenland.
Hann kvaðst eigi heldr ætla þette Grænland en it fyrra, "því at jöklar eru mjök miklir sagðir á Grænlandi".	He said not rather supposed this Greenland as the first "because the glaciers are very large said in Greenland"	He said that he did not think this was Greenland as the first "because there are said to be very large glaciers in Greenland".
Þeir nálguðust brátt þetta land ok sá þat vera slétt land ok viði vaxit.	They approached soon this land and saw it was flat land and woods growing.	They soon approached this land and saw that it was flat and wooded.
Þá tók af byr fyrir þeim.	Then took of fair-wind before them.	Then the wind died.
Þá ræddu hásetar þat, at þeim þótti þat ráð at taka þat land, en Bjarni vill þat eigi.	Then advised crew that to them thought that advised to take that land but Bjarni willed that not.	Then the crew advised that they put ashore, but Bjarni did not want to.

The Vinland Sagas   *The Saga of the Greenlanders (Old Norse)*

Old Norse	Literal	English
Þeir þóttust bæði þurfa við ok vatn.	They thought both needed wood and water.	They said that they needed wood and water.
At engu eruð þér því óbirgir, segir Bjarni, en þó fekk hann af því nökkut ámæli af hásetum sínum.	"In nothing are you for without-supplies" said Bjarni but though got he of for some reproach from crew his.	"There are no supplies you are lacking" said Bjarni, but he was criticised by his crew for this.
Hann bað þá vinda segl, ok svá var gert, ok settu framstafn frá landi ok sigla í haf útsynnings byr þrjú dægr ok sá þá landit it þriðja.	He bid them wind sails and so was done and set prow from land and sailing to sea south-west-wind three days and saw then land third.	He told them to hoist the sail and they did so, setting the bow away from land and sailing seawards, for three days they sailed with wind from the south west and then saw a third land.
En þat land var hátt ok fjöllótt ok jökull á.	And this land was high and mountainous and glaciers on.	And this land was high and mountainous and was capped by glaciers.
Þeir spyrja þá, ef Bjarni vildi at landi láta þar, en hann kvaðst eigi þat vilja, "því at mér lízt þetta land ógagnvænligt".	They asked then if Bjarni willed to land put there but he said not that willed "for to me appears this land uninviting".	They asked if Bjarni wished to make land here, but he said that he did not "for this land appears uninviting".
Nú lögðu þeir eigi segl sitt, halda með landinu fram ok sá, at þat var eyland, settu enn stafn við því landi ok heldu í haf inn sama byr.	Now lay they not sails these, held along land from and saw it that was island, turned yet stern with for land and held to sea the same fair-wind.	Now they did not lower the sail, but followed along the shore until they saw that it was an island, they turned the stern landwards and sailed out to sea with the same breeze.
En veðr óx í hönd, ok bað Bjarni þá svipta ok eigi sigla meira en bæði dygði vel skipi þeira ok reiða, sigldu nú fjögr dægr.	But weather grew at hand and bid Bjarni then shorten and not sail greater than both enough well ships theirs and decided, sailed now four days.	But the wind grew and Bjarni told them to lower the sail and not sail faster than the ship could manage, they sailed for four days.
Þá sá þeir land it fjórða.	Then saw they land the fourth.	Then they saw a fourth land.
Þá spurðu þeir Bjarna, hvárt hann ætlaði þetta vera Grænland, eða eigi.	Then asked they Bjarni whether he supposed this was Greenland or not.	They asked Bjarni if he thought this was Greenland or not.
Bjarni svarar: "Þetta er líkast því, er mér er sagt frá Grænlandi, ok hér munum vér at landi halda".	Bjarni answered: "This is like therefore which to-me was said from Greenland and here should we by land hold".	Bjarni answered: "This land appears to me as was was described about Greenland, and we'll head for the shore here".

Old Norse	Literal	English
Svá gera þeir ok taka land undir einhverju nesi at kveldi dags, ok var þar bátr á nesinu.	So did they and took land under some headland at evening day, and was there boat by headland.	So they did and took land under some headland in the evening of the day, and there was a boat by the headland.
En þar bjó Herjólfr, faðir Bjarna, á því nesi, ok af því hefir nesit nafn tekit ok er síðan kallat Herjólfsnes.	But there lived Herjolf, father Bjarni's, on that headland, and of because has headland name taken and was since called Herjolfsnes.	And there lived Herjolf, Bjarni's father, on that headland, and because of this the headland was taken and was since called Herjolfsnes.
Fór Bjarni nú til föður síns ok hættir nú siglingum ok er með föður sínum, meðan Herjólfr lifði, ok síðan bjó hann þar eftir föður sinn.	Went Bjarni now to father his and gave-up now sailing and was with father his, while Herjolf lived, and afterwards dwelt he there after father his.	Bjarni went now to his father and gave up his sailing, and afterwards settled he there after his father had died.

3

Þat er nú þessu næst, at Bjarni Herjólfsson kom útan af Grænlandi á fund Eiríks jarls, ok tók jarl við honum vel.	It is now this next that Bjarni Son-of-Herjolf came out of Greenland to meet Erik earl and took earl with him well.	It now happened that Bjarni Herjolfson came to Greenland to meet earl Erik, and the earl received him well.
Sagði Bjarni frá ferðum sínum, er hann hafði lönd sét, ok þótti mönnum hann verit hafa óforvitinn, er hann hafði ekki at segja af þeim löndum, ok fekk han af því nökkut ámæli.	Said Bjarni from voyages his that he had land seen and thought men he had-been having no-curiosity when he had nothing to say of these lands and got he of therefore some reproach.	Bjarni told of his voyages and that he had seen land, and people thought he had lacked curiosity when he had nothing much to say about these lands, and he received criticism for this.
Bjarni gerðist hirðmaðr jarls ok fór út til Grænlands um sumarit eftir.	Bjarni became court-man earl's and travelled out to Greenland about summer after.	Bjarni became one of the earl's followers and travelled out to Greenland the next summer.
Var nú mikil umræða um landaleitan.	Was now much talk about land-exploring.	There was now much talk of exploring these lands.
Leifr, sonr Eiríks rauða ór Brattahlíð, fór á fund Bjarna Herjólfssonar ok keypti skip at honum ok réð til háseta, svá at þeir váru hálfr fjórði tögr manna saman.	Leif son Erik's the-Red from Brattahlid travelled to meet Bjarni Herjolfsson and bought ship of his and appointed to men so that there were half fourth twenty men together.	Leif, Erik the Red's son from Brattahlid, travelled to meet Bjarni Herjolfsson and bought his ship and hired a crew of thirty five men altogether.
Leifr bað föður sinn, Eirík, at hann mundi enn fyrir vera förinni.	Leif bid father his Erik that he would still for be voyage.	Leif asked his father Erik to lead the expedition.
Eiríkr talðist heldr undan, kveðst þá vera hniginn í aldr ok kveðst minna mega við vási öllu en var.	Erik told rather away, saying then being declining in age and said less able with cold-and-wet all but was.	Erik was reluctant, saying that he was getting old and less able to cope with the cold weather as he once was.

The Vinland Sagas   *The Saga of the Greenlanders (Old Norse)*

Old Norse	Literal	English
Leifr kveðr hann enn mundu mestri heill stýra af þeim frændum.	Leif said he still would most luck steer of them kinsmen.	Leif said that he still had the most luck of all his kinsmen.
Ok þetta lét Eiríkr eftir Leifi ok ríðr heiman, þá er þeir eru at því búnir, ok var þá skammt at fara til skipsins.	And this allowed Erik after Leif and rode home then as they were to for prepared and was then short to go to ship.	Erik gave in to Leif, and they rode from home as they were ready and had a short distance to go to the ship.
Drepr hestrinn fæti, sá er Eiríkr reið, ok fell hann af baki, ok lestist fótr hans.	Failed horse's feet, that was Erik riding, and fell he from back and injured foot his.	The horse that Erik was riding stumbled, and Erik fell injuring his foot.
Þá mælti Eiríkr: "Ekki mun mér ætlat at finna lönd fleiri enn þetta, er nú byggjum vér.	Then said Erik "Not should to-me intend to find land more but this that now inhabit we.	Then Erik said "I am not intended to find any other land than the one where we now live.
Munum vér nú ekki lengr fara allir samt".	Should we now nothing longer go all together".	This will be the end of our travelling together".
Fór Eiríkr heim í Brattahlíð, en Leifr réðst til skips, ok félagar hans með honum, hálfr fjórði tögr manna.	Travelled Erik home to Brattahlid but Leif rode to ship and companions his with him, half fourth twenty men.	Erik travelled home to Brattahlid but Leif rode to the ship with his companions, thirty five men.
Þar var Suðrmaðr einn í ferð, er Tyrkir hét.	There was southern-man one on voyage was Tyrkir named.	There was a southern man on the voyage who was named Tyrkir.
Nú bjuggu þeir skip sitt ok sigldu í haf, þá er þeir váru búnir, ok fundu þá þat land fyrst, er þeir Bjarni fundu síðast.	Now prepared they ship theirs and sailed to sea then when they were ready and found then that land first which there Bjarni found last.	Now they prepared their ship and sailed to sea, then they were ready and found first land that Bjarni had found last.
Þar sigla þeir at landi, ok köstuðu akkerum ok skkutu báti ok fóru á land ok sá þar eigi gras.	There sailed they to land and cast anchor and launched boats and travelled to land and saw there not grass.	They sailed to the land, cast anchor, put out a boat and rowed ashore, and saw there was no grass.
Jöklar miklir váru allt it efra, en sem ein hella væri allt til jöklanna frá sjónum, ok sýndist þeim þat land vera gæðalaust.	Glaciers great were all the over but which a stone-slab was all to mountains from the-sea and seemed to-them that land was without-quality.	Large glaciers covered the highlands, but the land was like a stone slab from the mountains to the sea, and it seemed to them that this land was of little use.
Þá mælti Leifr: "Eigi er oss nú þat orðit um þetta land sem Bjarna, at vér hafim eigi komit á landit.	Then said Leif: "Not are we now that word about this land as Bjarna that we have not come on land.	Then Leif said: "Now we cannot have word about this land like Bjarni that we did not come on land.
Nú mun ek gefa nafn landinu, ok kalla Helluland".	Now will I give name land and call Helluland".	Now I will give the land a name and call it Helluland".
Síðan fóru þeir til skips.	Since travelled they to ship.	Afterwards they returned to the ship.

The Vinland Sagas   *The Saga of the Greenlanders (Old Norse)*

Old Norse	Literal	English
Eftir þetta sigla þeir í haf ok fundu land annat, sigla enn at landi ok kasta akkerum, skjóta síðan báti ok ganga á landit.	After that sailed they to sea and found land another, sailed yet to land and cast anchor, launched then boats and went to land.	After that they sailed to sea and found another land, sailed close to the land and cast anchor, put out a boat and went to shore.
Þat land var slétt ok skógi vaxit, ok sandar hvítir víða, þar sem þeir fóru, ok ósæbratt.	That land was flat and forest grown and sands white widely there as they travelled and unbroken-sea.	This land was flat and forested, with many white beaches, wide as they travelled and unbroken by the sea.
Þá mælti Leifr: "Af kostum skal þessu landi nafn gefa ok kalla Markland", fóru síðan ofan aftr til skips sem fljótast.	Then said Leif: "Of benefit shall this land name give and call Markland". Travelled since on back to ship as immediately.	Then Leif said: "This land shall be named by its benefit, and will be called Markland". Afterwards they travelled back to the ship immediately.
Nú sigla þeir þaðan í haf landnyrðingsveðr ok váru úti tvau dægr, áðr þeir sá land, ok sigldu at landi ok kómu at ey einni, er lá norðr af landinu, ok gengu þar upp ok sást um í góðu veðri ok fundu þat, at dögg var á grasinu, ok varð þeim þat fyrir, at þeir tóku höndum sínum í döggina ok brugðu í munn sér ok þóttust ekki jafnsætt kennt hafa sem þat var.	Now sailed they from-there to sea North-East-Wind and were out two days before they saw land and sailed to land and came to island one which lay north from land and went there up and looked about in good weather and found that to dew was on grass and were they that at-hand that they took hands theirs to dew and brought to mouths theirs and thought not as-sweet known have as that was.	Now they sailed from there to the sea with a north east wind, and sailed for two days before they saw land, they sailed towards it and came to an island that lay to the north of the land, they went up to the shore and looked about, in fine weather they found dew on the grass, that they took in their hands, and brought to their mouths, and they thought nothing was as sweet as that was.
Síðan fóru þeir til skip síns ok sigldu í sund þat, er lá milli eyjarinnar ok ness þess, er norðr gekk af landinu, stefndu í vestrætt fyrir nesit.	Since travelled they to ship theirs and sailed to strait that which lay between island and headland this was north going of land, steered at westwards before headland.	Afterwards they travelled to their ship and sailed to the strait that lay between the island and the headland that stretched out north from the land, they steered westwards around the headland.
Þar var grunnsævi mikit at fjöru sjávar, ok stóð þá uppi skip þeira, ok var þá langt til sjávar at sjá frá skipinu.	There were shallows much at tide sea and stood then up ship theirs and was then long to sea to see from ship.	There were many shallows at low tide and their ship was stranded, and then the sea was a long way out as seen by those on the ship.
En þeim var svá mikil forvitni á at fara til landsins, at þeir nenntu eigi þess at bíða, at sjór felli undir skip þeira, ok runnu til lands, þar er á ein fell ór vatni einu.	But they were so much curiosity of to travel to land, that they bothered not this to wait, by sea rising under ship theirs, and ran to land, there was on one lake from river one.	Their curiosity to travel to land was so great, that they did not bother to wait for the sea to rise under their ship, and ran aground where there was a river from a lake.

The Vinland Sagas   *The Saga of the Greenlanders (Old Norse)*

Old Norse	Literal	English
En þegar sjór fell undir skip þeira, þá tóku þeir bátinn ok reru til skipsins ok fluttu þat upp í ána, síðan í vatnit, ok köstuðu þar akkerum ok báru af skipi húðföt sín ok gerðu þar búðir, tóku þat ráð síðan at búast þar um þann vetr ok gerðu þar hús mikil.	But then sea fell under ship theirs, then took they boat and rowed to ship and floated that up into river, then into lake, and cast there anchor and brought off ship skin-cots theirs and made there booths, took they counsel then to stay there about then winter and make there houses large.	But when the sea flowed under their ship, they took the boat and rowed it to the ship, and floated up into the river, then into the lake, and cast anchor there, and brought off the ship their sleeping-sacks and built booths, they then decided to stay there for the winter and make large houses there.
Hvárki skorti þar lax í ánni né í vatninu ok stærra lax en þeir hefði fyrr sét.	Neither shortage there salmon in river nor in lake and larger salmon than they have before seen.	There was no shortage of salmon there, neither in the river nor in the lake, and larger salmon than they had seen before.
Þar var svá góðr landskostr, at því er þeim sýndist, at þar mundi engi fénaðr fóðr þurfa á vetrum.	There was so good land-benefits, in therefore as they seemed, that there would not cattle fodder need in winter.	The land was so good, that it seemed to them that cattle would not need fodder in winter.
Þar kómu engi frost á vetrum, ok lítt rénuðu þar grös.	There came no frost in winter, and little receded there grass.	There was no frost in winter, and the grass only receded a little.
Meira var þar jafndægri en á Grænlandi eða Íslandi.	More was there equal-day than on Greenland or Iceland.	The days and nights were more equal in length than in Greenland or Iceland.
Sól hafði þar eyktar stað ok dagmála stað um skammdegi.	Sun had there three-hours stood and morning stood during short-time-of-day.	The sun stood by mid morning and stood during mid afternoon, during winter and the shortest time of day.
En er þeir höfðu lokit húsgerð sinni, þá mælti Leifr við föruneyti sitt: "Nú vil ek skipta láta liði váru í tvá staði, ok vil ek kanna láta landit, ok skal helmingr liðs vera við skála heima, enn annarr helmingr skal kanna landit ok fara eigi lengra en þeir komi heim at kveldi, ok skilist eigi".	And when they had ended house-building theirs then talked Leif with companions his: "Now will I divide let company ours into two parts and will I explore let land and shall half company be with cabin home but another half shall explore land and go not further than they come home by evening and separate not".	And when they had finished their house building, Leif said to his companions: "Now I wish to have our company divided into two groups and explore the land, I wish that half the company shall be home at the cabin, and the other half shall explore the land and go no further than they can come home by evening, and no one separate".
Nú gerðu þeir svá um stund. Leifr gerði ýmisst, at hann fór með þeim eða var heima at skála.	Now did they so about awhile. Leif did either, that he travelled with them or was home at cabin.	Now they did this for a while. Leif either travelled with them or he was home at the cabin.

The Vinland Sagas   *The Saga of the Greenlanders (Old Norse)*

Old Norse	Literal	English
Leifr var mikill maðr ok sterkr, manna sköruligastr at sjá, vitr maðr ok góðr hófsmaðr um alla hluti.	Leif was great man and strong, man striking to see, wise man and good moderate-man about all things.	Leif was a great and strong man, striking in appearance, and a wise man who was moderate about all things.
4	4	4
Á einhverju kveldi bar þat til tíðenda, at manns var vant af liði þeira, ok var þat Tyrkir Suðrmaðr.	On some evening bore that to news, that man was missing of team theirs, and was that Tyrkir southern-man.	One evening came the news that a man was missing from their team, and that was Tyrkir the southerner.
Leifr kunni því stórilla, því at Tyrkir hafði lengi verit með þeim feðgum, ok elskat mjök Leif í barnæsku.	Leif knew therefore greatly, because for Tyrkir had long been with them father-and-son, and loved much Leif in childhood.	Leif was affected by this, because Tyrkir had spent many years with him and his father, and he had treated Leif very affectionately as a child.
Taldi Leifr nú mjök á hendr förunautum sínum ok bjóst til ferðar at leita hans ok tólf menn með honum.	Told Leif now much to hand people his and prepared to go to seek him and twelve men with him.	Leif told off his people and prepared to seek him with twelve men.
En er þeir váru skammt komnir frá skála, þá gekk Tyrkir í mót þeim, ok var honum vel fagnat.	But when they were short came from cabin, then going Tyrkir in meeting them, and was he well welcomed.	But when they were a short way away from the cabin, Tyrkir came towards them, and he was gladly welcomed.
Leifr fann þat brátt, at fóstra hans var skapgott.	Leif found that soon, that foster-father his was well-tempered.	Leif soon found that his foster-father was in a good mood.
Hann var brattleitr ok lauseygr, smáskitlegr í andliti, lítill vexti ok vesallegr, en íþróttamaðr á alls konar hagleik.	He was steep-looking and loose-eyed, dirty in face, little grown and poor-wretch, but excellent in all kinds-of pursuits.	He had a protruding forehead and darting eyes, with dark wrinkles in his face, he was short and frail looking, but excellent in many pursuits.
Þá mælti Leifr til hans: "Hví varstu svá seinn, fóstri minn, ok fráskili föruneytinu?"	Then said Leif to him: "Why were so late, foster mine, and separated companions?"	Then Leif said to him: "Why were you so late, foster-father, and how were you separated from your companions?".
Hann talaði þá fyrst lengi á þýzku ok skaut marga vega augunum ok gretti sik.	He talked then first long in German and shot many ways eyes and frowned himself.	He talked at length first in German with his eyes darting in many directions and frowning.
En þeir skilðu eigi, hvat er hann sagði.	But they knew not, what was he said.	The others did not know what he was saying.
Hann mælti þá á norrænu, er stund leið: "Ek var genginn eigi miklu lengra en þit. Kann ek nökkur nýnæmi at segja.	He said then in Norse, a while way: "I was going not much longer than you. Know I something new to say.	After a while, he spoke in Norse: "I had only gone a little farther than you. I know some news to tell you:

The Vinland Sagas   *The Saga of the Greenlanders (Old Norse)*

Old Norse	Literal	English
Ek fann vínvið ok vínber".	I found vines and grapes".	I found grapevines and grapes".
Mun þat satt, fóstri minn? kvað Leifr.	"Would that true, foster mine?" said Leif.	"Is this true, foster-father?" said Lef.
At vísu er þat satt, kvað hann, "því at ek var þar fæddr, er hvárki skorti vínvið né vínber".	"To know is that true", said he, "because that I was there fathered, where neither shortage vines nor grapes".	"I know this is true", said he, "because where I was brought up, there was no shortage of grapevines and grapes".
Nú sváfu þeir af þá nótt, en um morguninn mælti Leifr við háseta sína: "Nú skal hafa tvennar sýslur fram, ok skal sinn dag hvárt, lesa vínber eða höggva við ok fella mörkina, svá at þat verði farmr til skips míns". Ok þetta var ráðs tekit.	Now slept they of then night, but about morning said Leif to crew his: "Now shall have two pursuits from, and shall the day either, gather grapes or fell with and fell trees, so by that be cargo to ship mine". And that was counsel taken.	They went to sleep that night, and around morning Leif said to his crew: "No we shall have two pursuits each day, either picking grapes or cutting vines, or felling trees to make cargo for my ship". And that advice was taken.
Svá er sagt, at eftirbátr þeira var fylldr af vínberjum.	So is said, that boat theirs was filled of grapes.	So it was said that their boat was filled with grapes.
Nú var höggvinn farmr á skipit.	Now was cut-down cargo for ship.	Now they cut down wood as cargo for the ship.
Ok er várar, þá bjuggust þeir ok sigldu burt, ok gaf Leifr nafn landinu eftir landkostum ok kallaði Vínland, sigla nú síðan í haf, ok gaf þeim vel byri, þar til er þeir sá Grænland ok fjöll undir jöklum.	And when spring, then prepared they and sailed away, and gave Leif named land after land-benefits and called Vinland, sailed now since into sea, and gave them well fair-wind, there until was they saw Greenland and mountains below glaciers.	And when spring came, they made ready and sailed away, and Leif named the lanf after its features and called it Vinland, they now sailed to sea, and they were given fair wind until they saw Greenland and the mountains under glaciers.
Þá tók einn maðr til máls ok mælti við Leif: "Hví stýrir þú svá undir veðr skipinu?"	Then took one man to speak and said to Leif: "Why steer you so up-to wind the-ship?	Then one man said to Leif: "Why do you steer the ship so close to the wind?"
Leifr svarar: "Ek hygg at stjórn minni, en þó enn at fleira,	Leif answered: "I think to steering less, but though still to more,	Leif answered: "I am aware of my course, but there is more to it than that,
eðr hvat sjáið þér til tíðenda?".	or what see you to news?".	do you see anything of note?".
Þeir kváðust ekki sjá, þat er tíðindum sætti.	They said not see, that which news agreed.	They said that they did not see anything of note.
Ek veit eigi, segir Leifr, "hvárt ek sé skip eðr sker".	"I know not", said Leif, "Whether I see ship or skerry".	"I don't know", said Leif, "whether I see a ship or a rock".

The Vinland Sagas   *The Saga of the Greenlanders (Old Norse)*

Old Norse	Literal	English
Nú sjá þeir ok kváðu sker vera.	Now looked they and said skerry was.	Now they looked and said that it was a rock.
Hann sá því framar en þeir, at hann sá menn í skerinu.	He saw that from but they, that he saw men on the-skerry.	He saw so much better than them, that he could see men on the rock.
Nú vil ek, at vér beitim undir veðrit, segir Leifr, "svá at vér náim til þeira, ef menn eru þurftugir at ná várum fundi, ok er nauðsyn á at duga þeim. En með því at þeir sé eigi friðmenn, þá eigum vér allan kost undir oss, en þeir ekki undir sér".	"Now will I, that we apply up-to wind", said Leif, "So that we near to them, if men are in-need by near we meet, and is necessity to that help them. But as-well for by they so not peaceful-men, then own we all advantage behind us, but they not behind them".	"Now I wish to steer us close to the wind", said Leif, "so that we are near to them, if these men are in need of help, we must help them. But equally if they are hostile, then we have all the advantages, and they have none".
Nú sækja þeir undir skerit ok lægðu segl sitt, ok köstuðu akkeri ok skutu litlum báti öðrum, er þeir höfðu haft með sér.	Now sought they under the-skerry and lowered sails theirs, and cast anchor and launched little boat other, that they had had with them.	Now they searched about the rock, lowered their sails, cast anchor, and launched the second of their small boats that they had with them.
Þá spurði Tyrkir, hverr þar réði fyrir liði.	Then asked Tyrkir, who there leader present team.	Then Tyrkir asked who there was the leader of their company.
Sá kveðst Þórir heita, ok vera norrænn maðr at kyni.	So said Thorir called, and was north man by kin.	The man who replied said his name was Thorir, and that he was of Norwegian origin.
"Eða hvert er þitt nafn?"	"But what is your name?"	"But what is your name?"
Leifr segir til sín.	Leif said to them.	Leif told them.
Ertu sonr Eiríks rauða ór Brattahlíð? segir hann.	"Are-you son-of Erik's the-Red out-of Brattahlid?" said he.	"Are you the son of Erik the Red from Brattahlid?" he said.
Leifr kvað svá vera.	Leif said so was.	Leif said it was so.
"Nú vil ek", segir Leifr, "bjóða yðr öllum á mitt skip, ok fémunum þeim, er skipit má við taka".	"Now will I", said Leif, "Invite you all on my ship, and goods those, which ship may with take".	"Now I wish", said Leif, "to invite you all on to my ship and any goods, which the ship may carry".
Þeir þágu þann kost ok sigldu síðan til Eiríksfjarðar með þeim farmi, þar til er þeir kómu til Brattahlíðar, báru farminn af skipi.	They accepted that choice and sailed afterwards to Eriksfjord with them cargo, there to then they came to Brattahlid, brought cargo off ship.	They accepted his offer and then they sailed to Eriksfjord with their cargo, until they reached Brattahlid, where they brought the cargo off the ship.

The Saga of the Greenlanders (Old Norse)

Old Norse	Literal	English
Síðan bauð Leifr Þóri til vistar með sér ok Guðríði, konu hans, ok þremr mönnum öðrum, en fekk vistir öðrum hásetum, bæði Þóris ok sínum félögum.	Afterwards invited Leif Thorir to stay with him and Guthrid, wife his, and three men other, but got provisions other seamen, as-well Thorir and his companions.	Afterwards Leif invited Thorir to stay with him, along with Thorir's wife Gudrid, and three other men, and found provisions for the other seamen, both Thorir's and his companions.
Leifr tók fimmtán menn ór skerinu.	Leif took fifteen men from the-skerry.	Leif rescued fifteen men from the rock.
Hann var síðan kallaðr Leifr inn heppni.	He was afterwards called Leif the lucky.	After this he was called Leif the Lucky.
Leifi varð nú bæði gott til fjár ok mannvirðingar.	Leif was now both benefited to wealth and worthiness.	Leif now became very wealthy and gained much respect.
Þann vetr kom sótt mikil í lið Þóris, ok andist hann Þórir ok mikill hluti liðs hans.	That winter came sickness great among team Thorir, and died he Thorir and much part-of men his.	That winter there came a great sickness among Thorir's companions, and Thorir died along with many of his company.
Þann vetr andaðist ok Eiríkr rauði.	That winter died also Erik the-Red.	That winter Erik the Red also died.
Nú var umræða mikil um Vínlandsför Leifs, ok þótti Þorvaldi bróður hans, of óvíða kannat hafa verit landit.	Now was talk much about Vinland-voyage Leif's, and thought Thorvald brother his, about little-wide explored had been land.	There was great discussion of Leif's Vinland-voyage, and his brother Thorvald thought that the land had been little explored.
Þá mælti Leifr við Þorvald: "Þú skalt fara með skip mitt, bróðir, ef þú vill, til Vínlands, ok vil ek þó, at skipit fari áðr eftir viði þeim, er Þórir átti á skerinu".	Then said Leif to Thorvald: "You shall go with ship mine, brother, if you will, to Vinland, and will I though, that ship go return after timber that, was Thorir had on the-skerry".	Leif then said to Thorvald: "You go to Vinland, brother, if you wish, but I wish for that ship to return after the timber, that Thorir had on that rock".
Ok svá var gert.	And so was done.	And so it was done.
5	5	5
Nú bjóst Þorvaldr til þeirar ferðar með þrjá tigu manna með umráði Leifs, bróður síns.	Now prepared Thorvald to their voyage with three ten men with counsel Leif, brother his.	Now Thorvald prepared their voyage with advice from his brother Leif, with thirty companions.
Síðan bjuggu þeir skip sitt ok heldu í haf, ok er engi frásögn um ferð þeira, fyrr en þeir koma til Vínlands, til Leifsbúða, ok bjuggu þar um skip sitt ok sátu um kyrrt þann vetr ok veiddu fiska til matar sér.	After prepared they ship theirs and held to sea, and is nothing said about voyage theirs, before but they came to Vinland, to Leif's-camp, and settled there about ship theirs and sat about still they winter and caught fish for food theirs.	They made their ship ready and put to sea, and nothing is said about their voyage before they came to Vinland, to Leif's camp, and they settled their ship, and stayed in place that winter and caught fish for their food.

The Vinland Sagas   *The Saga of the Greenlanders (Old Norse)*

Old Norse	Literal	English
En um várit mælti Þorvaldr, at þeir skyldu búa skip sitt ok skyldi eftirbátr skipsins ok nökkurir menn með fara fyrir vestan landit ok kanna þar um sumarit.	But about spring said Thorvald, that they should prepare ship theirs and should boat ship's and some men with travel for western land and explore there about summer.	Then about spring Thorvald said that they should prepare their ship, and with the ship's boat some men should travel west of the land and explore there during the summer.
Þeim sýndist landit fagrt ok skógótt ok skammt milli skógar ok sjávar ok hvítir sandar.	They seemed land beautiful and wooded and short between woods and sea and white sands.	To them the land seemed beautiful and well forested, and a short distance between the woods and the sea were white sands.
Þar var eyjótt mjök ok grunnsævi mikit.	There were islands much and shallows much.	There were many islands and large stretches of shallow sea.
Þeir fundu hvergi manna vistir né dýra. *En í eyju einni vestarliga fundu þeir kornhjálm af tré.*	They found neither men food nor animals. But on island one westward found they corn-shed of wood.	The found neither sign of men nor animals. But on one of the westward islands they found a wooden corn shed.
Eigi fundu þeir fleiri mannaverk ok fóru aftr ok kómu til Leifsbúða at hausti.	Not found they more men's-work and went back and came to Leif's-camp in autumn.	They did not find any more work by human hands and came back to Leif's camp in the autumn.
En at sumri öðru fór Þorvaldr fyrir austan með kaupskipit ok it nyrðra fyrir landit. *Þá gerði at þeim veðr hvasst fyrir andnesi einu, ok rak þá þar upp, ok brutu kjölinn undan skipinu ok höfðu þar langa dvöl ok bættu skip sitt.*	But at summer the-next went Thorvald for eastward with ship and the north for land. Then was to them weather stormy before headland one, and driven then there up, and broke keel under ship and had there long dwelled and repaired ship theirs.	The next summer Thorvald journeyed eastwards with the ship and north around the land. Then they encountered stormy weather around one of the headlands, and they were driven ashore, and their keel brooke under their ship, and they stayed there a long time repairing their ship.
Þá mælti Þorvaldr við förunauta sína: "Nú vil ek, at vér reisim hér upp kjölinn á nesinu ok kallim Kjalarnes". *Ok svá gerðu þeir.*	Then said Thorvald to companions his: "Now will I, that we raise here up keel on headland and call Kjalarnes". And so did they.	Then Thorvald said to his companions: "Now I wish that we raise the keel up on the headland and call it Kjalarnes". And so they did.
Síðan sigla þeir þaðan í braut ok austr fyrir landit ok inn í fjarðarkjafta þá, er þar váru næstir, ok at höfða þeim, er þar gekk fram. *Hann var allr skógi vaxinn.*	Afterwards sailed they there to away and eastern for land and then into fjord-mouth then, which there was nearest, and to headland they, which there going from. It was all wood grown.	Afterwards they sailed away to the east of the land and then into the mouth of the next fjords, and then to a cape stretching out from there to the sea. It was covered with forest.

The Vinland Sagas   *The Saga of the Greenlanders (Old Norse)*

Old Norse	Literal	English
Þá leggja þeir fram skip sitt í lægi ok skjóta bryggjum á land, ok gengr Þorvaldr þar á land upp með alla förunauta sína.	There let they from ship theirs to lay and launched bridge to land, and went Thorvald there to land up with all companions his.	There they lay their ship and set out gangways to the land, and Thorvald and his companions went to shore.
Hann mælti þá: "Hér er fagrt, ok hér vilda ek bæ minn reisa",	He said then: "Here is beautiful, and here will I settlement mine raise",	Then he said: "It is beautiful here, and I wish to build a farm here",
ganga síðan til skips ok sjá á sandinum inn frá höfðanum þrjár hæðir, ok fóru til þangat ok sjá þar húðkeipa þrjá ok þrjá menn undir hverjum.	Went then to ship and saw on sands in from headland three heights, and went to there and saw there hide-boats three and three men under each.	Afterwards as they went back to the ship, they saw three hillocks on the beach inland from the cape, and saw three canoes with three men under each of them.
Þá skiptu þeir liði sínu ok höfðu hendr á þeim öllum, nema einn komst á burt með keip sinn.	Then divided they people theirs and had caught to they all, taken one came to away with canoe his.	They divided their forces and caught all of them, except one who escaped with his canoe.
Þeir drepa hina átta ok ganga síðan aftr á höfðann ok sjást þar um ok sjá inn í fjörðinn hæðir nökkurar, ok ætluðu þeir þat vera byggðir.	They killed the eight and went since back to headland and looked there about and saw that in fjord heights some, and supposed they that were dwellings.	They killed the other eight and afterwards went back to the cape, and they looked and saw that in some of the fjord heights, what they assumed to be settlements.
Eftir þat sló á þá höfga svá miklum, at þeir máttu eigi vöku halda, ok sofna þeir allir.	After that struck on then heaviness so much, that they may not awake keep, and slept they all.	After that they became so heavy with weariness, that they could not stay awake, and the all fell asleep.
Þá kom kall yfir þá, svá at þeir vöknuðu allir.	Then came shout over then, so that they awoke all.	Then a voice called to them, and they all awoke.
Svá segir kallit: "Vaki þú, Þorvaldr, ok allt föruneyti þitt, ef þú vill líf þitt hafa, ok far þú á skip þitt ok allir menn þínir, ok farit frá landi sem skjótast".	So said call: "Wake you, Thorvald, and all companions yours, if you will lives yours have, and go you to ship yours and all men yours, and travel from land which quickly".	The voice called: "Wake up, Thorvald, and all your companions, if you wish to save your lives, get to your ship and all your men, and leave this land as quickly as you can".
Þá fór innan eftir firðinum ótal húðkeipa, ok lögðu at þeim.	Then went within behind fjord countless hide-boats, and lay at them.	Then from within the fjord came countless canoes heading towards them.
Þorvaldr mælti þá: "Vér skulum færa út á borð vígfleka ok verjast sem bezt, en vega lítt í mót".	Thorvald said then: "We should bring out to board battle and defend as best, but fight little to against".	Then Thorvald said: "We should bring out breastworks along the sides of the ship and defend as best we can, but fight back as little as we can".

21

The Vinland Sagas   *The Saga of the Greenlanders (Old Norse)*

Old Norse	Literal	English
Svá gera þeir, en Skrælingar skutu á þá um stund, en flýja síðan burt sem ákafast, hverr sem mátti.	So did they, but Skraelings shot towards then about awhile, but fled afterwards away as fast, each as may.	So they did, but the Skraelings shot at them for a while, they fled as rapidly as they could.
Þá spurði Þorvaldr menn sína, ef þeir væri nökkut sárir.	Then asked Thorvald men his, if they had any wounds.	Then Thorvald asked his men if any of them had been wounded.
Þeir kváðust eigi sárir vera.	They said not wounded were.	They said that they were not wounded.
"Ek hefi fengit sár undir hendi", segir hann, "ok fló ör milli skipborðsins ok skjaldarins undir hönd mér, ok er hér örin, en mun mik þetta til bana leiða.	"I have caught wound under arm", said he, "And flew arrow between ship's-berth and shield under arm to-me, and is here arrow, then should me this to death lead.	"I have been wounded under my arm", he said, "and an arrow flew between the ship's berth and the shield into my armpit, and this shall lead to my death.
Nú ræð ek, at þér búið ferð yðra sem fljótast aftr á leið, en þér skuluð færa mik á höfða þann, er mér þótti byggiligast vera.	Now advise I, to you prepare travel depart as quickly return to journey, but you should bring me to headland that, which me thinks dwelling shall-be.	Now I advise you to prepare for your return journey as quickly as possible, but take me to that cape that I thought would make a good farm.
Má þat vera, at mér hafi satt á munn komit, at ek muni þar búa á um stund.	May that be, by me have true to mouth come, that I should there dwell on for awhile.	Maybe the words I spoke shall prove true, that I shall dwell there for awhile.
Þar skuluð þér mik grafa ok setja krossa at höfði mér ok at fótum, ok kallið þat Krossanes jafnan síðan".	There should you me engrave and set cross at head mine and at feet, and call that Krossanes ever after".	There you should bury me and put a cross at my head and feet, and call that Krossanes ever after".
Grænland var þá kristnat, en þó andaðist Eiríkr rauði fyrir kristni.	Greenland was then Christian, but though died Erik the-Red before Christianity.	Greenland was then Christian, but Erik died before the conversion to Christianity.
Nú andaðist Þorvaldr, en þeir gerðu allt eftir því, sem hann hafði mælt, ok fóru síðan ok hittu þar förunauta sína, ok sögðu hvárir öðrum slík tíðendi sem vissu ok bjuggu þar þann vetr ok fengu sér vínber ok vínvið til skipsins.	Now died Thorvald, but they did all after according, which he had said, and went since and met their companions theirs, and said each other such tidings which knew and dwelt there that winter and gathered they grapes and vines to ship.	Now Thorvald died, and they did everything as he had said, and afterwards they went to meet their companions, and each group told its news to the others, and they stayed there that winter and gathered grapes and vines in their ship.
Nú búast þeir þaðan um várit eftir til Grænlands ok kómu skipi sínu í Eiríksfjörð ok kunnu Leifi at segja mikil tíðendi.	Now prepared they there about spring after to Greenland and came ship theirs in Eriksfjord and known Leif that said much tidings.	Now they prepared their ship about spring to return to Greenland, and their ship came in to Eriksfjord and had much news to tell Leif.

The Vinland Sagas   *The Saga of the Greenlanders (Old Norse)*

Old Norse	Literal	English
Þat hafði gerzt til tíðenda meðan á Grænlandi, at Þorsteinn í Eiríksfirði hafði kvángazt ok fengit Guðríðar Þorbjarnardóttur, er átt hafði Þórir Austmaðr, er fyrr var frá sagt.	It had made to news meanwhile to Greenland, that Thorstein in Eriksfjord had married and married Guthrid Thorbjarnardottur, who had married Thorir Easterner, as before was from said.	Among the news meanwhile in Greenland was that Thorstein in Eriksfjord had married Gudrid Thorbjornadottir, who had previously been married to Thorir the Easterner who was spoken of earlier.
Nú fýstist Þorsteinn Eiríksson at fara til Vínlands eftir líki Þorvalds, bróður síns, ok bjó skip it sama, ok valði hann lið at afli ok vexti ok hafði með sér hálfan þriðja tög manna ok Guðríði, konu sína, ok sigla í haf, þegar þau eru búin, ok ór landsýn.	Now desired Thorstein Eriksson to travel to Vinland after body Thorvald's, brother his, and prepared ship the same, and chose he team in strength and well-built and had with him half third twenty men and Guthrid, wife his, and sailed to sea, then they were ready, and out-of land-sight.	Now Thorstein Eriksson wished to travel to Vinland and retrieve the body of his brother Thorvald, and made the same ship ready, and he chose his company for their strength and size, and had with him twenty five men and his wife Gudrid, and when they were ready the sailed to sea, and out of sight of land.
Þau velkði úti allt sumarit, ok vissu eigi, hvar þau fóru.	They drove about all summer, and knew not, where they went.	They were driven about all summer, and they did not know where they went.
Ok er vika var af vetri, þá tóku þeir land í Lýsufirði á Grænlandi í inni vestri byggð.	And when week was of winter, then took they land in Lysufjord in Greenland in the western settlement.	And when the first week of winter had passed, they made land in Lysufjord, in the Western Settlement of Greenland.
Þorsteinn leitaði þeim um vistir ok fekk vistir öllum hásetum sínum. *En hann var vistlauss ok kona hans.* *Nú váru þau eftir at skipi tvau nökkurar nætr.* *Þá var enn ung kristni á Grænlandi.*	Thorstein sought them about shelter and got lodging all crew his. But he was without-lodging and wife his. Now were they remained in ship two some nights. Then was yet young Christianity in Greenland.	Thorstein found them shelter and got lodgings for all of his crew. But he and his wife were without lodgings. Now they remained on the ship for several nights. Then Christianity was still young in Greenland.
Þat var einn dag, at menn kómu at tjaldi þeira snemma. *Sá spurði, er fyrir þeim var, hvat manna væri í tjaldinu.*	It was one day, that people came by tent theirs early. So asked, who present they were, what men were in tent.	One day some men came early to their tent. The asked what men were in the tent.
Þorsteinn svarar: "Tveir menn", segir hann, "eða hverr spyrr at?"	Thorstein answered: "Two people", said he, "But who asks to?"	Thorstein answered: "Two people", he said, "but who is asking?".

Old Norse	Literal	English
"Þorsteinn heiti ek, ok em ek kallaðr Þorsteinn svartr. En þat er erendi mitt hingat, at ek vil bjóða ykkr báðum hjónunum til vistar til mín".	"Thorstein called I, and am I called Thorstein the-Black. But that is errand mine here, that I will bid you both couple to lodging to mine".	"I am called Thorstein, Thorstein the Black. My reason for coming here is to invite you both to stay with me".
Þorsteinn kveðst vilja hafa umræði konu sinnar, en hon bað hann ráða, ok nú játar hann þessu.	Thorstein said will have discussion wife his, but she bid he decide, and now accepted he this.	Thorstein said he wished to discuss this with his wife, but she asked him to decide, and he now accepted.
"Þá mun ek koma eftir ykkur á morgin með eyki, því at skortir ekki til at veita ykkr vist, en fásinni er mikit með mér at vera, því at tvau erum vit þar hjón, því at ek em einþykkr mjök".	"Then should I come back to-you in morning with animals, for by shortage not to by supply you provisions, but remote is very with me by being, for that two we-are with there couple, because that I am solitary much".	"Then I shall come back to you in the morning with oxen, I have no shortage of supplies for you, but it is remote being here with me, because there are only two of us, my wife and I, and I am very much a solitary man.
Annan sið hefi ek ok en þér hafið, ok ætla ek þann þó betra, er þér hafið.	Another tradition have I and than you have, and suppose I that yet better, is you have".	Also I have another faith than you, but I suspect yours is the better of the two".
Nú kom hann eftir þeim um morgininn með eyki, ok fóru þau með Þorsteini svarta til vistar, ok veitti hann þeim vel.	Now came he after them about morning with animals, and went they with Thorstein the-Black to lodge, and supported he them well.	Now he came back to them around morning with oxen, and they went to stay with Thorstein the Black, and he provided for them generously.
Guðríðr var skörulig kona at sjá ok vitr kona ok kunni vel at vera með ókunnum mönnum.	Guthrid was strong woman to see and wise woman and knew well at being with unknown people.	Gudrid was a strong woman, of striking appearance, and a wise woman who knew how to behave among strangers.
Þat var snemma vetrar, at sótt kom í lið Þorsteins Eiríkssonar, ok önduðust þar margir förunautar hans.	That was early winter, that sickness came to companions Thorstein's Eriksson, and died there many companions his.	It was early that winter that sickness came to Thorstein Eriksson's companions, and many of them died there.
Þorsteinn bað gera kistur at líkum þeira, er önduðust, ok færa til skips ok búa þar um, "því at ek vil láta flytja til Eiríksfjarðar at sumri öll líkin".	Thorstein asked made coffins for bodies theirs, who died, and brought to ship and laid there about, "For that I will lay carry to Eriksfjord in summer all bodies".	Thorstein asked that coffins be made for their bodies who had died, and brought back to the ship and laid there, "For I will carry all of them to Eriksfjord in the summer".

The Vinland Sagas   *The Saga of the Greenlanders (Old Norse)*

Old Norse	Literal	English
Nú er þess skammt at bíða, at sótt kemr í hýbýli Þorsteins, ok tók kona hans sótt fyrst, er hét Grímhildr.	Now was this short to wait, that sickness came into dwelling Thorstein's, and took wife his sickness first, who called Grimhild.	It was not long until the sickness came to Thorstein the Black's house, and his wife Grimhild was the first to fall ill.
Hon var ákafliga mikil ok sterk sem karlar, en þó kom sóttin henni undir.	She was very large and strong as men, but yet came sickness her under.	She was a very large woman, strong as a man, yet she bowed to the sickness.
Ok brátt eftir þat tók sóttina Þorsteinn Eiríksson, ok lágu þau bæði senn, ok andaðist Grímhildr, kona Þorsteins svarta.	And soon after that took sickness Thorstein Eriksson, and lay they both same, and died Grimhild, wife Thorstein the-Black's.	And soon after that Thorstein Eriksson was stricken, and both of them laid there, and Grimhild, the wife of Thorstein the Black died.
En er hon var dauð, þá gekk Þorsteinn fram ór stofunni eftir fjöl at leggja á líkit.	But when she was dead, then went Thorstein from out room after plank to lay on body.	And when she had died, Thorstein the Black went from the main room to look for a plank to lay her body on.
Guðríðr mælti þá: "Vertu litla hríð á brott, Þorsteinn minn", segir hon. *Hann kvað svá vera skyldu.*	Guthrid said then: "Be little time to away, Thorstein mine", said she. He said so be should.	Gudrid then spoke: "Don't be away long, dear Thorstein" she said. He said so it would be.
Þá mælti Þorsteinn Eiríksson: "Með undarligum hætti er nú um húsfreyju vára, því at nú örglast hon upp við ölnboga ok þokar fótum sínum frá stokki ok þreifar til skúa sinna".	Then said Thorstein Eriksson: "With strange way is now about housewife going, for that now rises she up with elbows and stretches feet hers from bed and feels for shoes hers".	Then Thorstein Eriksson said: "Strange are the actions of the mistress of the house now, she's struggling to raise herself up on her elbows, and stretches her feet from the bed and feels for her shoes".
Ok í því kom Þorsteinn bóndi inn, ok lagðist Grímhildr niðr í því, ok brakaði þá í hverju tré í stofunni.	And in for came Thorstein farmer the, and lay Grimhild down in for, and creaked then in each beam in room.	And in came Thorstein the farmer, and Grimhild fell back down, and every beam in the room creaked.
Nú gerir Þorsteinn kistu at líki Grímhildr ok færði í brott ok bjó um. *Hann var bæði mikill maðr ok sterkr, ok þurfti hann þess alls, áðr hann kom henni burt af bænum.*	Now made Thorstein coffin for body Grimhild's and took it out and dwelling about. He was both large man and strong, and needed he this all, before he came her away out-of dwelling.	Thorstein then made a coffin for Grimhild's body and took it away from the house. He was a large and strong man, and he needed all his strenngth to carry her out of the house.
Nú elnaði sóttin Þorsteini Eiríkssyni, ok andaðist hann. *Guðríðr, kona hans, kunni því lítt.*	Now attacked sickness Thorstein Eriksson, and died he. Guthrid, wife his, knew therefore little.	Now the sickness attacked Thorstein Eriksson, and he died. Gudrid, his wife, was overtaken with grief and knew little else.

The Vinland Sagas   *The Saga of the Greenlanders (Old Norse)*

Old Norse	Literal	English
Þá váru þau öll í stofunni.	Then were they all in room.	All of them were in the main room.
Guðríðr hafði setit á stóli frammi fyrir bekknum, er hann hafði legit, Þorsteinn, bóndi hennar.	Guthrid had sat on stool from before bench, which he had laid, Thorstein, husband hers.	Gudrid sat on a stool in front of the bench where her husband Thorstein had lain.
Þá tók Þorsteinn bóndi Guðríði af stólinum í fang sér ok settist í annan bekkinn með hana gegnt líki Þorsteins ok talði um fyrir henni marga vega ok huggaði hana ok hét henni því, at hann mundi fara með henni til Eiríksfjarðar með líki Þorsteins, bónda hennar, ok förunauta hans.	Then took Thorstein the-farmer Guthrid from stool into grasp his and sat on another bench with he opposite body Thorstein's and talked about before her many ways and comforted he and called her therefore, that he would go with her to Eriksfjord with body Thorstein's, husband hers, and companions his.	Thorstein the farmer then took Gudrid from the stool into his arms and sat with her on the bench across from her husband Thorstein's corpse and said many comforting things, consoling her and promising her that he would take her to Eriksfjord with her husband Thorstein's body, and those of his companions.
Ok svá skal ek taka hingat hjón fleiri, segir hann, "þér til hugganar ok skemmtanar".	"And so shall I take there couple more", said he, "You to comfort and entertain".	"And we'll invite other people to stay here", he said, "to provide you with solace and companionship".
Hon þakkaði honum.	She thanked him.	She thanked him.
Þorsteinn Eiríksson settist þá upp ok mælti: "Hvar er Guðríðr?"	Thorstein Eriksson sat then up and said: "Where is Guthrid?"	Thorstein Eriksson then sat up and said: "Where is Gudrid?"
Þrjá tíma mælti hann þetta, en hon þagði.	Three times said he this, but she silent.	Three times he said this, but she remained silent.
Þá mælti hon við Þorstein bónda: "Hvárt skal ek svör veita hans máli eða eigi?"	Then said she to Thorstein the-farmer: "However shall I answer know his speech or not?"	Then she said to Thorstein the farmer: "Shall I answer him or not?",
Hann bað hana eigi svara.	He bid she not answer.	He told her not to answer.
Þá gekk Þorsteinn bóndi yfir gólfit ok settist á stólinn, en Guðríðr sat í knjám honum.	Then went Thorstein the-farmer over floor and sat on stool, but Guthrid sat on knees his.	Thorstein the farmer then crossed the floor and sat on the stool, and Gudrid on his knee.
Ok þá mælti Þorsteinn bóndi: "Hvat viltu, nafni?" segir hann.	And then said Thorstein the-farmer "What will-you, namesake?" said he.	Then Thorstein the farmer spoke: "What is it that you want, namesake?", he said.

The Vinland Sagas   *The Saga of the Greenlanders (Old Norse)*

Old Norse	Literal	English
Hann svarar, er stund leið: "Mér er annt til þess, at segja Guðríði forlög sín, til þess at hon kunni þá betr andláti mínu, því at ek em kominn til góðra hvíldastaða.	He answered, at time way: "I who wish to this, to say Guthrid fortune hers, to this by she could then better death mine, for that I am come to good resting-place.	He answered after a short while: "I want to tell Gudrid her fate, to make it easier for her to deal with my death, for I have gone to a good resting place.
En þat er þér at segja, Guðríðr, at þú munt gift vera íslenzkum manni, ok munu langar vera samfarir ykkrar, ok margt manna mun frá ykkr koma, þroskasamt, bjart ok ágætt, sætt ok ilmat vel.	But this is you to say, Guthrid, that you shall married be Icelander man, and shall long be together you, and many people shall from you come, promising, bright and fine, settled and favoured well.	I say this to you, Gudrid, that you shall marry an Icelander, and you will long be together, and you shall have many descendants, promisinig, bright, and fine, sweet and well favoured.
Munuð þit fara af Grænlandi til Nóregs ok þaðan til Íslands ok gera bú á Íslandi.	Shall you travel from Greenland to Norway and from-there to Iceland and make settlement on Iceland.	You will travel from Greenland to Norway, and from there to Iceland, and settle on Iceland.
Þar munuð þit lengi búa, ok muntu honum lengr lifa.	There shall you long live, and shall him longer live.	There you will live a long time, longer than your husband.
Þú munt útan fara ok ganga suðr ok koma út aftr til Íslands til bús þíns, ok þá mun þar kirkja reist vera, ok muntu þar vera ok taka nunnuvígslu, ok þar muntu andast".	You shall out travel and go south and come from return to Iceland to home yours, and then shall there church raised be, and shall there be and take nun's-vows, and there shall die".	You will travel and go south, and return to Iceland to your farm, and there a church will be raised, and there you will take a nun's vows, and there you will die".
Ok þá hnígr Þorsteinn aftr, ok var búit um lík hans ok fært til skips.	And then fell Thorstein back, and was prepared about body his and taken to ship.	And then Thorstein Eriksson fell back, and his corpse was prepared and taken to the ship.
Þorsteinn bóndi efndi vel við Guðríði allt þat, er hann hafði heitit. *Hann seldi um várit jörð sína ok kvikfé ok fór til skips með Guðríði með allt sitt, bjó skipit ok fekk menn til ok fór síðan til Eiríksfjarðar.* *Váru nú líkin jörðuð at kirkju.*	Thorstein the-farmer kept well with Guthrid all that, which he had promised. He sold about spring land his and livestock and went to ship with Guthrid with all his, prepared ship and got men to and went then to Eriksfjord. Were now bodies buried by church.	Thorstein the farmer kept all his promises to Gudrid. In the spring he sold his land and livestock, and went to the ship with all his posessions, prepared the ship, hired a crew, and sailed to Eriksfjord. The bodies were now buried by a church.
Guðríðr fór til Leifs í Brattahlíð, en Þorsteinn svarti gerði bú í Eiríksfirði ok bjó þar, meðan hann lifði, ok þótti vera inn vaskasti maðr.	Guthrid travelled to Leif in Brattahlid, but Thorstein the-Black made dwelling at Eriksfjord and dwelt there, meantime he lived, and thought was he capable man.	Gudrid travlelled to Leif in Brattahlid, and Thorstein the Black built a farm in Eriksfjord and settled there as long as he lived, and he was thought of as a most capable man.

7   7   7

The Vinland Sagas   *The Saga of the Greenlanders (Old Norse)*

Old Norse	Literal	English
Þat sama sumar kom skip af Nóregi til Grænlands.	That same summer came ship from Norway to Greenland.	That same summer a ship came from Norway and arrived in Greenland.
Sá maðr hét Þorfinnr karlsefni, er því skipi stýrði.	The man called Thorfin Karlsefni, who for ship steered.	The captain of the ship was named Thorfin Karlsefni.
Hann var sonr Þórðar hesthöfða Snorrasonar, Þórðarsonar frá Höfða.	He was son-of Thord Horse-Head Snorrason, Thordarson from Hofdi.	He was the son of Thord Horse-Head, the son of Snorri Thordarson of Hofdi.
Þorfinnr karlsefni var stórauðigr at fé, ok var um vetrinn í Brattahlíð með Leifi Eiríkssyni. Brátt felldi hann hug til Guðríðar ok bað hennar, en hon veik til Leifs svörum fyrir sik.	Thorfin Karlsefni was wealthy in cattle, and was about winter in Brattahlid with Leif Eriksson. Soon fell he thoughts to Guthrid and asked her, but she referred to Leif's answer to him.	Thorfin Karlsefni was wealth in cattle, and he spent the winter in Brattahlid with Leif Eriksson. He was soon attracted to Gudrid and asked her to marry him, but she referred him to Leif for his answer.
Síðan var hon honum föstnuð ok gert brúðlaup þeira á þeim vetri.	Afterwards was she to-him betrothed and was wedding theirs in that winter.	Afterwards she was engaged to him and their wedding was that winter.
In sama var umræða á Vínlandsför sem fyrr, ok fýstu menn Karlsefni mjök þeirar ferðar, bæði Guðríðr ok aðrir menn.	The same was discussed to Vinland-voyage as before, and urged people Karlsefni much there to-journey, both Guthrid and other people.	The discussion of a voyage to Vinland continued as before, and people urged Karlsefni to make the journey, both Gudrid and others.
Nú var ráðin ferð hans, ok réð hann sér skipverja sex tigu karla ok konur fimm.	Now was agreed travel his, and hired he the crew six ten men and women five.	Now he was decided to travel, he hired a crew of sixty men and five women.
Þann máldaga gerðu þeir Karlsefni ok hásetar hans, at jöfnum höndum skyldi þeir hafa allt þat, er þeir fengi til gæða.	Then agreed was they Karlsefni and crew his, that even handed should they have all that, which they get to quality.	Then Karlsefni and his crew agreed that all goods they obtained would be divided equally among them.
Þeir höfðu með sér allskonar fénað, því at þeir ætluðu at byggja landit, ef þeir mætti þat.	They have with them all-kinds livestock, for that they intended to settle land, if they may that.	They had with them all kinds of livestock, for they intended to settle the land if they could.
Karlsefni bað Leif húsa á Vínlandi, en hann kveðst ljá mundu húsin, en gefa eigi.	Karlsefni asked Leif houses in Vinland, but he said loan would houses, but give not.	Karlsefni asked Leif for his houses in Vinland, and Leif said he would lend them, but not give them to him.
Síðan heldu þeir í haf skipinu ok kómu til Leifsbúða með heilu ok höldnu ok báru þar upp húðföt sín.	Then held they to sea ship and came to Leif's-camp with whole and safe and carried there up skin-cots theirs.	Then they put the ship to sea and all arrived at Leif's camp safely and unloaded their sleeping-sacks.

The Vinland Sagas   *The Saga of the Greenlanders (Old Norse)*

Old Norse	Literal	English
Þeim bar brátt í hendr mikil föng ok góð, því at reyðr var þar upp rekin, bæði mikil ok góð, fóru til síðan ok skáru hvalinn, skorti þá eigi mat.	They bore soon to hand much provisions and good, for a rorqual was there up driven, both large and good, went to then and cut whale, shortage then not food.	They soon had plenty of good provisions, since a large and fine rorqual was driven up to shore, they had no shortage of food.
Skorti þá eigi mat.	Shortage then not food.	They had no shortage of food.
Fénaðr gekk þar á land upp, en þat var brátt, at graðfé varð úrigt ok gerði mikit um sik.	Cattle went there to land up, but that was soon, the cattle were irritable and made greatly about themselves.	The livestock went inland, but the males were soon irritable and hard to handle.
Þeir höfðu haft með sér griðung einn.	They had had with them bull one.	They had with them a bull.
Karlsefni lét fella viðu ok telgja til skips síns ok lagði viðinn á bjarg eitt til þurrkunar.	Karlsefni let fell wood and hewn to ships theirs and lay trees on rock along to dry.	Karlsefni had trees felled and hewn for their ships, and lay the timber on a rock to dry.
Þeir höfðu öll gæði af landkostum, þeim er þar váru, bæði af vínberjum ok alls konar veiðum ok gæðum.	They had all quality of land-benefits, they which there were, both of grapes and all kinds fish and quality.	They had all kinds of benefit from the land, which included grapes, all kinds of fish and game, and other quality things.
Eftir þann vetr inn fyrsta kom sumar.	After that winter the first came summer.	After the first winter passed and summer came,
Þá urðu þeir varir við Skrælinga, ok fór þar ór skógi fram mikill flokkr manna.	Then became they aware with Skraelings, and went there out woods from large group men.	They became aware of the Skraelings, a large group of men came out of the woods.
Þar var nær nautfé þeira, en graðungr tók at belja ok gjalla ákafliga hátt.	There was near cattle there, but bull took to bellowing and snorting very loudly.	There cattle were near, and the bull took to bellowing and snorting very loudly.
En þat hræddust Skrælingar ok lögðu undan með byrðar sínar, en þat var grávara ok safali ok alls konar skinnavara, ok snúa til bæjar Karlsefnis ok vildu þar inn í húsin, en Karlsefni lét verja dyrrnar.	But that frightened Skraelings and laid away with burdens theirs, but they were grey-skins and sables and all kinds furs, and turned towards farm Karlsefni's and willed there the into house, but Karlsefni laid protection door.	Then this frightened the Skraelings and they ran away with their burdens, which included grey skins, sables, and all kinds of fur, they turned towards Karlsefni's farm and wanted to get into the house, but Karlsefni had protected the door.
Hvárigir skilðu annars mál.	Neither knew others' language.	Neither knew the others' language.
Þá tóku Skrælingar ofan bagga sína ok leystu ok buðu þeim ok vildu vápn helzt fyrir, en Karlsefni bannaði þeim at selja vápnin.	Then took Skraelings off bags theirs and loosened and offered they and willed weapons preferably for, but Karlsefni banned they to sell weapons.	Then the Skraelings took off their bags and opened them, offering their goods, preferably in exchange for weapons, but Karlsefni forbade them to trade weapons.

The Vinland Sagas — *The Saga of the Greenlanders (Old Norse)*

Old Norse	Literal	English
Ok nú leitar hann ráðs með þeim hætti, at hann bað konur bera út búnyt at þeim, ok þegar er þeir sá búnyt, þá vildu þeir kaupa þat, en ekki annat.	And now sought he solution with them to-stop, that he asked women bring out milk-products by them, and then when they saw milk-products, then willed they buy that, and nothing else.	And now he sought a solution to this, he asked the women to bring out milk-products, and when they saw these milk-products, they wanted to buy that and nothing else.
Nú var sú kaupför Skrælinga, at þeir báru sinn varning í brott í mögum sínum, en Karlsefni ok förunautar hans höfðu eftir bagga þeira ok skinnvöru.	Now were their trading-with Skraelings, by them bearing their goods in away in stomachs theirs, but Karlsefni and companions his had after bags theirs and skin-wares.	The trading with the Skraelings resulted in them carrying away their purchases in their stomachs, leaving their packs and skins with Karlsefni.
Fóru þeir við svá búit í burt.	Went they with so settlement to away.	When this was done, they went away.
Nú er frá því at segja, at Karlsefni lætr gera skíðgarð rammligan um bæ sinn, ok bjuggust þar um.	Now was from therefore to say, that Karlsefni laid made fence strong about farm theirs, and prepared there about.	Now from this is to be told, that Karlsefni had a strong fence made around their farm to be prepared.
Í þann tíma fæddi Guðríðr sveinbarn, kona Karlsefnis, ok hét sá sveinn Snorri.	In that time bore Guthrid baby-boy, wife Karlsefni's, and called the boy Snorri.	At this time Karlsefni's wife Gudrid gave birth to a baby boy who was named Snorri.
Á öndverðum öðrum vetri þá kómu Skrælingar til móts við þá ok váru miklu fleiri en fyrr ok höfðu slíkan varnað sem fyrr.	The beginning next winter then came Skraelings to meet with then and were much more than before and had such wares as before.	At the beginning of the next winter the Skraelings came to meet with them in much greater numbers than before.
Þá mælti Karlsefni við konur: "Nú skuluð þér bera út slíkan mat sem fyrr var rífastr, en ekki annat".	Then said Karlsefni to women: "Now should you bring out such food as before was demanded, but nothing else".	Karlsefni then spoke to the women: "Now you should bring out whatever food was most in demand, and nothing else".
Ok er þeir sá þat, þá köstuðu þeir böggunum sínum inn yfir skíðgarðinn.	And when they saw that, they threw they bags theirs the over fence.	And when the natives saw this, they cast their bags over the fence.
En Guðríðr sat í durum inni með vöggu Snorra, sonar síns.	But Guthrid sat in doorway in with cradle Snorri, son hers.	But Gudrid sat in the doorway with the cradle of her son Snorri.
Þá bar skugga í dyrrin, ok gekk þar inn kona í svörtum námkyrtli, heldr lág, ok hafði dregil um höfuð ok ljósjörp á hár, fölleit ok mjök eygð, svá at eigi hafði jafnmikil augu sét í einum mannshausi.	Then carried shadow in doorway, and going there the woman in dark gown, held tightly, and had shawl about head and bright-chestnut of hair, pale and much eyed, so that not had equal eyes seen in any people's-heads.	Then a shadow fell across the doorway, and there came a woman in a dark gown, held tightly, and had a shawl around her head of bright chestnut hair, pale and large eyes, such that no one had seen eyes like them in anyone's head.

The Vinland Sagas *The Saga of the Greenlanders (Old Norse)*

Old Norse	Literal	English
Hon gekk þar at, er Guðríðr sat, ok mælti: "Hvat heitir þú?" segir hon.	She went there by, was Guthrid sat, and spoke: "What called-are you?" said she.	She came to where Gudrud sat, and spoke: "What is your name?", she said.
"Ek heiti Guðríðr, eða hvert er þitt heiti?".	"I am-called Guthrid, but what is your name?".	"I am called Gudrid, but what is your name?".
"Ek heiti Guðríðr", segir hon.	"I am-called Guthrid", said she.	"I am called Gudrid", she said.
Þá rétti Guðríðr húsfreyja hönd sína til hennar, at hún sæti hjá henni, en þat bar allt saman, at þá heyrði Guðríðr brest mikinn, ok var þá konan horfin, ok í því var ok veginn einn Skrælingr af einum húskarli Karlsefnis, því at hann hafði viljat taka vápn þeira, ok fóru nú brott sem tíðast, en klæði þeira lágu þar eftir ok varningr.	Then extended Guthrid housewife hand hers to her, that she sit by her, but that bore all together, that then heard Guthrid crash great, and was then woman disappeared, and in therefore was also slain one Skraeling from one houseman Karlsefnis, because that he had willed take weapon theirs, and went now away that swiftly, but clothing theirs laid there left and goods.	Then Gudrid the housewife extended her hand to her, to sit by her, but then there was a great crash, and the woman disappeared, at that moment one of the natives had been killed by one of Karlsefni's men, because he had tried to take their weapons, and they went away swiftly, but their clothing lay there behind with other goods.
Engi maðr hafði konu þessa sét útan Guðríðr ein.	No man had woman this seen of Guthrid alone.	No one had seen the woman except for Gudrid.
Nú munum vér þurfa til ráða at taka, segir Karlsefni, "því at ek hygg, at þeir muni vitja vár it þriðja sinn með ófriði ok fjölmenni. Nú skulum vér taka þat ráð, at tíu menn fari fram á nes þetta ok sýni sik þar, en annat lið várt skal fara í skóg ok höggva þar rjóðr fyrir nautfé váru, þá er liðit kemr fram ór skóginum.	"Now should we need to plan to take", said Karlsefni, "Because that I think, that they shall visit will the third they with warlike and many. Now should we take that plan, that ten men go from to headland this and show themselves there, while second team ours shall go into forest and strike there clearing for cattle ours, then as team come from out forest.	"Now we need to make a plan", said Karlsefni, "because I think that they will visit us a third time with hostility and in many numbers. Now shall we follow this plan, that ten men will go out on this headland and show themselves there, while our second team will go into the forest and strike there a clearing for the cattle, then as a team come from out of the forest.
Vér skulum ok taka gríðung várn ok láta hann fara fyrir oss".	We shall also take bull ours and let him go ahead-of us".	We shall also take our bull and let him go before us".
En þar var svá háttat, er fundr þeira var ætlaðr, at vatn var öðrum megin, en skógr á annan veg. Nú váru þessi ráð höfð, er Karlsefni lagði til.	But there was so the-way where battle theirs was intended, by water was the-other side, but forest on-the other way. Now was this plan taken, as Karlsefni had to.	There where their battle was intended, there was water on one side, and a forest on the other. Now the followed the plan that Karlsefni had made.

The Vinland Sagas   *The Saga of the Greenlanders (Old Norse)*

Old Norse	Literal	English
Nú kómu Skrælingar í þann stað, er Karlsefni hafði ætlat til bardaga.	Now came Skraelings to the place, where Karlsefni had intended to battle.	Now the Skraelings came to the place where Karlsefni had intended to battle.
Nú var þar bardagi, ok fell fjölði af liði Skrælinga.	Now was there battle, and fell many of people Skraelings.	Now was there a battle, and many of the Skraeling people fell.
Einn maðr var mikill ok vænn í liði Skrælinga, ok þótti Karlsefni, sem hann mundi vera höfðingi þeira.	One man was tall and handsome in group Skraelings, and thought Karlsefni, that he would be leader theirs.	One of them men in their group was tall and handsome, and Karlsefni thought that he was probably their leader.
Nú hafði einn þeira Skrælinga tekit upp öxi eina ok leit á um stund ok reiddi at félaga sínum ok hjó til hans.	Now had one of-them Skraelings taken up axe one and looked to about awhile and aimed at companion his and struck to him.	Now one of the Skraelings took up an axe and looked around awhile and aimed at one of his companions and struck him.
Sá fell þegar dauðr.	So fell then dead.	So he then fell dead.
Þá tók sá inn mikli maðr við öxinni ok leit á um stund ok varp henni síðan á sjóinn, sem lengst mátti hann.	Then took so the tall man to axe and looked to about awhile and threw he then to sea, as long as-may he.	Then the tall man took the axe and looked around for awhile, and then he thew it into the sea as far as he could.
En síðan flýja þeir á skóginn, svá hverr sem fara mátti, ok lýkr þar nú þeira viðskiptum.	But afterwards fled they to woods, so each as went may, and ended there now their dealings.	After that they fled into the woods as fast as they could, and they had no more dealings with them.
Váru þeir Karlsefni þar þann vetr allan.	Were they Karlsefni there that winter all.	Karlsefni and his companions were there all winter.
En at vári þá lýsir Karlsefni, at hann vill eigi þar vera lengr ok vill fara til Grænlands.	But at spring then declared Karlsefni, that he willed not there be longer and will travel to Greenland.	But in the spring, Karlsefni declared that he did not wish to be there any longer and wished to travel to Greenland.
Nú búa þeir ferð sína ok höfðu þaðan mörg gæði í vínviði ok berjum ok skinnvöru.	Now prepared they journey theirs and had there many quality in vines and berries and skin-wares.	Now they prepared for their journey and they had much good quality vines, berries, and skins.
Nú sigla þeir í haf ok kómu til Eiríksfjarðar skipi sínu heilu ok váru þar um vetrinn.	Now sailed they to sea and came to Eriksfjord ship theirs whole and were there about winter.	Now they sailed to sea and their ship came safely to Eriksfjord and they stayed there over the winter.
8	8	8
Nú tekst umræða at nýju um Vínlandsferð, því at sú ferð þykkir bæði góð til fjár ok virðingar.	Now took discussion that again about Vinland-voyage, since by that trip seemed both good to wealth and worthiness.	Now the discussion was taken to again about a Vinland voyage, since the trip seemed to bring both wealth and respect.

Old Norse	Literal	English
Þat sama sumar kom skip af Nóregi til Grænlands, er Karlsefni kom af Vínlandi.	That same summer came ship of Norway to Greenland, when Karlsefni came of Vinland.	That same summer a ship came from Norway when Karlsefni came back from Vinland.
Því skipi stýrðu bræðr tveir, Helgi ok Finnbogi, ok váru þann vetr á Grænlandi.	For ship steered brothers two, Helgi and Finnbogi, and were they wintered in Greenland.	The captains were two brothers, Helgi and Finnbogi, and they spent the winter in Greenland.
Þeir bræðr váru íslenzkir at kyni ok ór Austfjörðum.	Those brothers were Icelanders by kin and from Austfjord.	The brothers were Icelanders, from the East Fjords.
Þar er nú til at taka, at Freydís Eiríksdóttir gerði ferð sína heiman ór Görðum ok fór til fundar við þá bræðr, Helga ok Finnboga, ok beiddi þá, at þeir færi til Vínlands með farkost sinn ok hafa helming gæða allra við hana, þeira er þar fengist.	There is now to that take, that Freydis Eriksdottir made journey hers home from Gardar and went to meet with then brothers, Helgi and Finnbogi, and propose then, that they journey to Vinland with vessel theirs and have half quality everyone's with her, their which there caught.	Now we turn to Freydis Eriksdottir, who journeyed from here home at Gardar and then travelled to meet with the brothers, Helgi and Finnbogi, to invite them to travel to Vinland with their vessel and have a half share of any profits from it.
Nú játtu þeir því.	Now agreed they accordingly.	They agreed to this.
Þaðan fór hon á fund Leifs, bróður síns, ok bað, at hann gæfi henni hús þau, er hann hafði gera látit á Vínlandi.	There travelled she to meet Leif, brother hers, and asked, to him give her houses those, which he had made laid in Vinland.	There she travelled to meet Leif, her brother, to ask him to give her those houses which he had made in Vinland.
En hann svarar inu sama, kveðst ljá mundu hús, en gefa eigi.	But he answered the same, said loan would houses, but give not.	But he answered the same as before, he said that he would loan the houses, but not give them to her.
Sá var máldagi með þeim bræðrum ok Freydísi, at hvárir skyldu hafa þrjá tigu vígra manna á skipi ok konur um fram.	So were matters with they brothers and Freydis, that each should have three ten fighting men on ship and women about from.	So were matters between the brothers and Freydis, that each should have thirty fighting men on their ships and women in addition.
En Freydís brá af því þegar ok hafði fimm mönnum fleira ok leyndi þeim, ok urðu þeir bræðr eigi fyrri við þá varir en þeir kómu til Vínlands.	But Freydis drew off for already and had five men more and concealed them, and became they brothers not before to then foreseen but they came to Vinland.	But Freydis broke the agreement straight away and had five extra men, concealing them so that the brothers would not be aware of this until they came to Vinland.
Nú létu þau í haf ok höfðu til þess mælt áðr, at þau myndi samflota hafa, ef svá vildi verða, ok þess var lítill munr.	Now laid they to sea and had to this said before, that they should together have, if so will be, and this was little difference.	Now they put to sea and had said before that they should be together if they could, which they almost did.

The Saga of the Greenlanders (Old Norse)

Old Norse	Literal	English
En þó kómu þeir bræðr nökkuru fyrri ok höfðu upp borit föng sín til húsa Leifs.	But though came they brothers sometime before and had up carried possessions theirs to houses Leif's.	Though the brothers arrived sometime before and carried their possessions to Leif's houses.
En er Freydís kom at landi, þá ryðja þeir skip sitt ok bera upp til húss föng sín.	But when Freydis came to land, then cleared they ship theirs and carried up to houses possessions theirs.	Then when Freydis came to land, they cleared their ship and carried their possessions up to their houses.
Þá mælti Freydís: "Hví báruð þér inn hér föng yður?"	Then spoke Freydis: "Why carried you in here possessions yours?"	Then Freydis spoke: "Why have you carried your posessions in here?".
"Því, at vér hugðum", segja þeir, "at haldast mundi öll ákveðin orð með oss".	"Because that we thought", said they, "That hold would all agreed word with us".	"Because we thought", they said, "that you would keep your agreement with us".
Mér léði Leifr húsanna, segir hon, "en eigi yðr".	"To-me lent Leif houses", said she, "But not you".	"Leif lent the houses to me", she said, "not you".
Þá mælti Helgi: "Þrjóta mun okkr bræðr illsku við þik",	Then said Helgi: "Scarcely would-be we brothers ill-will with you",	Then Helgi said: "We brothers would scarcely be a match for your ill-will".
báru nú út föng ok gerðu sér skála ok settu þann skála firr sjónum á vatnsströndu ok bjuggu vel um.	Carried now out possessions and made they cabin and placed they cabin further-from the-sea towards a-lake and settled well about.	They removed their posessions and they made a longhouse further from the sea towards a lake, and settled in well.
En Freydís lét fella viðu til skips síns.	Then Freydis had wood felled for ship hers.	Then Freydis had wood cut to make a load for her ship.
Nú tók at vetra, ok töluðu þeir bræðr, at takast myndi upp leikar ok væri höfð skemmtan.	Now took in winter, and talked they brothers, that take should up games and would have amusement.	Now winter took, and the brothers talked of taking up games that would bring entertainment.
Svá var gert um stund, þar til er menn bárust verra í milli.	So was done about awhile, there until were men brought worse in between.	And so they did for a while, until disagreements arose between them.
Ok þá gerðist sundrþykki með þeim, ok tókust af leikar, ok engar gerðust kvámur milli skálanna,	And then made disagreement with them, and took of games, and none did come between cabins	And then was a rift between them, and the activities ceased, and none came or went between their cabins,
ok fór svá fram lengi vetrar.	and went so from long winter.	and so it went all winter long.

The Vinland Sagas   *The Saga of the Greenlanders (Old Norse)*

Old Norse	Literal	English
Þat var einn morgin snemma, at Freydís stóð upp ór rúmi sínu ok klæddist ok fór eigi í skóklæðin, en veðri var svá farit, at dögg var fallin mikil.	It was one morning early, that Freydis stood up out-of room theirs and dressed and went not in shoes, but weather was such going, that dew was fallen much.	It was early one morning, that Freydis got up and dressed, but did not wear any shoes, but the weather had left much dew fallen on the ground.
Hon tók kápu bónda síns ok fór í, en síðan gekk hon til skála þeira bræðra ok til dura.	She took cape husband hers and went into, but then went she to cabin theirs brothers and to door.	She took her husband's cape and went out, and then she went to the door of the brothers' cabin.
En maðr einn hafði út gengit litlu áðr ok lokit hurð aftr á miðjan klofa.	But man one had out gone little before and left door back to middle gap.	One of the men had gone out shortly before and left the door half open.
Hon lauk upp hurðinni ok stóð í gáttum stund þá ok þagði.	She closed up door and stood in doorway awhile then and silent.	She closed the door and stood silently in the doorway awhile.
En Finnbogi lá innstr í skálanum ok vakði.	But Finnbogi lay inside in cabin and awoke.	Finnbogi lay inside the cabin and awoke.
Hann mælti: "Hvat villtu hingat, Freydís?"	He said: "What will-you here, Freydis?".	He said: "What do you want here Freydis?".
Hon svarar: "Ek vil, at þú standir upp ok gangir út með mér, ok vil ek tala við þik".	She answered: "I will, that you stand up and go out with me, and will I speak with you".	She answered: "I want you to get up and come outside, and I want to speak with you".
Svá gerir hann.	So did he.	So he did.
Þau ganga at tré, er lá undir skálavegginum, ok settust þar niðr.	They went to tree, that lay near cabins, and sat there down.	They went to a tree that lay near the cabins, and there sat down.
Hversu líkar þér? segir hon.	"How like you?" said she.	"How do you like it here?" she said.
Hann svarar: "Góðr þykkir mér landkostr, en illr þykkir mér þústr sá, er vár á milli er, því ek kalla ekki hafa til orðit".	He answered: "Good think me land-benefits, but ill think me discord so, that sprung to between as, for I call not have to word".	He answered: "I think the land here has much benefit, but I don't like the ill feeling that has arisen between us, as I have no words for it".
Þá segir þú sem er, segir hon,	"Then say you as is", said she,	"What you say is true", she said,
"ok svá þykkir mér. En þat er erendi mitt á þinn fund, at ek vilda kaupa skipum við ykkr bræðr, því at þit hafið meira skip en ek, ok vilda ek í brott heðan".	"And so think I. But that which business mine to you find, that I will purchase ship with you brothers, because that you have more ship than I, and will I to away hence".	"And I agree. But my purpose in meeting with you, is that I wish to buy yours and your brother's ship, because you have more ship than I, and I wish to leave soon".

The Vinland Sagas   *The Saga of the Greenlanders (Old Norse)*

Old Norse	Literal	English
Þat mun ek láta gangast, segir hann, "ef þér líkar þá vel".	"That should I let go", said he, "If you like then well".	"That I could agree to", he said, "If that pleases you".
Nú skilja þau við þat, gengr hon heim, en Finnbogi til hvílu sinnar.	Now separated they with that, went she home, and Finnbogi to bed his.	Now with that they separated, and she went home, and Finnbogi to his bed.
Hon stígr upp í rúmit köldum fótum, ok vaknar hann Þorvarðr við ok spyrr, hví at hon væri svá köld ok vát.	She climbed up into room cold feet, and awoke he Thorvald to and asked, why that she was so cold and wet.	She climbed up into the room with cold feet, and Thorvard woke and asked why she was so cold and wet.
Hon svarar með miklum þjósti: "Ek var gengin", segir hon, "til þeira bræðra at fala skip af þeim, ok vilda ek kaupa meira skip. En þeir urðu við þat svá illa, at þeir börðu mik ok léku sárliga, en þú, vesall maðr, munt hvárki vilja reka minnar skammar né þinnar, ok mun ek þat nú finna, at ek em í brottu af Grænlandi, ok mun ek gera skilnað við þik, útan þú hefnir þessa".	She answered with much vehemence: "I was gone", said she, "To the brothers to bargain ship of them, and wished I purchase bigger ship. But they became with that so bad, that they beat me and played woundingly, but you, miserable man, would neither will expel my shame nor yours, and should I that now find, that I am in gone from Greenland, and should I make separate with you, outside-of you avenge this".	She answered vehemently: "I was gone", she said, "to the brothers to purchase their ship from them, and wished I to buy a bigger ship. With that they became so angry, that they beat me, and struck me woundingly, but you, miserable man, will neither expel my shame or yours, and if that's the case, then I will leave Greenland, and divorce you, unless you avenge this".
Ok nú stóðst hann eigi átölur hennar ok bað menn upp standa sem skjótast ok taka vápn sín,	And now stood he not reproaches hers and ordered men up stand while quickly and take weapons theirs,	And now, unable to withstand her reproaches, he ordered that the men get up quickly and get their weapons,
Ok svá gera þeir ok fara þegar til skála þeira bræðra ok gengu inn at þeim soföndum ok tóku þá ok færðu í bönd ok leiddu svá út hvern, sem bundinn var.	And so did they and went straightaway to cabin they brothers and went in by them sleeping and took then and went in binding and lead so out each, who bound was.	And so they did, travelling straightaway to the brothers' cabin, and went in while they were sleeping, took them, bound them, and led them outside as they were bound.
En Freydís lét drepa hvern, sem út kom.	Then Freydis had killled each, who out came.	Then Freydis had each one killed as they came out.
Nú váru þar allir karlar drepnir, en konur váru eftir, ok vildi engi þær drepa.	Now were there all men killed, but women were left, and willed none they kill.	Now all the men were killed, there remained the women, but no one wanted to kill them.
Þá mælti Freydís: "Fái mér öxi í hönd".	Then said Freydis: "Give me axe into hand".	Then Freydis said: "Give me the axe in my hand".
Svá var gert.	So was done.	So was it done.

Old Norse	Literal	English
Síðan vegr hon at konum þeim fimm, er þar váru, ok gekk af þeim dauðum.	Then slayed she that women they five, who there were, and went of them dead.	Then she slayed the five women who were there, and all of them were dead.
Nú fóru þau til skála síns eftir þat it illa verk, ok fannst þat eitt á, at Freydís þóttist allvel hafa um ráðit, ok mælti við félaga sína: "Ef oss verðr auðit at koma til Grænlands", segir hon, "þá skal ek þann mann ráða af lífi, er segir frá þessum atburðum.	Now went they to cabin theirs after that the evil work, and found that one all, that Freydis thought all-well have about resolved, and said to companions hers: "If we worth fated to come to Greenland", said she, "Then shall I then men rule of life, who says from these events.	Now they went back to their cabin after that evil work, and they all found that Freydis thought all was well done, and she spoke to her companions: "If we are fated to return to Greenland", she said, "Then I shall have killed any man who says anything about these events.
Nú skulum vér þat segja, at þau búi hér eftir, þá er vér fórum í brott".	Now should we this say, that they remained here behind, when were we travelling to away".	Now shall we say of this that they remained here, when we travelled away".
Nú bjuggu þeir skipit snemma um várit, þat er þeir bræðr höfðu átt, með þeim öllum gæðum, er þau máttu til fá ok skipit bar, sigla síðan í haf ok urðu vel reiðfara ok kómu í Eiríksfjörð skipi sínu snemma sumars.	Now readied they ship early about spring, that was the brothers had had, with them all quality, that they may to get and ship carry, sailed after to sea and became well voyage and came to Eriksfjord ship theirs early summer.	Early in the spring they prepared the ship which the brothers had owned, with all the goods that the ship could carry, then afterwards sailed to sea and they had a good voyage and their ship came into Eriksfjord early in the summer.
Nú var þar Karlsefni fyrir ok hafði albúit skip sitt til hafs ok beið byrjar, ok er þat mál manna, at eigi mundi auðgara skip gengit hafa af Grænlandi en þat, er hann stýrði.	Now was there Karlsefni already and had prepared ship his to sea and waited begin, and is that said men, that not would richer ship go sea off Greenland but that, which he steered.	Karlsefni was there already, and had his ship all prepared for sea, waiting for a favourable wind, and it was said that none would go to sea with a richer ship from Greenland than that which he captained.
9	9	9
Freydís fór nú til bús síns, því at þat hafði staðit meðan óskatt.	Freydis travelled now to dwelling hers, for as that had stood meantime uninjured.	Freydis travelled now to her farm, which withstood her absence without injury.
Hon fekk mikinn feng fjár öllu föruneyti sínu, því at hon vildi leyna láta ódáðum sínum.	She gave great gifts wealth all companions hers, for that she would conceal let dishonour hers.	She gave great gifts of wealth to all her companions, so that she could conceal her dishonour.
Sitr hon nú í búi sínu.	Sat she now in house hers.	She remained at her farm.

The Vinland Sagas   *The Saga of the Greenlanders (Old Norse)*

Old Norse	Literal	English
Eigi urðu allir svá haldinorðir, at þegði yfir ódáðum þeira eða illsku, at eigi kæmi upp um síðir.	Not became all so held-words, by silence over dishonour theirs or evil, that not came up about eventually.	Not all words were held in silence over their dishonour or evil, that didn't come up eventually.
Nú kom þetta upp um síðir fyrir Leif, bróður hennar, ok þótti honum þessi saga allill.	Now came this up about eventually before Leif, brother hers, and thought he this story evil.	Now this came up before Leif, her brother, and he thought this story was most evil.
Þá tók Leifr þrjá menn af liði þeira Freydísar ok píndi þá til sagna um þenna atburð allan jafnsaman, ok var með einu móti sögn þeira.	Then took Leif three men of band theirs Freydis and tortured then to say about these events all equally, and was with one towards story theirs.	Then Leif took three men from Freydis's company and tortured them to talk about those events, they were all equal and as one in their telling.
Eigi nenni ek, segir Leifr, "at gera þat við Freydísi, systur mína, sem hon væri verð, en spá mun ek þeim þess, at þeira afkvæmi muni lítt at þrifum verða".	"Not bother I", said Leif, "To do that to Freydis, sister mine, which she would deserve, but prophecy should I that these, by their offspring should little by thriving be".	"I am not the one", said Leif, "to do to Freydis, my sister, that which she deserves, but I should prophecise this, that their offspring shall little thriving become".
Nú leið þat svá fram, at engum þótti um þau vert þaðan í frá nema ills.	Now laid that so from, that none thought about them worthy there in from taking ill.	Now as it happened, none thought anything of them except evil.
Nú er at segja frá því, er Karlsefni býr skip sitt ok sigldi í haf. *Honum fórst vel ok kom til Nóregs með heilu ok höldnu ok sat þar um vetrinn ok seldi varning sinn ok hafði þar gott yfirlæti ok þau bæði hjón af inum göfgustum mönnum í Nóregi,* *en um várit eftir bjó hann skip sitt til Íslands.*	Now is to say from therefore, when Karlsefni prepared ship his and sailed to sea. He travelled well and came to Norway with whole and safe and sat there about winter and sold wares his and had there benefit respectable and they both couple of the respectable people in Norway, but about spring after prepared he ship his to Iceland.	Now to turn to Karlsefni, he prepared his ship and sailed to sea. He travelled well and came to Norway safe an well, and remained there over the winter and sold his goods, and both him and his wife were treated well by the noble people in Norway, and after about spring, he prepared his ship for Iceland.
Ok er hann var albúinn ok skip hans lá til byrjar fyrir bryggjunum, þá kom þar at honum Suðrmaðr einn, ættaðr af Brimum ór Saxlandi. *Hann falar at Karlsefni húsasnotru hans.*	And when he was ready and ship his lay to fair-wind for bridge, then came there to him southern-man one, descended from Bremen of Saxony. He bargained-for that Karlsefni carved decoration his.	And when he was ready and his ship waited for a fair wind on the gangways, then came a southern man, descended from Bremen of Saxony. He asked Karlsefni to sell him the carved decoration on the prow.
Ek vil eigi selja", sagði hann.	"I will not sell", said he.	"I don't care to sell it", he said.

The Vinland Sagas *The Saga of the Greenlanders (Old Norse)*

Old Norse	Literal	English
Ek mun gefa þér við hálfa mörk gulls, segir Suðrmaðr.	"I would give you to half mark gold", said southern-man.	"I'll give you half a mark of gold for it", said the southern man.
Karlsefni þótti vel við boðit, ok keyptu síðan.	Karlsefni thought well with offer, and sold afterwards.	Karlsefni thought this was a good offer, and then sold it.
Fór Suðrmaðr í burt með húsasnotruna, en Karlsefni vissi eigi, hvat tré var.	Went southern-man to away with carved-decoration, but Karlsefni knew not, what wood was.	The southern man went away with his carved decoration, but Karlsefni did not know what wood it was made of.
En þat var mösurr, kominn af Vínlandi.	But that was burl-wood, coming from Vinland.	But it was made of burl wood, which came from Vinland.
Nú siglir Karlsefni í haf ok kom skipi sínu fyrir norðan land í Skagafjörð, ok var þar upp sett skip hans um vetrinn.	Now sailed Karlsefni to sea and came ship his for north land to Skagafjord, and was there up set ship his about winter.	Now Karlsefni sailed to sea and his ship came to the north of the land to Skagafjord, and he set up his ship there for the winter.
En um várit keypti hann Glaumbæjarland ok gerði bú á ok bjó þar, meðan hann lifði, ok var it mesta göfugmenni, ok er margt manna frá honum komit ok Guðríði, konu hans, ok góðr ættbogi.	Then about spring bought he Glaumbær and made dwelling on and lived there, long-as he lived, and was the most greatest, and which many people from him came and Guthrid, wife his, and good descendents.	Then in the spring he purchased land at Glaumbaer and made a farm there, as long as he lived, and was the the most respected, and many pepople are came from him and his wife Gudrid, with good descendents.
Ok er Karlsefni var andaðr, tók Guðríðr við búsvarðveizlu ok Snorri, sonr hennar, er fæddr var á Vínlandi.	And when Karlsefni was dead, took Guthrid to farming and Snorri, son hers, who born was in Vinland.	And when Karlsefni died, Gudrid took over the farm with her son Snorri, who had been born in Vinland.
Ok er Snorri var kvángaðr, þá fór Guðríðr útan ok gekk suðr ok kom út aftr til bús Snorra, sonar síns, ok hafði hann þá látit gera kirkju í Glaunbæ.	And when Snorri was married, then went Guthrid out and went south and came out returning to house Snorri, son hers, and had he then caused made church in Glaumbær.	And when Snorri was married, Gudrid travelled abroad, and went south, returning to her son Snorri's farm, and he had built a church in Glaumbaer.
Síðan varð Guðríðr nunna ok einsetukona ok var þar, meðan hon lifði.	Afterwards was Guthrid a-nun and recluse and was there, long-as she lived.	Later Gudrid became a nun and an anchoress and remained there as long as she lived.
Snorri átti son þann, er Þorgeirr hét. *Hann var faðir Yngvildar, móður Brands biskups.*	Snorri had son that, was Thorgeir named. He was father-of Yngvild, mother Brand Bishop's	Snorri has a son who was named Thorgeir. He was the father of Yngvild, who was mother to Bishop Brand.

The Vinland Sagas   *The Saga of the Greenlanders (Old Norse)*

Old Norse	Literal	English
Dóttir Snorra Karlsefnissonar hét Hallfríðr.	Daughter Snorri Karlsefnison's was-called Hallfrid.	Snorri Karlsefnison's daughter was called Hallfrid.
Hon var kona Runólfs, föður Þorláks biskups.	She was wife Runolf's, father Thorlak Bishop's	She was the wife of Runolf, father of Bishop Thorlak.
Björn hét sonr Karlsefnis ok Guðríðar.	Bjorn was-called son-of Karlsefni's and Guthrid's.	Karlsefni and Gudrid had a son called Bjorn.
Hann var faðir Þórunnar, móður Bjarnar biskups.	He was father-of Thorun, mother Bjarn Bishop's	He was the father of Thorun, mother to Bishop Bjorn.
Fjölði manna er frá Karlsefni kominn, ok er hann kynsæll maðr orðinn.	Many people were from Karlsefni come, and was he kin-blessed man become.	Many people are descended from Karlesfni, and his was a prosperous clan.
Ok hefir Karlsefni gerst sagt allra manna atburði um farar þessar allar, er nú er nökkut orði á komit.	And has Karlsefni made said every people's events about voyages these all, which now is somewhat recited to came.	It was Karlsefni who told of people's events about these voyages, some of which came to words.

The Saga of the Greenlanders (*Old Icelandic*)

Old Icelandic	Literal	English
1	1	1
Þorvaldur hét maður, sonur Ásvalds Úlfssonar, Öxna-Þórissonar.	Thorvald was-named a-man, son-of Asvald's Son-of-Ulfson, Son-of-Oxna-Thorri.	There was a man named Thorvald, son of Asvald, son of Ulf, son of Oxna-Thorri.
Þorvaldur og Eiríkur hinn rauði, sonur hans, fóru af Jaðri til Íslands fyrir víga sakir.	Thorvald and Erik the Red, son his, travelled from Jaeren to Iceland because-of-a killing conviction.	Thorvald and Erik the Red, his son, travelled from Jaeran to Iceland because of a conviction for a killing.
Þá var víða byggt Ísland.	Then was widely settled Iceland.	Then Iceland was widely settled.
Þeir bjuggu fyrst að Dröngum á Hornströndum.	They lived first at Drangar on Hornstrandir.	They lived first at Drangar in Hornstrandir.
Þar andaðist Þorvaldur.	There died Thorvald.	There Thorvald died.
Eiríkur fekk þá Þjóðhildar, dóttur Jörundar Úlfssonar og Þorbjargar knarrarbringu, er þá átti Þorbjörn hinn haukdælski.	Erik married then Thjodhild, daughter-of Jorund Son-of-Ulf and Thorbjorg Knarrarbringu, who then married Thorbjorn of Haukadal.	Erik then married Thjodhild, daughter of Jorund, son of Ulf, and Thorbjorg Knarrabringu, who then married Thorbjorn of Haukadal.
Réðst Eiríkur þá norðan og bjó á Eiríksstöðum hjá Vatnshorni.	Went Erik then northwards and lived at Eriksstadir near Vatnshorn.	Erik then went northwards and lived at Eriksstadir near Vantshorn.
Sonur Eiríks og Þjóðhildar hét Leifur.	Son-of Erik's and Thjodhild's was-named Leif.	Erik and Thjodhild's son was named Leif.
Enn eftir víg Eyjólfs saurs og Hólmgöngu-Hrafns var Eiríkur gerður brott úr Haukadal.	But after killing-of Eyolf's the-Foul and Raven-the-dueller was Erik made away from Haukadal.	But after the killing of Eyolf the Foul and Raven the Dueller, Erik was made to leave Haukadal.
Fór hann vestur til Breiðafjarðar og bjó í Öxney á Eiríksstöðum.	Travelled he west to Breidafjord and lived at Oxney on Eriksstadir.	He then travelled west to Breidafjord and lived at Oxney in Eriksstadir.
Hann léði Þorgesti á Breiðabólstað setstokka og náði eigi, er hann kallaði til.	He lent Thorgest to Upholstery seat-posts and got not, when he called to.	He lent Thorgest some upholstery seat posts, and when he asked for them back, he did not get them.
Þaðan af gerðust deilur og bardagar með þeim Þorgesti, sem segir í sögu Eiríks.	From-there from made disputes and battle between them Thorgest, as said in saga Erik's.	From then on there were disputes and battles between him and Thorgest, as told in Erik's Saga.
Styrr Þorgrímsson veitti Eiríki að málum og Eyjólfur úr Svíney, og synir Þorbrands úr Álftafirði og Þorbjörn Vífilsson.	Styrr Thorgrimson supported Erik in the-matter and Eyjolf of Sviney, and sons Thorbrand's of Alftafjord and Thorbjorn Vifilson.	Styrr Thorgrimson supported Erik in the matter, and Eyolf of Sviney, and Thorbrand's sons of Alftafjord, and Thorbjorn Vifilson.

The Saga of the Greenlanders (Old Icelandic)

Old Icelandic	Literal	English
En Þorgestlingum veittu synir Þórðar Gellis ok Þorgeir úr Hítardal.	But Thorgest's-sons supported sons Thord Howler and Thorgeir of Hitardal.	But Thorgest's sons were supported by Thord Howler, and Thorgeir of Hitardal.
Eiríkur varð sekur á Þórsnessþingi.	Erik was outlawed at-the Thorsness-assembly.	Erik was outlawed at the Thorsness assembly.
Bjó Eiríkur þá skip sitt til hafs í Eiríksvogi.	Prepared Erik then ship his to sea at Eriksvog.	He then prepared his ship to go to sea at Eriksvog.
En er hann var búinn, fylgdu þeir Styrr honum út um eyjar.	And when he was ready, followed they Styrr him out about the-island.	And when he was ready, Styrr followed them about the island.
Eiríkur sagði þeim, að hann ætlaði at leita lands þess, er Gunnbjörn, sonur Úlfs kráku, sá, er hann rak vestur um haf, þá er hann fann Gunnbjarnarsker.	Erik told them, that he intended to search land this, which Gunnbjorn, son-of Ulf Crow, saw, when he driven west at sea, when was he found Gunnbjarnarsker.	Erik told them that he intended to search for a land, which Gunnbjorn, son of Ulf Crow, saw when he was driven west at sea, when he found Gunnbjorn's Skerries.
Kveðst hann aftur mundu leita til vina sinna, ef hann fyndi landið.	Said he return would seek to friends his, if he found land.	He said he would return to seek his friends if he found land.
Eiríkur sigldi undan Snæfellsjökli.	Erik sailed from Snaefellsjokli.	Erik sailed from Snaefellsjokli.
Hann fann landið, og kom utan að því, þar sem hann kallaði Miðjökul.	He found land, and came out of for, there which he called Midjokul.	He found land, and came out therefore, there he called Modjokul.
Sá heitir nú Bláserkur.	This is-named now Blaserkur.	This is now named Blaserkur.
Hann fór þá þaðan suður með landinu at leita, ef þaðan væri byggjandi landið.	He travelled then from-there south along land to seek, if there was habitable land.	He travelled south from there along land to see if there was habitable land.
Hann var hinn fyrsta vetur í Eiríksey, nær miðri hinni eystri byggð.	He was the first winter in Eriksey, near-the middle of-the Eastern Settlement.	The first winter he was at Eriksey, near the middle of the Eastern Settlement.
Um vorið eftir fór hann til Eiríksfjarðar og tók sér þar bústað.	About spring after travelled he to Eriksfjord and took he there abode.	After about spring he travelled to Eriksfjord and took he there a dwelling.
Hann fór það sumar í hina vestri óbyggð og gaf víða örnefni.	He travelled that summer to the western settlement and gave many place-names.	He travelled that summer to the Western Settlement and gave many places names.
Hann var annan vetur í Hólmum við Hvarfsgnípu, en hið þriðja sumar fór allt norður til Snæfells og inn í Hrafnsfjörð.	He was second winter at Holm in Hvarfsgnipu, but the third summer travelled all North to Snaefell and then to Hrafnsfjord.	The second winter he was at Holm in Hvarfsgnipu, but the third summer travelled all the way north to Snaefell and then to Hrafnsfjord.
Þá kvaðst hann kominn fyrir botn Eiríksfjarðar.	Then said he coming for-the bottom-of Eriksfjord.	Then he said he came to the bottom of Eriksfjord.

The Saga of the Greenlanders (Old Icelandic)

Old Icelandic	Literal	English
Hvarf hann þá aftur og var hinn þriðja vetur í Eiríksey fyrir mynni Eiríksfjarðar.	Disappeared he then after and was the third winter in Eriksey before the-inlet Eriksfjord.	After that he then disappeared and was for the third winter in Eriksey before the inlet Eriksfjord.
Eftir um sumarið fór hann til Íslands og kom skipi sínu í Breiðafjörð.	After about summer travelled he to Iceland and came ship his to Breidafjord.	After about summer he travelled to Iceland and his ship came to Breidajord.
Hann kallaði land það, er hann hafði fundið, Grænland, því að hann kvað það mundu fýsa menn þangað, ef landið héti vel.	He called land that, which he had found, Greenland, because as he said it would attract men there, if the-land was-named well.	He called the land which he had found Greenland, because as he said, it would attract people there if it was named well.
Eiríkur var á Íslandi um veturinn, en um sumarið eftir fór hann að byggja landið.	Erik was in Iceland about winter, but about summer after travelled he to settle land.	Erik was in Iceland over winter, but after around summer he travelled to settle the land.
Hann bjó í Brattahlíð í Eiríksfirði.	He dwelt at Brattahlid in Eriksfjord.	He lived at Brattahlid in Eriksfjord.
Svo segja fróðir menn, að á því sama sumri, er Eiríkur rauði fór að byggja Grænland, þá fór hálfur þriði tugur skipa úr Breiðafirði og Borgarfirði, en fjórtán komust út þangað.	So say wise men, that at since same summer, that Erik the-Red travelled to settle Greenland, then travelled half-of thirty twenty ships from Breidafjord and Borgafjord, but fourteen arrived out there.	So wise men say that after that same summer, Erik the Red travelled to settle Greenland, then half of thirty and twenty ships travelled from Breidafjord and Borgafjord, but fourteen arrived there.
Sum rak aftur, en sum týndust.	Some driven back, but some lost.	Some were driven back, but some were lost.
Það var fimmtán vetrum fyrr en kristni var lögtekin á Íslandi.	This was fifteen winters before that christianity was law-taken on Iceland.	This was fifteen winters before Christianity became law in Iceland.
Á því sama sumri fór utan Friðrekur biskup og Þorvaldur Koðránsson.	Then since same summer travelled out Fridrek bishop and Thorvald Kodranson.	After that same summer travelled out Bishop Fridrek and Thorvald Kodranson.
Þessir menn námu land á Grænlandi, er þá fóru út með Eiríki: Herjólfur Herjólfsfjörð, - hann bjó á Herjólfsnesi, - Ketill Ketilsfjörð, Hrafn Hrafnsfjörð, Sölvi Sölvadal, Helgi Þorbrandsson Álftafjörð, Hafgrímur Hafgrímsfjörð og Vatnahverfi, Arnlaugur Arnlaugsfjörð.	These men took land in Greenland, when then travelled out with Erik: Herjolf Herjolfsfjord, - he lived on Herjólfsnes, - Ketil Ketilsfjord, Hrafn Hrafnsfjord, Sölvi Solvadal, Helgi Thorbrandson Alftafjord, Hafgrim Hafgrimsfjord and Vatnahverfi, Arnlaug Arnlaugsfjord.	These men took land in Greenland, when they travelled out with Erik: Herjolf took Herjolfsfjord, he lived on Herjolfsnes, Ketil took Ketilsfjord, Hrafn took Hrafnsfjord, Solvi took Solvadal, Helgi Thorbrandson took Alftafjord, Hafgrim took Hafgrimsfjord and Vatnahverfi, and Arnlaug took Arnlaugsfjord.
En sumir fóru til Vestribyggðar.	But some travelled to Western-settlement.	But some travelled to the Western Settlement.

The Vinland Sagas   *The Saga of the Greenlanders (Old Icelandic)*

Old Icelandic	Literal	English
Herjúlfur var Bárðarson Herjúlfssonar. Hann var frændi Ingólfs landnámamanns. Þeim Herjúlfi gaf Ingólfur land á milli Vogs og Reykjaness.	Herjolf was Bard's-son Son-of-Herjolf. He was kinsman Ingolf's land-taking-man. To-them Herjolf gave Ingolf land on between Vogs and Reykjanes.	Herjolf was Bard's son, the son of Herjolf. He was kinsman to Ingolf the land taking man. Ingolf gave to them land between Vogs and Reykjanes.
Herjúlfur bjó fyrst á Drepstokki. Þorgerður hét kona hans en Bjarni son þeirra og var hinn efnilegsti maður. Hann fýstist utan þegar á unga aldri. Varð honum gott bæði til fjár og mannvirðingar og var sinn vetur hvort, utan lands eða með föður sínum. Brátt átti Bjarni skip í förum. Og hinn síðasta vetur er hann var í Noregi þá brá Herjúlfur til Grænlandsferðar með Eiríki og brá búi sínu.	Herjolf lived first on Drepstokk. Thorgerd was-named wife his but Bjarni son theirs and was a promising man. He desired out-travel already at young age. Was he good both to wealth and man-worthiness and was he winter either, out-of lands or with father his. Soon had Bjarni ship to travel. And the last winter that he was in Norway then prepared Herjolf to Greenland-voyage with Erik and prepared farm his.	Herjolf lived first at Drepstokk. His wife was named Thorgerd and their son Bjarni was a promising man. He desired to travel out at a young age. He was good in both wealth and worthiness, and in winter he was either travelling or with his father. Soon Bjarni had a ship to travel. And the last winter that he was in Norway, then Herjolf prepared for the voyage to Greenland with Erik and prepared his farm.
Með Herjúlfi var á skipi suðureyskur maður, kristinn, sá er orti Hafgerðingadrápu.	With Herjolf was in ship south-islander man, christian, that who wrote Sea-poem.	With Herjolf in his ship was a man from the southern islands, a Christian who wrote a sea poem.
Þar er þetta stef í:	There which this stave is:	There is this stave:
Mínar bið eg að munka reyni meinalausan farar beina, heiðis haldi hárrar foldar hallar drottinn yfir mér stalli.	My bid I that monks tester harmlessly travel assist, heath hold high folds hall master over my altar.	I ask you, monks' tester to assist my travel harmless, holding the heath's high folds hall master over my altar.
Herjúlfur bjó á Herjúlfsnesi. Hann var hinn göfgasti maður.	Herjolf lived on Herjolfsness. He was a respectable man.	Herjolf lived at Herjolfsness. He was a respectable man.
Eiríkur rauði bjó í Brattahlíð.	Erik the-Red settled at Brattahlid.	Erik the Red settled at Brattahlid.
Hann var þar með mestri virðingu og lutu allir til hans. Þessi voru börn Eiríks: Leifur, Þorvaldur og Þorsteinn en Freydís hét dóttir hans.	He was there with most worthiness and lent all to his. These were children Erik's: Leif, Thorvald also, and Thorstein but Freydis was-named daughter his.	He was there given the most respect by all. Erik's children were: Leif, Thorvald, and Thorstein, and his daughter was named Freydis.

The Saga of the Greenlanders (Old Icelandic)

Old Icelandic	Literal	English
Hún var gift þeim manni er er Þorvarður hét og bjuggu þau í Görðum þar sem nú er biskupsstóll.	She was married they a-man who was Thorvard was-named and lived they at Gardar there as now who bishop's-seat.	She was married to a man named Thorvard, and they lived at Gardar, where the bishop's seat now is.
Hún var svarri mikill en Þorvarður var lítilmenni.	She was haughty very but Thorvard was little-man.	She was haughty, but Thorvard was not much of a man.
Var hún mjög gefin til fjár.	Was she much married to wealth.	She married him very much for this wealth.
Heiðið var fólk á Grænlandi í þann tíma.	Heathen were folk in Greenland at this time.	Heathen were the people in Greenland at this time.
Það sama sumar kom Bjarni skipi sínu á Eyrar er faðir hans hafði brott siglt um vorið.	That same summer came Bjarni ship his to Eyrar where father his had away sailed about spring.	That same summer came Bjarni's ship to Eyrar, where his father had sailed from in the spring.
Þau tíðindi þóttu Bjarna mikil og vildi eigi bera af skipi sínu.	These tidings thought Bjarni great and willed not unload from ship his.	This news greatly affected Bjarni and he did not want to unload his ship.
Þá spurðu hásetar hans hvað er hann bærist fyrir en hann svaraði að hann ætlaði að að halda siðvenju sinni og þiggja að föður sínum veturvist "og vil eg halda skipinu til Grænlands ef þér viljið mér fylgd veita".	Then asked crew he what was he bearing for but he answered that he intended that to hold custom his and receive by father his winter "and will I hold ship to Greenland if you will me follow lead".	His crew asked him what he wanted to do but he answered that he wanted to keep his custom of spending the winter with his father "and I want sail to Greenland if you will follow me".
Allir kváðust hans ráðum fylgja vilja.	All said his counsel follow would.	All of them said the would follow his counsel.
Þá mælti Bjarni: "Óviturleg mun þykja vor ferð þar sem engi vor hefir komið í Grænlandshaf".	Then said Bjarni: "Unwisely will seem our voyage there since none been have come to Greenland-sea".	Then Bjarni said: "Our voyage will look unwise, since none of us have sailed the Greenland sea".
En þó halda þeir nú í haf þegar þeir voru búnir og sigldu þrjá daga þar til er landið var vatnað en þá tók af byrina og lagði á norrænur og þokur og vissu þeir eigi hvert að þeir fóru og skipti það mörgum dægrum.	But though held they now to sea when they were ready and sailed three days there until was land was water-taken but then took of fair-wind and lay on north-wind and fog and knew they not where that they travelled and time that many days.	But they set sail once they were ready and sailed for three days, until the land disappeared below the horizon, but then the fair wind dropped, and they were met with winds from the north and fog, and they did not know where they were travelling for many days.

The Vinland Sagas — *The Saga of the Greenlanders (Old Icelandic)*

Old Icelandic	Literal	English
Eftir það sáu þeir sól og máttu þá deila áttir, vinda nú segl og sigla þetta dægur áður þeir sáu land og ræddu um með sér hvað landi þetta mun vera en Bjarni kveðst hyggja að það mundi eigi Grænland.	After that saw they the-sun and could then share direction, wind now sails and sailed this day before they saw land and discussed among with them what land that could be but Bjarni said thought it that could not-be Greenland.	After that they saw the sun and took their bearings, they hoisted their sails and sailed for the rest of the day before they saw land, and they discussed among themselves what land it could be, but Bjarni said that it could not be Greenland.
Þeir spyrja hvort hann vill sigla að þessu landi eða eigi.	They asked whether he wished sail to this land or not.	They asked whether he wished to sail close to the land or not.
"Það er mitt ráð að sigla í nánd við landið".	"It is my advice to sail to close with land".	"I advise that we sail close to the land".
Og svo gera þeir og sáu það brátt að landið var ófjöllótt og skógi vaxið og smár hæðir á landinu og létu landið á bakborða og létu skaut horfa á land.	And so did they and saw that soon that land was without-mountains and forests grown and small heights on land and left land on port-side and let stern turn on land.	And so they did, and saw that the land was not mountainous, but did have small hills and was covered with forests, so keeping land on their port side, they turned their sail-end landwards and angled away from the shore.
Síðan sigla þeir tvö dægur áður þeir sáu land annað.	Afterwards sailed they two days before they saw land another.	Then they sailed for two days before they saw any more land.
Þeir spyrja hvort Bjarni ætlaði það enn Grænland.	They asked if Bjarni supposed this was Greenland.	They asked Bjarni if he thought this land was Greenland.
Hann kvaðst eigi heldur ætla þetta Grænland en hið fyrra "því að jöklar eru mjög miklir sagðir á Grænlandi"	He said not rather supposed this Greenland as the first "because the glaciers are very large said in Greenland"	He said that he did not think this was Greenland as the first "because there are said to be very large glaciers in Greenland".
Þeir nálguðust brátt þetta land og sáu það vera slétt land og viði vaxið. *Þá tók af byr fyrir þeim.*	They approached soon this land and saw it was flat land and woods growing. Then took of fair-wind before them.	They soon approached this land and saw that it was flat and wooded. Then the wind died.
Þá ræddu hásetar það að þeim þótti það ráð að taka það land en Bjarni vill það eigi. *Þeir þóttust bæði þurfa við og vatn.*	Then advised crew that to them thought that advised to take that land but Bjarni willed that not. They thought both needed wood and water.	Then the crew advised that they put ashore, but Bjarni did not want to. They said that they needed wood and water.

The Saga of the Greenlanders (Old Icelandic)

Old Icelandic	Literal	English
"Að öngu eruð þér því óbirgir" segir Bjarni en þó fékk hann af því nokkuð ámæli af hásetum sínum.	"In nothing are you for without-supplies" said Bjarni but though got he of for some reproach from crew his.	"There are no supplies you are lacking" said Bjarni, but he was criticised by his crew for this.
Hann bað þá vinda segl og svo var gert og settu framstafn frá landi og sigla í haf útsynningsbyr þrjú dægur og sáu þá landið þriðja.	He bid them wind sails and so was done and set prow from land and sailing to sea south-west-wind three days and saw then land third.	He told them to hoist the sail and they did so, setting the bow away from land and sailing seawards, for three days they sailed with wind from the south west and then saw a third land.
En það land var hátt og fjöllótt og jökull á.	And this land was high and mountainous and glaciers on.	And this land was high and mountainous and was capped by glaciers.
Þeir spyrja þá ef Bjarni vildi að landi láta þar en hann kvaðst eigi það vilja "því að mér líst þetta land ógagnvænlegt".	They asked then if Bjarni willed to land put there but he said not that willed "for to me appears this land uninviting".	They asked if Bjarni wished to make land here, but he said that he did not "for this land appears uninviting".
Nú lögðu þeir eigi segl sitt, halda með landinu fram og sáu að það var eyland, settu enn stafn við því landi og héldu í haf hinn sama byr.	Now lay they not sails these, held along land from and saw it that was island, turned yet stern with for land and held to sea the same fair-wind.	Now they did not lower the sail, but followed along the shore until they saw that it was an island, they turned the stern landwards and sailed out to sea with the same breeze.
En veður óx í hönd og bað Bjarni þá svipta og eigi sigla meira en bæði dygði vel skipi þeirra og reiða, sigldu nú fjögur dægur.	But weather grew at hand and bid Bjarni then shorten and not sail greater than both enough well ships theirs and decided, sailed now four days.	But the wind grew and Bjarni told them to lower the sail and not sail faster than the ship could manage, they sailed for four days.
Þá sáu þeir land hið fjórða.	Then saw they land the fourth.	Then they saw a fourth land.
Þá spurðu þeir Bjarna hvort hann ætlaði þetta vera Grænland eða eigi.	Then asked they Bjarni whether he supposed this was Greenland or not.	They asked Bjarni if he thought this was Greenland or not.
Bjarni svarar: "Þetta er líkast því er mér er sagt frá Grænlandi og hér munum vér að landi halda".	Bjarni answered: "This is like therefore which to-me was said from Greenland and here should we by land hold".	Bjarni answered: "This land appears to me as was was described about Greenland, and we'll head for the shore here".

3	3	3
Það er nú þessu næst að Bjarni Herjúlfsson kom utan af Grænlandi á fund Eiríks jarls og tók jarl við honum vel.	It is now this next that Bjarni Son-of-Herjolf came out of Greenland to meet Erik earl and took earl with him well.	It now happened that Bjarni Herjolfson came to Greenland to meet earl Erik, and the earl received him well.

The Saga of the Greenlanders (Old Icelandic)

Old Icelandic	Literal	English
Sagði Bjarni frá ferðum sínum er hann hafði lönd séð og þótti mönnum hann verið hafa óforvitinn er hann hafði ekki að segja af þeim löndum og fékk hann af því nokkuð ámæli.	Said Bjarni from voyages his that he had land seen and thought men he had-been having no-curiosity when he had nothing to say of these lands and got he of therefore some reproach.	Bjarni told of his voyages and that he had seen land, and people thought he had lacked curiosity when he had nothing much to say about these lands, and he received criticism for this.
Bjarni gerðist hirðmaður jarls og fór út til Grænlands um sumarið eftir. Var nú mikil umræða um landaleitan.	Bjarni became court-man earl's and travelled out to Greenland about summer after. Was now much talk about land-exploring.	Bjarni became one of the earl's followers and travelled out to Greenland the next summer. There was now much talk of exploring these lands.
Leifur son Eiríks rauða úr Brattahlíð fór á fund Bjarna Herjúlfssonar og keypti skip að honum og réð til háseta svo að þeir voru hálfur fjórði tugur manna saman. Leifur bað föður sinn Eirík að hann mundi enn fyrir vera förinni.	Leif son Erik's the-Red from Brattahlid travelled to meet Bjarni Herjolfsson and bought ship of his and appointed to men so that there were half fourth twenty men together. Leif bid father his Erik that he would still for be voyage.	Leif, Erik the Red's son from Brattahlid, travelled to meet Bjarni Herjolfsson and bought his ship and hired a crew of thirty five men altogether. Leif asked his father Erik to lead the expedition.
Eiríkur taldist heldur undan, kveðst þá vera hniginn í aldur og kveðst minna mega við vosi öllu en var. Leifur kveður hann enn mundu mestri heill stýra af þeim frændum. Og þetta lét Eiríkur eftir Leifi og ríður heiman þá er þeir eru að því búnir og var þá skammt að fara til skipsins. Drepur hesturinn fæti, sá er Eiríkur reið, og féll hann af baki og lestist fótur hans.	Erik told rather away, saying then being declining in age and said less able with cold-and-wet all but was. Leif said he still would most luck steer of them kinsmen. And this allowed Erik after Leif and rode home then as they were to for prepared and was then short to go to ship. Failed horse's feet, that was Erik riding, and fell he from back and injured foot his.	Erik was reluctant, saying that he was getting old and less able to cope with the cold weather as he once was. Leif said that he still had the most luck of all his kinsmen. Erik gave in to Leif, and they rode from home as they were ready and had a short distance to go to the ship. The horse that Erik was riding stumbled, and Erik fell injuring his foot.
Þá mælti Eiríkur "Ekki mun mér ætlað að finna lönd fleiri en þetta er nú byggjum vér. Munum vér nú ekki lengur fara allir samt".	Then said Erik "Not should to-me intend to find land more but this that now inhabit we. Should we now nothing longer go all together".	Then Erik said "I am not intended to find any other land than the one where we now live. This will be the end of our travelling together".
Fór Eiríkur heim í Brattahlíð en Leifur réðst til skips og félagar hans með honum, hálfur fjóði tugur manna.	Travelled Erik home to Brattahlid but Leif rode to ship and companions his with him, half fourth twenty men.	Erik travelled home to Brattahlid but Leif rode to the ship with his companions, thirty five men.

The Saga of the Greenlanders (Old Icelandic)

Old Icelandic	Literal	English
Þar var suðurmaður einn í ferð er Tyrkir hét.	There was southern-man one on voyage was Tyrkir named.	There was a southern man on the voyage who was named Tyrkir.
Nú bjuggu þeir skip sitt og sigldu í haf þá er þeir voru búnir og fundu þá það land fyrst er þeir Bjarni fundu síðast.	Now prepared they ship theirs and sailed to sea then when they were ready and found then that land first which there Bjarni found last.	Now they prepared their ship and sailed to sea, then they were ready and found first land that Bjarni had found last.
Þar sigla þeir að landi og köstuðu akkerum og skutu báti og fóru á land og sáu þar eigi gras.	There sailed they to land and cast anchor and launched boats and travelled to land and saw there not grass.	They sailed to the land, cast anchor, put out a boat and rowed ashore, and saw there was no grass.
Jöklar miklir voru allt hið efra en sem ein hella væri allt til jöklanna frá sjónum og sýndist þeim það land vera gæðalaust.	Glaciers great were all the over but which a stone-slab was all to mountains from the-sea and seemed to-them that land was without-quality.	Large glaciers covered the highlands, but the land was like a stone slab from the mountains to the sea, and it seemed to them that this land was of little use.
Þá mælti Leifur: "Eigi er oss nú það orðið um þetta land sem Bjarna að vér höfum eigi komið á landið. Nú mun eg gefa nafn landinu og kalla Helluland".	Then said Leif: "Not are we now that word about this land as Bjarni that we have not come on land. Now will I give name land and call Helluland".	Then Leif said: "Now we cannot have word about this land like Bjarni that we did not come on land. Now I will give the land a name and call it Helluland".
Síðan fóru þeir til skips.	Since travelled they to ship.	Afterwards they returned to the ship.
Eftir þetta sigla þeir í haf og fundu land annað, sigla enn að landi og kasta akkerum, skjóta síðan báti og ganga á landið. Það land var slétt og skógi vaxið og sandar hvítir víða þar sem þeir fóru og ósæbratt.	After that sailed they to sea and found land another, sailed yet to land and cast anchor, launched then boats and went to land. That land was flat and forest grown and sands white widely there as they travelled and unbroken-sea.	After that they sailed to sea and found another land, sailed close to the land and cast anchor, put out a boat and went to shore. This land was flat and forested, with many white beaches, wide as they travelled and unbroken by the sea.
Þá mælti Leifur: "Af kostum skal þessu landi nafn gefa og kalla Markland".	Then said Leif: "Of benefit shall this land name give and call Markland".	Then Leif said: "This land shall be named by its benefit, and will be called Markland".
Fóru síðan ofan aftur til skips sem fljótast.	Travelled since on back to ship as immediately.	Afterwards they travelled back to the ship immediately.

Old Icelandic	Literal	English
Nú sigla þeir þaðan í haf landnyrðingsveður og voru úti tvö dægur áður þeir sáu land og sigldu að landi og komu að ey einni er lá norður af landinu og gengu þar upp og sáust um í góðu veðri og fundu það að dögg var á grasinu og varð þeim það fyrir að þeir tóku höndum sínum í döggina og brugðu í munn sér og þóttust ekki jafnsætt kennt hafa sem það var.	Now sailed they from-there to sea North-East-Wind and were out two days before they saw land and sailed to land and came to island one which lay north from land and went there up and looked about in good weather and found that to dew was on grass and were they that at-hand that they took hands theirs to dew and brought to mouths theirs and thought not as-sweet known have as that was.	Now they sailed from there to the sea with a north east wind, and sailed for two days before they saw land, they sailed towards it and came to an island that lay to the north of the land, they went up to the shore and looked about, in fine weather they found dew on the grass, that they took in their hands, and brought to their mouths, and they thought nothing was as sweet as that was.
Síðan fóru þeir til skips síns og sigldu í sund það er lá milli eyjarinnar og ness þess er norður gekk af landinu, stefndu í vesturátt fyrir nesið.	Since travelled they to ship theirs and sailed to strait that which lay between island and headland this was north going of land, steered at westwards before headland.	Afterwards they travelled to their ship and sailed to the strait that lay between the island and the headland that stretched out north from the land, they steered westwards around the headland.
Þar var grunnsævi mikið að fjöru sjóvar og stóð þá uppi skip þeirra og var þá langt til sjóvar að sjá frá skipinu.	There were shallows much at tide sea and stood then up ship theirs and was then long to sea to see from ship.	There were many shallows at low tide and their ship was stranded, and then the sea was a long way out as seen by those on the ship.
En þeim var svo mikil forvitni á að fara til landsins að þeir nenntu eigi þess að bíða að sjór félli undir skip þeirra og runnu til lands þar er á ein féll úr vatni einu. En þegar sjór féll undir skip þeirra þá tóku þeir bátinn og réru til skipsins og fluttu það upp í ána, síðan í vatnið og köstuðu þar akkerum og báru af skipi húðföt sín og gerðu þar búðir, tóku það ráð síðan að búast þar um þann vetur og gerðu þar hús mikil.	But they were so much curiosity of to travel to land, that they bothered not this to wait, by sea rising under ship theirs, and ran to land, there was on one lake from river one. But then sea fell under ship theirs, then took they boat and rowed to ship and floated that up into river, then into lake, and cast there anchor and brought off ship skin-cots theirs and made there booths, took they counsel then to stay there about then winter and make there houses large.	Their curiosity to travel to land was so great, that they did not bother to wait for the sea to rise under their ship, and ran aground where there was a river from a lake. But when the sea flowed under their ship, they took the boat and rowed it to the ship, and floated up into the river, then into the lake, and cast anchor there, and brought off the ship their sleeping-sacks and built booths, they then decided to stay there for the winter and make large houses there.
Hvorki skorti þar lax í ánni né í vatninu og stærra lax en þeir hefðu fyrr séð.	Neither shortage there salmon in river nor in lake and larger salmon than they have before seen.	There was no shortage of salmon there, neither in the river nor in the lake, and larger salmon than they had seen before.

The Vinland Sagas   *The Saga of the Greenlanders (Old Icelandic)*

Old Icelandic	Literal	English
Þar var svo góður landskostur, að því er þeim sýndist, að þar mundi engi fénaður fóður þurfa á vetrum. Þar komu engi frost á vetrum og lítt rénuðu þar grös. Meira var þar jafndægri en á Grænlandi eða Íslandi. Sól hafði þar eyktarstað og dagmálastað um skammdegi.	There was so good land-benefits, in therefore as they seemed, that there would not cattle fodder need in winter. There came no frost in winter, and little receded there grass. More was there equal-day than on Greenland or Iceland. Sun had there three-hours stood and morning stood during short-time-of-day.	The land was so good, that it seemed to them that cattle would not need fodder in winter. There was no frost in winter, and the grass only receded a little. The days and nights were more equal in length than in Greenland or Iceland. The sun stood by mid morning and stood during mid afternoon, during winter and the shortest time of day.
En er þeir höfðu lokið húsgerð sinni þá mælti Leifur við föruneyti sitt: "Nú vil eg skipta láta liði voru í tvo staði og vil eg kanna láta landið og skal helmingur liðs vera við skála heima en annar helmingur skal kanna landið og fara eigi lengra en þeir komi heim að kveldi og skiljist eigi".	And when they had ended house-building theirs then talked Leif with companions his: "Now will I divide let company ours into two parts and will I explore let land and shall half company be with cabin home but another half shall explore land and go not further than they come home by evening and separate not".	And when they had finished their house building, Leif said to his companions: "Now I wish to have our company divided into two groups and explore the land, I wish that half the company shall be home at the cabin, and the other half shall explore the land and go no further than they can come home by evening, and no one separate".
Nú gerðu þeir svo um stund. Leifur gerði ýmist, að hann fór með þeim eða var heima að skála.	Now did they so about awhile. Leif did either, that he travelled with them or was home at cabin.	Now they did this for a while. Leif either travelled with them or he was home at the cabin.
Leifur var mikill maður og sterkur, manna skörulegastur að sjá, vitur maður og góður hófsmaður um alla hluti.	Leif was great man and strong, man striking to see, wise man and good moderate-man about all things.	Leif was a great and strong man, striking in appearance, and a wise man who was moderate about all things.
4	4	4
Á einhverju kveldi bar það til tíðinda að manns var vant af liði þeirra og var það Tyrkir suðurmaður. Leifur kunni því stórilla því að Tyrkir hafði lengi verið með þeim feðgum og elskað mjög Leif í barnæsku.	At one-such evening bore that to news that man was missing from company theirs and was that Tyrkir southern-man. Leif knew therefore greatly because that Tyrkir had long been with them father-and-son and loved much Leif in childhood.	One evening came the news that a man was missing from their team, and that was Tyrkir the southerner. Leif was affected by this, because Tyrkir had spent many years with him and his father, and he had treated Leif very affectionately as a child.

The Vinland Sagas   *The Saga of the Greenlanders (Old Icelandic)*

Old Icelandic	Literal	English
Taldi Leifur nú mjög á hendur förunautum sínum og bjóst til ferðar að leita hans og tólf menn með honum.	Told Leif now much on hand travelling-men his and prepared to go to seek him and twelve men with him.	Leif told off his people and prepared to seek him with twelve men.
En er þeir voru skammt komnir frá skála þá gekk Tyrkir í mót þeim og var honum vel fagnað.	But when they were short came from cabin, then going Tyrkir in meeting them, and was he well welcomed.	But when they were a short way away from the cabin, Tyrkir came towards them, and he was gladly welcomed.
Leifur fann það brátt að fóstra hans var skapgott.	Leif found that soon, that foster-father his was well-tempered.	Leif soon found that his foster-father was in a good mood.
Hann var brattleitur og lauseygur, smáskitlegur í andliti, lítill vexti og vesallegur en íþróttamaður á alls konar hagleik.	He was steep-looking and loose-eyed, dirty in face, little grown and poor-wretch, but excellent in all kinds-of pursuits.	He had a protruding forehead and darting eyes, with dark wrinkles in his face, he was short and frail looking, but excellent in many pursuits.
Þá mælti Leifur til hans: "Hví varstu svo seinn fóstri minn og fráskili föruneytinu?"	Then said Leif to him: "Why were so late, foster mine, and separated companions?"	Then Leif said to him: "Why were you so late, foster-father, and how were you separated from your companions?".
Hann talaði þá fyrst lengi á þýsku og skaut marga vega augunum og gretti sig. *En þeir skildu eigi hvað er hann sagði.*	He talked then first long in German and shot many ways eyes and frowned himself. But they knew not, what was he said.	He talked at length first in German with his eyes darting in many directions and frowning. The others did not know what he was saying.
Hann mælti þá á norrænu er stund leið: "Eg var genginn eigi miklu lengra en þið. *Kann eg nokkur nýnæmi að að segja.* *Eg fann vínvið og vínber".*	He said then in Norse, a while way: "I was going not much longer than you. Know I something new to say. I found vines and grapes".	After a while, he spoke in Norse: "I had only gone a little farther than you. I know some news to tell you: I found grapevines and grapes".
"Mun það satt fóstri minn?" kvað Leifur.	"Would that true, foster mine?" said Leif.	"Is this true, foster-father?" said Lef.
Að vísu er það satt, kvað hann, "því að eg var þar fæddur er hvorki skorti vínvið né vínber".	"To know is that true", said he, "because that I was there fathered, where neither shortage vines nor grapes".	"I know this is true", said he, "because where I was brought up, there was no shortage of grapevines and grapes".

The Saga of the Greenlanders (Old Icelandic)

Old Icelandic	Literal	English
Nú sváfu þeir af þá nótt en um morguninn mælti Leifur við háseta sína: "Nú skal hafa tvennar sýslur fram og skal sinn dag hvort, lesa vínber eða höggva vínvið og fella mörkina svo að það verði farmur til skips míns".	Now slept they of then night, but about morning said Leif to crew his: "Now shall have two pursuits from, and shall the day either, gather grapes or fell with and fell trees, so by that be cargo to ship mine".	They went to sleep that night, and around morning Leif said to his crew: "No we shall have two pursuits each day, either picking grapes or cutting vines, or felling trees to make cargo for my ship".
Og þetta var ráðs tekið.	And that was counsel taken.	And that advice was taken.
Svo er sagt að eftirbátur þeirra var fylltur af vínberjum.	So is said, that boat theirs was filled of grapes.	So it was said that their boat was filled with grapes.
Nú var hogginn farmur á skipið.	Now was cut-down cargo for ship.	Now they cut down wood as cargo for the ship.
Og er vorar þá bjuggust þeir og sigldu burt og gaf Leifur nafn landinu eftir landkostum og kallaði Vínland, sigla nú síðan í haf og gaf þeim vel byri þar til er þeir sáu Grænland og fjöll undir jöklum.	And when spring, then prepared they and sailed away, and gave Leif named land after land-benefits and called Vinland, sailed now since into sea, and gave them well fair-wind, there until was they saw Greenland and mountains below glaciers.	And when spring came, they made ready and sailed away, and Leif named the lanf after its features and called it Vinland, they now sailed to sea, and they were given fair wind until they saw Greenland and the mountains under glaciers.
Þá tók einn maður til máls og mælti við Leif: "Hví stýrir þú svo mjög undir veður skipinu?"	Then took one man to speak and said to Leif: "Why steer you so up-to wind the-ship?	Then one man said to Leif: "Why do you steer the ship so close to the wind?"
Leifur svaraði: "Eg hygg að stjórn minni en þó enn að fleira. Eða hvað sjáið þér til tíðinda?"	Leif answered: "I think to steering less, but though still to more, or what see you to news?".	Leif answered: "I am aware of my course, but there is more to it than that, do you see anything of note?".
Þeir kváðust ekki sjá það er tíðindum sætti.	They said not see, that which news agreed.	They said that they did not see anything of note.
Eg veit eigi, segir Leifur, "hvort eg sé skip eða sker".	"I know not", said Leif, "Whether I see ship or skerry".	"I don't know", said Leif, "whether I see a ship or a rock".
Nú sjá þeir og kváðu sker vera.	Now looked they and said skerry was.	Now they looked and said that it was a rock.
Hann sá því framar en þeir að hann sá menn í skerinu.	He saw that from but they, that he saw men on the-skerry.	He saw so much better than them, that he could see men on the rock.

The Vinland Sagas — The Saga of the Greenlanders (Old Icelandic)

Old Icelandic	Literal	English
Nú vil eg að vér beitum undir veðrið, segir Leifur, "svo að vér náum til þeirra ef menn eru þurftugir að ná vorum fundi og er nauðsyn á að duga þeim. En með því að þeir séu eigi friðmenn þá eigum vér allan kost undir oss en þeir ekki undir sér".	"Now will I, that we apply up-to wind", said Leif, "So that we near to them, if men are in-need by near we meet, and is necessity to that help them. But as-well for by they so not peaceful-men, then own we all advantage behind us, but they not behind them".	"Now I wish to steer us close to the wind", said Leif, "so that we are near to them, if these men are in need of help, we must help them. But equally if they are hostile, then we have all the advantages, and they have none".
Nú sækja þeir undir skerið og lægðu segl sitt, köstuðu akkeri og skutu litlum báti öðrum er þeir höfðu haft með sér.	Now sought they under the-skerry and lowered sails theirs, and cast anchor and launched little boat other, that they had had with them.	Now they searched about the rock, lowered their sails, cast anchor, and launched the second of their small boats that they had with them.
Þá spurði Leifur hver þar réði fyrir liði.	Then asked Leif who there leader for company.	Then Leif asked who there was the leader of their company.
Sá kveðst Þórir heita og vera norænn maður að kyni,	So said Thorir called, and was north man by kin.	The man who replied said his name was Thorir, and that he was of Norwegian origin.
"eða hvert er þitt nafn?"	"But what is your name?"	"But what is your name?"
Leifur segir til sín.	Leif said to them.	Leif told them.
"Ertu son Eiríks rauða úr Brattahlíð?" segir hann.	"Are-you son-of Erik's the-Red out-of Brattahlid?" said he.	"Are you the son of Erik the Red from Brattahlid?" he said.
Leifur kvað svo vera: *"Nú vil eg", segir Leifur, "bjóða yður öllum á mitt skip og fémunum þeim er skipið má við taka".*	Leif said so was. "Now will I", said Leif, "Invite you all on my ship, and goods those, which ship may with take".	Leif said it was so. "Now I wish", said Leif, "to invite you all on to my ship and any goods, which the ship may carry".
Þeir þágu þann kost og sigldu síðan til Eiríksfjarðar með þeim farmi þar til er þeir komu til Brattahlíðar, báru farminn af skipi. Síðan bauð Leifur Þóri til vistar með sér og Guðríði konu hans og þrem mönnum öðrum en fékk vistir öðrum hásetum, bæði Þóris og sínum félögum.	They accepted that choice and sailed afterwards to Eriksfjord with them cargo, there to then they came to Brattahlid, brought cargo off ship. Afterwards invited Leif Thori to stay with him and Guthrid, wife his, and three men other, but got provisions other seamen, as-well Thori and his companions.	They accepted his offer and then they sailed to Eriksfjord with their cargo, until they reached Brattahlid, where they brought the cargo off the ship. Afterwards Leif invited Thorir to stay with him, along with Thorir's wife Gudrid, and three other men, and found provisions for the other seamen, both Thorir's and his companions.
Leifur tók fimmtán menn úr skerinu.	Leif took fifteen men from the-skerry.	Leif rescued fifteen men from the rock.

Old Icelandic	Literal	English
Hann var síðan kallaður Leifur hinn heppni. Leifi varð nú bæði gott til fjár og mannvirðingar.	He was afterwards called Leif the lucky. Leif was now both benefited to wealth and worthiness.	After this he was called Leif the Lucky. Leif now became very wealthy and gained much respect.
Þann vetur kom sótt mikil í lið Þóris og andaðist hann Þórir og mikill hluti liðs hans.	That winter came sickness great among team Thorir, and died he Thorir and much part-of men his.	That winter there came a great sickness among Thorir's companions, and Thorir died along with many of his company.
Þann vetur andaðist og Eiríkur rauði.	That winter died also Erik the-Red.	That winter Erik the Red also died.
Nú var umræða mikil um Vínlandsför Leifs og þótti Þorvaldi bróður hans of óvíða kannað hafa verið landið.	Now was talk much about Vinland-voyage Leif's, and thought Thorvald brother his, about little-wide explored had been land.	There was great discussion of Leif's Vinland-voyage, and his brother Thorvald thought that the land had been little explored.
Þá mælti Leifur við Þorvald: "Þú skalt fara með skip mitt bróðir ef þú vilt til Vínlands og vil eg þó að skipið fari áður eftir viði þeim er Þórir átti í skerinu".	Then said Leif to Thorvald: "You shall go with ship mine, brother, if you will, to Vinland, and will I though, that ship go return after timber that, was Thorir had on the-skerry".	Leif then said to Thorvald: "You go to Vinland, brother, if you wish, but I wish for that ship to return after the timber, that Thorir had on that rock".
Og svo var gert.	And so was done.	And so it was done.
5	5	5
Nú bjóst Þorvaldur til þeirrar ferðar með þrjá tigi manna með umráði Leifs bróður síns.	Now prepared Thorvald to their voyage with three ten men with counsel Leif, brother his.	Now Thorvald prepared their voyage with advice from his brother Leif, with thirty companions.
Síðan bjuggu þeir skip sitt og héldu í haf og er engi frásögn um ferð þeirra fyrr en þeir koma til Vínlands til Leifsbúða og bjuggu þar um skip sitt og sátu um kyrrt þann vetur og veiddu fiska til matar sér.	After prepared they ship theirs and held to sea, and is nothing said about voyage theirs, before but they came to Vinland, to Leif's-camp, and settled there about ship theirs and sat about still they winter and caught fish for food theirs.	They made their ship ready and put to sea, and nothing is said about their voyage before they came to Vinland, to Leif's camp, and they settled their ship, and stayed in place that winter and caught fish for their food.
En um vorið mælti Þorvaldur að þeir skyldu búa skip sitt og skyldi eftirbátur skipsins og nokkurir menn með fara fyrir vestan landið og kanna þar um sumarið.	But about spring said Thorvald, that they should prepare ship theirs and should boat ship's and some men with travel for western land and explore there about summer.	Then about spring Thorvald said that they should prepare their ship, and with the ship's boat some men should travel west of the land and explore there during the summer.

The Saga of the Greenlanders (Old Icelandic)

Old Icelandic	Literal	English
Þeim sýndist landið fagurt og skógótt, og skammt milli skógar og sjóvar, og hvítir sandar.	They seemed land beautiful and wooded and short between woods and sea and white sands.	To them the land seemed beautiful and well forested, and a short distance between the woods and the sea were white sands.
Þar var eyjótt mjög og grunnsævi mikið.	There were islands much and shallows much.	There were many islands and large stretches of shallow sea.
Þeir fundu hvergi mannavistir né dýra,	They found neither men food nor animals.	The found neither sign of men nor animals.
en í eyju einni vestarlega fundu þeir kornhjálm af tré.	But on island one westward found they corn-shed of wood.	But on one of the westward islands they found a wooden corn shed.
Eigi fundu þeir fleiri mannaverk og fóru aftur og komu til Leifsbúða að hausti.	Not found they more men's-work and went back and came to Leif's-camp in autumn.	They did not find any more work by human hands and came back to Leif's camp in the autumn.
En að sumri öðru fór Þorvaldur fyrir austan með kaupskipið og hið nyrðra fyrir landið.	But at summer the-next went Thorvald for eastward with ship and the north for land.	The next summer Thorvald journeyed eastwards with the ship and north around the land.
Þá gerði að þeim veður hvasst fyrir andnesi einu og rak þá þar upp og brutu kjölinn undan skipinu og höfðu þar langa dvöl og bættu skip sitt.	Then was to them weather stormy before headland one, and driven then there up, and broke keel under ship and had there long dwelled and repaired ship theirs.	Then they encountered stormy weather around one of the headlands, and they were driven ashore, and their keel brooke under their ship, and they stayed there a long time repairing their ship.
Þá mælti Þorvaldur við förunauta sína: "Nú vil eg að vér reisum hér upp kjölinn á nesinu og köllum Kjalarnes". Og svo gerðu þeir.	Then said Thorvald to companions his: "Now will I, that we raise here up keel on headland and call Kjalarnes". And so did they.	Then Thorvald said to his companions: "Now I wish that we raise the keel up on the headland and call it Keel Point". And so they did.
Síðan sigla þeir þaðan í braut og austur fyrir landið og inn í fjarðarkjafta þá er þar voru næstir og að höfða þeim er þar gekk fram.	Afterwards sailed they there to away and eastern for land and then into fjord-mouth then, which there was nearest, and to headland they, which there going from.	Afterwards they sailed away to the east of the land and then into the mouth of the next fjords, and then to a cape stretching out from there to the sea.
Hann var allur skógi vaxin.	It was all wood grown.	It was covered with forest.
Þá leggja þeir fram skip sitt í lægi og skjóta bryggjum á land og gengur Þorvaldur þar á land upp með alla förunauta sína.	There let they from ship theirs to lay and launched bridge to land, and went Thorvald there to land up with all companions his.	There they lay their ship and set out gangways to the land, and Thorvald and his companions went to shore.
Hann mælti þá: "Hér er fagurt og hér vildi eg bæ minn reisa".	He said then: "Here is beautiful, and here will I settlement mine raise",	Then he said: "It is beautiful here, and I wish to build a farm here",

The Vinland Sagas — The Saga of the Greenlanders (Old Icelandic)

Old Icelandic	Literal	English
Ganga síðan til skips og sjá á sandinum inn frá höfðanum þrjár hæðir og fóru til þangað og sjá þar húðkeipa þrjá og þrjá menn undir hverjum.	Went then to ship and saw on sands in from headland three heights, and went to there and saw there hide-boats three and three men under each.	Afterwards as they went back to the ship, they saw three hillocks on the beach inland from the cape, and saw three canoes with three men under each of them.
Þá skiptu þeir liði sínu og höfðu hendur á þeim öllum nema einn komst í burt með keip sinn.	Then divided they people theirs and had caught to they all, taken one came to away with canoe his.	They divided their forces and caught all of them, except one who escaped with his canoe.
Þeir drepa hina átta og ganga síðan aftur á höfðann og sjást þar um og sjá inn í fjörðinn hæðir nokkurar og ætluðu þeir það vera byggðir.	They killed the eight and went since back to headland and looked there about and saw that in fjord heights some, and supposed they that were dwellings.	They killed the other eight and afterwards went back to the cape, and they looked and saw that in some of the fjord heights, what they assumed to be settlements.
Eftir það sló á þá höfga svo miklum að þeir máttu eigi vöku halda og sofna þeir allir.	After that struck on then heaviness so much, that they may not awake keep, and slept they all.	After that they became so heavy with weariness, that they could not stay awake, and the all fell asleep.
Þá kom kall yfir þá svo að þeir vöknuðu allir.	Then came shout over then, so that they awoke all.	Then a voice called to them, and they all awoke.
Svo segir kallið: "Vaki þú Þorvaldur og allt föruneyti þitt ef þú vilt líf þitt hafa og far þú á skip þitt og allir menn þínir og farið frá landi sem skjótast".	So said call: "Wake you, Thorvald, and all companions yours, if you will lives yours have, and go you to ship yours and all men yours, and travel from land which quickly".	The voice called: "Wake up, Thorvald, and all your companions, if you wish to save your lives, get to your ship and all your men, and leave this land as quickly as you can".
Þá fór innan eftir firðinum ótal húðkeipa og lögðu að þeim.	Then went within behind fjord countless hide-boats, and lay at them.	Then from within the fjord came countless canoes heading towards them.
Þorvaldur mælti þá: "Vér skulum færa út á borð vígfleka og verjast sem best en vega lítt í mót".	Thorvald said then: "We should bring out to board battle and defend as best, but fight little to against".	Then Thorvald said: "We should bring out breastworks along the sides of the ship and defend as best we can, but fight back as little as we can".
Svo gera þeir en Skrælingjar skutu á þá um stund en flýja síðan í burt sem ákafast hver sem mátti.	So did they, but Skraelings shot towards then about awhile, but fled afterwards away as fast, each as may.	So they did, but the Skraelings shot at them for a while, they fled as rapidly as they could.
Þá spurði Þorvaldur menn sína ef þeir væru nokkuð sárir.	Then asked Thorvald men his, if they had any wounds.	Then Thorvald asked his men if any of them had been wounded.

The Saga of the Greenlanders (Old Icelandic)

Old Icelandic	Literal	English
Þeir kváðust eigi sárir vera.	They said not wounded were.	They said that they were not wounded.
Ég hef fengið sár undir hendi, segir hann, "og fló ör milli skipborðsins og skjaldarins undir hönd mér og er hér örin, en mun mig þetta til bana leiða.	"I have caught wound under arm", said he, "And flew arrow between ship's-berth and shield under arm to-me, and is here arrow, then should me this to death lead.	"I have been wounded under my arm", he said, "and an arrow flew between the ship's berth and the shield into my armpit, and this shall lead to my death.
Nú ræð ég að þér búið ferð yðra sem fljótast aftur á leið en þér skuluð færa mig á höfða þann er mér þótti byggilegast vera.	Now advise I, to you prepare travel depart as quickly return to journey, but you should bring me to headland that, which me thinks dwelling shall-be.	Now I advise you to prepare for your return journey as quickly as possible, but take me to that cape that I thought would make a good farm.
Má það vera að mér hafi satt á munn komið að eg muni þar búa á um stund.	May that be, by me have true to mouth come, that I should there dwell on for awhile.	Maybe the words I spoke shall prove true, that I shall dwell there for awhile.
Þar skuluð þér mig grafa og setja krossa að höfði mér og að fótum og kallið það Krossanes jafnan síðan".	There should you me engrave and set cross at head mine and at feet, and call that Krossanes ever after".	There you should bury me and put a cross at my head and feet, and call that Krossanes ever after".
Grænland var þá kristnað en þó andaðist Eiríkur rauði fyrir kristni.	Greenland was then Christian, but though died Erik the-Red before Christianity.	Greenland was then Christian, but Erik died before the conversion to Christianity.
Nú andaðist Þorvaldur en þeir gerðu allt eftir því sem hann hafði mælt og fóru síðan og hittu þar förunauta sína og sögðu hvorir öðrum slík tíðindi sem vissu og bjuggu þar þann vetur og fengu sér vínber og vínvið til skips síns.	Now died Thorvald, but they did all after according, which he had said, and went since and met their companions theirs, and said each other such tidings which knew and dwelt there that winter and gathered they grapes and vines to ship.	Now Thorvald died, and they did everything as he had said, and afterwards they went to meet their companions, and each group told its news to the others, and they stayed there that winter and gathered grapes and vines in their ship.
Nú búast þeir þaðan um vorið eftir til Grænlands og komu skipi sínu í Eiríksfjörð og kunnu Leifi að segja mikil tíðindi.	Now prepared they there about spring after to Greenland and came ship theirs in Eriksfjord and known Leif that said much tidings.	Now they prepared their ship about spring to return to Greenland, and their ship came in to Eriksfjord and had much news to tell Leif.

6

Það hafði gerst til tíðinda meðan á Grænlandi að Þorsteinn í Eiríksfirði hafði kvongast og fengið Guðríðar Þorbjarnardóttur er átt hafði Þórir austmaður er fyrr var frá sagt.	It had made to news meanwhile to Greenland, that Thorstein in Eriksfjord had married and married Guthrid Thorbjarnardottur, who had married Thorir Easterner, as before was from said.	Among the news meanwhile in Greenland was that Thorstein in Eriksfjord had married Gudrid Thorbjornadottir, who had previously been married to Thorir the Easterner who was spoken of earlier.

The Vinland Sagas — The Saga of the Greenlanders (Old Icelandic)

Old Icelandic	Literal	English
Nú fýstist Þorsteinn Eiríksson að fara til Vínlands eftir líki Þorvalds bróður síns og bjó skip hið sama og valdi hann lið að afli og vexti og hafði með sér hálfan þriðja tug manna og Guðríði konu sína og sigla í haf þegar þau eru búin og úr landsýn.	Now desired Thorstein Eriksson to travel to Vinland after body Thorvald's, brother his, and prepared ship the same, and chose he team in strength and well-built and had with him half third twenty men and Guthrid, wife his, and sailed to sea, then they were ready, and out-of land-sight.	Now Thorstein Eriksson wished to travel to Vinland and retrieve the body of his brother Thorvald, and made the same ship ready, and he chose his company for their strength and size, and had with him twenty five men and his wife Gudrid, and when they were ready the sailed to sea, and out of sight of land.
Þau velkti úti allt sumarið og vissu eigi hvar þau fóru.	They drove about all summer, and knew not, where they went.	They were driven about all summer, and they did not know where they went.
Og er vika var af vetri þá tóku þeir land í Lýsufirði á Grænlandi í hinni vestri byggð.	And when week was of winter, then took they land in Lysufjord in Greenland in the western settlement.	And when the first week of winter had passed, they made land in Lysufjord, in the Western Settlement of Greenland.
Þorsteinn leitaði þeim um vistir og fékk vistir öllum hásetum sínum.	Thorstein sought them about shelter and got lodging all crew his.	Thorstein found them shelter and got lodgings for all of his crew.
En hann var vistlaus og kona hans.	But he was without-lodging and wife his.	But he and his wife were without lodgings.
Nú voru þau eftir að skipi tvö nokkurar nætur.	Now were they remained in ship two some nights.	Now they remained on the ship for several nights.
Þá var enn ung kristni á Grænlandi.	Then was yet young Christianity in Greenland.	Then Christianity was still young in Greenland.
Það var einn dag að menn komu að tjaldi þeirra snemma.	It was one day, that people came by tent theirs early.	One day some men came early to their tent.
Sá spurði er fyrir þeim var hvað manna væri í tjaldinu.	So asked, who present they were, what men were in tent.	The asked what men were in the tent.
Þorsteinn svarar: "Tveir menn", segir hann, "eða hver spyr að?"	Thorstein answered: "Two people", said he, "But who asks to?"	Thorstein answered: "Two people", he said, "but who is asking?".
"Þorsteinn heiti eg og er eg kallaður Þorsteinn svartur.	"Thorstein called I, and am I called Thorstein-the-Black.	"I am called Thorstein, Thorstein the Black.
En það er erindi mitt hingað að eg vil bjóða ykkur báðum hjónum til vistar til mín".	But that is errand mine here, that I will bid you both couple to lodging to mine".	My reason for coming here is to invite you both to stay with me".

The Saga of the Greenlanders (Old Icelandic)

Old Icelandic	Literal	English
Þorsteinn kveðst vilja hafa umræði konu sinnar en hún bað hann ráða og nú játar hann þessu.	Thorstein said will have discussion wife his, but she bid he decide, and now accepted he this.	Thorstein said he wished to discuss this with his wife, but she asked him to decide, and he now accepted.
"Þá mun eg koma eftir ykkur á morgun með eyki því að mig skortir ekki til að veita ykkur vist en fásinni er mikið með mér að vera því að tvö erum við þar hjón því að eg er einþykkur mjög.	"Then should I come back to-you in morning with animals, for by shortage not to by supply you provisions, but remote is very with me by being, for that two we-are with there couple, because that I am solitary much".	"Then I shall come back to you in the morning with oxen, I have no shortage of supplies for you, but it is remote being here with me, because there are only two of us, my wife and I, and I am very much a solitary man.
Annan sið hefi eg og en þér hafið og ætla eg þann þó betra er þér hafið".	Another tradition have I and than you have, and suppose I that yet better, is you have".	Also I have another faith than you, but I suspect yours is the better of the two".
Nú kom hann eftir þeim um morguninn með eyki og fóru þau með Þorsteini svarta til vistar og veitti hann þeim vel.	Now came he after them about morning with animals, and went they with Thorstein the-Black to lodge, and supported he them well.	Now he came back to them around morning with oxen, and they went to stay with Thorstein the Black, and he provided for them generously.
Guðríður var sköruleg kona að sjá og vitur kona og kunni vel að vera með ókunnugum mönnum.	Guthrid was strong woman to see and wise woman and knew well at being with unknown people.	Gudrid was a strong woman, of striking appearance, and a wise woman who knew how to behave among strangers.
Það var snemma vetrar að sótt kom í lið Þorsteins Eiríkssonar og önduðust þar margir förunautar.	That was early winter, that sickness came to companions Thorstein's Eriksson, and died there many companions his.	It was early that winter that sickness came to Thorstein Eriksson's companions, and many of them died there.
Þorsteinn bað gera kistur að líkum þeirra er önduðust og færa til skips og búa þar um "því að eg vil láta flytja til Eiríksfjarðar að sumri öll líkin".	Thorstein asked made coffins for bodies theirs, who died, and brought to ship and laid there about, "For that I will lay carry to Eriksfjord in summer all bodies".	Thorstein asked that coffins be made for their bodies who had died, and brought back to the ship and laid there, "For I will carry all of them to Eriksfjord in the summer".
Nú er þess skammt að bíða að sótt kemur í híbýli Þorsteins og tók kona hans sótt fyrst er hét Grímhildur.	Now was this short to wait, that sickness came into dwelling Thorstein's, and took wife his sickness first, who called Grimhild.	It was not long until the sickness came to Thorstein the Black's house, and his wife Grimhild was the first to fall ill.
Hún var ákaflega mikil og sterk sem karlar en þó kom sóttin henni undir.	She was very large and strong as men, but yet came sickness her under.	She was a very large woman, strong as a man, yet she bowed to the sickness.

The Vinland Sagas — The Saga of the Greenlanders (Old Icelandic)

Old Icelandic	Literal	English
Og brátt eftir það tók sóttina Þorsteinn Eiríksson og lágu þau bæði senn og andaðist Grímhildur kona Þorsteins svarta.	And soon after that took sickness Thorstein Eriksson, and lay they both same, and died Grimhild, wife Thorstein the-Black's.	And soon after that Thorstein Eriksson was stricken, and both of them laid there, and Grimhild, the wife of Thorstein the Black died.
En er hún var dauð þá gekk Þorsteinn fram úr stofunni eftir fjöl að leggja á líkið.	But when she was dead, then went Thorstein from out room after plank to lay on body.	And when she had died, Thorstein the Black went from the main room to look for a plank to lay her body on.
Guðríður mælti þá: "Vertu litla hríð í brott Þorsteinn minn", segir hún.	Guthrid said then: "Be little time to away, Thorstein mine", said she.	Gudrid then spoke: "Don't be away long, dear Thorstein" she said.
Hann kvað svo vera skyldu.	He said so be should.	He said so it would be.
Þá mælti Þorsteinn Eiríksson: "Með undarlegum hætti er nú um húsfreyju vora því að nú örglast hún upp við ölnboga og þokar fótum sínum frá stokki og þreifar til skúa sinna".	Then said Thorstein Eriksson: "With strange way is now about housewife going, for that now rises she up with elbows and stretches feet hers from bed and feels for shoes hers".	Then Thorstein Eriksson said: "Strange are the actions of the mistress of the house now, she's struggling to raise herself up on her elbows, and stretches her feet from the bed and feels for her shoes".
Og í því kom Þorsteinn bóndi inn og lagðist Grímhildur niður í því og brakaði þá í hverju tré í stofunni.	And in for came Thorstein farmer the, and lay Grimhild down in for, and creaked then in each beam in room.	And in came Thorstein the farmer, and Grimhild fell back down, and every beam in the room creaked.
Nú gerir Þorsteinn kistu að líki Grímhildar og færði í brott og bjó um. Hann var bæði mikill maður og sterkur og þurfti hann þess alls áður hann kom henni burt af bænum.	Now made Thorstein coffin for body Grimhild's and took it out and dwelling about. He was both large man and strong, and needed he this all, before he came her away out-of dwelling.	Thorstein then made a coffin for Grimhild's body and took it away from the house. He was a large and strong man, and he needed all his strenngth to carry her out of the house.
Nú elnaði sóttin Þorsteini Eiríkssyni og andaðist hann.	Now attacked sickness Thorstein Eriksson, and died he.	Now the sickness attacked Thorstein Eriksson, and he died.
Guðríður kona hans kunni því lítt.	Guthrid, wife his, knew therefore little.	Gudrid, his wife, was overtaken with grief and knew little else.
Þá voru þau öll í stofunni.	Then were they all in room.	All of them were in the main room.
Guðríður hafði setið á stóli frammi fyrir bekknum er hann hafði legið Þorsteinn bóndi hennar.	Guthrid had sat on stool from before bench, which he had laid, Thorstein, husband hers.	Gudrid sat on a stool in front of the bench where her husband Thorstein had lain.

The Vinland Sagas — *The Saga of the Greenlanders (Old Icelandic)*

Old Icelandic	Literal	English
Þá tók Þorsteinn bóndi Guðríði af stólinum í fang sér og settist í bekkinn annan með hana gegnt líki Þorsteins og taldi um fyrir henni marga vega og huggaði hana og hét henni því að hann mundi fara með henni til Eiríksfjarðar með líki Þorsteins bónda hennar og förunauta hans.	Then took Thorstein the-farmer Guthrid from stool into grasp his and sat on another bench with he opposite body Thorstein's and talked about before her many ways and comforted he and called her therefore, that he would go with her to Eriksfjord with body Thorstein's, husband hers, and companions his.	Thorstein the farmer then took Gudrid from the stool into his arms and sat with her on the bench across from her husband Thorstein's corpse and said many comforting things, consoling her and promising her that he would take her to Eriksfjord with her husband Thorstein's body, and those of his companions.
Og svo skal eg taka hingað hjón fleiri, segir hann, "þér til huggunar og skemmtanar".	"And so shall I take there couple more", said he, "You to comfort and entertain".	"And we'll invite other people to stay here", he said, "to provide you with solace and companionship".
Hún þakkaði honum.	She thanked him.	She thanked him.
Þorsteinn Eiríksson settist þá upp og mælti: "Hvar er Guðríður?"	Thorstein Eriksson sat then up and said: "Where is Guthrid?"	Thorstein Eriksson then sat up and said: "Where is Gudrid?"
Þrjá tíma mælti hann þetta en hún þagði.	Three times said he this, but she silent.	Three times he said this, but she remained silent.
Þá mælti hún við Þorstein bónda: "Hvort skal eg svör veita hans máli eða eigi?"	Then said she to Thorstein the-farmer: "However shall I answer know his speech or not?"	Then she said to Thorstein the farmer: "Shall I answer him or not?",
Hann bað hana eigi svara.	He bid she not answer.	He told her not to answer.
Þá gekk Þorsteinn bóndi yfir gólfið og settist á stólinn en Guðríður sat í knjám honum.	Then went Thorstein the-farmer over floor and sat on stool, but Guthrid sat on knees his.	Thorstein the farmer then crossed the floor and sat on the stool, and Gudrid on his knee.
Og þá mælti Þorsteinn bóndi: "Hvað viltu nafni?" segir hann.	And then said Thorstein the-farmer "What will-you, namesake?" said he.	Then Thorstein the farmer spoke: "What is it that you want, namesake?", he said.
Hann svarar er stund leið: "Mér er annt til þess að segja Guðríði forlög sín til þess að hún kunni þá betur andláti mínu því að eg er kominn til góðra hvíldarstaða.	He answered, at time way: "I who wish to this, to say Guthrid fortune hers, to this by she could then better death mine, for that I am come to good resting-place.	He answered after a short while: "I want to tell Gudrid her fate, to make it easier for her to deal with my death, for I have gone to a good resting place.

The Vinland Sagas   *The Saga of the Greenlanders (Old Icelandic)*

Old Icelandic	Literal	English
En það er þér að segja Guðríður að þú munt gift vera íslenskum manni og munu langar vera samfarir ykkar og mart manna mun frá ykkur koma, þroskasamt, bjart og ágætt, sætt og ilmað vel.	But this is you to say, Guthrid, that you shall married be Icelander man, and shall long be together you, and many people shall from you come, promising, bright and fine, settled and favoured well.	I say this to you, Gudrid, that you shall marry an Icelander, and you will long be together, and you shall have many descendants, promisinig, bright, and fine, sweet and well favoured.
Munuð þið fara af Grænlandi til Noregs og þaðan til Íslands og gera bú á Íslandi.	Shall you travel from Greenland to Norway and from-there to Iceland and make settlement on Iceland.	You will travel from Greenland to Norway, and from there to Iceland, and settle on Iceland.
Þar munuð þið lengi búa og muntu honum lengur lifa.	There shall you long live, and shall him longer live.	There you will live a long time, longer than your husband.
Þú munt utan fara og ganga suður og koma út aftur til Íslands til bús þíns og þá mun þar kirkja reist vera og muntu þar vera og taka nunnuvígslu og þar muntu andast".	You shall out travel and go south and come from return to Iceland to home yours, and then shall there church raised be, and shall there be and take nun's-vows, and there shall die".	You will travel and go south, and return to Iceland to your farm, and there a church will be raised, and there you will take a nun's vows, and there you will die".
Og þá hnígur Þorsteinn aftur og var búið um lík hans og fært til skips.	And then fell Thorstein back, and was prepared about body his and taken to ship.	And then Thorstein Eriksson fell back, and his corpse was prepared and taken to the ship.
Þorsteinn bóndi efndi vel við Guðríði allt það er hann hafði heitið.	Thorstein the-farmer kept well with Guthrid all that, which he had promised.	Thorstein the farmer kept all his promises to Gudrid.
Hann seldi um vorið jörð sína og kvikfé og fór til skips með Guðríði með allt sitt, bjó skipið og fékk menn til og fór síðan til Eiríksfjarðar.	He sold about spring land his and livestock and went to ship with Guthrid with all his, prepared ship and got men to and went then to Eriksfjord.	In the spring he sold his land and livestock, and went to the ship with all his posessions, prepared the ship, hired a crew, and sailed to Eriksfjord.
Voru nú líkin jörðuð að kirkju.	Were now bodies buried by church.	The bodies were now buried by a church.
Guðríður fór til Leifs í Brattahlíð en Þorsteinn svarti gerði bú í Eiríksfirði og bjó þar meðan hann lifði og þótti vera hinn vaskasti maður.	Guthrid travelled to Leif in Brattahlid, but Thorstein the-Black made dwelling at Eriksfjord and dwelt there, meantime he lived, and thought was he capable man.	Gudrid travlelled to Leif in Brattahlid, and Thorstein the Black built a farm in Eriksfjord and settled there as long as he lived, and he was thought of as a most capable man.
7	7	7
Það sama sumar kom skip af Noregi til Grænlands.	That same summer came ship from Norway to Greenland.	That same summer a ship came from Norway and arrived in Greenland.
Sá maður hét Þorfinnur karlsefni er því skipi stýrði.	The man called Thorfin Karlsefni, who for ship steered.	The captain of the ship was named Thorfin Karlsefni.

The Vinland Sagas *The Saga of the Greenlanders (Old Icelandic)*

Old Icelandic	Literal	English
Hann var son Þórðar hesthöfða Snorrasonar, Þórðarsonar frá Höfða.	He was son-of Thord Horse-Head Snorrason, Thordarson from Hofdi.	He was the son of Thord Horse-Head, the son of Snorri Thordarson of Hofdi.
Þorfinnur karlsefni var stórauðigur að fé og var um veturinn í Brattahlíð með Leifi Eiríkssyni.	Thorfin Karlsefni was wealthy in cattle, and was about winter in Brattahlid with Leif Eriksson.	Thorfin Karlsefni was wealth in cattle, and he spent the winter in Brattahlid with Leif Eriksson.
Brátt felldi hann hug til Guðríðar og bað hennar en hún veik til Leifs svörum fyrir sig.	Soon fell he thoughts to Guthrid and asked her, but she referred to Leif's answer to him.	He was soon attracted to Gudrid and asked her to marry him, but she referred him to Leif for his answer.
Síðan var hún honum föstnuð og gert brúðhlaup þeirra á þeim vetri.	Afterwards was she to-him betrothed and was wedding theirs in that winter.	Afterwards she was engaged to him and their wedding was that winter.
Hin sama var umræða á Vínlandsför sem fyrr og fýstu menn Karlsefni mjög þeirrar ferðar, bæði Guðríður og aðrir menn.	The same was discussed to Vinland-voyage as before, and urged people Karlsefni much there to-journey, both Guthrid and other people.	The discussion of a voyage to Vinland continued as before, and people urged Karlsefni to make the journey, both Gudrid and others.
Nú var ráðin ferð hans og réð hann sér skipverja, sex tigi karla og konur fimm.	Now was agreed travel his, and hired he the crew six ten men and women five.	Now he was decided to travel, he hired a crew of sixty men and five women.
Þann máldaga gerðu þeir Karlsefni og hásetar hans að jöfnum höndum skyldu þeir hafa allt það er þeir fengju til gæða.	Then agreed was they Karlsefni and crew his, that even handed should they have all that, which they get to quality.	Then Karlsefni and his crew agreed that all goods they obtained would be divided equally among them.
Þeir höfðu með sér alls konar fénað því að þeir ætluðu að byggja landið ef þeir mættu það.	They have with them all-kinds livestock, for that they intended to settle land, if they may that.	They had with them all kinds of livestock, for they intended to settle the land if they could.
Karlsefni bað Leif húsa á Vínlandi en hann kveðst ljá mundu húsin en gefa eigi.	Karlsefni asked Leif houses in Vinland, but he said loan would houses, but give not.	Karlsefni asked Leif for his houses in Vinland, and Leif said he would lend them, but not give them to him.
Síðan héldu þeir í haf skipinu og komu til Leifsbúða með heilu og höldnu og báru þar upp húðföt sín.	Then held they to sea ship and came to Leif's-camp with whole and safe and carried there up skin-cots theirs.	Then they put the ship to sea and all arrived at Leif's camp safely and unloaded their sleeping-sacks.
Þeim bar brátt í hendur mikil föng og góð því að reyður var þar upp rekin, bæði mikil og góð, fóru til síðan og skáru hvalinn.	They bore soon to hand much provisions and good, for a rorqual was there up driven, both large and good, went to then and cut whale, shortage then not food.	They soon had plenty of good provisions, since a large and fine rorqual was driven up to shore, they had no shortage of food.
Skorti þá eigi mat.	Shortage then not food.	They had no shortage of food.

The Vinland Sagas — *The Saga of the Greenlanders (Old Icelandic)*

Old Icelandic	Literal	English
Fénaður gekk þar á land upp en það var brátt að graðfé varð úrigt og gerði mikið um sig.	Cattle went there to land up, but that was soon, the cattle were irritable and made greatly about themselves.	The livestock went inland, but the males were soon irritable and hard to handle.
Þeir höfðu haft með sér griðung einn.	They had had with them bull one.	They had with them a bull.
Karlsefni lét fella viðu og telgja til skips síns og lagði viðinn á bjarg eitt til þurrkanar.	Karlsefni let fell wood and hewn to ships theirs and lay trees on rock along to dry.	Karlsefni had trees felled and hewn for their ships, and lay the timber on a rock to dry.
Þeir höfðu öll gæði af landkostum þeim er þar voru, bæði af vínberjum og alls konar veiðum og gæðum.	They had all quality of land-benefits, they which there were, both of grapes and all kinds fish and quality.	They had all kinds of benefit from the land, which included grapes, all kinds of fish and game, and other quality things.
Eftir þann vetur hinn fyrsta kom sumar.	After that winter the first came summer.	After the first winter passed and summer came,
Þá urðu þeir varir við Skrælingja og fór þar úr skógi fram mikill flokkur manna.	Then became they aware with Skraelings, and went there out woods from large group men.	They became aware of the Skraelings, a large group of men came out of the woods.
Þar var nær nautfé þeirra en graðungur tók að belja og gjalla ákaflega hátt.	There was near cattle there, but bull took to bellowing and snorting very loudly.	There cattle were near, and the bull took to bellowing and snorting very loudly.
En það hræddust Skrælingjar og lögðu undan með byrðar sínar en það var grávara og safali og alls konar skinnavara og snúa til bæjar Karlsefnis og vildu þar inn í húsin en Karlsefni lét verja dyrnar.	But that frightened Skraelings and laid away with burdens theirs, but they were grey-skins and sables and all kinds furs, and turned towards farm Karlsefni's and willed there the into house, but Karlsefni laid protection door.	Then this frightened the Skraelings and they ran away with their burdens, which included grey skins, sables, and all kinds of fur, they turned towards Karlsefni's farm and wanted to get into the house, but Karlsefni had protected the door.
Hvorigir skildu annars mál.	Neither knew others' language.	Neither knew the others' language.
Þá tóku Skrælingjar ofan bagga sína og leystu og buðu þeim og vildu vopn helst fyrir en Karlsefni bannaði þeim að selja vopnin.	Then took Skraelings off bags theirs and loosened and offered they and willed weapons preferably for, but Karlsefni banned they to sell weapons.	Then the Skraelings took off their bags and opened them, offering their goods, preferably in exchange for weapons, but Karlsefni forbade them to trade weapons.
Og nú leitar hann ráðs með þeim hætti að hann bað konur bera út búnyt að þeim og þegar er þeir sáu búnyt þá vildu þeir kaupa það en ekki annað.	And now sought he solution with them to-stop, that he asked women bring out milk-products by them, and then when they saw milk-products, then willed they buy that, and nothing else.	And now he sought a solution to this, he asked the women to bring out milk-products, and when they saw these milk-products, they wanted to buy that and nothing else.

The Saga of the Greenlanders (Old Icelandic)

Old Icelandic	Literal	English
Nú var sú kaupför Skrælingja að þeir báru sinn varning í brott í mögum sínum en Karlsefni og förunautar hans höfðu eftir bagga þeirra og skinnavöru.	Now were their trading-with Skraelings, by them bearing their goods in away in stomachs theirs, but Karlsefni and companions his had after bags theirs and skin-wares.	The trading with the Skraelings resulted in them carrying away their purchases in their stomachs, leaving their packs and skins with Karlsefni.
Fóru þeir við svo búið í burt.	Went they with so settlement to away.	When this was done, they went away.
Nú er frá því að segja að Karlsefni lætur gera skíðgarð rammlegan um bæ sinn og bjuggust þar um.	Now was from therefore to say, that Karlsefni laid made fence strong about farm theirs, and prepared there about.	Now from this is to be told, that Karlsefni had a strong fence made around their farm to be prepared.
Í þann tíma fæddi Guðríður sveinbarn, kona Karlsefnis, og hét sá sveinn Snorri.	In that time bore Guthrid baby-boy, wife Karlsefni's, and called the boy Snorri.	At this time Karlsefni's wife Gudrid gave birth to a baby boy who was named Snorri.
Á öndverðum öðrum vetri þá komu Skrælingjar til móts við þá og voru miklu fleiri en fyrr og höfðu slíkan varnað sem fyrr.	The beginning next winter then came Skraelings to meet with then and were much more than before and had such wares as before.	At the beginning of the next winter the Skraelings came to meet with them in much greater numbers than before.
Þá mælti Karlsefni við konur: "Nú skuluð þér bera út slíkan mat sem fyrr var rífastur en ekki annað".	Then said Karlsefni to women: "Now should you bring out such food as before was demanded, but nothing else".	Karlsefni then spoke to the women: "Now you should bring out whatever food was most in demand, and nothing else".
Og er þeir sáu það þá köstuðu þeir böggunum sínum inn yfir skíðgarðinn.	And when they saw that, they threw they bags theirs the over fence.	And when the natives saw this, they cast their bags over the fence.
En Guðríður sat í dyrum inni með vöggu Snorra sonar síns.	But Guthrid sat in doorway in with cradle Snorri, son hers.	But Gudrid sat in the doorway with the cradle of her son Snorri.
Þá bar skugga í dyrin og gekk þar inn kona í svörtum námkyrtli, heldur lág, og hafði dregil um höfuð, og ljósjörp á hár, fölleit og mjög eygð svo að eigi hafði jafnmikil augu séð í einum mannshausi.	Then carried shadow in doorway, and going there the woman in dark gown, held tightly, and had shawl about head and bright-chestnut of hair, pale and much eyed, so that not had equal eyes seen in any people's-heads.	Then a shadow fell across the doorway, and there came a woman in a dark gown, held tightly, and had a shawl around her head of bright chestnut hair, pale and large eyes, such that no one had seen eyes like them in anyone's head.
Hún gekk þar er Guðríður sat og mælti: "Hvað heitir þú?" segir hún.	She went there by, was Guthrid sat, and spoke: "What called-are you?" said she.	She came to where Gudrud sat, and spoke: "What is your name?", she said.
"Ég heiti Guðríður eða hvert er þitt heiti?"	"I am-called Guthrid, but what is your name?".	"I am called Gudrid, but what is your name?".

The Vinland Sagas — The Saga of the Greenlanders (Old Icelandic)

Old Icelandic	Literal	English
"Ég heiti Guðríður", segir hún.	"I am-called Guthrid", said she.	"I am called Gudrid", she said.
Þá rétti Guðríður húsfreyja hönd sína til hennar að hún sæti hjá henni en það bar allt saman að þá heyrði Guðríður brest mikinn og var þá konan horfin og í því var og veginn einn Skrælingi af einum húskarli Karlsefnis því að hann hafði viljað taka vopn þeirra og fóru nú í brott sem tíðast en klæði þeirra lágu þar eftir og varningur.	Then extended Guthrid housewife hand hers to her, that she sit by her, but that bore all together, that then heard Guthrid crash great, and was then woman disappeared, and in therefore was also slain one Skraeling from one houseman Karlsefnis, because that he had willed take weapon theirs, and went now away that swiftly, but clothing theirs laid there left and goods.	Then Gudrid the housewife extended her hand to her, to sit by her, but then there was a great crash, and the woman disappeared, at that moment one of the natives had been killed by one of Karlsefni's men, because he had tried to take their weapons, and they went away swiftly, but their clothing lay there behind with other goods.
Engi maður hafði konu þessa séð utan Guðríður ein.	No man had woman this seen of Guthrid alone.	No one had seen the woman except for Gudrid.
Nú munum vér þurfa til ráða að taka, segir Karlsefni, "því að eg hygg að þeir muni vitja vor hið þriðja sinni með ófriði og fjölmenni. *Nú skulum vér taka það ráð að tíu menn fari fram á nes þetta og sýni sig þar en annað lið vort skal fara í skóg og höggva þar rjóður fyrir nautfé vort þá er liðið kemur framúr skóginum.*	"Now should we need to plan to take", said Karlsefni, "Because that I think, that they shall visit will the third they with warlike and many. Now should we take that plan, that ten men go from to headland this and show themselves there, while second team ours shall go into forest and strike there clearing for cattle ours, then as team come from out forest.	"Now we need to make a plan", said Karlsefni, "because I think that they will visit us a third time with hostility and in many numbers. Now shall we follow this plan, that ten men will go out on this headland and show themselves there, while our second team will go into the forest and strike there a clearing for the cattle, then as a team come from out of the forest.
Vér skulum og taka griðung vorn og láta hann fara fyrir oss".	We shall also take bull ours and let him go ahead-of us".	We shall also take our bull and let him go before us".
En þar var svo háttað er fundur þeirra var ætlaður að vatn var öðru megin en skógur á annan veg. *Nú voru þessi ráð höfð er Karlsefni lagði til.*	But there was so the-way where battle theirs was intended, by water was the-other side, but forest on-the other way. Now was this plan taken, as Karlsefni had to.	There where their battle was intended, there was water on one side, and a forest on the other. Now the followed the plan that Karlsefni had made.
Nú komu Skrælingjar í þann stað er Karlsefni hafði ætlað til bardaga. *Nú var þar bardagi og féll fjöldi af liði Skrælingja.*	Now came Skraelings to the place, where Karlsefni had intended to battle. Now was there battle, and fell many of people Skraelings.	Now the Skraelings came to the place where Karlsefni had intended to battle. Now was there a battle, and many of the Skraeling people fell.

The Vinland Sagas — The Saga of the Greenlanders (Old Icelandic)

Old Icelandic	Literal	English
Einn maður var mikill og vænn í liði Skrælingja og þótti Karlsefni sem hann mundi vera höfðingi þeirra.	One man was tall and handsome in group Skraelings, and thought Karlsefni, that he would be leader theirs.	One of them men in their group was tall and handsome, and Karlsefni thought that he was probably their leader.
Nú hafði einn þeirra Skrælingja tekið upp öxi eina og leit á um stund og reiddi að félaga sínum og hjó til hans.	Now had one of-them Skraelings taken up axe one and looked to about awhile and aimed at companion his and struck to him.	Now one of the Skraelings took up an axe and looked around awhile and aimed at one of his companions and struck him.
Sá féll þegar dauður.	So fell then dead.	So he then fell dead.
Þá tók sá hinn mikli maður við öxinni og leit á um stund og varp henni síðan á sjóinn sem lengst mátti hann.	Then took so the tall man to axe and looked to about awhile and threw he then to sea, as long as-may he.	Then the tall man took the axe and looked around for awhile, and then he thew it into the sea as far as he could.
En síðan flýja þeir á skóginn svo hver sem fara mátti og lýkur þar nú þeirra viðskiptum.	But afterwards fled they to woods, so each as went may, and ended there now their dealings.	After that they fled into the woods as fast as they could, and they had no more dealings with them.
Voru þeir Karlsefni þar þann vetur allan.	Were they Karlsefni there that winter all.	Karlsefni and his companions were there all winter.
En að vori þá lýsir Karlsefni að hann vill eigi þar vera lengur og vill fara til Grænlands.	But at spring then declared Karlsefni, that he willed not there be longer and will travel to Greenland.	But in the spring, Karlsefni declared that he did not wish to be there any longer and wished to travel to Greenland.
Nú búa þeir ferð sína og höfðu þaðan mörg gæði í vínviði og berjum og skinnavöru.	Now prepared they journey theirs and had there many quality in vines and berries and skin-wares.	Now they prepared for their journey and they had much good quality vines, berries, and skins.
Nú sigla þeir í haf og komu til Eiríksfjarðar skipi sínu heilu og voru þar um veturinn.	Now sailed they to sea and came to Eriksfjord ship theirs whole and were there about winter.	Now they sailed to sea and their ship came safely to Eriksfjord and they stayed there over the winter.

8

Old Icelandic	Literal	English
Nú tekst umræða að nýju um Vínlandsferð því að sú ferð þykir bæði góð til fjár og virðingar.	Now took discussion that again about Vinland-voyage, since by that trip seemed both good to wealth and worthiness.	Now the discussion was taken to again about a Vinland voyage, since the trip seemed to bring both wealth and respect.
Það sama sumar kom skip af Noregi til Grænlands er Karlsefni kom af Vínlandi.	That same summer came ship of Norway to Greenland, when Karlsefni came of Vinland.	That same summer a ship came from Norway when Karlsefni came back from Vinland.

The Vinland Sagas — *The Saga of the Greenlanders (Old Icelandic)*

Old Icelandic	Literal	English
Því skipi stýrðu bræður tveir, Helgi og Finnbogi, og voru þann vetur á Grænlandi.	For ship steered brothers two, Helgi and Finnbogi, and were they wintered in Greenland.	The captains were two brothers, Helgi and Finnbogi, and they spent the winter in Greenland.
Þeir bræður voru íslenskir að kyni og úr Austfjörðum.	Those brothers were Icelanders by kin and from Austfjord.	The brothers were Icelanders, from the East Fjords.
Þar er nú til að taka að Freydís Eiríksdóttir gerði ferð sína heiman úr Görðum og fór til fundar við þá bræður Helga og Finnboga og beiddi þá að þeir færu til Vínlands með farkost sinn og hafa helming gæða allra við hana, þeirra er þar fengjust.	There is now to that take, that Freydis Eriksdottir made journey hers home from Gardar and went to meet with then brothers, Helgi and Finnbogi, and propose then, that they journey to Vinland with vessel theirs and have half quality everyone's with her, their which there caught.	Now we turn to Freydis Eriksdottir, who journeyed from here home at Gardar and then travelled to meet with the brothers, Helgi and Finnbogi, to invite them to travel to Vinland with their vessel and have a half share of any profits from it.
Nú játtu þeir því.	Now agreed they accordingly.	They agreed to this.
Þaðan fór hún á fund Leifs bróður síns og bað að hann gæfi henni hús þau er hann hafði gera látið á Vínlandi.	There travelled she to meet Leif, brother hers, and asked, to him give her houses those, which he had made laid in Vinland.	There she travelled to meet Leif, her brother, to ask him to give her those houses which he had made in Vinland.
En hann svarar hinu sama, kveðst ljá mundu hús en gefa eigi.	But he answered the same, said loan would houses, but give not.	But he answered the same as before, he said that he would loan the houses, but not give them to her.
Sá var máldagi með þeim bræðrum og Freydísi að hvorir skyldu hafa þrjá tigi vígra manna á skipi og konur umfram.	So were matters with they brothers and Freydis, that each should have three ten fighting men on ship and women about from.	So were matters between the brothers and Freydis, that each should have thirty fighting men on their ships and women in addition.
En Freydís brá af því þegar og hafði fimm mönnum fleira og leyndi þeim og urðu þeir bræður eigi fyrri við þá varir en þeir komu til Vínlands.	But Freydis drew off for already and had five men more and concealed them, and became they brothers not before to then foreseen but they came to Vinland.	But Freydis broke the agreement straight away and had five extra men, concealing them so that the brothers would not be aware of this until they came to Vinland.
Nú létu þau í haf og höfðu til þess mælt áður að þau mundu samflota hafa ef svo vildi verða, og þess var lítill munur.	Now laid they to sea and had to this said before, that they should together have, if so will be, and this was little difference.	Now they put to sea and had said before that they should be together if they could, which they almost did.
En þó komu þeir bræður nokkuru fyrri og höfðu upp borið föng sín til húsa Leifs.	But though came they brothers sometime before and had up carried possessions theirs to houses Leif's.	Though the brothers arrived sometime before and carried their possessions to Leif's houses.

The Vinland Sagas — The Saga of the Greenlanders (Old Icelandic)

Old Icelandic	Literal	English
En er Freydís kom að landi þá ryðja þeir skip sitt og bera upp til húss föng sín.	But when Freydis came to land, then cleared they ship theirs and carried up to houses possessions theirs.	Then when Freydis came to land, they cleared their ship and carried their possessions up to their houses.
Þá mælti Freydís: "Hví báruð þér inn hér föng yður?"	Then spoke Freydis: "Why carried you in here possessions yours?"	Then Freydis spoke: "Why have you carried your posessions in here?".
Því að vér hugðum, segja þeir, "að haldast muni öll ákveðin orð með oss".	"Because that we thought", said they, "That hold would all agreed word with us".	"Because we thought", they said, "that you would keep your agreement with us".
Mér léði Leifur húsanna, segir hún, "en eigi yður".	"To-me lent Leif houses", said she, "But not you".	"Leif lent the houses to me", she said, "not you".
Þá mælti Helgi: "Þrjóta mun okkur bræður illsku við þig".	Then said Helgi: "Scarcely would-be we brothers ill-will with you",	Then Helgi said: "We brothers would scarcely be a match for your ill-will".
Báru nú út föng og gerðu sér skála og settu þann skála firr sjónum á vatnsströndu og bjuggu vel um.	Carried now out possessions and made they cabin and placed they cabin further-from the-sea towards a-lake and settled well about.	They removed their posessions and they made a longhouse further from the sea towards a lake, and settled in well.
En Freydís lét fella viðu til skips síns.	Then Freydis had wood felled for ship hers.	Then Freydis had wood cut to make a load for her ship.
Nú tók að vetra og töluðu þeir bræður að takast mundu upp leikar og væri höfð skemmtan.	Now took in winter, and talked they brothers, that take should up games and would have amusement.	Now winter took, and the brothers talked of taking up games that would bring entertainment.
Svo var gert um stund þar til er menn bárust verra í milli.	So was done about awhile, there until were men brought worse in between.	And so they did for a while, until disagreements arose between them.
Og þá gerðist sundurþykki með þeim og tókust af leikar og öngar gerðust komur milli skálanna.	And then made disagreement with them, and took of games, and none did come between cabins	And then was a rift between them, and the activities ceased, and none came or went between their cabins,
Og fór svo fram lengi vetrar.	and went so from long winter.	and so it went all winter long.
Það var einn morgun snemma að Freydís stóð upp úr rúmi sínu og klæddist og fór eigi í skóklæðin en veðri var svo farið að dögg var fallin mikil.	It was one morning early, that Freydis stood up out-of room theirs and dressed and went not in shoes, but weather was such going, that dew was fallen much.	It was early one morning, that Freydis got up and dressed, but did not wear any shoes, but the weather had left much dew fallen on the ground.

The Vinland Sagas *The Saga of the Greenlanders (Old Icelandic)*

Old Icelandic	Literal	English
Hún tók kápu bónda síns og fór í en síðan gekk hún til skála þeirra bræðra og til dyra.	She took cape husband hers and went into, but then went she to cabin theirs brothers and to door.	She took her husband's cape and went out, and then she went to the door of the brothers' cabin.
En maður einn hafði út gengið litlu áður og lokið hurð aftur á miðjan klofa.	But man one had out gone little before and left door back to middle gap.	One of the men had gone out shortly before and left the door half open.
Hún lauk upp hurðinni og stóð í gáttum stund þá og þagði.	She closed up door and stood in doorway awhile then and silent.	She closed the door and stood silently in the doorway awhile.
En Finnbogi lá innstur í skálanum og vakti.	But Finnbogi lay inside in cabin and awoke.	Finnbogi lay inside the cabin and awoke.
Hann mælti: "Hvað viltu hingað Freydís?"	He said: "What will-you here, Freydís?".	He said: "What do you want here Freydis?".
Hún svarar: "Eg vil að þú standir upp og gangir út með mér og vil eg tala við þig".	She answered: "I will, that you stand up and go out with me, and will I speak with you".	She answered: "I want you to get up and come outside, and I want to speak with you".
Svo gerir hann.	So did he.	So he did.
Þau ganga að tré er lá undir skálavegginum og settust þar niður.	They went to tree, that lay near cabins, and sat there down.	They went to a tree that lay near the cabins, and there sat down.
"Hversu líkar þér?" segir hún.	"How like you?" said she.	"How do you like it here?" she said.
Hann svarar: "Góður þykir mér landskostur en illur þykir mér þústur sá er vor í milli er því að eg kalla ekki hafa til orðið".	He answered: "Good think me land-benefits, but ill think me discord so, that sprung to between as, for I call not have to word".	He answered: "I think the land here has much benefit, but I don't like the ill feeling that has arisen between us, as I have no words for it".
Þá segir þú sem er, segir hún,	"Then say you as is", said she,	"What you say is true", she said,
"og svo þykir mér. En það er erindi mitt á þinn fund að eg vildi kaupa skipum við ykkur bræður því að þið hafið meira skip en eg og vildi eg í brott héðan".	"And so think I. But that which business mine to you find, that I will purchase ship with you brothers, because that you have more ship than I, and will I to away hence".	"And I agree. But my purpose in meeting with you, is that I wish to buy yours and your brother's ship, because you have more ship than I, and I wish to leave soon".
Það mun eg láta gangast, segir hann, "ef þér líkar þá vel".	"That should I let go", said he, "If you like then well".	"That I could agree to", he said, "If that pleases you".
Nú skilja þau við það.	Now separated they with that,	Now with that they separated,

71

The Vinland Sagas   *The Saga of the Greenlanders (Old Icelandic)*

Old Icelandic	Literal	English
Gengur hún heim en Finnbogi til hvílu sinnar.	went she home, and Finnbogi to bed his.	and she went home, and Finnbogi to his bed.
Hún stígur upp í rúmið köldum fótum og vaknar hann Þorvarður við og spyr hví að hún væri svo köld og vot.	She climbed up into room cold feet, and awoke he Thorvald to and asked, why that she was so cold and wet.	She climbed up into the room with cold feet, and Thorvard woke and asked why she was so cold and wet.
Hún svarar með miklum þjósti: "Eg var gengin", segir hún, "til þeirra bræðra að fala skip að þeim og vildi eg kaupa meira skip. En þeir urðu við það svo illa að þeir börðu mig og léku sárlega en þú, vesæll maður, munt hvorki vilja reka minnar skammar né þinnar og mun eg það nú finna að eg er í brottu af Grænlandi og mun eg gera skilnað við þig utan þú hefnir þessa".	She answered with much vehemence: "I was gone", said she, "To the brothers to bargain ship of them, and wished I purchase bigger ship. But they became with that so bad, that they beat me and played woundingly, but you, miserable man, would neither will expel my shame nor yours, and should I that now find, that I am in gone from Greenland, and should I make separate with you, outside-of you avenge this".	She answered vehemently: "I was gone", she said, "to the brothers to purchase their ship from them, and wished I to buy a bigger ship. With that they became so angry, that they beat me, and struck me woundingly, but you, miserable man, will neither expel my shame or yours, and if that's the case, then I will leave Greenland, and divorce you, unless you avenge this".
Og nú stóðst hann eigi átölur hennar og bað menn upp standa sem skjótast og taka vopn sín. Og svo gera þeir og fara þegar til skála þeirra bræðra og gengu inn að þeim sofundum og tóku þá og færðu í bönd og leiddu svo út hvern sem bundinn var en Freydís lét drepa hvern sem út kom.	And now stood he not reproaches hers and ordered men up stand while quickly and take weapons theirs, And so did they and went straightaway to cabin they brothers and went in by them sleeping and took then and went in binding and lead so out each, who bound was. Then Freydis had killled each, who out came.	And now, unable to withstand her reproaches, he ordered that the men get up quickly and get their weapons, And so they did, travelling straightaway to the brothers' cabin, and went in while they were sleeping, took them, bound them, and led them outside as they were bound. Then Freydis had each one killed as they came out.
Nú voru þar allir karlar drepnir en konur voru eftir og vildi engi þær drepa.	Now were there all men killed, but women were left, and willed none they kill.	Now all the men were killed, there remained the women, but no one wanted to kill them.
Þá mælti Freydís: "Fái mér öxi í hönd".	Then said Freydis: "Give me axe into hand".	Then Freydis said: "Give me the axe in my hand".
Svo var gert. Síðan vegur hún að konum þeim fimm er þar voru og gekk af þeim dauðum.	So was done. Then slayed she that women they five, who there were, and went of them dead.	So was it done. Then she slayed the five women who were there, and all of them were dead.

The Saga of the Greenlanders (Old Icelandic)

Old Icelandic	Literal	English
Nú fóru þau til skála síns eftir það hið illa verk og fannst það eitt á að Freydís þóttist allvel hafa um ráðið og mælti við félaga sína: "Ef oss verður auðið að koma til Grænlands", segir hún, "þá skal eg þann mann ráða af lífi er segir frá þessum atburðum.	Now went they to cabin theirs after that the evil work, and found that one all, that Freydis thought all-well have about resolved, and said to companions hers: "If we worth fated to come to Greenland", said she, "Then shall I then men rule of life, who says from these events.	Now they went back to their cabin after that evil work, and they all found that Freydis thought all was well done, and she spoke to her companions: "If we are fated to return to Greenland", she said, "Then I shall have killed any man who says anything about these events.
Nú skulum vér það segja að þau búi hér eftir þá er vér förum í brott".	Now should we this say, that they remained here behind, when were we travelling to away".	Now shall we say of this that they remained here, when we travelled away".
Nú bjuggu þeir skipið snemma um vorið, það er þeir bræður höfðu átt, með þeim öllum gæðum er þau máttu til fá og skipið bar, sigla síðan í haf og urðu vel reiðfara og komu í Eiríksfjörð skipi sínu snemma sumars.	Now readied they ship early about spring, that was the brothers had had, with them all quality, that they may to get and ship carry, sailed after to sea and became well voyage and came to Eriksfjord ship theirs early summer.	Early in the spring they prepared the ship which the brothers had owned, with all the goods that the ship could carry, then afterwards sailed to sea and they had a good voyage and their ship came into Eriksfjord early in the summer.
Nú var þar Karlsefni fyrir og hafði albúið skip sitt til hafs og beið byrjar og er það mál manna að eigi mundi auðgara skip gengið hafa af Grænlandi en það er hann stýrði.	Now was there Karlsefni already and had prepared ship his to sea and waited begin, and is that said men, that not would richer ship go sea off Greenland but that, which he steered.	Karlsefni was there already, and had his ship all prepared for sea, waiting for a favourable wind, and it was said that none would go to sea with a richer ship from Greenland than that which he captained.

9

Freydís fór nú til bús síns því að það hafði staðið meðan óskatt.	Freydis travelled now to dwelling hers, for as that had stood meantime uninjured.	Freydis travelled now to her farm, which withstood her absence without injury.
Hún fékk mikinn feng fjár öllu föruneyti sínu því að hún vildi leyna láta ódáðum sínum.	She gave great gifts wealth all companions hers, for that she would conceal let dishonour hers.	She gave great gifts of wealth to all her companions, so that she could conceal her dishonour.
Situr hún nú í búi sínu.	Sat she now in house hers.	She remained at her farm.
Eigi urðu allir svo haldinorðir að þegðu yfir ódáðum þeirra eða illsku að eigi kæmi upp um síðir.	Not became all so held-words, by silence over dishonour theirs or evil, that not came up about eventually.	Not all words were held in silence over their dishonour or evil, that didn't come up eventually.
Nú kom þetta upp um síðir fyrir Leif bróður hennar og þótti honum þessi saga allill.	Now came this up about eventually before Leif, brother hers, and thought he this story evil.	Now this came up before Leif, her brother, and he thought this story was most evil.

The Vinland Sagas — *The Saga of the Greenlanders (Old Icelandic)*

Old Icelandic	Literal	English
Þá tók Leifur þrjá menn af liði þeirra Freydísar og píndi þá til sagna um þenna atburð allan jafnsaman og var með einu móti sögn þeirra.	Then took Leif three men of band theirs Freydis and tortured then to say about these events all equally, and was with one towards story theirs.	Then Leif took three men from Freydis's company and tortured them to talk about those events, they were all equal and as one in their telling.
"Eigi nenni eg", segir Leifur, "að gera það að við Freydísi systur mína sem hún væri verð en spá mun eg þeim þess að þeirra afkvæmi mun lítt að þrifum verða".	"Not bother I", said Leif, "To do that to Freydis, sister mine, which she would deserve, but prophecy should I that these, by their offspring should little by thriving be".	"I am not the one", said Leif, "to do to Freydis, my sister, that which she deserves, but I should prophecise this, that their offspring shall little thriving become".
Nú leið það svo fram að öngum þótti um þau vert þaðan í frá nema ills.	Now laid that so from, that none thought about them worthy there in from taking ill.	Now as it happened, none thought anything of them except evil.
Nú er að segja frá því er Karlsefni býr skip sitt og sigldi í haf. Honum fórst vel og kom til Noregs með heilu og höldnu og sat þar um veturinn og seldi varning sinn og hafði þar gott yfirlæti og þau bæði hjón af hinum göfgustum mönnum í Noregi. En um vorið eftir bjó hann skip sitt til Íslands.	Now is to say from therefore, when Karlsefni prepared ship his and sailed to sea. He travelled well and came to Norway with whole and safe and sat there about winter and sold wares his and had there benefit respectable and they both couple of the respectable people in Norway, but about spring after prepared he ship his to Iceland.	Now to turn to Karlsefni, he prepared his ship and sailed to sea. He travelled well and came to Norway safe an well, and remained there over the winter and sold his goods, and both him and his wife were treated well by the noble people in Norway, and after about spring, he prepared his ship for Iceland.
Og er hann var albúinn og skip hans lá til byrjar fyrir bryggjunum þá kom þar að honum Suðurmaður einn, ættaður af Brimum úr Saxlandi. Hann falar af Karlsefni húsasnotru hans.	And when he was ready and ship his lay to fair-wind for bridge, then came there to him southern-man one, descended from Bremen of Saxony. He bargained-for that Karlsefni carved decoration his.	And when he was ready and his ship waited for a fair wind on the gangways, then came a southern man, descended from Bremen of Saxony. He asked Karlsefni to sell him the carved decoration on the prow.
"Eg vil eigi selja", sagði hann.	"I will not sell", said he.	"I don't care to sell it", he said.
"Eg mun gefa þér við hálfa mörk gulls", segir Suðurmaður.	"I would give you to half mark gold", said southern-man.	"I'll give you half a mark of gold for it", said the southern man.
Karlsefni þótti vel við boðið og keyptu síðan.	Karlsefni thought well with offer, and sold afterwards.	Karlsefni thought this was a good offer, and then sold it.

The Saga of the Greenlanders (Old Icelandic)

Old Icelandic	Literal	English
Fór Suðurmaður í burt með húsasnotruna en Karlsefni vissi eigi hvað tré var. En það var mösur kominn af Vínlandi.	Went southern-man to away with carved-decoration, but Karlsefni knew not, what wood was. But that was burl-wood, coming from Vinland.	The southern man went away with his carved decoration, but Karlsefni did not know what wood it was made of. But it was made of burl wood, which came from Vinland.
Nú siglir Karlsefni í haf og kom skipi sínu fyrir norðan land í Skagafjörð og var þar upp sett skip hans um veturinn.	Now sailed Karlsefni to sea and came ship his for north land to Skagafjord, and was there up set ship his about winter.	Now Karlsefni sailed to sea and his ship came to the north of the land to Skagafjord, and he set up his ship there for the winter.
En um vorið keypti hann Glaumbæjarland og gerði bú á og bjó þar meðan hann lifði og var hið mesta göfugmenni og er mart manna frá honum komið og Guðríði konu hans og góður ættbogi.	Then about spring bought he Glaumbær and made dwelling on and lived there, long-as lived, and was the most greatest, and which many people from him came and Guthrid, wife his, and good descendents.	Then in the spring he purchased land at Glaumbaer and made a farm there, as long as he lived, and was the the most respected, and many pepople are came from him and his wife Gudrid, with good descendents.
Og er Karlsefni var andaður tók Guðríður við búsvarðveislu og Snorri son hennar er fæddur var á Vínlandi.	And when Karlsefni was dead, took Guthrid to farming and Snorri, son hers, who born was in Vinland.	And when Karlsefni died, Gudrid took over the farm with her son Snorri, who had been born in Vinland.
Og er Snorri var kvongaður þá fór Guðríður utan og gekk suður og kom út aftur til bús Snorra sonar síns og hafði hann þá látið gera kirkju í Glaumbæ.	And when Snorri was married, then went Guthrid out and went south and came out returning to house Snorri, son hers, and had he then caused made church in Glaumbær.	And when Snorri was married, Gudrid travelled abroad, and went south, returning to her son Snorri's farm, and he had built a church in Glaumbaer.
Síðan varð Guðríður nunna og einsetukona og var þar meðan hún lifði.	Afterwards was Guthrid a-nun and recluse and was there, long-as she lived.	Later Gudrid became a nun and an anchoress and remained there as long as she lived.
Snorri átti son þann er Þorgeir hét. Hann var faðir Yngveldar móður Brands biskups.	Snorri had son that, was Thorgeir named. He was father-of Yngvild, mother Brand Bishop's	Snorri has a son who was named Thorgeir. He was the father of Yngvild, who was mother to Bishop Brand.
Dóttir Snorra Karlsefnissonar hét Hallfríður. Hún var kona Runólfs föður Þorláks biskups. Björn hét sonur Karlsefnis og Guðríðar. Hann var faðir Þórunnar móður Bjarnar biskups.	Daughter Snorri Karlsefnison's was-called Hallfrid. She was wife Runolf's, father Thorlak Bishop's Bjorn was-called son-of Karlsefni's and Guthrid's. He was father-of Thorun, mother Bjarn Bishop's	Snorri Karlsefnison's daughter was called Hallfrid. She was the wife of Runolf, father of Bishop Thorlak. Karlsefni and Gudrid had a son called Bjorn. He was the father of Thorun, mother to Bishop Bjorn.

Old Icelandic	Literal	English
Fjöldi manna er frá Karlsefni komið og er hann kynsæll maður orðinn.	Many people were from Karlsefni come, and was he kin-blessed man become.	Many people are descended from Karlesfni, and his was a prosperous clan.
Og hefir Karlsefni gerst sagt allra manna atburði um farar þessar allar er nú er nokkuð orði á komið.	And has Karlsefni made said every people's events about voyages these all, which now is somewhat recited to came.	It was Karlsefni who told of people's events about these voyages, some of which came to words.

The Saga of Erik the Red (*Old Norse*)

Old Norse	Literal	English
1	1	1
Óláfr hét herkonungr, er kallaðr var Óláfr hvíti.	Olaf was-named warrior-king, that called was Olaf the-White.	There was a warrior king named Olaf, that was called Olaf the White.
Hann var sonr Ingjalds konungs Helgasonar, Óláfssonar, Guðröðarsonar, Hálfdanarsonar hvítbeins Upplendingakonungs.	He was son-of Ingjald's the-king son-of-Helga, son-of-Olaf, son-of-Gudrod, son-of-Halfdan White-Leg Opplands-king.	He was the son of Ingjald, the son of Helga, the son of Olaf, the son of Gudrod, the son of Halfdan White Leg, the king of the Opplands.
Óláfr herjaði í vestrvíking ok vann Dyflinni á Írlandi ok Dyflinnarskíri.	Olaf harried to west-raiding and won Dublin in Ireland and Dublinshire.	Olaf harried on raids to the west and conquered Dublin in Ireland and Dublinshire.
Þar gerðist hann konungr yfir.	There made himself king over.	He made himself king there.
Hann fekk Auðar djúpúðgu, dóttur Ketils flatnefs, Bjarnarsonar bunu, ágæts manns ór Nóregi.	He married Aud the-Deep-Minded, daughter Ketil's Flat-Nose son-of-Bjorn Buna, excellent man from Norway.	He married Aud the Deep Minded, daughter of Ketil Flat Nose, the son of Bjorn Buna, an excellent man from Norway.
Þorsteinn rauðr hét sonr þeira.	Thorstein the-Red was-named son theirs.	Their son was named Thorstein the Red.
Óláfr fell á Írlandi í orrostu, en Auðr ok Þorsteinn fóru þá í Suðreyjar.	Olaf fell in Ireland in battle, then Aud and Thorstein went they to Sudreyar.	Olaf fell in Ireland in battle, then Aud and Thorstein went to the Southern Islands.
Þar fekk Þorsteinn Þuríðar, dóttur Eyvindar Austmanns, systur Helga ins magra.	There married Thorstein Thorid, daughter-of Eyvind the-Easternman sister-of Helga the Lean.	There Thorstein married Thorid, daughter of Eyvind the Easterner, sister of Helga the Lean.
Þau áttu mörg börn.	They had many children.	They had many children.
Þorsteinn gerðist herkonungr.	Thorstein became-a warrior-king.	Thorstein became a warrior king.
Hann réðst til lags með Sigurði jarli inum ríka, syni Eysteins glumru.	He appointed to position with Sigurd Earl the Rich, son-of Eystein Glumra.	He teamed up with Earl Sigurd the Rich, son of Eystein Glumra.
Þeir unnu Katanes ok Suðrland, Ross ok Meræfi ok meir en hálft Skotland.	They won Caithness and Sutherland, Ross and Moray and more than half-of Scotland.	They conquered Caithness, Sutherland, Ross, Moray, and more than half of Scotland.
Gerðist Þorsteinn þar konungr yfir, áðr Skotar sviku hann, ok fell hann þar í orrostu.	Became Thorstein there king over, until Scots betrayed him, and fell he there in battle.	Thorstein became king there until the Scots betrayed him and he fell in battle.

Old Norse	Literal	English
Auðr var þá á Katanesi, er hon spurði fall Þorsteins.	Aud was then in Caithness, when she heard-of fall Thorstein's.	Aud was then at Caithness when she learned of Thorstein's falling.
Hon lét þá gera knörr í skógi á laun, ok er hon var búin, helt hon út í Orkneyjar.	She had then made ship in woods of hired, and when she was ready, held she out to Orkney.	She then hired a ship to be made in the woods, and when she was ready, she set out to Orkney.
Þar gifti hon Gró, dóttur Þorsteins rauðs.	There gave she Gro, daughter Thorstein the-Red's.	There she gave in marriage Gro, daughter of Thorstein the Red.
Hon var móðir Grélaðar, er Þorfinnr jarl hausakljúfr átti.	She was mother-of Grelod, who Thorfin Earl Scull-Cleaver married.	She was the mother of Grelod, who was married to Earl Thorfinn the Skull-Cleaver.
Eftir þat fór Auðr at leita Íslands.	After that went Aud to seek Iceland.	After that Aud went to seek Iceland.
Hon hafði á skipi tuttugu karla frjálsa.	She had in ship twenty men free.	She had twenty free men on her ship.
Auðr kom til Íslands ok var inn fyrsta vetr í Bjarnarhöfn með Birni, bróður sínum.	Aud came to Iceland and was the first winter in Bjarnarhofn with Bjorn, brother hers.	Aud came to Iceland and spent the first winter in Bjarnarhofn with her brother Bjorn.
Síðan nam Auðr öll Dalalönd milli Dögurðarár ok Skraumuhlaupsár.	Since took Aud all Dale-land between Dogurdara and Skraumuhlaupsa.	After that, Aud took all of the Dale lane between Dogurdara and Skraumuhlapusa.
Hon bjó í Hvammi.	She settled at Hvamm.	She settled at Hvam.
Hon hafði bænahald í Krosshólum.	She had prayer-holdings at Krossholar.	She held prayers at Krossholar.
Þar lét hon reisa krossa, því at hon var skírð ok vel trúuð.	Where had she raise crosses, for that she was baptised and well religious.	There she had crosses raised, for she was baptised and a devout Christian.
Með henni kómu út margir göfgir menn, þeir er herteknir höfðu verit í vestrvíking ok váru kallaðir ánauðgir.	With her came out many noble people, they which war-taken had been among west-raiding and were called bondsmen.	Many noble people came with her, who had been taken prisoner in viking raids and they were called bondsmen.
Einn af þeim hét Vífill.	One of them was called Vifil.	One of them was called Vifil.
Hann var ættstórr maðr ok hafði verit hertekinn fyrir vestan haf ok var kallaðr ánauðigr, áðr Auðr leysti hann.	He was high-family man and had been war-taken before western sea and was-called bondsman, before Aud released him.	He was a man of noble birth and had been taken prisoner by the western sea and was called a bondsman until Aud gave him his freedom.
Ok er Auðr gaf bústaði skipverjum sínum, þá spurði Vífill, hví Auðr gæfi honum engan bústað sem öðrum mönnum.	And when Aud gave farms crew hers, then asked Vifil, why Aud gave him no abode as other people.	When Aud gave her crew farm sites, then Vifil asked why Aud had not given him a farm as she had other people.

Old Norse	Literal	English
Auðr kvað þat eigi mundu skipta, kallaði hann þar göfgan mundu þykkja, sem hann væri.	Aud said that not would change, called he there esteemed would-be valued, wherever he was.	Aud said that it made no difference, as he would be considered a fine man, wherever he was.
Hon gaf honum Vífilsdal, ok bjó hann þar.	She gave him Vifilsdal, and settled he there.	She gave him Vifilsdal, and he settled there.
Hann átti þá konu, er hét -- --.	He married then wife, was called -- --.	He married a woman who was called -- --.
Þeira synir váru þeir Þorbjörn ok Þorgeirr.	Their sons were they Thorbjorn and Thorgeir.	Their sons were Thorbjorn and Thorgeir.
Þeir váru efniligir menn ok óxu upp með föður sínum.	They were promising men and grew up with father theirs.	They were promising men and grew up with their father.
2	2	2
Þorvaldr hét maðr.	Thorvald was-called a-man.	There was a man called Thorvald.
Hann var sonr Ásvalds Úlfssonar, Öxna-Þórissonar.	He was son Asvald's son-of-Ulf, son-of-Ox-Thorir	He was the son of Asvald, the son of Ulf, the son of Ox-Thorir.
Eiríkr rauði hét sonr hans.	Erik the-Red was-called son his	His son was called Erik the Red.
Þeir feðgar fóru af Jaðri til Íslands fyrir víga sakar ok námu land á Hornströndum ok bjuggu at Dröngum.	They father-and-son travelled from Jaeren to Iceland because-of killing conviction and took land in Hornstrandir and settled at Drangar.	Father and son travelled from Jaeran to Iceland because of a conviction for a slaying, and they took land at Hornstrandir and settled at Drangar.
Þar andaðist Þorvaldr.	There died Thorvald.	There Thorvald died.
Eiríkr fekk þá Þjóðhildar, dóttur Jörundar Úlfssonar ok Þorbjargar knarrarbringu, er þá átti Þorbjörn inn haukdælski.	Erik married then Thjodhild, daughter-of Jorund Ulfson and Thorbjorg Knarrarbringu, who then married Thorbjorn of Haukadal.	Erik then married Thjodhild, the daughter of Jorund Ulfson and Thorbjorn Knarrarbringu, who had since married Thorbjorn of Haukadal.
Réðst Eiríkr þá norðan ok ruddi land í Haukadal ok bjó á Eiríksstöðum hjá Vatnshorni.	Rode Erik then north and cleared land in Haukadal and settled at Eriksstadir near Vatnshorn.	Erik then rode north and cleared land in Haukadal and settled at Eriksstadir near Vatnshorn.
Þá felldu þrælar Eiríks skriðu á bæ Valþjófs á Valþjófsstöðum.	Then fell thralls Erik's landslide on farm Vallthjof at Vathjolfsstadr.	Then Erik's slaves caused a landslide to fall on the farm at Vallthjof at Vatnhjolfsstadr.
Eyjólfr saurr, frændi hans, drap þrælana hjá Skeiðsbrekkum upp frá Vatnshorni.	Eyolf the-Foul, kinsman his, killed thralls beside Skeidsbrekkur up from Vatnshorn.	His kinsman Eyolf the Foul killed the slaves near Skeidsbrekkur above Vatnshorn.

The Saga of Erik the Red (Old Norse)

Old Norse	Literal	English
Fyrir þat vá Eiríkr Eyjólf saur.	For that slew Erik Eyolf the-Foul.	For that Erik killed Eyolf the Foul.
Hann vá ok Hólmgöngu-Hrafn at Leikskálum.	He slew also Raven-the-Dueller at Leikskalar.	He also killed Raven the Dueller at Leikskalar.
Geirsteinn ok Oddr á Jörva, frændi Eyjólfs, mæltu eftir hann.	Gerstein and Odd of Jorfi, kinsman Eyolf's, spoke after him.	Gerstein and Odd of Jorvi, Eyolf's kinsmen sought judgement for his killing.
Þá var Eiríkr gerr brott ór Haukadal.	Then was Erik made out from Haukadal.	Then Erik was outlawed from Haukadal.
Hann nam þá Brokey ok Öxney ok bjó at Tröðum í Suðrey inn fyrsta vetr.	He took then Brokey and Oxney and settled at Tradir in Sudrey the first winter.	He took the islands Brokey and Oxney and settled at Tradir on Sudurey island that first winter.
Þá léði hann Þorgesti setstokka.	Then lent he Thorgest seat-posts.	Then he lent Thorgest bedstead boards.
Síðan fór Eiríkr í Öxney ok bjó á Eiríksstöðum.	Afterwards travelled Erik to Oxney and settled at Eriksstadir.	Afterwards Erik travelled to Oxney and settled at Eriksstadir.
Þá heimti hann setstokkana ok náði eigi.	Then claimed he seat-posts and got not.	Then he asked for the bedstead boards back, but did not get them.
Eiríkr sótti setstokkana á Breiðabólstað, en Þorgestr fór eftir honum.	Erik took seat-posts from Breidabolstad, but Thorgest went after him.	Erik went to Breidabolstad and took the bedstead boards, but Thorgest went after him.
Þeir börðust skammt frá garði at Dröngum.	There fought short from garden at Drangar.	They fought a short distance from the farm at Drangar.
Þar fellu tveir synir Þorgests ok nökkurir menn aðrir.	There fell two sons Thorgest's and some men other.	There Thorgest's two sons fell along with several other men.
Eftir þat höfðu hvárirtveggju setu fjölmenna.	After that had either-side sitting many-men.	After that, both sides kept a large following of many men.
Styrr veitti Eiríki ok Eyjólfr ór Svíney, Þorbjörn Vífilsson ok synir Þorbrands ór Álftafirði, en Þorgesti veittu synir Þórðar gellis ok Þorgeirr ór Hítardal, ok Áslákr ór Langadal ok Illugi, sonr hans.	Styrr supported Erik and Eyolf of Sviney, Thorbjorn Vifilson and sons Thorbrand's from Alftafjord, but Thorgest supported sons Thord Gellir and Thorgeir of Hitardal, and Aslak of Langadal and Illugi, son his.	Erik had the support of Styrr, Eyolf of Sviney, Thorbjorn Vifilsson, and the sons of Thorbrand of Alftafjord, while Thorgest was supported by Thord Bellower, Thorgeir of Hitardal, Aslak of Langdal, and his son Illugi.
Þeir Eiríkr urðu sekir á Þórsnessþingi.	They and Erik became outlawed at Thorsnes-Thing.	Erik and his companions became outlawed at the Thorsnes Assembly.

The Saga of Erik the Red (Old Norse)

Old Norse	Literal	English
Hann bjó skip í Eiríksvági, en Eyjólfr leyndi honum í Dímunarvági, meðan þeir Þorgestr leituðu hans um eyjarnar.	He prepared ship in Eriksvog, and Eyolf hid him in Dimunarvog, while they Thorgest sought him about islands.	He prepared a ship at Eriksvog, and Eyolf hid him in Dimunarvog while Thorgest and his men searched the islands for him.
Þeir Þorbjörn ok Eyjólfr ok Styrr fylgðu Eiríki út um eyjarnar, ok skilðust þeir með inni mestu vináttu.	There Thorbjorn and Eyolf and Styrr followed Erik back around islands, and separated they with the most friendship.	Thorbjorn, Eyolf, and Styrr followed Erik through the islands, and they separated with the most friendship.
Kveðst Eiríkr þeim skyldu verða at þvílíku trausti, ef hann mætti sér við koma ok kynni þeir hans at þurfa.	Said Erik to-them should be to likewise trust, if he may them with come and circumstance they him to need.	Erik said to them that they should trust that he would help them in any way if they ever needed him.
Hann sagði þeim, at hann ætlaði at leita lands þess, er Gunnbjörn, sonr Úlfs kráku, sá, er hann rak vestr um haf ok hann fann Gunnbjarnarsker.	He told them, that he intended to seek lands these, which Gunnbjorn, son-of Ulf Crow, saw, when he-was driven west about sea and he found Gunnbjarnarsker.	He said to them that he intended to search for the lands which Gunnbjorn son of Ulf Crow saw, when he was driven west at sea and found Gunnbjarbarsker.
Hann kveðst aftr mundu leita til vina sinna, ef hann fyndi landit.	He said return would seek to friends his, if he found land.	He said that he would return to seek them out if he found land.
Sigldi Eiríkr á haf undan Snæfellsjökli.	Sailed Erik to sea from Snaefellsjokli.	Erik sailed to sea from Snaefellsjokli.
Hann kom útan at jökli þeim, er heitir Bláserkr.	He came out of glacier that, was named Blaserkur.	He came out from a glacier that was named Blaserkr.
Hann fór þaðan suðr at leita, ef þar væri byggjanda.	He travelled from-there south to seek, if there was habitable.	He travelled south from there to see if there was any habitable land.
Hann var inn fyrsta vetr í Eiríksey nær miðri inni eystri byggð.	He was the first winter at Eriksey near the-middle of-the eastern settlement.	For the first winter he was at Eriksey, near the middle of the Eastern Settlement.
Um várit eftir fór hann til Eiríksfjarðar ok tók sér þar bústað.	About spring after travelled he to Eriksfjord and took he there settlement.	After about spring he travelled to Eriksfjord and took settlement there.
Hann fór þat sumar í ina vestri óbyggð ok gaf víða örnefni.	He travelled that summer into the western settlement and gave widely place-names.	That summer he travelled into the Western Settlement and gave place names widely.
Hann var annan vetr í Eiríkshólmum við Hvarfsgnípu en it þriðja sumar fór hann allt norðr til Snæfells ok inn í Hrafnsfjörð.	He was second winter at Eriksholmar off Hvarfsgnipu and the third summer went he altogether north to Snaefell and then into Hrafnsfjord.	The second winter he was at Eriksholmar near Hvarfsgnipu, and the third summer he travelled all the way north to Snaefell and into Hrafnsfjord.

The Vinland Sagas
The Saga of Erik the Red (Old Norse)

Old Norse	Literal	English
Þá þóttist hann kominn fyrir botn Eiríksfjarðar.	Then thought he came before the-bottom-of Eriksfjord.	There he thought he had reached the head of Eriksfjord.
Hverfr hann þá aftr ok var inn þriðja vetr í Eiríksey fyrir mynni Eiríksfjarðar.	Turned he then back and was in third winter at Eriksey before the-mouth-of Eriksfjord.	Then he returned to winter at Eriksey at the mouth of Eriksfjord.
En eftir um sumarit fór hann til Íslands ok kom í Breiðafjörð.	But afterwards about summer travelled he to Iceland and came to Breidafjord.	Then after about summer he travelled to Iceland and came to Breidafjord.
Hann var þann vetr með Ingólfi á Hólmlátri.	He was that winter with Ingolf at Holmlatr.	That winter he was with Ingolf at Holmlatr.
Um várit börðust þeir Þorgestr, ok fekk Eiríkr ósigr.	About spring fought they Thorgest, and got Erik defeat.	About spring Erik and Thorgest fought, and Erik was defeated.
Eftir þat váru þeir sættir.	After that were they reconciled.	After that they were reconciled.
Þat sumar fór Eiríkr at byggja land þat, er hann hafði fundit ok hann kallaði Grænland, því at hann kvað menn þat mjök mundu fýsa þangat, ef landit héti vel.	That summer went Erik to settle land that, which he had found and he called Greenland, because as he said people that much would desire there, if land named well.	That summer Erik went to settle the land that he had found, which he called Greenland, because as he said, people would be attracted if the land was named well.
[Svá segir Ari Þorgilsson, at þat sumar fór hálfr þriði tögr skipa til Grænlands ór Breiðafirði og Borgarfirði, en fjórtán kómust út.	So said Ari Thorgilson, by that summer came half-of thirty-and twenty ships to Greenland from Breidafjord and Borgafjord, and fourteen arrived from.	So said Ari Thorgilson, that summer thirty five ships travelled to Greenland from Breidafjord and Borgafjord, but fourteen arrived.
Sum rak aftr, en sum týndust.	Some driven back, but some lost.	Some were driven back, but some were lost.
Þat var fimmtán vetrum fyrr en kristni var í lög tekin á Íslandi.	That was fifteen winters before that Christianity was in law taken in Iceland.	That was fifteen winters before Christianity was taken into law in Iceland.
Eiríkr nam síðan Eiríksfjörð ok bjó í Brattahlíð.].	Erik took then Eriksfjord and settled in Brattahlid.	Erik then took Eriksfjord and settled in Brattahlid.
3	3	3
Þorgeirr Vífilsson kvángaðist ok fekk Arnóru, dóttur Einars frá Laugarbrekku, Sigmundarsonar, Ketilssonar þistils, er numit hafði Þistilsfjörð.	Thorgeir Vifilson married and got Arnora, daughter Einar's from Laugarbrekka, son-of-Sigmund, son-of-Ketil Thistle who taken had Thistilsfjord.	Thorgeir Vifilson took as his wife Arnora, daughter of Einar from Laugarbrekk, the son of Sigmund, the son of Ketil Thistle who had taken Thistilsfjord.
Önnur dóttir Einars hét Hallveig.	Second daughter Einar's was-named Hallveig.	Einar's second daughter was named Hallveig.

The Vinland Sagas   *The Saga of Erik the Red (Old Norse)*

Old Norse	Literal	English
Hennar fekk Þorbjörn Vífilsson ok tók með land á Laugarbrekku, á Hellisvöllum.	She married Thorbjorn Vifilson and took with land in Laugarbrekka, at Hellisvellir.	She married Thorbjorn Vifilson and took land at Laugarbrekku in Hellisvellir.
Réðst Þorbjörn þangat byggðum ok gerðist göfugmenni mikit.	Moved Thorbjorn there settlement and became noble much.	Thorbjorn moved his settlement there and became a great nobleman.
Hann var góðr bóndi ok hafði rausnarráð.	He was a-good farmer and had great-estate.	He was a good farmer and had a great estate.
Guðríðr hét dóttir Þorbjarnar.	Guthrid was-called daughter Thorbjorn's.	Thorbjorn's daughter was called Gudrid.
Hon var kvenna vænst ok inn mesti skörungr í öllu athæfi sínu.	She was woman fair and the most noble in all behaviour hers.	She was a fair woman and the most noble in all her behaviour.
Maðr hét Ormr, er bjó at Arnarstapa.	A-man was-called Orm, who settled at Arnarstapi.	There was a man called Orm who settled at Arnarstapi.
Hann átti konu, er Halldís hét.	He had a-wife, was Halldis named.	He had a wife who was named Halldis.
Ormr var góðr bóndi ok vinr Þorbjarnar mikill, ok var Guðríðr þar löngum at fóstri með honum.	Orm was a-good farmer and friend of-Thorbjorn great, and was Guthrid there long to foster with him.	Orm was a good farmer and a great friend of Thorbjorn, and Gudrid was fostered there and stayed for long periods of time with him.
Þorgeirr hét maðr.	Thorgeir was-named a-man.	There was a man named Thorgeir.
Hann bjó at Þorgeirsfelli.	He lived at Thorgeirsfell.	He lived at Thorgeirsfell.
Hann var auðigr at fé ok hafði verit leysingi.	He was wealthy in cattle and had-been made a-freed-man.	He was rich in cattle and had been made a free man.
Hann átti son, er Einarr hét.	He had a-son who-was Einar named.	He had a son who was named Einar.
Hann var vænn maðr ok vel mannaðr.	He was a-fair man and well mannered.	He was a fair man and well mannered.
Hann var ok skartsmaðr mikill.	He was also jewelled-man much.	He was also much bejewelled.
Einarr var í siglingum meðal landa, ok tókst honum þat vel.	Einar was among sailing between lands, and took him that well.	Einar was sailing between lands, and he took to it well.
Var hann jafnan sinn vetr hvárt á Íslandi eða í Nóregi.	Was he equally the winter either to Iceland or to Norway.	In winter he was equally in either Iceland or Norway.
Nú er frá því at segja eitt haust, þá er Einarr var á Íslandi, at hann fór með varning sinn út eftir Snæfellströnd ok vildi selja.	Now is from that to say one autumn, then that Einar was in Iceland, as he came with wares his out along Snaefellstrond and wished to-sell.	From that is there now to say that one autumn when Einar was in Iceland, he came with goods to Snaefellstrond wishing to sell.

The Vinland Sagas *The Saga of Erik the Red (Old Norse)*

Old Norse	Literal	English
Hann kemr til Arnarstapa.	He came to Arnarstapi.	He came to Arnarstapi.
Ormr býðr honum þar at vera, ok þat þiggr Einarr, því at þar var vinátta við körin.	Orm invited him there to be, and that accepted Einar, because that there was friendship with chosen.	Orm invited him to be there, and Einar accepted, as friendship was also chosen.
Var borinn inn varningr hans í eitt útibúr.	Were carried in wares his into an out-house.	His goods were carried into an outhouse.
Einarr braut upp varning sinn ok sýndi Ormi ok heimamönnum ok bauð honum af at hafa slíkt er hann vildi.	Einar divided up wares his and showed Orm and housemen and invited him of to have such that he willed.	Einar divided up his goods and showed Orm and his housemen, inviting them to have whatever they wished.
Ormr þá þetta ok talði Einar vera góðan fardreng ok auðnumann mikinn.	Orm then that also told Einar was good traveller-generous and fortune much.	Orm accepted and told Einar that he was a good merchant, generous, and of great fortune.
En er þeir heldu á varninginum, gekk kona fyrir útibúrsdyrrin.	When were they busy of wares, walked woman before out-house-door.	While they were occupied with the goods, a woman walked in front of the outhouse door.
Einarr spurði Orm, hver væri sú in fagra kona, er þar gekk fyrir dyrrin, - "ek hefi eigi hana hér fyrr sét".	Einar asked Orm, who was that in fair woman, was there going before doorway, - "I have not her here before seen".	Einar asked Orm who that fair woman was who walked in front of the doorway: "I have not seen her here before".
Ormr svaraði: "Þat er Guðríðr, fóstra mín, dóttir Þorbjarnar at Laugarbrekku".	Orm answered: "That is Guthrid, foster-child mine, daughter Thorbjorn's from Laugarbrekka".	Orm answered: "That is Gudrid, my foster child, daughter of Thorbjorn from Laugarbrekka".
Einarr mælti: "Hon mun vera kostr góðr.	Einar said: "She would be choice good.	Einar said: "She would be a good choice.
Eða hafa nökkurir menn til komit at biðja hennar?"	Or have some men towards come to propose her?"	Or have any men come forward to propose to her?"
Ormr svarar: "Beðit hefir hennar víst verit, ok liggr þat eigi laust fyrir. Finnst þat á, at hon mun vera mannvönd ok svá faðir hennar".	Orm answered: "Proposals have for-her made been, and lies that not less for. Finding that of, that she should be husband and so father hers".	Orm answered: "Proposals have been made to her, but without success. She shall choose her husband, and so will her father".
"Svá, með því", sagði Einarr, "at hér er sú kona, er ek ætla mér at biðja, ok vilda ek, at þessa mála leitaðir þú við Þorbjörn, föður hennar, ok legðir allan hug á, at þetta mætti framgengt verða.	"So with therefore", said Einar, "That she is the woman, that I intend me to propose, and will I, to this matter seek you with Thorbjorn, father hers, and lay all thoughts to, that this may from-going be.	"So be it", said Einar, "she's the woman I intend to propose to, and I would like you to seek the matter with her father Thorbjorn, and give it your thoughts, how this may be so.

The Vinland Sagas   *The Saga of Erik the Red (Old Norse)*

Old Norse	Literal	English
Skal ek þér fullkomna vináttu fyrir gjalda, ef ek get táðit.	Shall I you full-come friendship for expenses, if I can say.	I will repay you with the fullest friendship, that I can say.
Má Þorbjörn bóndi þat sjá, at okkr væri vel hentar tengðir, því at hann er sómamaðr mikill ok á staðfestu góða, en lausafé hans er mér sagt heldr á förum.	May Thorbjorn farmer that see, to ours would-be well suits joined, for to he is famous-man great and of established good, but liquidity his is to-me said rather to going.	Thorbjorn the farmer may see we would be well joined, as he is a man of high regard with a good farm, but it is said that his means are rather depleting".
En mik skortir hvárki land né lausafé ok okkr feðga, ok myndi Þorbirni verða at þessu inn mesti styrkr, ef þetta tækist".	But my shortage neither land nor liquidity and us father-and-son, and should Thorbjorn be therefore this the most strength, if this takes".	But my father and I lack neither land or means, and would therefore give the most support, if this is concluded.
Ormr segir: "Víst þykkjumst ek vinr þinn vera, en þó em ek eigi við mitt ráð fúss, at vit berim þetta upp, því at Þorbjörn er skapstórr ok þó metnaðarmaðr mikill".	Orm said: "Knowing think-us I friend yours be, but though am I not with my advice willing, of to bring this up, because that Thorbjorn is temperamental and though ambitious-man much".	Orm said: "Knowing that I consider myself your friend, I am though not willing to bring up this discussion, because Thorbjorn is temperamental and a very ambitious man".
Einarr kveðst ekki vilja annat en upp væri borit bónorðit.	Einar said not willing another but up would-be carried proposal.	Einar said that he would not be satisfied unless the proposal was brought up.
Ormr kvað hann ráða skyldu.	Orm said his decision shall-be.	Orm said that his decision would be so.
Ferr Einarr suðr aftr, unz hann kemr heim.	Travelled Einar south back, until he came home.	Einar travelled back south until he came home.
Nökkuru síðar hafði Þorbjörn haustboð, sem hann átti vanða til, því at hann var stórmenni mikit.	Sometime since had Thorbjorn harvest-feast, that he had accustomed to, because to him were great-men much.	Sometime after Thorbjorn had a harvest feast, that was his custom, as he was a great man.
Kom þar Ormr frá Arnarstapa ok margir aðrir vinir Þorbjarnar.	Came there Orm from Arnarstapi and many other friends Thorbjorn's.	Orm came from Arnarstapi and many of Thorbjorn's other friends.
Ormr kom at máli við Þorbjörn ok sagði, at Einarr var þar skömmu, frá Þorgeirsfelli, ok gerðist inn efniligsti maðr.	Orm came to speak with Thorbjorn and said, that Einar was there recently, from Thorgeirsfell, and became the promising man.	Orm came to speak with Thorbjorn and said, that Einar from Thorgeirsfell had been there recently, and he had become a promising man.

The Vinland Sagas — The Saga of Erik the Red (Old Norse)

Old Norse	Literal	English
Hefr Ormr nú upp bónorðit fyrir hönd Einars ok segir þat vel hent fyrir sumra hluta sakar.	Had Orm now upped proposal for hand Einar's and said that well joined for some part's sake.	Orm now brought up Einar's marriage proposal and said that it would be well joined on several accounts.
"Má þér, bóndi, verða at styrkr mikill fyrir fjárkosta sakar".	"May to-you, farmer, be in strength much for financial-cost's sake".	"It may be to you be strong support in financial terms".
Þorbjörn svarar: "Eigi varði mik slíkra orða af þér, at ek mynda gifta þrælssyni dóttur mína.	Thorbjorn answered: "Not expected I such words from you, that I should give thrall's-son daughter mine.	Thorbjorn answered: "I did not expect to hear such words from you, that I should give my daughter to a slave's son.
Ok þat finnið þér nú, at fé mitt þverr, er slíkt ráð gefið mér.	And that find you now, that wealth mine decreases, is such counsel given to-me.	As you now suggest, that my wealth is decreasing, to give such advice to me.
Ok eigi skal hon með þér vera lengr, er þér þótti hon svá lítils gjaforðs verð".	And not shall she with you be longer, as you thought she such little marriage-offer deserve".	And no longer shall she be with you, as you thought she deserved such a lowly marriage offer".
Síðan fór Ormr heim ok hverr annarr boðsmanna til sins heimilis.	Afterwards went Orm home and each other guests to their households.	Afterwards Orm went home an each of the other guests went to their homes.
Guðríðr var eftir með föður sínum ok var heima þann vetr.	Guthrid was remained with father hers and stayed home that winter.	Gudrid stayed behind with her father and spent that winter at home.
En at vári hafði Þorbjörn vinaboð, ok kom þar margt manna, ok var in bezta veizla.	But in spring had Thorbjorn friend-invites, and came there many people, and was the best feast.	Then when spring came Thorbjorn invited his friends to come with many people, and there was the best feast.
Ok at veizlunni krafði Þorbjörn sér hljóðs ok mælti: "Hér hefi ek búit langa ævi, ok hefi ek reynt góðvilja manna við mik ok ástúð.	And at the-feast called Thorbjorn he be-heard and spoke: "Here have I lived long life, and have I experienced good-will men's to me and affection.	During the feast, Thorbjorn asked to be heard and spoke: "Here I have lived a long life, and I have enjoyed the good will and affection.
Kalla ek vel farit hafa vár skipti.	Call I well gone have been exchanges.	I call all our dealings well done.
En nú tekr hagr minn at óhægjast fyrir lausafjár sakar, en hér til hefir kallat verit heldr virðingarráð.	But now take benefits mine to maintain for liquidity's sake, that here until has called have-been rather worthiness.	But now my benefit begins to be uneasy for the sake of means, though so far it has been called worthy.
Nú vil ek fyrr búinu bregða en sæmðinni týna.	Now will I for settlement foreclose before honour lose.	Now I wish to foreclose before I lose my honour.

The Vinland Sagas   *The Saga of Erik the Red (Old Norse)*

Old Norse	Literal	English
Ætla ek fyrr af landi fara en ætt mína svívirða ok vitja heita Eiríks ins rauða, vinar míns, er hann hafði, þá er vit skilðum á Breiðafirði.	Intend I for of land travel but-for lineage mine shame and visit called Erik the Red, friend mine, that he had, then was with separated at Breidafjord.	I intend to travel from this land, rather than shame my lineage, and visit my friend Erik the Red who I was separated from at Breidafjord.
Ætla ek nú at fara til Grænlands í sumar, ef svá ferr sem ek vilda".	Intend I now to travel to Greenland in summer, if so goes as I wish".	I now intend to travel to Greenland I summer, if it goes as I wish".
Mönnum þótti mikil þessi ráðabreytni, því at Þorbjörn var vinsæll maðr, en þóttust vita, at Þorbjörn mundi svá fremi þetta upp hafa kveðit, at ekki myndi tjóa at letja hann.	People thought great this change, for that Thorbjorn was befriended man, but thought knowing, that Thorbjorn would so provide that up had declared, that not should avail to discourage him.	People thought this was a great change, because Thorbjorn was a popular man, but they thought that once Thorbjorn had declared this, it would be to no avail to discourage him.
Gaf Þorbjörn mönnum gjafar, ok var brugðit veizlunni.	Gave Thorbjorn people gifts, and was brought-out feast.	Thorbjorn gave people gifts, and a feast was brought out.
Síðan fór hverr til síns heima.	Afterwards went each to their homes.	Afterwards everyone went to their homes.
Þorbjörn selr lönd sín ok kaupir sér skip, er uppi stóð í Hraunhafnarósi.	Thorbjorn sold land his and bought himself ship, which up stood at Hraunhafnaros.	Thorbjorn sold his land and bought himself a ship, which stood at Hraunhafnaros.
Réðust til ferðar með honum þrír tigir manna.	Hired to travel with him three tens men.	He hired thirty men to travel with him.
Var þar í ferð Ormr frá Arnarstapa ok kona hans ok aðrir vinir Þorbjarnar, þeir er eigi vildu við hann skilja.	Was there to travel Orm from Arnarstapi and wife his and other friends Thorbjorn's, they were not willing with him separate.	There to travel with him was Orm from Arnarstapi, and his wife, and Thorbjorn's other friends, they were not willing to separate with him.
Síðan létu þeir í haf, ok er þeir váru í hafi, tók af byri.	Afterwards left they to sea, and then they were to sea, taken of fair-wind.	Afterwards they put to sea, and when they were at sea, the fair wind disappeared.
Fengu þeir hafvillur, ok fórst þeim ógreitt um sumarit.	Caught they open-sea, and went they not-without-obstacle about summer.	They were caught in the open sea, and they were not without obstacle all summer.
Því næst kom sótt í lið þeira, ok andaðist Ormr ok Halldís, kona hans, ok helmingr liðs þeira.	For next came sickness among team theirs, and died Orm and Halldis, wife his, and half team theirs.	Because next there came a sickness among their crew, and Orm died, and his wife Halldis, along with half of the crew.

The Vinland Sagas   *The Saga of Erik the Red (Old Norse)*

Old Norse	Literal	English
Sjó tók at stæra, ok þolðu menn it mesta vás ok vesöld á marga vega, en tóku þó Herjólfsnes á Grænlandi við vetr sjálfan.	Sea took to greatly, and endured men the most toil and misery in many ways, but took though Herjolfsnes to Greenland by winter itself.	The sea swelled, and people endured the most toil and misery in many ways, but they took land at Herjolfsnes in Greenland during the Winter Nights.
Sá maðr hét Þorkell, er bjó á Herjólfsnesi.	So a-man was-named Thorkell, who settled at Herjolfsnes.	There was a man named Thorkell, who lived at Herjolfsnes.
Hann var inn bezti bóndi.	He was the best farmer.	He was the best farmer.
Hann tók við Þorbirni ok öllum skipverjum hans um vetrinn.	He took with Thorbjorn and all crew his about winter.	He took with Thorbjorn and all his crew for the winter.
Þorkell veitti þeim sköruliga.	Thorkell provided-for them boldly.	Thorkell provided for them generously.
4	4	4
Í þann tíma var hallæri mikit á Grænlandi.	In that time was famine much in Greenland.	At that time there was much famine in Greenland.
Höfðu menn fengit lítit fang, þeir er í veiðiferðir höfðu farit, en sumir ekki aftr komnir.	Had people caught little, they which to hunting had been, and some not after returning.	People that had been hunting had caught little, and some of them had not returned.
Sú kona var þar í byggð, er Þorbjörg hét.	The woman was there in settlement, was Thorbjorg called.	There was a woman in the settlement who was named Thorbjorg.
Hon var spákona ok var kölluð lítilvölva.	She was prophetess and was called Little-Prophetess.	She was a prophetess, and was called Little Prophetess.
Hon hafði átt sér níu systr, ok váru allar spákonur, en hon ein var þá á lífi.	She had descendents hers nine sisters, and were all prophetesses, and she alone was then yet living.	Among her family were nine sisters, and all were prophetesses, and she was the only one yet living.
Þat var háttr Þorbjargar um vetrum, at hon fór at veizlum, ok buðu þeir menn henni mest heim, er forvitni var á at vita forlög sín eða árferð.	It was way Thorbjorg's about winter, that she went to feasts, and invited they people her most homes, that curious were for to know fortune theirs or season.	It was a custom of Thorbjorg's during winter, that she went to feasts, and to homes that people had invited her to, who were curious to know their fortune for the season.
Ok með því at Þorkell var þar mestr bóndi, þá þótti til hans koma at vita, hvé nær létta myndi óárani þessu, sem yfir stóð.	And with because that Thorkell was there greatest landowner, then thought to him came to know, how near relieve should scarcity this, which over stood.	And with Thorkell being the greatest landowner, it was thought that he should come to know when the scarcity that stood over them would be relieved.

The Saga of Erik the Red (Old Norse)

Old Norse	Literal	English
Býðr Þorkell spákonunni heim, ok er henni þar vel fagnat, sem siðr var til, þá er við þess háttar konum skyldi taka.	Invited Thorkell prophetess home, and was she there well welcomed, as custom was to, then was with this kind woman should take.	Thorkell invited the prophetess to his home, and she was well welcomed, as was the custom, when this kind of woman was received as a guest.
Var henni búit hásæti ok lagt undir hana hægendi.	Was she prepared a-high-seat and laid under her a-cushion.	A high seat was prepared for her, and under it a cushion.
Þar skyldi í vera hænsafiðri.	There should in be hen's-feathers.	This was to be filled with hen's feathers.
En er hon kom um kveldit ok sá maðr, er móti henni var sendr, þá var hon svá búin, at hon hafði yfir sér tuglamöttul blán, ok var settr steinum allt í skaut ofan.	Then when she came about evening and saw a-man, who meeting her was sent, then was she such ready, for she had over her mantle blue, and was set stones all in lap of.	Then when she arrived around evening, with the man who was sent to meet her when she was ready, she had over her a blue mantle, which was set with stones in the lap.
Hon hafði á hálsi sér glertölur, lambskinnskofra svartan á höfði ok við innan kattarskinn hvít.	She had on neck hers glass-beads, lamb-skin-hood black on head and with in cat-skin white.	She had glass beads on her neck, and on her head a hood of black lamb skin, lined with white cat skin.
Ok hon hafði staf í hendi, ok var á knappr.	And she had staff in hand, and was on a-knob	And she had in her hand a staff, which had a knob on the top.
Hann var búinn með messingu ok settr steinum ofan um knappinn.	It was set with brass and set stones on about knob.	It was set with brass and had stones set about the knob.
Hon hafði um sik hnjóskulinda, ok var þar á skjóðupungr mikill, ok varðveitti hon þar í töfr sín, þau er hon þurfti til fróðleiks at hafa.	She had about herself a-girdle and was there on skin-purse great, and kept she there in magic hers, those which she needed to knowledge of have.	She wore a girdle with a large skin purse, and she kept her magic in there, which she needed to have knowledge of.
Hon hafði á fótum kálfskinnsskúa loðna ok í þvengi langa ok á tinknappar miklir á endunum.	She had on feet calf-skin-shoes fur and in tied long and in pewter-buttons great on ends.	She had calf skin shoes lined with fur, with long laces with pewter knobs on the ends.
Hon hafði á höndum sér kattskinnsglófa, ok váru hvítir innan ok loðnir.	She had on hands hers cat-skin-gloves, and were white inside and furry.	She had cat skin gloves on her hands and they were white and furry inside.
En er hon kom inn, þótti öllum mönnum skylt at velja henni sæmiligar kveðjur.	Then when she came in, thought all people should to will her honourable greetings.	When she came in, everyone was supposed to give her honourable greetings.
Hon tók því sem henni váru menn geðjaðir til.	She received therefore as she was people agreeable to.	She responded to people according to how the person appealed to her.

The Saga of Erik the Red (Old Norse)

Old Norse	Literal	English
Tók Þorkell bóndi í hönd henni ok leiddi hana til þess sætis, sem henni var búit.	Took Thorkell the-Farmer in hand hers and led her to this seat, which she was prepared.	Thorkell the Farmer took her hand and led her to the seat which was prepared for her.
Þorkell bað hana þá renna þar augum yfir hjú ok hjörð ok svá híbýli.	Thorkell asked her then run there eyes over herd and hearth and so settlement.	Thorkell asked her to run her eyes over the herd, the hearth, and the settlement.
Hon var fámálug um allt.	She was silent about all.	She was silent about all of it.
Borð váru upp tekin um kveldit, ok er frá því at segja, hvat spákonunni var matbúit.	Tables were up taken about evening, and was from since to say, what prophetess was food-prepared.	That evening tables were set up, and afterwards it was to say, what food was prepared for the prophetess.
Henni var gerr grautr af kiðjamjólk ok matbúin hjörtu ór öllum kykvendum, þeim er þar váru til.	She was made porridge of kid's-milk and food-prepared hearts of all creatures, they that there were to.	She was made a porridge of kid's milk and hearts of all animals available there.
Hon hafði messingarspón ok hníf tannskeftan, tvíhólkaðan af eiri, ok var brotinn af oddrinn.	She had brass-spoon and knife walrus-tusk, two-ringed of bronze, and was broken of tip.	She had a brass spoon and a knife with a walrus tusk, two halves ringed with bronze, and the tip had been broken off.
En er borð váru upp tekin, þá gengr Þorkell bóndi fyrir Þorbjörgu ok spyrr, hversu henni þykki þar um at lítast eða hversu skapfelld henni eru þar híbýli eða hættir manna eða hversu fljótliga hon mun vís verða þess, er hann hefir spurt hana ok mönnum er mest forvitni at vita.	Then when table was up taken, then went Thorkell farmer before Thorbjorg and asked, how she thought there about it looked or how agreeable to-her were there settlements or manner people's or how soon she could aware be this, that he had asked her and men were most curious to know.	And when the tables were taken up, then Thorkell the Farmer went before Thorbjorg and asked her what she thought of the conduct of the household, the manner of people, and how soon she would know what he had asked her, and what people were most curious to know.
Hon kallast ekki mundu segja fyrr en um morgininn eftir, er hon hafði áðr sofit um nóttina.	She considered not would say before that about morning after, when she had after slept for night.	She said that she would not say before the following morning, when she had slept about the night.
En um morgininn at áliðnum degi var henni veittr sá umbúningr, sem hon þurfti at hafa til at fremja seiðinn.	Then from morning to following day was she given that clothing, which she needed to have for to perform enchantments.	Then the following morning she was given the clothing that she needed to have to perform her enchantments.
Hon bað ok fá sér konur þær, er kynni fræði þat, sem til seiðsins þarf ok Varðlokur hétu.	She asked also get the women there, who knew wisdom that, which for enchantments needed and warlock-songs called.	She asked for women who had the wisdom of the enchantments needed, which were called warlock songs.
En þær konur fundust eigi.	But those women were-found not.	But those women were not found.

The Vinland Sagas — The Saga of Erik the Red (Old Norse)

Old Norse	Literal	English
Þá var at leitat at um bæinn, ef nökkurr kynni.	They were to seek to about household, if anyone knew.	The people of the household searched for anyone who knew.
Þá segir Guðríðr: "Hvárki em ek fjölkunnig né vísendakona, en þó kenndi Halldís, fóstra mín, mér á Íslandi þat kvæði, er hon kallaði Varðlokur".	Then said Guthrid: "Neither am I of-magic nor fore-knowing-woman, but though taught Halldis, foster mine, to-me in Iceland that poem, that she called warlock-songs".	Then Gudrid said: "I am neither of magic nor prophecy, but my foster mother, Halldis, taught me chants that she called warlock songs.
Þorkell segir: "Þá ertu happfróð".	Thorkell said: "Then are-you lucky-wise".	Thorkell said: "Then you are luckily wise".
Hon segir: "Þetta er þat eitt atferli, er ek ætla í engum atbeina at vera, því at ek em kristin kona".	She said: "That is the one ceremony, that I intend to no assistance in being, because that I am Christian woman".	She said: "That is one ceremony that I do not intend to be assisting because I am a Christian woman".
Þorbjörg segir: "Svá mætti verða, at þú yrðir mönnum at liði hér um, en þú værir þá kona ekki verri en áðr.	Thorbjorg said: "So may be, that you become people to help here about, but you would-be then woman not worse than before.	Thorbjorg said: "So it may be that you may come to help here, but you would be no worse a woman than before.
En við Þorkel mun ek meta at fá þá hluti til, er hafa þarf".	But with Thorkell should I evaluate to get the things for, which have need".	But I will appreciate getting the things from Thorkell that are needed".
Þorkell herðir nú at Guðríði, en hon kveðst gera mundu sem hann vildi.	Thorkell hardened now to Guthrid, but she said do would as he wished.	Thorkell now hardened towards Gudrid, and said that she should do as he wished.
Slógu þá konur hring um hjallinn, en Þorbjörg sat á uppi.	Formed then women a-ring around the-platform, while Thorbjorg sat on up.	The women then formed a ring around the platform, while Thorbjorg sat above.
Kvað Guðríðr þá kvæðit svá fagrt ok vel, at engi þóttist heyrt hafa með fegri rödd kvæði kveðit, sá er þar var hjá.	Said Guthrid then recited so beautiful and well, that none thought heard had with more-beautiful voice poem sung, so as there was heard.	Gudrid then recited so beautifully and so well, that no one thought they had head a poem sung with more beautiful a voice, than that which they heard.

Old Norse	Literal	English
Spákonan þakkar henni kvæðit ok kvað margar þær náttúrur nú til hafa sótt ok þykkja fagrt at heyra, er kvæðit var svá vel flutt, - "er áðr vildu við oss skiljast ok enga hlýðni oss veita.	Prophetess thanked her poem and said many they spirits now to have attended and think beautiful to hear, that poem was so well performed, - "Who before would by us separate and none homage us grant.	The prophetess thanked her for the poem and said that the many spirits have now attended who thought it beautiful to hear, as it was so well performed: "those who before turned their backs on us and refused to grant us assistance.
En mér eru nú margir þeir hlutir auðsýnir, er áðr var ek duldið, ok margir aðrir.	And to-me are now many those things shown, which before were I hidden, and many others.	And there are now many things shown to me which before were hidden from me and others.
En ek kann þér þat at segja, Þorkell, at hallæri þetta mun ekki haldast lengr en í vetr, ok mun batna árangr, sem várar.	And I can to-you that to say, Thorkell, to famine this should not hold longer than to winter, and should better harvest, then spring.	And I can now say to you, Thorkell, that this famine should not hold longer than to winter, and there should be a better harvest in the spring.
Sóttarfar þat, sem á hefir legit, mun ok batna vánu bráðara.	Sickness that, which to has laid, should also better-than hope sooner.	That sickness which has happened, should hopefully be better sooner.
En þér, Guðríðr, skal ek launa í hönd liðsinni þat, er oss hefir af þér staðit, því at þín forlög eru mér nú allglöggsæ.	And you, Guthrid, shall I reward in hand assistance that, for us have of you stood, because that your fortunes are to-me now clear.	And you, Gudrid, I shall reward in hand for the assistance that you placed, because to me your fortunes are now clear.
Þú munt gjaforð fá hér á Grænlandi, þat er sæmiligast er, þó at þér verði þat eigi til langæðar, því at vegir þínir liggja út til Íslands, ok mun þar koma frá þér bæði mikill ætt ok góð, ok yfir þínum kynkvíslum skína bjartari geislar en ek hafa megin til at geta slikt vandliga sét.	You shall married be here in Greenland, that which honourable is, though for you will-be that not for long, because the way yours lies out to Iceland, and shall there come from you both great descendents and good, and over your family shine bright rays but I have most towards that can such closely seen.	You shall be married here in Greenland, and honourably, though you will not be married for long, because your way lies out to Iceland, and there shall come from you good descendents, and bright rays will shine over your family, towards that I can clearly see.
Enda far þú nú heil ok vel, dóttir".	End go you now whole and well, daughter".	After all, travel you now whole and well, daughter".
Síðan gengu menn at vísendakonunni, ok frétti þá hverr þess, er mest forvitni var á at vita.	Afterwards went people to wise-woman, and heard then each these, were most curious was of to know.	Afterwards people went to the wise woman, and then each heard that which they were most curious to know.
Hon var ok góð af frásögnum. Gekk þat ok lítt í tauma, er hon sagði.	She was also good of account. Went that also little of reins, that she said.	She gave a good answer. Things went little from the reins of what she had said.

Old Norse	Literal	English
Þessu næst var komit eftir henni af öðrum bæ.	This next were come after her from another farm.	Following this, someone came for her from another farm.
Fór hon þá þangat.	Went she then from-there.	She then went from there.
Þá var sent eftir Þorbirni, því at hann vildi eigi heima vera, meðan slík hindrvitni var framið.	Then was sent after Thorbjorn, because that she willed not home be, while such hindered-knowledge was committed.	Then Thorbjorn was sent for, because she did not want to be at home while such hindered knowledge was committed.
Veðrátta batnaði skjótt, sem Þorbjörg hafði sagt.	Weather bettered shortly, as Thorbjorg had said.	The weather soon bettered, as Thorbjorg had said.
Býr Þorbjörn skip sitt ok ferr þar til, er hann kemr í Brattahlíð.	Prepared Thorbjorn ship his and travelled there to, that he came to Brattahlid.	Thorbjorn prepared his ship and travelled until he came to Brattahlid.
Eiríkr tekr vel við honum með blíðu ok kvað þat vel, er hann var þar kominn.	Erik took well with him with friendliness and saying that well, that he was there coming.	Erik received him well with friendliness and said how good it was that he had come.
Var Þorbjörn með honum um vetrinn ok skuldalið hans, en þeir vistuðu háseta með bóndum.	Was Thorbjorn with him about winter and household his, then they sheltered men among farms.	Thorbjorn was with him over the winter and his household was sheltered among the farms.
Eftir um várit gaf Eiríkr Þorbirni land á Stokkanesi, ok var þar gerr sæmiligr bær, ok bjó hann þar síðan.	After about spring gave Erik Thorbjorn land in Stokkanes, and was there made honourable farm, and settled he there since.	After about spring, Erik gave Thorbjorn land in Stokkanes, and there was made an honourable farm, and he settled there since.
5	5	5
Eiríkr átti þá konu, er Þjóðhildr hét, ok við henni tvá sonu.	Erik had then a-wife, was Thjodhild named, and with her two sons.	Erik had then a wife, who was named Thjodhild, and with her two sons.
Hét annarr Þorsteinn, en annarr Leifr.	Was called-one Thorstein, and another Leif.	One was called Thorstein, and another Leif.
Þeir váru báðir efniligir menn.	They were both promising men.	They were both promising men.
Var Þorsteinn heima með föður sínum, ok var eigi sá maðr á Grænlandi, er jafnmannvænn þótti sem hann.	Was Thorstein home with father his, and was not so a-man in Greenland, as equally-handsome thought as he.	Thorstein lived at home with his father, and there was no man in Greenland thought as equally handsome as him.
Leifr hafði siglt til Nóregs ok var með Óláfi konungi Tryggvasyni.	Leif had sailed to Norway and was with Olaf king Tryggvason.	Leif had sailed to Norway and was with King Olaf Tryggvason.
En er Leifr sigldi af Grænlandi um sumarit, urðu þeir sæhafa til Suðreyja.	But when Leif sailed from Greenland about summer, became they sea-scattered to Sudreyar.	But when Leif sailed from Greenland that summer, the ship was driven off course to Sudreyar.

The Saga of Erik the Red (Old Norse)

Old Norse	Literal	English
Þaðan byrjaði þeim seint, ok dvölðust þeir þar lengi um sumarit.	From-there began they late, and dwelled they there long about summer.	From there they began late, and they dwelled their a long time through the summer.
Leifr lagði þokka á konu þá, er Þórgunna hét.	Leif laid thoughts to a-woman there, was Thorgun called.	Leif fell in love with a woman there, who was named Thorgun.
Hon var kona ættstór, ok skildi Leifr, at hon mundi vera margkunnig.	She was woman noble, and understood Leif, that she would be many-knowing.	She was a noble woman, and Leif understood that she knew much.
En er Leifr bjóst brott, beiddist Þórgunna at fara með honum.	When was Leif prepared away, asked Thorgun to travel with him.	When Leif was preparing to leave, Thorgun asked to travel with him.
Leifr spurði, hvárt þat væri nökkut vili frænda hennar.	Leif asked, if that was something wished kinsmen hers.	Leif asked if that was something her kinsmen would agree to.
Hon kveðst þat ekki hirða.	She said that not consider.	She said that she did not care.
Leifr kveðst eigi þat kunna at sjá at sínu ráði at gera hertekna svá stórættaða konu í ókunnu landi, - "en vér liðfáir".	Leif said not that know-how to see of her advice to make captive such noble woman in unknown land, - "as we-are few".	Leif said that he did not know how to see to it that he make a captive such a noble woman in an unknown land - "as we have few troops".
Þórgunna mælti: "Eigi er víst, at þér þykki því betr ráðit".	Thorgun spoke: "Not is certain, that to-you seems therefore better decision".	Thorgun spoke: "I am not sure there is for you a better choice".
"Á þat mun ek þó hætta", sagði Leifr.	"At that should I though stop", said Leif.	"I will stop at that", said Leif.
"Þá segi ek þér", sagði Þórgunna, "at ek mun fara kona eigi ein saman, ok em ek með barni.	"Then say I to-you", said Thorgun, "That I should travel as-a-woman not alone together, and am I with child.	"Then I say to you", said Thorgun, "That I travel not alone, and I am with child.
Segi ek þat af þínum völdum.	Say I this of your doing.	And I say that this is your doing.
Get ek, at þat muni vera sveinbarn, þá er fæðist.	Guess I, of that shall be boy, then to born.	I guess that a boy shall be born.
En þóttú vilir engan gaum at gefa, þá mun ek upp fæða sveininn ok þér senda til Grænlands, þegar fara má með öðrum mönnum.	But though will-you no heed of give, then shall I up feed boy and to-you send to Greenland, when travel may with other people.	But though you will not heed him, I shall bring the boy up and send him to you in Greenland, when he may travel with other people.

The Vinland Sagas   *The Saga of Erik the Red (Old Norse)*

Old Norse	Literal	English
En ek get, at þér verði at þvílíkum nytjum sonareignin sem nú verðr skilnaðr okkarr til.	But I guess, that you will-be as for-like use son's-property as now worth parting ours to.	But I guess that he will serve you as well as you have served me with your departure.
En koma ætla ek mér til Grænlands, áðr lýkr".	But come intend I myself to Greenland, before it-ends".	But I intend to come to Greenland myself, before it all ends".
Leifr gaf henni fingrgull ok vaðmálsmöttul grænlenzkan ok tannbelti.	Leif gave her finger-gold and mantle Greenland-skin and tusk-belt.	He gave her gold for her finger and a mantle of Greenland-skin and a belt with ivory.
Þessi sveinn kom til Grænlands ok nefndist Þorgils.	This boy came to Greenland and named Thorgils.	The boy came to Greenland and was named Thorgils.
Leifr tók við honum at faðerni.	Leif took with him to paternity.	Leif recognised him as his son.
Ok er þat sumra manna sögn, at þessi Þorgils hafi komit til Íslands fyrir Fróðárundr um sumarit.	And was that summer people said, that this Thorgils had come to Iceland before hauntings about summer.	And that summer people said that Thorgils had come to Iceland before the hauntings in summer.
En sjá Þorgils var síðan á Grænlandi, ok þótti þar enn eigi kynjalaust um hann verða, áðr lauk.	Then seen Thorgils was since in Greenland, and thought there yet not extraordinary about him to-be, before end.	Then Thorgils was seen afterwards in Greenland, and it was thought that there was something unusual about him before it ended.
Þeir Leifr sigldu brott ór Suðreyjum ok tóku Nóreg um haustit.	There Leif sailed away from Sudreyar and took-to Norway about autumn.	There Leif sailed away from Sudreyar and took to land in Norway about autumn.
Fór Leifr til hirðar Óláfs konungs Tryggvasonar.	Travelled Leif to court Olaf king Tryggvason's.	Leif travelled to the court of King Olaf Tryggvason.
Lagði konungr á hann góða virðing ok þóttist sjá, at hann mundi vera vel menntr maðr.	Had the-king towards him good honour and thought saw, that he would be a well-educated man.	The King had good honour towards him, and thought that he was a well educated man.
Eitt sinn kom konungr at máli við Leif ok sagði: "Ætlar þú til Grænlands í sumar?"	Once he came king to speak to Leif and said: "Intend you to Greenland in summer?".	One time, the king spoke to Leif and said: "Do you intend to go to Greenland in summer?".
"Þat ætla ek", sagði Leifr, "ef þat er yðvarr vili".	"That intend I", said Leif, "If that is your will".	"That I do intend", said Leif, "If that is your will".
Konungr svarar: "Ek get, at þat muni vel vera, ok skaltu þangat fara með erendum mínum, at boða þar kristni".	King answered: "I do, for that should well be, and shall-you there travel with errand mine, to preach there Christianity".	The king answered: "I do, for that will be well, and you shall travel there with my purpose, to preach there Christianity".

The Vinland Sagas   *The Saga of Erik the Red (Old Norse)*

Old Norse	Literal	English
Leifr kvað hann ráða skyldu, en kveðst hyggja, at þat erendi myndi torflutt á Grænlandi.	Leif said he decide should, but said thought, it that errand would difficult-be in Greenland.	Leif said that the king should decide that, but that he thought the errand would be difficult in Greenland.
Konungr kveðst eigi þann mann sjá, er betr væri til fallinn en hann, - "ok muntu giftu til bera".	King said none that men seen, were better would-be to fall than he, - "And should luck towards carry".	The king said there was no one better for the task to fall to than him, "and luck shall carry you towards".
"Þat mun því at eins", segir Leifr, "ef ek nýt yðvar við".	"That should therefore by likewise", said Leif, "If I benefit yours with".	"That it should be", said Leif, "if I travel with your luck also".
Lætr Leifr í haf ok er lengi úti ok hitti á lönd þau, er hann vissi áðr enga ván til.	Put Leif to sea and was long out and met to lands those, that he knew before none looked to.	Leif put to sea when he was ready and after a long time at sea, he met lands that he knew none had seen before.
Váru þar hveitiakrar sjálfsánir ok vínviðr vaxinn.	Were there wheat-acres self-sowing and vine-trees growing.	There were acres of wheat that were self-sowing, and vine trees growing.
Þar váru þau tré, er mösurr heita, ok höfðu þeir af þessu öllu nökkur merki, sum tré svá mikil, at í hús váru lögð.	There were there trees, were maple called, and had they from this all some imprint, some trees so great, that to houses were laid.	There were trees there known as burl, and they took some specimens of all of them, and some trees were so large that houses could be laid in them.
Leifr fann menn á skipflaki ok flutti heim með sér.	Leif found people on shipwreck and brought home with him.	Leif found people on a shipwreck and brought them home with him.
Sýndi hann í því ina mestu stórmennsku ok drengskap sem mörgu öðru, er hann kom kristni á landit, ok var jafnan síðan kallaðr Leifr inn heppni.	Showed he to therefore the most greatness and honour as many other, as he came Christianity to land, and was ever after called Leif the lucky.	He showed his greatness and honour and boyishness, so as many others, when he brought Christianity to the land, and was ever after called Leif the Lucky.
Leifr tók land í Eiríksfirði ok fór heim síðan í Brattahlíð.	Leif took land in Eriksfjord and went home afterwards to Brattahlid.	Leif took land in Eriksfjord and went home afterwards to Brattahlid.
Tóku þar allir menn vel við honum.	Took there all people well with him.	People there all received him warmly.

Old Norse	Literal	English
Hann boðaði brátt kristni um landit ok almenniliga trú ok sýndi mönnum orðsending Óláfs konungs Tryggvasonar ok sagði, hversu mörg ágæti ok mikil dýrð fylgði þessum sið.	He preached soon Christianity about land and properly faith and showed people message Olaf king Tryggvason's and said, how much excellent and great glory followed this tradition.	He soon preached the faith of Christianity throughout the land and showed people the message that King Olaf Tryggvason who said how much excellence and glory followed this tradition.
Eiríkr tók því máli seint, at láta sið sinn, en Þjóðhildr gekk skjótt undir ok lét gera kirkju eigi allnær húsunum.	Erik took since matter late, to leave tradition his, but Thjodhild went quickly behind and had made church not all-near the-house.	Erik was reluctant to take to it and leave his tradition, but Thjodhild was quick to follow and had a church made a distance away from the house.
Þat hús var kallat Þjóðhildarkirkja.	That house was called Thjodhildakirkja.	That house was called Thjodhildakirkja.
Hafði hon þar fram bænir sínar ok þeir menn, sem við kristni tóku.	Had she there from prayers hers and they people, since with Christianity took.	She held her prayers there, and with people who had since converted to Christianity.
Þjóðhildr vildi ekki samræði við Eirík, síðan hon tók trú, en honum var þat mjök móti skapi.	Thjodhild willed not intercourse with Erik, since she took faith, but he was that much against mood.	Thjodhild did not want to have intercourse with Erik since she had taken the faith, which went very much against his mood.
Á því gerðist orð mikit, at menn myndi leita lands þess, er Leifr hafði fundit.	Then therefore made words much, to people would search lands these, that Leif had found.	Then there were many words about people searching these lands that Leif had found.
Var þar formaðr at Þorsteinn Eiríksson, fróðr maðr ok vinsæll.	Was there chief to Thorstein Eriksson, wise man and popular.	Chief among them was Thorstein Eriksson, a wise and popular man.
Eiríkr var ok til beðinn, ok trúðu menn hans gæfu framast ok forsjá.	Erik was and to asked, and believed people his gifted foremost and foresight.	Erik was also asked, and people believed he was gifted and a man of foresight.
Hann var lengi fyrir, en kvað eigi nei við, er vinir hans báðu hann til, bjuggu síðan skip þat, er Þorbjörn hafði út haft, ok váru til ráðnir tuttugu menn, ok höfðu lítit fé, eigi meir en vápn ok vistir.	He was long before, that saying not no with, then friends his asked him to, prepared since then ship that, Thorbjorn had out had, and were to appointed twenty people, and had little cattle, not more than weapons and provisions.	For a long time he was against going, but his friends bid him to go, and then a ship was prepared, which Thorbjorn had sailed out on, and twenty men were hired, and some cattle, not more than weapons and provisions.
Þann myrgin, er Eiríkr reið heiman, tók hann einn kistil, ok var þar í gull ok silfr.	That morning, was Erik riding home, took he one chest, and was there of gold and silver.	That morning, Erik was rode home, he took a chest, and therein was gold and silver.

The Saga of Erik the Red (Old Norse)

Old Norse	Literal	English
Fal hann þat ok fór síðan leiðar sinnar, ok bar svá til, at hann fell af baki, ok brotna rifin í síðunni, en lesti höndina í axlarliðnum.	Hid he that and went afterwards way his, and carrying such until, that he fell from back, and broke rib among his, and gripped hand to shoulder.	He hid that and then travelled his way, and carried such until, he fell back from the horse, and broke one of his ribs, and gripped his hand to his shoulder.
Af þeim atburð sagði hann Þjóðhildi, konu sinni, at hon tæki féit á brott, lézt þess hafa at goldit, er hann hafði féit fólgit.	Of these events said he Thjodhild, wife his, that she take treasure to away, should this have of gold, that he had wealth hidden.	He said to his wife Thjodhild what had happened, and asked her to take the treasure hidden away, and have this gold that he had hidden.
Síðan sigldu þeir út ór Eiríksfirði með gleði mikilli. *Þótti þeim allvænt um sitt efni.*	Since sailed they out from Eriksfjord with gladness much. Thought they expected about their prospects.	Afterwards they sailed out of Eriksfjord with much gladness. They thought expectantly about their prospects.
Þá velkði úti lengi í hafi, ok kómu þeir ekki á þær slóðir, sem þeir vildu.	Then drove about long at sea, and came they not to those routes, which they willed.	Then they were driven about at sea for a long time, and did not come to those routes which they had wished.
Þeir kómu í sýn við Ísland, ok svá höfðu þeir fugl af Írlandi.	They came it seemed to Iceland, and so had they birds of Ireland.	They came in sight of what seemed like Iceland they had birds of Ireland.
Rak þá skip þeira um haf innan, fóru aftr um haustit ok váru allmjök væstir ok þrekaðir, koma við vetr sjálfan á Eiríksfjörð.	Driven then ship theirs about sea within, travelled back about autumn and were all-very worn and exhausted, came in winter itself to Eriksfjord.	Their ship was driven about the sea, and they travelled back about autumn, and all were very weary and exhausted, as winter was coming to Eriksfjord.
Þá mælti Eiríkr: "Kátari sigldum vér í sumar út ór firðinum en nú erum vér, ok eru nú þó enn mörg góð at".	Then said Erik: "Merrier sailed we this summer out from fjord than now are we, and are now though still many good to".	Then Erik said: "We sailed more merrily in the summer out of this fjord than we now return to it, but there is still much good".
Þorsteinn svarar: "Þat er nú höfðingligt bragð at sjá nökkut gott ráð fyrir þeim mönnum öllum, sem hér eru nú ráðstafalausir, ok fá þeim vist í vetr".	Thorstein answered: "That is now having-like solution to see some good proposal for those people all, which here are now disposed, and get they provisions to winter".	Thorstein answered: "Now we should propose that these people here are given provisions for the winter".
Eiríkr svarar: "Þat er jafnan satt, sem mælt er, at eigi veit, fyrr en svarat er, ok svá mun hér fara.	Erik answered: "That is equally true, which said was, to not know, before but answered is, and so should here go.	Erik answered: "That is equally true, as is said, you can't know a question before it is answered, and so it will be here.

Old Norse	Literal	English
Skal nú hafa ráð þín um þetta".	Shall now have discussion with-you about that".	Now shall we have a discussion with you about that".
Fóru nú allir þeir, er eigi höfðu aðrar vistir, með þeim feðgum.	Went now all they, who not had other supplies, with they father-and-son.	All those who had no provisions with the father and son.
Síðan fóru þeir heim í Brattahlíð ok váru þar um vetrinn.	Afterwards travelled they home to Brattahlid and were there about winter.	Afterwards they travelled hoe to Brattahlid and were there for the winter.

6

Nú er frá því at segja, at Þorsteinn Eiríksson vakði bónorð við Guðríði, ok var því máli vel svarat bæði af henni ok af föður hennar.	Now is from accordingly to say, that Thorstein Eriksson awoke proposal to Guthrid, and was accordingly the-matter well answered both from her and of father hers.	Now following this is to say that Thorstein Eriksson brought up a marriage proposal to Gudrid, and accordingly the matter was well answered from both her and her father.
Er þetta at ráði gert.	Then that as advised was-done.	Then that which was planned was done.
Þorsteinn gengr at eiga Guðríði, ok var þetta brúðkaup í Brattahlíð um haustit.	Thorstein went to marry Guthrid, and was this wedding in Brattahlid about autumn.	Thorstein went to marry Gudrid, and this wedding was in Brattahlid around autumn.
Fór sjá veizla vel fram, ok var allfjölmennt.	Went seen the-feast well from, and were many-people.	The feast was well witnessed, and there were many people there.
Þorsteinn átti bú í Vestribyggð á bæ þeim, er heitir í Lýsufirði.	Thorstein had a-farm in Vestribyggd in town theirs, was named it Lysufjord.	Thorstein had a farm in the Western Settlement in the worn, which was named Lysufjord.
En sá maðr átti þar helming í búi, er Þorsteinn hét.	But so a-man had there half a farm, was Thorstein called.	There was a man there that had a half share of a farm, who was named Thorstein.
Sigríðr hét kona hans.	Sigrid was-called wife his.	His wife was named Sigrid.
Fór Þorsteinn í Lýsufjörð um haustit til nafna síns ok þau Guðríðr bæði.	Went Thorstein to Lysufjord about autumn to namesake his and they Guthrid both.	They went to Lysufjord around autumn to both his namesake and Gudrid.
Var þar við þeim vel tekit.	Were there with them well taken.	They were well received by them.
Váru þau þar um vetrinn.	Were they there about winter.	They were there around winter.
Þat gerðist til tíðenda, at sótt kom í bæ þeira, er lítit var af vetri.	That happened until news, that sickness came among settlement theirs, that little was from winter.	Then came the news, that sickness came among their settlement, shortly after the beginning of winter.

The Saga of Erik the Red (Old Norse)

Old Norse	Literal	English
Garðarr hét þar verkstjóri.	Gardi was-called there a-foreman.	There was a foreman there who was named Gardi.
Hann var ekki vinsæll maðr.	He was not popular a-man.	He was not a popular man.
Hann tók fyrst sótt ok andaðist.	He took first sickness and died.	He was the first to become ill, and he died.
Síðan var skammt at bíða, at hverr lézt at öðrum.	Since was short to wait, that each died the others.	It was not long after that, that each of the others died.
Þá tók sótt Þorsteinn Eiríksson ok Sigríðr, kona Þorsteins, nafna hans.	Then took sickness Thorstein Eriksson and Sigrid, wife Thorstein's, namesake his.	Then the sickness took Thorstein Eriksson, and his namesake's wife Sigrid.
Ok eitt kveld fýstist Sigríðr at ganga til náðahúss, er stóð í gegnt útidurum.	And one evening desired Sigrid to go to outhouse, which stood about opposite the-out-door.	And one evening, Sigrid wanted to go to the outhouse, which stood opposite the farmhouse door.
Guðríðr fylgði henni, ok horfðu þær móti útidurunum.	Guthrid followed her, and looked they towards the-out-door.	Gudrid followed her, and they looked towards the farmhouse door.
Þá kvað hon við hátt, Sigríðr.	Then cried-out she with loud, Sigrid.	Then Sigrid cried out loudly.
Guðríðr mælti: "Vit höfum óvarliga farit, ok áttu engan stað við, at kalt komi á þik, ok förum vit heim sem skjótast".	Guthrid said: "We have unwisely gone, and have-you none stand with, that cold comes to you, and go into home then quickly".	Gudrid said: "We have acted carelessly, you should not stand in the cold, and we must go inside quickly".
Sigríðr svarar: "Eigi er fært at svá búnu.	Sigrid answered: "Not am-i going-out as so are.	Sigrid answered: "I won't go out with things as they are.
Hér er nú liðit þat allt it dauða fyrir durunum ok Þorsteinn, bóndi þinn, ok þar kenni ek mik.	Here is now company that all to death before the-door and Thorstein, husband yours, and there recognise I me.	Here are now all the companions that died standing there before the door, and Thorstein your husband, and there I recognise myself.
Ok er slíkt hörmung at sjá".	And is such horrible to see".	And it is such a horrible thing to see".
Ok er þetta leið af, mælti hon: "Förum vit nú, Guðríðr.	And when that passed out-of, spoke she: "Gone known now, Guthrid.	And when it had passed, she spoke: "They are gone now Gudrid".
Nú sé ek ekki liðit".	Now see I not company".	Now I don't see those companions".
Var þá Þorsteinn horfinn.	Was then Thorstein disappeared.	It was then that Thorstein had disappeared.

Old Norse	Literal	English
Henni þótti hann áðr haft hafa svipu í hendi ok vilja berja liðit.	She thought he returned had having whip in hand and willing to-bear the-company.	She thought he had returned with a whip in hand ready and willing to strike those companions.
Síðan gengu þær inn, ok áðr morginn kæmi, þá var hon látin, ok var ger kista at líkinu.	Afterwards went they in, and before morning came, then was she dead, and was made coffin for body.	Afterwards they went inside, and before the morning came, she was dead, and a coffin was made for her body.
Ok þenna sama dag ætluðu menn at róa, ok leiddi Þorsteinn þá til vara, ok í annan lit fór hann at sjá veiðiskap þeira.	And then same day intended people to row, and led Thorstein then to wares, and to others the-team went he to see fishing there.	And then that same day people intended to row and go fishing, and led Thorstein to where the goods were kept, and to the others in the company he went to see how the fishing was going.
Þá sendi Þorsteinn Eiríksson nafna sínum orð, at hann kæmi til hans, ok sagði svá, at þar væri varla kyrrt ok húsfreyja vildi færast á fætr ok vildi undir klæðin hjá honum.	Then sent Thorstein Eriksson namesake his word, that he come to him, and said such, that there was hardly peace and housewife willed move to feet and willing under bed-clothes by him.	Then Thorstein Eriksson sent his namesake his word to come to him, and said that there was no peace at home and his housewife was trying to rise up and get into bed with him.
Ok er hann kom inn, var hon komin upp á rekkjustokkinn.	And when he came in, was she coming up to sideboards.	And when he came in, she had reached the sideboards of the bed.
Þá tók hann hana höndum ok lagði bolöxi fyrir brjóst henni.	Then took he her hand and laid a-pole-axe for breast hers.	Then he took her hand and drove an axe into her breast.
Þorsteinn Eiríksson andaðist nær dagsetri.	Thorstein Eriksson died near day-setting.	Thorsteinn Eriksson died close to sunset.
Þorsteinn bóndi bað Guðríði leggjast niðr ok sofa, en hann kveðst vaka mundu um nóttina yfir líkinu.	Thorstein farmer asked Guthrid ti-lie down and sleep, and he said awake would-be about night over the-bodies.	Thorstein the Farmer told Gudrid to lie down and sleep, and he said that he would keep watch over the bodies.
Hon gerir svá.	She did so.	She did so.
Ok er skammt leið á nóttina, settist Þorsteinn Eiríksson upp ok mælti, kveðst vilja, at Guðríðr væri þangat kölluð, ok kveðst vilja tala við hana: "Guð vill, at þessi stund sé mér gefin til leyfis ok umbótar míns ráðs".	And that short way in night, sat Thorstein Eriksson up and spoke, saying willed, that Guthrid was there called, and saying he-willed to-speak with her: "God wills, that this time so me given to leave and offer my plans".	A short way into the night, Thorstein Eriksson sat up and spoke, saying that he wished for Gudrid to be called, as he willed to speak with her. "God wills that this time has been given to me to better my prospects".

The Vinland Sagas — *The Saga of Erik the Red (Old Norse)*

Old Norse	Literal	English
Þorsteinn bóndi gengr á fund Guðríðar ok vakði hana, biðr hana signa sik ok biðja sér guð hjálpar ok segir, hvat Þorsteinn Eiríksson hafði talat við hann, - "ok hann vill finna þik.	Thorstein the-farmer went to find Guthrid and woke her, asked her to-sign herself and ask herself God's help and said, what Thorstein Eriksson had told to him, - "And he wills find you.	Thorstein the Farmer went to find Gudrid and woke her, asking her to sign herself with the cross, and to ask for God's help, telling her what Thorstein Eriksson had told him: "And he wishes to meet you.
Verðr þú ráð fyrir at sjá, hvat þú vill upp taka, því at ek kann hér um hvárkis at fýsa".	Become you obliged for to see, what you will up take, because that I know here about neither to desire".	Are you obliged to see what you will learn from this?, for I will not advise you either way".
Hon svaraði: "Vera kann, at þetta sé ætlat til nökkurra þeira hluta, er síðan sé í minni hafðir, þessi inn undarligi hlutr, en ek vænti, at guðs gæzla mun yfir mér standa.	She answered: "Be it possible that this intends to something part there which afterwards are to mine have, this the strange lot, but I expect that God's herding shall over me stand.	She answered: "Could it possibly be that there is some purpose to this, which afterwards will have consequences for me, this strange occurrence, but I hope that God will shepherd over me".
Mun ek ok á hætta með guðs miskunn at fara til móts við hann ok vita, hvat hann vill tala, því at ek mun eigi forðast mega, ef mér skal mein at verða.	Should I to danger with God's mercy to speak with him because that I may now not avoid harm to mine.	I will to chance, with God's mercy, to speak with him, because I may not escape any threat to myself.
Vil ek síðr, at hann gangi víðara.	Will I less that he go far-and-wide.	I do not wish for him to have to go further and wider.
En mik grunar, at þat mun á liggja".	But I suspect that it so to other choice".	And I suspect that it would be the alternative choice".
Nú fór Guðríðr ok hittir Þorstein.	Now came Guthrid and met Thorstein.	Now Gudrid came and met Thorstein.
Sýndist henni sem hann felldi tár.	Seemed to-her that he shed tears.	It seemed to her that he had shed tears.
Hann mælti í eyra henni nökkur orð hljótt, svá at hon ein vissi, en þat mælti hann, svá at allir heyrðu, at þeir menn væri sælir, er trúna heldu, ok henni fylgði öll hjálp ok miskunn, ok sagði þó, at margir heldi hana illa.	He spoke in ear hers some words quietly, so that she alone knew, and that spoke he, so as all heard, that they men were happy, that faith held, and him followed all help and mercy, and said though, that many held it badly.	He spoke some words in her ear quietly, so that she alone knew, and he said that those men who had kept their faith well rejoiced as it brought them mercy and salvation, but he said that some had kept their faith badly though.

The Vinland Sagas   *The Saga of Erik the Red (Old Norse)*

Old Norse	Literal	English
"Er þat engi háttr, sem hér hefir verit á Grænlandi, síðan kristni kom hér, at setja menn niðr í óvígða mold við litla yfirsöngva.	"Is that no way, which here has been in Greenland, after Christianity came here, to set people down among unconsecrated dust with little burial-service.	"It is no way to set people down among unconsecrated dust with little burial service, which people have done here in Greenland since Christianity came here.
Vil ek mik láta flytja til kirkju ok aðra þá menn, sem hér hafa andazt, en Garðar vil ek brenna láta á báli sem skjótast, því at hann veldr öllum aftrgöngum þeim, sem hér hafa verit í vetr".	Will I me laid carried to church and others they people, which here have died, but Gardar will I burn let to fire that quickly, because that he caused all hauntings those, which here have been in winter".	I wish that I be carried to church, along with the other people who have died here, but Gardi should be burned on a pyre straight away, because he caused all those hauntings which were here in winter".
Hann sagði henni ok um sína hagi ok kvað hennar forlög mikil mundu verða, en bað hana varast at giftast grænlenzkum mönnum, bað, at hon legði fé þeira til kirkju ok sumt fátækum mönnum.	He told her and about his state and said her fortune great would be, but asked she avoid to marry Greenlander men, asked, that she leave wealth theirs to the-church and some poor people.	He told her about his situation and said that her fortune would be great, but warned her against marrying a Greenlander, he also asked that she donate their wealth to the church, and to the poor.
Ok þá hné hann aftr öðru sinni.	And then knee he back second his.	And then he sank back down for the second time.
Sá hafði háttr verit á Grænlandi, síðan kristni kom þangat, at menn váru grafnir á bæjum, þar sem önduðust, í óvígðri moldu.	So had the-way been in Greenland, since Christianity came there, that people were buried in farms, there which died, in unconsecrated ground.	So had been the way in Greenland, since Christianity arrived there, that people were buried in farms where they died in unconsecrated ground.
Skyldi setja staur upp af brjósti inum dauða, en síðan, er kennimenn kómu til, þá skyldi upp kippa staurinum ok hella þar í vígðu vatni ok veita þar yfirsöngva, þótt þat væri miklu síðar.	As-should-be set poles up on breast in the-dead, then after, a priest came to, then should-be up pulled poles and flat-stones there among ground water and supplied there burial-service, though that was much later.	A pole was set up on the breast of each corpse, then afterwards there came a priest, then the poles were pulled up, and flat stones placed on the ground, and consecrated water poured into the hole with a burial service, even though this was done much later.
Lík þeira Þorsteins váru færð til kirkju í Eiríksfjörð ok veittir þar yfirsöngvar af kennimönnum.	Body there Thorstein's was taken to church in Eriksfjord and supplied there burial-service from priests.	There Thorstein's body was taken to church in Eriksfjord and priests held burial services for them.
Tók Eiríkr við Guðríði ok var henni í föður stað.	Took Erik with Guthrid and was she at father's place.	Erik received Gudrid and she stayed at her father's place.

Old Norse	Literal	English
Litlu síðar andaðist Þorbjörn. Bar þá fé allt undir Guðríði.	Little later died Thorbjorn. Bore then wealth all up-to Guthrid.	A little later Thorbjorn died. All of his wealth was given up to Gudrid.
Tók Eiríkr hana til sín ok sá vel um hennar kost.	Took Erik her to his and saw well about her provided.	Erik invited her to live with him, and saw that she was well provided for.

7

Old Norse	Literal	English
Þórðr hét maðr, er bjó at Höfða á Höfðaströnd.	Thord was-called a-man who lived at Hofda in Hofdastrond.	There was a man called Thord who lived at Hofda in Hofdastrond.
Hann átti Þorgerði, dóttur Þóris hímu ok Friðgerðar, dóttur Kjarvals Írakonungs.	He married Thorgerd, daughter-of Thori's aunt and Fridgerdar, daughter-of Kjarval Ireland-King.	He married Thorgerd, daughter of Thori's aunt and Fridgerar, the daughter of King Kjarval of Ireland.
Þórðr var sonr Bjarnar byrðusmjörs Hróaldssonar hryggs, Áslákssonar, Bjarnarsonar járnsíðu, Ragnarssonar loðbrókar.	Thord was son-of Bjarn Byrdusmjors Roaldsson the-Sad, son-of-Aslak, son-of-Bjorn Ironside son-of-Ragnar Lothbrok	Thord was the son of Bjarn Byrdusmjors, the son of Roald the Sad, the son of Aslak, the son of Bjorn Ironside, the son of Ragnar Lothbrok.
Þau áttu son, er Snorri hét.	They had a-son who-was Snorri named.	They had a son who was named Snorri.
Hann átti Þórhildi rjúpu, dóttur Þórðar gellis.	He married Thorhild Rjupa, daughter-of Thord Gellis.	He married Thorhild Rjupa, the daughter of Thord Gellis.
Þeira sonr var Þórðr hesthöfði.	Their son was Thord Horse-head.	Their son was Thord Horse-Head.
Þorfinnr karlsefni hét sonr Þórðar.	Thorfin Karlsefni was-called son-of Thord.	Thord's son was called Thorfin Karlsefni.
Móðir Þorfinns hét Þórunn.	Mother Thorfin's was-called Thorun.	Thorfin's mother was called Thorun.
Þorfinnr var í kaupferðum ok þótti góðr fardrengr.	Thorfin was on trading-journeys and thought a-good travelling-companion.	Thorfin went on trading journeys and was thought of as a good travelling companion.
Eitt sumar býr Karlsefni skip sitt ok ætlar til Grænlands.	One summer prepared Karlsefni ship his and intended to Greenland.	One summer Karlsefni intended to go to Greenland and prepared his ship.
Snorri Þorbrandsson ferr með honum, ór Álftafirði, ok váru fjórir tigir manna á skipi.	Snorri Thorbrandson travelled with him, from Alftafjord, and was four tens men on ship.	Snorri Thorbrandson travelled with him from Alftafjord, and there were forty men on his ship.
Maðr hét Bjarni Grímólfsson, breiðfirzkr at ætt.	A-man was-called Bjarni Grimolfson, Breidafjord man ancestry.	There was a man called Bjarni Grimolfson, a man from Breidafjord by ancestry.

The Vinland Sagas — *The Saga of Erik the Red (Old Norse)*

Old Norse	Literal	English
Annarr hét Þórhallr Gamlason, austfirzkr maðr.	Another was-called Thorhall Gamlason, east-fjords man.	Another was called Thorhall Gamlason, a man from the East Fjords.
Þeir bjuggu it sama sumar skip sitt ok ætluðu til Grænlands.	There prepared the same summer ship his and intended to Greenland.	There they prepared their ship that summer, intending to go to Greenland.
Þeir váru ok fjórir tigir manna á skipi.	They were and four tens men on ship.	There were forty men on the ship.
Láta þeir Karlsefni í haf þessum tveim skipum, þegar þeir váru búnir.	Had they Karlsefni to sea these two ships, as-soon-as they were ready.	Karlsefni had these two ships put to sea as soon as they were ready.
Ekki er um þat getit, hversu langa útivist þeir höfðu, en frá því er at segja, at bæði þessi skip kómu á Eríksfjörð um haustit.	Not is about that told-of, how long out-journey they had, but from since was to say, that both these ships came to Eriksfjord about autumn.	Not much was said about how long a journey they had, but since was said that both these ships came to Eriksfjord about autumn.
Eiríkr reið til skips ok aðrir landsmenn.	Erik rode to ships and other landsmen.	Erik rode to the ships along with other men of the land.
Tókst með þeim greiðlig kaupstefna.	Took with them promptly trading-posts.	They promptly took trading posts with them.
Buðu stýrimenn Eiríki at hafa slíkt af varningi sem hann vildi.	Invited steersmen Erik to have such of wares that he willed.	The captains invited Erik to have whatever goods he wanted.
En Eiríkr sýnir þeim stórmennsku af sér í móti, því at hann bauð þessum tveim skipshöfnum til sín heim um vetrinn í Brattahlíð.	Then Erik showed them great-man-ness of him among towards, for that he invited these two ships-ports to his home about winter to Brattahlid.	Erik then showed them great generosity, as he invited these two ships to his home for the winter at Brattahlid.
Þetta þágu kaupmenn ok þökkuðu honum.	This accepted trading-men and thanked him.	The traders accepted this and thanked him.
Síðan var fluttr heim varningr þeira í Brattahlíð.	Then were transported home goods theirs to Brattahlid.	Later their goods were transported to Brattahlid.
Skorti þar eigi útibú stór til at varðveita í varning þeira.	Shortage there was-not out-houses great for in supplies to wares theirs.	There was no shortage of large outhouses for the to store their goods in.
Skorti þar ekki margt þat, er hafa þurfti, ok líkaði kaupmönnum vel um vetrinn.	Shortage there not many that, were had needed, and liked trading-men well about winter.	There no shortage of anything that they needed, and the traders very much enjoyed their winter.
En er dró at jólum, tók Eiríkr fæð mikla ok var óglaðari en hann átti vana til.	But as drew to Yule, took Erik sadness much and was without-gladness that he had custom to.	But as it drew closer to Yule, Erik became sad and was without the cheerfulness that he usually had.

The Vinland Sagas *The Saga of Erik the Red (Old Norse)*

Old Norse	Literal	English
Eitt sinn kom Karlsefni at máli við Eirík ok mælti: "Er þér þungt, Eiríkr bóndi? Menn þykkjast finna, at þú ert óglaðari en þú átt vana til.	Along then came Karlsefni to speak with Erik and said: "Are you unhappy, Erik farmer people think find, that you are un-glad than you have custom to.	Then along came Karlsefni to talk to Erik and said: "Are you unhappy, Erik the farmer? People seem to find that you are unhappier than usual.
Þú hefir veitt oss með inni mestu rausn, ok erum vér skyldir til at launa þér slíku góðu sem vér höfum föng á.	You have given us well the most generosity, and are we obliged to that repay you such good as we have possessions of.	You have provided for us most generously, and we are obliged to repay you as best we can with everything we have.
Nú segðu, hvat ógleði þinni veldr".	Now say, what sadness yours brought-about".	Now tell me, what is it that makes you sad?".
Eiríkr svarar: "Þér þiggið vel ok góðmannliga.	Erik answered: "You accepted well and good-man-like.	Erik answered: "You have accepted with gratitude and respect.
Nú leikr mér þat eigi í hug, at á yðr verði hallat um vár skipti.	Now like I that not in mind, that for you have-been inclined about what-was exchanged.	To my mind, you have not been lacking in our exchanges.
Hitt er heldr, at mér þykkir uggligt, þá er þér komið annars staðar, at þat flytist, at þér hafið engi jól verri haft en þessi, er nú koma ok Eiríkr inn rauði veitti yðr í Brattahlíð á Grænlandi".	I find rather, that to-me seems fearful, then that you come to-another place, by that flows, that you have not Yule worse had than this, when now came and Erik the Red supported you in Brattahlid in Greenland".	I worry to think that it will get around that you have not had a Yule worse than this, when Erik the Red came and supported you in Brattahlid in Greenland".
"Þat mun eigi svá fara, bóndi", segir Karlsefni.	"That shall not so go, farmer", said Karlsefni.	"It shall not be that way, farmer", said Karlsefni.
Vér höfum á skipi váru bæði malt ok korn, hafið þar af slíkt er þér vilið ok gerið veizlu svá stórmannliga sem yðr líkar fyrir því".	"We have in ships ours both malt and corn, have there of such that you will and make feast such great-man-ness as you like for according".	"We have malt and flour and grain aboard our ships, and you will have whatever you wish to make such a great feast according to your generosity".
Þetta þiggr Eiríkr, ok var þá búit til jólaveizlu, ok var hon in sæmiligsta, svá at menn þóttust trautt þvílíka rausn sét hafa í fátæku landi.	This accepted Erik, and were then preparations for Yule-feast, and was it in honourable, such that people thought scarcely spectacular generous seen had among poor land.	Erik accepted this, and then the preparations were made for the Yule feast, and it was honourable, so much so that people thought the had scarcely seen such spectacular generosity in such a poor land.

Old Norse	Literal	English
Ok eftir jólin vekr Karlsefni bónorð fyrir Eiríki um Guðríði, því at honum leizt sem hann mundi forræði á hafa.	And after Yule awoke Karlsefni proposal to Erik about Guthrid, because to him looked-like that he would power of have.	And after Yule, Karlsefni brought up a marriage proposal about Gudrid, as it seemed to him that Erik had protection of her.
Eiríkr svaraði vel ok segir, at hon mun sínum forlögum verða at fylgja, ok kveðst góða eina frétt af honum hafa.	Erik answered well and said, that she could her fortune be to follow, and said good only news of him had.	Erik answered favourably and said that she could follow her fortune, and said only good things about him.
Ok lauk svá, at Þorfinnr festi Guðríði, ok var þá aukin veizlan ok drukkit brullaup þeira, ok váru þau í Brattahlíð um vetrinn.	And ended so, that Thorfin joined Guthrid, and was then increased the-feast and drink wedding theirs, and were they in Brattahlid about winter.	And so it concluded, that Thorfin and Gudrid joined in marriage, and the feast was expanded to include toasting their wedding, and they were in Brattahlid over the winter.

8

Old Norse	Literal	English
Í Brattahlíð hófust miklar umræður, at menn skyldi leita Vínlands ins góða, ok var sagt, at þangat myndi vera at vitja góðra landkosta.	In Brattahlid began much discussion, that people should seek Vinland the good, and was said, that there would be to visit good land-benefits.	There began much discussion in Brattahlid about people seeking Vinland the good, and it was said that there would be good benefits.
Ok þar kom, at Karlsefni ok Snorri bjuggu skip sitt at leita landsins um várit.	And there came, that Karlsefni and Snorri prepared ship theirs to seek lands about spring.	And then it came, that Karlsefni and Snorri prepared their ship to seek lands during the spring.
Til þeirar ferðar réðust þeir Bjarni ok Þórhallr með skip sitt ok þat föruneyti, er þeim hafði fylgt.	To their travel appointed they Bjarni and Thorhall with ship theirs and that companions, that they had followed.	For their voyage, they hired Bjarni and Thorhall with their own ship, and their companions who followed them.
Maðr hét Þorvarðr.	A-man was-called Thorvard.	There was a man called Thorvard.
Hann átti Freydísi, dóttur Eiríks rauða, laungetna.	He married Freydis, daughter Erik the-Red's, illegitimate.	He married Freydis, the illegitimate daughter of Erik the Red.
Hann fór ok með þeim ok Þorvaldr, sonr Eiríks, ok Þórhallr, er kallaðr var veiðimaðr.	He went also with them and Thorvald, son Erik's, and Thorhall, who called was hunter.	He also travelled with them, along with Thorvald, Erik's son, and Thorhall, who was called the hunter.
Hann hafði lengi verit með Eiríki, veiðimaðr hans um sumrum, en bryti um vetrum.	He had long been with Erik, hunter his about summer, but breaks about winter.	He had long been with Erik, hunting during the summer, and breaks during the winter.

The Vinland Sagas — The Saga of Erik the Red (Old Norse)

Old Norse	Literal	English
Hann var mikill maðr ok sterkr ok svartr ok þursligr, hljóðlyndr ok illorðr, þat er hann mælti, ok eggjaði jafnan Eirík ins verra.	He was great man and strong and dark and giant, quiet and difficult-of-words, that when he spoke, and urged ever Erik the worse.	He was a great and strong man, dark and giant, a man of few words, but when he spoke, he usually desired to make trouble.
Hann var illa kristinn.	He was a-bad Christian.	He was a bad Christian.
Honum var víða kunnigt í óbyggðum.	He was widely known to unsettled-land.	He knew the unsettled land widely.
Hann var á skipi með Þorvarði ok Þorvaldi.	He was in ship with Thorvard and Thorvald.	He was in a ship with Thorvard and Thorvald.
Þeir höfðu þat skip, er Þorbjörn hafði út haft.	They had that ship, which Thorbjorn had back had.	They had the ship which Thorbjorn had brought back.
Þeir höfðu alls fjóra tigu manna ok hundrað, er þeir sigldu til Vestribyggðar ok þaðan til Bjarneyjar.	They had all forty ten men and hundred, when they sailed to Vestribyggd and there to Bjarney.	They had among all a hundred and forty men, then they sailed to the Western Settlement and from there to Bjarney.
Þaðan sigldu þeir tvau dægr suðr.	From-there sailed they two days south.	From there they sailed south for two days.
Þá sá þeir land ok skutu báti ok könnuðu landit, fundu þar hellur stórar ok margar tólf álna víðar.	Then saw they land and launched boat and explore land, found they slabs large and as-much-as twelve cubits wide.	Then they saw land and launched a boat to explore the land, and they found large slabs as wide as twelve cubits.
Fjölði var þar melrakka.	Many were there melrakka.	There were many melrakka.
Þeir gáfu þar nafn ok kölluðu Helluland.	They gave there name and called Helluland.	They gave there a name and called it Helluland.
Þaðan sildu þeir tvau dægr, ok brá þá landsuðrs ór suðri, ok fundu land skógvaxit ok mörg dýr á.	From-there sailed they two days, and drew they south-east from south, and found land forest-grown and many wild-animals on.	From there they sailed for two days, and drew southeast and south, and found forested land with many wild animals on.
Ey lá þar undan í landsuðr.	Island lay there from among south-east.	An island lay south east from there.
Þar drápu þeir einn björn ok kölluðu þar síðan Bjarney, en landit Markland.	There killed they a bear and called they since Bjarney, and land Markland.	They killed a bear there and afterwards they called it Bjarney, and called the land Markland.
Þaðan silgdu þeir suðr með landinu langa stund ok kómu at nesi einu.	From-there sailed they south along land long while and came to headland one.	From there they sailed south along the land, and after a long while they came to a headland.
Lá landit á stjórn.	Lay land to stern.	They kept the land to their stern.
Váru þar strandir langar ok sandar.	Were there beaches long and sandy.	The beaches were long and sandy.

The Saga of Erik the Red (Old Norse)

Old Norse	Literal	English
Þeir reru til lands ok fundu þar á nesinu kjöl af skipi ok kölluðu þar Kjalarnes.	They rowed towards land and found there on headland keel from ship and called they Kjalarnes.	They rowed towards the land and found that there on the headland was the keep from a ship, and they called it Kjalarnes.
Þeir kölluðu ok strandirnar Furðustrandir, því at langt var með at sigla.	They called and beaches Furdustrandir, because by long was along to sail.	The called the beaches Furdustrandir because they were long to sail by.
Þá gerðist landit vágskorit.	Then became land creek-indented.	Then the land became indented with creeks.
Þeir heldu skipunum í einn vág.	They held ship into one inlet.	They kept the ship in an inlet.
Óláfr konungr Tryggvason hafði gefit Leifi tvá menn skozka.	Olaf king Tryggvason had given Leif two men Scottish.	King Olaf Tryggvason had given Leif two Scottish people.
Hét karlmaðrinn Haki, en konan Hekja.	Called servants Haki, and woman Hekja.	The servants were called Haki, and a woman Hekja.
Þau váru dýrum skjótari.	They were wild-animals faster-than.	They were faster than wild animals.
Þessir menn váru á skipi með Karlsefni.	These people were on the-ship with Karlsefni.	They were on the ship with Karlsefni.
En er þeir höfðu siglt fyrir Furðustrandir, þá létu þeir ina skozku menn á land ok báðu þau hlaupa suðr á landit at leita landskosta ok koma aftr, áðr þrjú dægr væru liðin.	Then when they had sailed for Furdustrandir, they let they the Scottish people to land and asked them run south of land to seek land-benefits and coming back, before three days would-be passed.	Then when they had sailed along Furdustrandir, the put the Scottish people on land and asked them to run southwards and explore the land and come back before three days were passed.
Þau höfðu þat klæði, er þau kölluðu kjafal.	They had the clothes, that they called kjafal.	They had clothing which was called a kjafal.
Þat var svá gert, at höttr var á upp ok opit at hliðunum ok engar ermar á ok kneppt saman milli fóta með knappi ok nezlu, en ber váru þau annars staðar.	That was so made, that hood was for up and opened at sides and no sleeves of and fastened together between feet with fastening and nettle, but bare were they other places.	It was made with a hood at the top, with an opening at the sides and no sleeves, and fastened together between the feet, with a button and a loop, they were bare in other places.
Þeir biðuðu þar þá stund.	Then settled they then awhile.	Then they settled there awhile.
En er þau kómu aftr, hafði annat í hendi vínbejaköngul, en annat hveitiax sjálfsáit.	Then when they came back, had one in hand grape-vines, and another wheat self-sowing.	Then when they came back, one had grape vines in hand, and the other self-sowing wheat.
Gengu þau á skip út, ok silgdu þeir síðan leiðar sinnar.	Went they to ship back, and sailed they since route theirs.	They went back to their ship and then sailed on their way.

The Vinland Sagas — The Saga of Erik the Red (Old Norse)

Old Norse	Literal	English
Þeir silgdu inn á fjörð einn.	They sailed the to fjord one.	They sailed to a fjord.
Þar lá ein ey fyrir útan.	There lay an island before out-of.	There lay before it an island.
Þar um váru straumar miklir.	There about were streams great.	There were great streams surrounding it.
Því kölluðu þeir hana Straumey.	Therefore called they it Straumsey.	Therefore they called it Straumsey.
Svá var mörg æðr í eynni, at varla mátti ganga fyrir eggjum.	So was many eider-birds on island, that rarely may walk for eggs.	There were so many eider-birds on the island, that they could hardly walk for eggs.
Þeir kölluðu þar Straumfjörð.	There called they Straumfjord.	There they called Straumfjord.
Þeir báru þar farm af skipum sínum ok bjuggust þar um.	They carried there from out-of ships theirs and settled there about.	They carried there cargo from their ship and settled thereabouts.
Þeir höfðu með sér alls konar fénað.	They had with them all kinds livestock.	They had with them all kinds of livestock.
Þar var fagrt landsleg.	There was beautiful landscape.	There the landscape was beautiful.
Þeir gáðu einskis útan at kanna landit.	They heeded nothing outside-of to explore land.	They observed nothing other than exploring the land.
Þeir váru þar um vetrinn, ok var ekki fyrir unnit um sumarit.	They were there about winter, and was not before spared about summer.	They were there during the winter, and nothing had been done in preparation during summer.
Tókust af veiðarnar, ok gerðist illt til matar.	Taken of fishing, and became disorderly for food.	They took to hunting, but became bad for food.
Þá hvarf brott Þórhallr veiðimaðr.	Then disappeared away Thorhall the-Hunter.	Then Thorhall the Hunter disappeared.
Þeir höfðu áðr heitit á guð til matar, ok varð eigi við svá skjótt sem sem þeir þóttust þurfa.	They had before called to God for food, and was not with so quickly that which they thought needed.	They had afterwards prayed to God for food, and it was not as quick in arriving as they needed.
Þeir leituðu Þórhalls um þrjú dægr ok fundu hann á hamargnípu einni.	They sought Thorhall about three days and found him on cliff-top alone.	They looked for Thorhall for three days and found him on top of a cliff.
Hann lá þar ok horfði í loft upp ok gapði bæði munni ok nösum ok þulði nökkut.	He lay there and looking to sky up and gaping both mouth and nose and rattling-off something.	He lay there looking up to the sky with his mouth and nose gaping, and he was reciting something.
Þeir spurðu, hví hann var þar kominn.	They asked, why he was there come.	They asked why he had come there.
Hann kvað þá engu þat varða.	He said to-them nothing that concerned.	He said to them that it was nothing of any concern.
Þeir báðu hann fara heim með sér, ok hann gerði svá.	They asked him travel home with them, and he did so.	They asked him to travel home with them, and he did so.

The Vinland Sagas   *The Saga of Erik the Red (Old Norse)*

Old Norse	Literal	English
Litlu síðar kom þar hvalr, ok fóru þeir til ok skáru, ok kenndi engi maðr, hvat hvala var.	Little afterwards came there a-whale, and went they to and cut, and knew no man, what whale was.	Shortly afterwards there came a whale, and they went to it and carve it, and no man knew what kind of whale it was.
Ok er matsveinar suðu, þá átu þeir, ok varð öllum illt af.	And when ship's-cook boiled, then ate they, and were all ill from.	And when the ship's cook boiled it, they ate it, and everyone was then from it.
Þá mælti Þórhallr: "Drjúgari varð inn rauðskeggjaði nú en Kristr yðvarr.	Then spoke Thorhall: "Ample was the Redbeard now than Christ yours.	Thorhall then spoke: "Ampler was the Red-Beard now than your Christ.
Hefi ek þetta nú fyrir skáldskap minn, er ek orta um Þór, fulltrúann.	Have I that now for poetry mine, that I wrote about Thor, patron.	I had this now for my poem, which I wrote about Thor, my guardian.
Sjaldan hefir hann mér brugðizt".	Seldom has he me broken".	Seldom has he broken me".
Ok er menn vissu þetta, báru þeir hvalinn allan á kaf ok skutu sínu máli til guðs.	And when people knew this, carried they whale all to submerge and launched they the-matter to God.	And when people knew this, they carried the whale to cast to sea, and threw themselves on God's mercy.
Batnaði þá veðrátta, ok gaf þeim útróðra, ok skorti þá síðan eigi föng, því at þá var dýraveiðr á landinu, en eggver í eynni, en fiski ór sjónum.	Bettered then weather, and gave they out-rowing, and shortage then since not supplies, because that then were animal-hunting to land, and eggs on island, and fishing from sea.	The weather improved, and they were given to rowing, and since then they had no shortage in supplies, because they hunted animals on land, gathered eggs on the island, and caught fish from the sea.
9	9	9
Svá er sagt, at Þórhallr veiðimaðr vill fara norðr fyrir Furðustrandir ok fyrir Kjalarnes at leita Vínlands, en Karlsefni vill fara suðr fyrir landit.	So was said, that Thorhall the-hunter willed travel north for Furdustrandir and for Kjalarnes to seek Vinland, but Karlsefni willed travel south along land.	So it was said that Thorhall the Hunter wished to travel north for Furdustrandir and for Kjalarnes to seek Vinland, but Karlsefni wished to travel south along the land.
Býst Þórhallr út undir eynni, ok verða þeir eigi fleiri saman en níu menn, en allt annat lið fór með Karlsefni.	Prepared Thorhall out under island, and were there not more together than nine people, and all other company went with Karlsefni.	Thorhall prepared his ship close to the island, and there were not more than nine people together, and all the other group went with Karlsefni.

The Saga of Erik the Red (Old Norse)

Old Norse	Literal	English
En er Þórhallr bar vatn á skip sitt ok drakk, þá kvað hann vísu:	And was Thorhall carrying water to ship his and drank, then said he verse:	And as Thorhall was carrying water to their ship, he drank from it and said this verse:
Hafa kváðu mik meiðar malmþings, es komk hingat,	Shores sang me hurt metal-assemblied, when coming here,	The shores sang me hurt Metal assembled, when I came here,
mér samir láð fyr lýðum	To-me same invited for people	I have the same advice for the people
lasta, drykk inn bazta	Load, drink the best.	Loaded, drink the best.
Bílds hattar verðr byttu beiði-Týr at reiða.	Axe hoods become replaced Bids-Tyr to ruling.	Axe hoods will be replaced Asking for Tyr's ruling.
Heldr's svát krýpk at keldu.	Rather is so that I creep to the well,	It is rather that I creep to the well,
Komat vín á grön mína.	Come wine to green mine.	Bring green wine to me.
Ok er þeir váru búnir, undu þeir upp segl. Þá kvað Þórhallr:	And when they were ready, hoisted they up sails. Then said Thorhall:	And when they were ready, they hoisted up the sails. Then Thorhall said:
Förum aftr, þar es órir	Travel-we back, there where others	We travel back to where the others
eru, sandhimins, landar,	are, sand-heaven's, land,	Are, the heavens of the sands, land,
látum kenni-Val kanna	let-us know-choose explore	Let us knowing choose to explore
knarrar skeið in breiðu, meðan bilstyggvir byggva bellendr ok hval vella Laufa veðrs, þeirs leyfa lönd, á Furðuströndum.	Ship sheathed-sword in wide, while space settle partakers and whale boil leaf weathered, they have land, to Furdustrandir.	Ship of swords in the wide, Among the space settle. Participants and boil the whale Leaf weathered, they have Land, in Furdustrandir.
Síðan sigldu þeir norðr fyrir Furðuströndir ok Kjalarnes ok vildu beita vestr fyrir.	Then sailed they north along Furdustrandir and Kjalarnes and willed applied west for.	Then they sailed north along Furdustrandir and Kjalarnes, and wished to head for the west.
Þá kom móti þeim vestanveðr, ok rak þá upp á Írlandi, ok váru þeir þar barðir ok þjáðir, ok lét Þórhallr þar líf sitt, eftir því sem kaupmenn hafa sagt.	Then came towards them west-wind, and driven they up to Ireland, and were they there beaten and enslaved, and lost Thorhall there life his, after for so trading-men have said.	Then the west wind came towards them, and they were driven up to Ireland, and there they were beaten and enslaved, and there Thorhall lost his life, so the trading men have said.

Old Norse	Literal	English
Nú er at segja af Karlsefni, at hann fór suðr fyrir landit ok Snorri ok Bjarni með sínu fólki.	Now is it said of Karlsefni, that he went south along land and Snorri and Bjarni with their folk.	Now it is said of Karlsefni, that he went south along the land, with Snorri and Bjarni and the rest of their company.
Þeir fóru lengi ok allt þar til, er þeir kómu at á einni, er fell af landi ofan ok í vatn eitt til sjóvar.	They travelled along and all there until, then they came to river one, which fell from land off and into lake single to sea.	They travelled along the land until they came to a river which fell from the land into a lake, and into the sea.
Eyrar váru þar miklar, ok mátti eigi komast inn í ána útan at háflæðum.	Islands were there great, and may not come in to river out of high-tide.	There were large islands there, and they could not come into the river outside of high tide.
Þeir Karlsefni silgdu í ósinn ok kölluðu í Hópi.	There Karlsefni sailed to inlet and called it Hop.	There Karlsefni sailed to the inlet and called it Hop.
Þeir fundu þar á landi sjálfsána hveitiakra, þar sem lægðir váru, en vínvið allt þar, sem holta vissi.	There found they of land self-sowing wheat-acres, there where low-ground was, and vines all there, which hills knew.	There they found acres of self-sowing wheat, where the low ground was, and vines growing on the hills.
Hverr lækr var þar fullr af fiskum.	Every stream was there full of fish.	Every stream there was full of fish.
Þeir gerðu grafar, þar sem mættist landit ok flóðit gekk ofast, ok þá er út fell sjórinn, váru helgir fiskar í gröfunum.	They made trenches, there which may land and tide went highest, and then when back fell sea, were flat fish in trenches.	They made trenches in the land where the tide reached its highest, and then when the sea fell back, there were flat fish in the trenches.
Þar var mikill fjölði dýra á skóginum með öllu móti.	There were great many animals in forest with all met.	There were a great many wild animals of all kinds in the forest.
Þeir váru þar hálfan mánuð ok skemmtuðu sér ok urðu við ekki varir.	They were there half month and entertained themselves and became with nothing aware.	They were there half a month and entertained themselves and were not aware of anything unusual.
Fé sitt höfðu þeir með sér.	Cattle theirs had they with them.	They had their livestock with them.
Ok einn morgin snemma, er þeir lituðust um, sá þeir mikinn fjölða húðkeipa, ok var veift trjám á skipunum, ok lét því líkast sem í hálmþúst, ok var veift sólarsinnis.	And one morning early, when they looked about, saw they great many skin-boats, and were waving poles from boats, and had accordingly like as to straw-staves, and were waved sun-wise-motion.	And early one morning, when they looked about, they saw a great many hide-boats, and there were poles waving from the boats, which made a sound like a straw man, and they were waved in a sun-wise motion.
Þá mælti Karlsefni: "Hvað mun þetta hafa at teikna?"	Then spoke Karlsefni: "What could this have to betoken?"	Then spoke Karlsefni: "What could this mean?"

Old Norse	Literal	English
Snorri Þorbrandsson svaraði honum: "Vera kann, at þetta sé friðarmark, ok tökum skjöld hvítan ok berum at móti".	Snorri Thorbrandson answered he: "Be-it can, that this so peace-mark, and take shield white and bear it towards".	Snorri Thorbrandson answered: "Maybe it can be a peace sign, and we should take a white shield and show it to them".
Ok svá gerðu þeir.	And so did they.	And so they did.
Þá reru þeir í mót ok undruðust þá, sem fyrir váru, ok gengu á land upp.	Then rowed they to meet and astonished they, as present were, and went to land up.	Then they rowed to meet them, and they were astonished as they came up on land to meet them.
Þeir váru svartir menn ok illiligir ok höfðu illt hár á höfði.	They were dark men and ill-looking and had disorderly hair on heads.	They were dark men, and looked threatening, with tangled hair on their heads.
Þeir váru mjök eygðir ok breiðir í kinnum.	They were much eyed and broad in cheeks.	They had large eyes and broad cheeks.
Dvölðust þeir of stund ok undruðust þá, sem fyrir váru, ok reru síðan brott ok suðr fyrir nesit.	Dwelled they about awhile and marvelled they, which present were, and rowed then away and south for headland.	They stayed around awhile and marvelled at those who were present, and then they rowed away and headed south around the headland.
Þeir Karlsefni höfðu gert búðir sínar upp frá vatninu, ok váru sumir skálarnir nær vatninu, en sumir firr.	They Karlsefni had made booths theirs up from lake, and were some cabins near lake, but some further.	Karlsefni's group made their booths up from the lake, and there were some cabins near the lake, but some further inland.
Nú váru þeir þar þann vetr.	Now were they there then winter.	They were there for the winter.
Þar kom enginn snjór, ok allt gekk fé þeira sjálfala fram.	There came no snow, and all going cattle they themselves from.	There was no snow there, and all the livestock could fend for themselves outside.

11

En er vára tók, sá þeir einn morgin snemma, at fjölði húðkeipa reri sunnan fyrir nesit, svá margt sem kolum væri sáit fyrir Hópit.	Then when spring took, saw they one morning early, that many skin-boats rowing south for headland, so many as coal were seen for group.	Then when spring came, early one morning they saw many hide boats rowing up from the south around the headland, so many that it looked like coal had been thrown across the water.
Var þá ok veift af hverju skipi trjánum.	Was then and waved of each ship poles.	They were also waving poles from each ship.

The Vinland Sagas   *The Saga of Erik the Red (Old Norse)*

Old Norse	Literal	English
Þeir Karlsefni brugðu þá skjöldum upp, ok er þeir fundust, tóku þeir kaupstefnu sín á milli, ok vildi þat fólk helzt hafa rautt skrúð.	Then Karlsefni brought then shields up, and were they met, taken their trading-posts theirs in between, and willed that people preferably have red cloth.	Then Karlsefni's company brought up their shields, and when they met them, they set up trading posts, and the people wanted to buy red cloth.
Þeir höfðu móti at gefa skinnavöru ok algrá skinn.	They had met to give skin-wares and grey skins.	They had met them with skins and gray skins.
Þeir vildu ok kaupa sverð ok spjót, en þat bönnuðu þeir Karlsefni ok Snorri.	They willed also purchase swords and spears, but that banned them Karlsefni and Snorri.	They also wanted to purchase swords and spears, but Karlsefni and Snorri banned them from purchasing them.
Þeir Skrælingar tóku spannarlangt rautt skrúð fyrir ófölvan belg ok bundu um höfuð sér.	They Skraelings took long-spanning red cloth for dark pelts and bound about heads theirs.	They Skraelings took spans of red cloth in return for dark pelts and tied the cloth around their heads.
Gekk svá kaupstefna þeira um hríð.	Went so trading-posts theirs about awhile.	And so the trading went on in this way for a while.
Þá tók at fættast skrúðit með þeim Karlsefni, ok skáru þeir þá svá smátt í sundr, at eigi var breiðara en þvers fingrar, ok gáfu Skrælingar þó jafnmikit fyrir sem áðr eða meira.	Then took to carry cloth with them Karlsefni, and cut they then so small to distribute, that not was broad but across finger, and gave Skraelings though equal for which before or more.	Then as the cloth was carried with them, Karlsefni's company cut the cloth smaller to distribute it further, so that it was narrower, about a finger's width, and the Skraelings paid just as much for it, or even more.
Þat bar til, at griðungr hljóp ór skógi, er þeir Karlsefni áttu, ok gellr hátt.	That bore towards, a bull ran from woods, which they Karlsefni owned, and bellowed loudly.	Then a bull that Karlsefni owned ran out of the woods and towards them, bellowing loudly.
Þetta fælast Skrælingar ok hlaupa út á keipana ok reru síðan suðr fyrir landit.	This frightened Skraelings and ran out of trading and rowed then south for land.	This frightened the Skraelings and they ran away from the trading posts and rowed away south around the headland.
Verðr þá ekki vart við þá þrjár vikur í samt.	Were they not noticed by them three weeks at together.	They did not notice them again for another three weeks.
En er sjá stund var liðin, sjá þeir fara sunnan mikinn fjölða Skrælingaskipa, svá sem straumr stæði.	And when seen awhile was company, saw there travelling south great many Skraelings, so as stream steady.	Then after a while their company saw travelling from the south, a great many Skraelings, like a steady stream.
Var þá trjánum öllum veift andsælis, ok ýla upp allir mjök hátt.	Were they poles all waving anti-sun-wise, and howling up all very loudly.	They were all waving their poles anti-sunwise now, and all were howling very loudly.

The Vinland Sagas — The Saga of Erik the Red (Old Norse)

Old Norse	Literal	English
Þá tóku þeir Karlsefni rauðan skjöld ok báru at móti.	Then took they Karlsefni red shields and bore to meet.	Then Karlsefni's company took their red shields and carried them up to meet them.
Skrælingar hlupu af skipum, ok síðan gengu þeir saman ok börðust.	Skraelings running from ship, and then went they together and battled.	The Skraelings ran from their ships, and then they went together to battle.
Varð þar skothríð hörð, því at Skrælingar höfðu valslöngur.	Were they launching hard, because the Skraelings had war-slings.	They were launching hard, because the Skraelings had catapults.
Þat sá þeir Karlsefni, at Skrælingar færðu upp á stöng knött stundar mikinn, því nær til at jafna sem sauðarvömb, ok helzt blán at lit, ok fleygðu af stönginni upp á landit yfir lið þeira Karlsefnis, ok lét illiliga við, þar sem niðr kom.	That saw they Karlsefni, that Skraelings went up to poles balls around as-big, as nearly to from equal that sheep's-stomach, and rather blue that around, and flew off poles up to land over team theirs Karlsefni's, and lay badly to, there where down came.	Karlsefni's company saw the Skraelings raised large round objects up on poles, about the size of a sheep's stomach, and blue all over, and they flew from the poles to land over Karlsefni's company, and landed terribly when they came down.
Við þetta sló ótta miklum á Karlsefni ok allt lið hans, svá at þá fýsti einskis annars en flýja ok halda undan upp með ánni, því at þeim þótti lið Skrælinga drífa at sér öllum megin, ok létta eigi fyrr en þeir koma til hamra nökkurra ok veittu þar viðtöku harða.	With that struck fear much in Karlsefni and all team his, such that they desired nothing else than fleeing and holding away up with river, because that they thought company Skraelings drove at them all ways, and let not before that they came to crags some and gave there resistance hard.	This struck great fear into Karlsefni and his men, so much so that they wanted nothing else but to flee up the river, since the Skraelings seemed to be attacking from all angles, and not stop until they reached a cliff where they could give a stiffer resistance.
Freydís kom út ok sá, at þeir Karlsefni heldu undan, ok kallaði: "Hví rennið þér undan þessum auvirðismönnum, svá gildir menn sem þér eruð, er mér þætti sem þér mættið drepa niðr svá sem búfé? Ok ef ek hefða vápn, þætti mér sem ek skylda betr berjast en einnhverr yðvar".	Freydis came out and saw, that they Karlsefni held ahead, and called: "Why run you away these un-worthy-men, so thick men that you are, that to-me seems that you may kill down such as livestock and if I had weapon, seems to-me that I should better fight than any-of you".	Freydis came out and saw that Karlsefni's company were fleeing, and called out: "Why are you running away from such unworthy opponents? such men that you are, who look to me like you could kill them as easily as livestock, and if I had a weapon I would fight them better than any of you".
Þeir gáfu engan gaum hennar orðum.	They gave no heed her words.	They paid no attention to what she said.

The Vinland Sagas — The Saga of Erik the Red (Old Norse)

Old Norse	Literal	English
Freydís vildi fylgja þeim ok varð seinni, því at hon var eigi heil.	Freydis willed follow them and became behind, because that she was not well.	Freydis wanted to follow them, and fell behind, because she was with child.
Gekk hon þó eftir þeim í skóginn, en Skrælingar sækja at henni.	Went she though after them into woods, but Skraelings sought towards her.	She went after them into the forest, but the Skraelings reached her.
Hon fann fyrir sér mann dauðan.	She found before their man dead.	She found in front of her one of their men who had died.
Þar var Þorbrandr Snorrason, ok stóð hellusteinn í höfði honum.	There was Thorbrand Snorrason, and stood slab-stone in head his.	It was Thorbrand Snorrason, and a stone slab was buried in his head.
Sverðit lá bert í hjá honum.	Sword lay uncovered to by him.	A sword lay unsheathed next to him.
Tók hon þat upp ok býst at verja sik.	Took she that up and prepared to protect herself.	She took that sword and prepared to protect herself.
Þá kómu Skrælingar at henni.	Then came Skraelings to her.	Then the Skraelings came to her.
Hon dró þá út brjóstit undan klæðunum ok slettir á beru sverðinu.	She pulled then out breast from clothes and slapped on open sword.	She pulled out one of her breasts from her clothes, and slapped the sword against it.
Við þetta óttast Skrælingar ok hljópu undan á skip sín ok reru í brott.	With that feared Skraelings and ran away to ships theirs and rowed to away.	With that the Skraelings became afraid and they ran away to their ships and rowed away.
Þeir Karlsefni finna hana ok lofa happ hennar.	There Karlsefni found her and praised zeal hers.	Here Karlsefni found her and praised her bravery.
Tveir menn fellu af þeim Karlsefni, en fjölði af þeim Skrælingum.	Two men fell of theirs Karlsefni, but many of them Skraelings.	Two men from Karlsefni's company fell and many of the Skraelings.
Urðu þeir Karlsefni ofrliði bornir ok fóru nú heim eftir þetta til búða sinna ok bundu sár sín ok íhuga, hvat fjölmenni þat mundi verit hafa, er at þeim sótti af landinu ofan.	Became they Karlsefni outnumbered borne and went now home after that to settlement theirs and bound wounds theirs and thought, what many that would been have, that which they encountered of land on.	Karlsefni's men were outnumbered, and they returned home to their settlement and bound their wounds, and thought what had been, which they encountered on the land.
Sýnist þeim nú sem þat eina mun liðit verit hafa, er af skipunum kom, en hitt fólkit mun verit hafa sjónhverfingar.	Seemed that now then that one could team have-been at-sea, where out-of ships came, but other people could been have illusions.	It seemed now that there could have been one team at sea where the ships came, but other people could have been illusions.
Þeir Skrælingar fundu ok mann dauðan, ok lá öx í hjá.	Then Skraelings found also man dead, and laying axe to near.	The Skraelings also found a man dead, and an axe laying near to him.

Old Norse	Literal	English
Einn þeira tók upp öxina ok höggr með tré ok þá hverr at öðrum, ok þótti þeim vera gersimi ok bíta vel.	One there took up axe and hewed with tree and then each to other, and thought they was treasure and bit well.	One of them there took up the axe and hewed at a tree, and then each of them took turns trying it, and they thought it was a treasure that cut so well.
Síðan tók einn ok hjó í stein, svá at brotnaði öxin, ok þá þótti þeim engu nýt, er eigi stóðst grjótit, ok köstuðu niðr.	Then took one and struck at stone, so that broke axe, and then thought they none use, was not withstood stones, and cast down.	Then one of them took up the axe and struck at stone with it, and the axe broke, and then they thought it was of no use, as it did not withstand stone, and they threw it down.
Þeir Karlsefni þóttust nú sjá, þótt þar væri landskostir góðir, at þar myndi jafnan ótti og ófriðr á liggja af þeim, er fyrir bjuggu.	There Karlsefni thought now looked, thought there was land-benefits good, but there should equal fear and without-peace to lay of them, as before inhabitants.	There Karlsefni's company thought that although there were many benefits in that land, they would always be without peace, fearing attack by the inhabitants.
Síðan bjuggust þeir á brottu ok ætluðu til síns lands ok sigldu norðr fyrir landit ok fundu fimm Skrælinga í skinnhjúpum, sofnaða, nær sjó.	Afterwards prepared they to leave and intended towards they land and sailed north along the land and found five Skraelings in skin-sacks, sleeping, near sea.	Afterwards they prepared to leave and intended to sail north around the land, and they found five Skraelings in skin sacks sleeping near the sea.
Þeir höfðu með sér stokka ok í dýramerg, dreyra blandinn.	They had with them stock of in animal-marrow, blood mixed.	They had with them a stock made of animal marrow mixed with blood.
Þóttust þeir Karlsefni þat skilja, at þessir menn myndi hafa verit gervir brott af landinu.	Thought they Karlsefni that separated, which these people would have been made away from land.	Karlsefni's company thought that they must have been outlaws.
Þeir drápu þá.	They killed then.	They then killed them.
Síðan fundu þeir Karlsefni nes eitt ok á fjölða dýra.	Afterwards found they Karlsefni headland one and of many animals.	Afterwards Karlsefni's company found a headland that had many wild animals.
Var nesit at sjá sem mykiskán væri, af því at dýrin lágu þar um nætrnar.	Was headland to see which muck-encrusted was, of therefore were wild-animals laying there about night.	The headland looked like it was covered with dung, as the deer gathered there at night to sleep.
Nú koma þeir Karlsefni aftr í Straumfjörð, ok váru þar fyrir alls gnóttir þess, er þeir þurftu at hafa.	Now came they Karlsefni back to Straumfjord, and were there before all abundance this, as they needed to have.	Now Karlsefni's company came back to Straumfjord, where they found all in abundance, everything that they needed.

Old Norse	Literal	English
Þat er sumra manna sǫgn, at þau Bjarni ok Guðríðr hafi þar eftir verit ok tíu tigir manna með þeim ok hafi eigi farit lengra, en þeir Karlsefni ok Snorri hafi suðr farit ok fjórir tigir manna með þeim ok hafi eigi lengr verit í Hópi en vart tvá mánuði ok hafi sama sumar aftr komit.	It was some men said, that those Bjarni and Guthrid had there after been and ten tens men with them and had not travelled further, but there Karlsefni and Snorri had south travelled and four ten men with them and have no longer been in tidal-pool but hardly two months and had the-same summer returned come.	Some say that Bjarni and Gudrid had remained behind with a hundred men and had not travelled further, and that it was Karlsefni and Snorri who went further south with forty men, stayed at Hop for not longer than two months, and returned that same summer.
Karlsefni fór þá einu skipi at leita Þórhalls veiðimanns, en annat liðit var eftir, ok fóru þeir norðr fyrir Kjalarnes, ok berr þá fyrir vestan fram, ok var landit á bakborða þeim.	Karlsefni travelled then one ship to seek Thorhall the-Hunter, but another team were remained, and travelled they north for Kjalarnes, and bore they for west from, and was the-land to larboard-side theirs.	Karlsefni then travelled with one ship to find Thorhall the Hunter, while the other tem stayed behind, and they travelled north around Kjalarnes, and they then bore west, and the land was to their port side.
Þar váru þá eyðimerkr einar allt at sjá fyrir þeim ok nær hvergi rjóðr í.	There was then deserted-forest only all to see before them and near neither clearing among.	There was then nothing to see except deserted forest before them, with no clearing among them.
Ok er þeir hǫfðu lengi farit, fellr á af landi ofan ór austri ok í vestr.	And were they had long travelled, falls to out-of land above out east and to west.	And after they had travelled for a long time, they reached a river flowing from east to west.
Þeir lǫgðu inn í árósinn ok lágu við inn syðra bakkann.	They laid in to river-mouth and laid to in southern bank.	They sailed into the mouth of the river and lay to near the south bank.

12	12	12
Þat var einn morgin, er þeir Karlsefni sá fyrir ofan rjóðrit flekk nǫkkurn, sem glitraði við þeim, ok æpðu þeir á þat.	It was one morning, that they Karlsefni saw before above clearing speck certain, that glittered by them, and shouted they at that.	It was one morning that Karlsefni's company saw a clearing before them, and a speck of light that glittered before them, and they shouted at it.
Þat hrærðist, ok var þat einfætingr ok skauzt ofan á þann árbakkann, sem þeir lágu við.	It stirred, and was it a-one-footer and launched down towards the river-bank, where they lay by.	It stirred, and it was a one legged creature, and it launched down towards the river bank there the ship was laid.
Þorvaldr Eiríksson rauða sat við stýri, ok skaut einfætingr ǫr í smáþarma honum.	Thorvald son-of-Erik the-Red sat by steering, and shot one-footer arrow into small-intestine his.	Thorvald, son of Erik the Red, sat at the helm, and the one legged creature shot an arrow into his intestine.

The Vinland Sagas   *The Saga of Erik the Red (Old Norse)*

Old Norse	Literal	English
Þorvaldr dró út örina ok mælti: "Feitt er um ístruna.	Thorvald dragged out arrow and spoke: "Bold is around belly-fat.	Thorvald dragged out the arrow and spoke: "Bold it is around the belly.
Gott land höfum vér fengit kostum, en þó megum vér varla njóta".	Good land have we found benefit, but though may we barely enjoy".	We have found good benefit from this land here, but we may scarcely be able to enjoy it".
Þorvaldr dó af sári þessu litlu síðar.	Thorvald died of wound his a-little later.	Thorvald died of his wound a little later.
Þá hleypr einfætingr á braut ok suðr aftr.	Then ran the-one-footer to away and south returning.	Then the one legged creature ran away and returned south.
Þeir Karlsefni fóru eftir honum ok sá hann stundum.	They Karlsefni went after him and saw him sometimes.	Karlsefni's company went after him and saw him sometimes.
Þat sá þeir síðast til hans, at hann hljóp á vág nökkurn.	That saw they last towards him, that he ran to inlet some.	The last time they saw him, he ran into an inlet.
Þá hurfu þeir Karlsefni aftr.	Then disappeared they Karlsefni returned.	Then he disappeared, and Karlsefni's company returned.
Þá kvað einn maðr kviðling þenna:	Then said one man verse this:	Then one man said this verse:
Eltu seggir, *allsatt vas þat,* *einn einfæting* *ofan til strandar,* *en kynligr maðr* *kostaði rásar* *hart of stopir.* *Heyr, Karlsefni.*	"Pursued said, true was that, a one-footer down to shore, but uncanny man exerted rushed rough about stopped. Hear, Karlsefni".	"Pursued it was said true it was a one-footer down to the shore, but the uncanny man rushed away hard of stopping. Hear us, Karlsefni".
Þeir fóru þá í brott ok norðr aftr ok þóttust sjá Einfætingaland.	They went then to away and north returning and thought saw One-Footer-Land.	Then they went away and headed back north and thought they saw One Footer Land.
Vildu þeir þá eigi hætta liði sínu lengra.	Willed they then not danger team theirs further.	They did not wish to put themselves in any further danger.
Þeir ætluðu öll ein fjöll, þau, er í Hópi váru, ok þessi, er nú fundu þeir, ok þat stæðist mjök svá á ok væri jafnlangt ór Straumfirði beggja vegna.	They supposed all same mountains, these, were among Hop was, and this, was now found they, and that place much so that also was equal-long from Straumfjord both ways.	They supposed that the mountains they saw were the same as the ones at Hop, and so that place was equally distant from Straumfjord.
Inn þriðja vetr váru þeir í Straumfirði.	The third winter were they in Straumfjord.	They spent the third winter in Straumfjord.

The Vinland Sagas   *The Saga of Erik the Red (Old Norse)*

Old Norse	Literal	English
Gengu menn þá mjök í sveitir, ok varð þeim til um konur, ok vildu þeir, er ókvæntir váru, sækja til í hendr þeim, sem kvæntir váru, ok stóð af því in mesta óró.	Went people then much to fighting, and became they to around women, and willed they, who unmarried were, seek to into hand that, who married were, and stood of therefore in most uneasiness.	Then there was much fighting among the men, as those that were not married sought after the women that were married, and there became the worst uneasiness.
Þar kom til it fyrsta haust Snorri, sonr Karlsefnis, ok var hann þá þrévetr, er þeir fóru brott.	There came to the first autumn Snorri, son Karlsefni's, and was he then three-winters, when they went away.	Karlsefni's son Snorri was born there the first autumn, and he was three winters old when they left.
Þá er þeir silgdu af Vínlandi, tóku þeir suðræn veðr ok hittu þá Markland ok fundu þar Skrælinga fimm, ok var einn skeggjaðr, konur váru tvær ok börn tvau.	Then when they sailed from Vinland, took they southern wind and met then Markland and found there Skraelings five, and was one bearded, women were two and children two.	Then they sailed from Vinland, and they were taken by a southerly wind and reached Markland, and found there five Skraelings, and one of them was bearded, two were women, and two were children.
Tóku þeir Karlsefni sveinana, en hinir kómust undan, ok sukku þeir Skrælingar í jörð niðr.	Took they Karlsefni young-men, and others went away, and sank they Skraelings among land down.	Karlsefni's company took the two boys, and the others went away, and then the Skraelings disappeared into the earth.
Sveina þessa tvá höfðu þeir með sér.	Young-men these two had they with them.	They kept these two with them.
Þeir kenndu þeim mál, ok váru skírðir.	They taught them language, and were baptised.	They taught them their language, and they were baptised.
Þeir nefndu móður sína Vethildi ok föður Óvægi.	They named mother theirs Vethild and father Ovaegi.	Their mother was named Vethildi and their father Ovaegi.
Þeir sögðu, at konungar stjórnuðu Skrælingum, ok hét annarr þeira Avaldamon, en annarr Avaldidida.	They said, that kings greatly-ruled-over Skraelings, and called one theirs Avaldamon, and another Valdidida.	They said that there were great kings who ruled over the Skraelings, one of them was called Avaldamon, and the other Valdidida.
Þeir kváðu þar engin hús. Lágu menn þar í hellum eða holum.	They said there no houses. Laid people there in caves or holes.	They said they had no houses. The people slept in caves or holes.

Old Norse	Literal	English
Þeir sögðu þar liggja land öðrum megin gagnvart sínu landi, er þeir menn byggðu, er váru í hvítum klæðum ok báru stangir fyrir sér, ok váru festar við flíkr ok æpðu hátt, ok ætla menn, at þat hafi verit Hvítramannaland eða Írland it mikla.	They said there lying land other side going-from their land, were their people settled, where were among white clothes and bore poles before them, and were fixed with banners and shouted loudly, and supposed people, that that had been White-man-land or Ireland the great.	The said there was another land across from theirs, where there were people settled, and they wore white clothes and carried poles before them, fixed with banners, and they shouted loudly, and they supposed that this was White Man Land or Great Ireland.
Nú kómu þeir til Grænlands ok eru með Eiríki rauða um vetrinn.	Now came they to Greenland and were with Erik the-Red about winter.	Now they came to Greenland and were with Erik the Red by about winter.
13	13	13
Þá Bjarna Grímólfsson bar í Írlandshaf ok kómu í maðksjó, ok sökk drjúgum skipit undir þeim.	Then Bjarni Grimolfson was-carried to the-Irish-Sea and came into ship-worms, and sank greatly ship under them.	Then Bjarni Grimolfson was carried to the Irish Sea and the ship was beset by worms, and the ship sank greatly beneath them.
Þeir höfðu bát þann, er bræddr var með seltjöru, því at þar fær eigi sjómaðkr á.	They had boat then, which spread was with seal-fat, because to there go not sea-worms to.	They had a boat, which had been spread with seal fat, so that the sea worms did not eat into it.
Þeir gengu í bátinn, ok sá þeir þá, at þeim mátti hann eigi öllum vinnast.	They went into the-boat, and saw they then, that they may it not all go-on.	They went into the boat, and realised that they could not all go aboard it.
Þá mælti Bjarni: "Af því at bátrinn tekr eigi meira en helming manna várra, þá er þat mitt ráð, at menn sé hlutaðir í bátinn, því at þetta skal ekki fara at mannvirðingu".	Then spoke Bjarni: "Of since the boat takes not more than half people ours, then is this my advice, that men see lots in boat, accordingly that this shall not go to rank".	Then Bjarni spoke: "Since the boat does not take more than half of our people, then I advise that we draw lots to enter the boat, and therefore this will not be decided by rank".
Þetta þótti öllum svá drengiliga boðit, at engi vildi móti mæla.	This thought all such bravely bid, that no-one willed against speak.	Everyone thought this was such a brave idea, that no one wanted to speak against it.
Gerðu þeir svá, at þeir hlutuðu mennina, ok hlaut Bjarni at fara í bátinn ok helmingr manna með honum, því at bátrinn tók ekki meira.	Did they so, to their lots men, and lot Bjarni to travel in the-boat and half the-men with him, because the boat took not more.	They did so, the people's lots were drawn, and it was Bjarni's lot to travel in the boat with half the men with him, because the boat would not take any more.

Old Norse	Literal	English
En er þeir váru komnir í bátinn, þá mælti einn íslenzkr maðr, er þá var í skipinu ok Bjarna hafði fylgt af Íslandi: "Ætlar þú, Bjarni, hér at skiljast við mik?"	But as they were coming into the-boat, then spoke one Icelander man, who then was in ship and Bjarni had followed from Iceland: "Intend you, Bjarni, here to separate with me?"	But as they were coming into the boat, then an Icelander who was in the ship spoke, who Bjarni had followed from Iceland: "Do you intend to separate with me now Bjarni?".
Bjarni svaraði: "Svá verðr nú at vera".	Bjarni answered: "So becomes now to be".	Bjarni answered: "So it has now come to be".
Hann svaraði: "Öðru hézt þú föður mínum, þá er ek fór af Íslandi með þér, en skiljast svá við mik, þá er þú sagðir, at eitt skyldi ganga yfir okkr báða".	He answered: "Otherwise promised you father mine, when as I travelled from Iceland with you, than separate so with me, then as you said, that one should go over us both".	He answered: "It dos not go with what you promised my father, then I travelled from Iceland with you, that you separate with me, for then you said that we would both go as one".
Bjarni svaraði: "Eigi skal ok svá vera. *Gakk þú hingat í bátinn, en ek mun upp fara í skipit, því at ek sé, at þú ert svá fúss til fjörsins".*	Bjarni answered: "Not shall and so be. Go you here in boat, and I will up go to ship, because that I see, that you are so willing to live".	Bjarni answered: "It shall not be so. You go here in the boat, and I will go up to the ship, because I see that you are so willing to live".
Gekk Bjarni þá upp í skipit, en þessi maðr í bátinn, ok fóru þeir síðan leiðar sinnar, til þess er þeir kómu til Dyflinnar í Írlandi, ok sögðu þar þessa sögu.	Went Bjarni then up into ship, while this man into boat, and went they afterwards way theirs, until this when they came to Dublin in Ireland, and told they this saga.	Bjarni then went up into the ship, while this man went into the boat, and afterwards they went their way, until they came to Dublin in Ireland, and they told this story.
En þat er flestra manna ætlan, at Bjarni ok þeir menn, sem í skipinu váru með honum, hafi látizt í maðksjónum, því at ekki spurðist til þeira síðan.	And that was most people's supposing, that Bjarni and those men, which in the-ship were with him, had died in the-worm-sea, because of nothing heard for they since.	And most people supposed that Bjarni and those men who were on the ship with him had died in the worm sea, because they were not heard of since.

14   14   14

Annat sumar eftir fór Karlsefni til Íslands ok Guðríðr með honum ok fór heim í Reynines.	Next summer after went Karlsefni to Iceland and Guthrid with him and went home to Reynines.	The next summer Karlsefni went to Iceland with Gudrid and went home to Reynines.

Old Norse	Literal	English
Móður hans þótti sem hann hefði lítt til kostar tekit, ok var hon eigi heima inn fyrsta vetr.	Mother his thought that he had little for choice taken, and was she not home the first winter.	His mother thought she had made a bad choice, and she did not stay at their home for the first winter.
En er hon reyndi, at Guðríðr var kvenskörungr mikill, fór hon heim, ok váru samfarar þeira góðar.	But when she experienced, that Guthrid was noble much, went she home, and was interaction theirs good.	But when she experienced that Gudrid was very noble, she went home, and their relationship was good.
Dóttir Snorra Karlsefnissonar var Hallfríðr, móðir Þorláks byskups Runólfssonar.	Daughter-of Snorri Karlsefnison was Hallfrid, Mother Thorlak's the-Bishop son-of-Runolf.	Snorri Karlsefnison's daughter was Hallfrid, mother to Thorlak the Bishop, son of Runolf.
Þau áttu son, er Þorbjörn hét.	They had a-son, was Thorbjorn named.	They had a son who was named Thorbjorn.
Hans dóttir hét Þórunn, móðir Bjarnar byskups.	His daughter was-called Thorun, mother Bjarn's the-Bishop.	His daughter was named Thorun, the mother of Bishop Bjarn.
Þorgeirr hét sonr Snorra Karlsefnissonar, faðir Yngvildar, móður Brands byskups ins fyrra.	Thorgeir was-called of Snorri son-of-Karlsefni, father-of Yngvild, mother-of Brand's Bishop the first.	Snorri Karlsefnison's son was named Thorgeir, he was the father of Yngvild, the mother of the first Bishop Brand.
Ok lýkr hér þessi sögu.	And ends here this saga.	And here ends this saga.

The Saga of Erik the Red (*Old Icelandic*)

Old Icelandic	Literal	English
1	1	1
Óleifur hét herkonungur er kallaður var Óleifur hvíti.	Olaf was-named warrior-king, that called was Olaf the-White.	There was a warrior king named Olaf, that was called Olaf the White.
Hann var son Ingjalds konungs Helgasonar, Ólafssonar, Guðröðarsonar, Hálfdanarsonar hvítbeins Upplendingakonungs.	He was son-of Ingjald's the-king son-of-Helga, son-of-Olaf, son-of-Gudrod, son-of-Halfdan White-Leg Opplands-king.	He was the son of Ingjald, the son of Helga, the son of Olaf, the son of Gudrod, the son of Halfdan White Leg, the king of the Opplands.
Óleifur herjaði í vesturvíking og vann Dyflinni á Írlandi og Dyflinnarskíri og gerðist konungur yfir.	Olaf harried to west-raiding and won Dublin in Ireland and Dublinshire and became king over.	Olaf harried on raids to the west and conquered Dublin in Ireland and Dublinshire, and made himself king there.
Hann fékk Auðar djúpúðgu dóttur Ketils Flatnefs Bjarnarsonar bunu, ágæts manns úr Noregi.	He married Aud the-Deep-Minded, daughter Ketil's Flat-Nose son-of-Bjorn Buna, excellent man from Norway.	He married Aud the Deep Minded, daughter of Ketil Flat Nose, the son of Bjorn Buna, an excellent man from Norway.
Þorsteinn rauður hét son þeirra.	Thorstein the-Red was-named son theirs.	Their son was named Thorstein the Red.
Óleifur féll á Írlandi í orustu en Auður og Þorsteinn fóru þá í Suðureyjar.	Olaf fell in Ireland in battle, then Aud and Thorstein went they to Sudreyar.	Olaf fell in Ireland in battle, then Aud and Thorstein went to the Southern Islands.
Þar fékk Þorsteinn Þuríðar dóttur Eyvindar austmanns, systur Helga hins magra.	There married Thorstein Thorid, daughter-of Eyvind the-Easternman sister-of Helga the Lean.	There Thorstein married Thorid, daughter of Eyvind the Easterner, sister of Helga the Lean.
Þau áttu mörg börn.	They had many children.	They had many children.
Þorsteinn gerðist herkonungur.	Thorstein became-a warrior-king.	Thorstein became a warrior king.
Hann réðst til lags með Sigurði jarli hinum ríka syni Eysteins glumru.	He appointed to position with Sigurd Earl the Rich, son-of Eystein Glumra.	He teamed up with Earl Sigurd the Rich, son of Eystein Glumra.
Þeir unnu Katanes og Suðurland, Ross og Meræfi og meir en hálft Skotland.	They won Caithness and Sutherland, Ross and Moray and more than half-of Scotland.	They conquered Caithness, Sutherland, Ross, Moray, and more than half of Scotland.
Gerðist Þorsteinn þar konungur yfir áður Skotar sviku hann og féll hann þar í orustu.	Became Thorstein there king over, until Scots betrayed him, and fell he there in battle.	Thorstein became king there until the Scots betrayed him and he fell in battle.

Old Icelandic	Literal	English
Auður var þá á Katanesi er hún spurði fall Þorsteins.	Aud was then in Caithness, when she heard-of fall Thorstein's.	Aud was then at Caithness when she learned of Thorstein's falling.
Hún lét þá gera knörr í skógi á laun en er hún var búin hélt hún út í Orkneyjar.	She had then made ship in woods of hired, and when she was ready, held she out to Orkney.	She then hired a ship to be made in the woods, and when she was ready, she set out to Orkney.
Þar gifti hún Gró dóttur Þorsteins rauðs.	There gave she Gro, daughter Thorstein the-Red's.	There she gave in marriage Gro, daughter of Thorstein the Red.
Hún var móðir Grélaðar er Þorfinnur jarl hausakljúfur átti.	She was mother-of Grelod, who Thorfin Earl Scull-Cleaver married.	She was the mother of Grelod, who was married to Earl Thorfinn the Skull-Cleaver.
Eftir það fór Auður að leita Íslands.	After that went Aud to seek Iceland.	After that Aud went to seek Iceland.
Hún hafði á skipi tuttugu karla frjálsa.	She had in ship twenty men free.	She had twenty free men on her ship.
Auður kom til Íslands og var hinn fyrsta vetur í Bjarnarhöfn með Birni bróður sínum.	Aud came to Iceland and was the first winter in Bjarnarhofn with Bjorn, brother hers.	Aud came to Iceland and spent the first winter in Bjarnarhofn with her brother Bjorn.
Síðan nam Auður öll Dalalönd milli Dögurðarár og Skraumuhlaupsár og bjó í Hvammi.	Since took Aud all Dale-land between Dogurdara and Skraumuhlaupsa and settled at Hvamm.	After that, Aud took all of the Dale lane between Dogurdara and Skraumuhlapusa and settled at Hvam.
Hún hafði bænahald í Krosshólum.	She had prayer-holdings at Krossholar.	She held prayers at Krossholar.
Þar lét hún reisa krossa því að hún var skírð og vel trúuð.	Where had she raise crosses, for that she was baptised and well religious.	There she had crosses raised, for she was baptised and a devout Christian.
Með henni komu út margir göfgir menn þeir er herteknir höfðu verið í vesturvíking og voru kallaðir ánauðgir.	With her came out many noble people, they which war-taken had been among west-raiding and were called bondsmen.	Many noble people came with her, who had been taken prisoner in viking raids and they were called bondsmen.
Einn af þeim hét Vífill.	One of them was called Vifil.	One of them was called Vifil.
Hann var ættstór maður og hafði verið hertekinn fyrir vestan haf og var kallaður ánauðigur áður Auður leysti hann.	He was high-family man and had been war-taken before western sea and was-called bondsman, before Aud released him.	He was a man of noble birth and had been taken prisoner by the western sea and was called a bondsman until Aud gave him his freedom.
Og er Auður gaf bústað skipverjum sínum þá spurði Vífill hví Auður gæfi honum öngvan bústað sem öðrum mönnum.	And when Aud gave farms crew hers, then asked Vifil, why Aud gave him no abode as other people.	When Aud gave her crew farm sites, then Vifil asked why Aud had not given him a farm as she had other people.

The Vinland Sagas   *The Saga of Erik the Red (Old Icelandic)*

Old Icelandic	Literal	English
Auður kvað eigi mundu skipta, kvað hann þar göfgan mundu þykja sem hann væri.	Aud said that not would change, called he there esteemed would-be valued, wherever he was.	Aud said that it made no difference, as he would be considered a fine man, wherever he was.
Honum gaf Auður Vífilsdal og bjó hann þar.	She gave him Vifilsdal, and settled he there.	She gave him Vifilsdal, and he settled there.
Hann átti konu.	He married a-woman.	He married a woman.
Þeirra synir voru þeir Þorgeir og Þorbjörn.	Their sons were they Thorbjorn and Thorgeir.	Their sons were Thorbjorn and Thorgeir.
Þeir voru efnilegir menn og óxu upp með föður sínum.	They were promising men and grew up with father theirs.	They were promising men and grew up with their father.
2	2	2
Þorvaldur hét maður.	Thorvald was-called a-man.	There was a man called Thorvald.
Hann var son Ásvalds Úlfssonar, Yxna-Þórissonar.	He was son Asvald's son-of-Ulf, son-of-Ox-Thorir	He was the son of Asvald, the son of Ulf, the son of Ox-Thorir.
Eiríkur rauði hét son hans.	Erik the-Red was-called son his	His son was called Erik the Red.
Þeir feðgar fóru af Jaðri til Íslands fyrir víga sakir og námu land á Hornströndum og bjuggu að Dröngum.	They father-and-son travelled from Jaeren to Iceland because-of killing conviction and took land in Hornstrandir and settled at Drangar.	Father and son travelled from Jaeran to Iceland because of a conviction for a slaying, and they took land at Hornstrandir and settled at Drangar.
Þar andaðist Þorvaldur.	There died Thorvald.	There Thorvald died.
Eiríkur fékk þá Þjóðhildar dóttur Jörundar Úlfssonar og Þorbjargar knarrarbringu er þá átti Þorbjörn hinn haukdælski.	Erik married then Thjodhild, daughter-of Jorund Ulfson and Thorbjorg Knarrarbringu, who then married Thorbjorn of Haukadal.	Erik then married Thjodhild, the daughter of Jorund Ulfson and Thorbjorn Knarrarbringu, who had since married Thorbjorn of Haukadal.
Réðst Eiríkur þá norðan og ruddi land í Haukadal og bjó á Eiríksstöðum hjá Vatnshorni.	Rode Erik then north and cleared land in Haukadal and settled at Eriksstadir near Vatnshorn.	Erik then rode north and cleared land in Haukadal and settled at Eriksstadir near Vatnshorn.
Þá felldu þrælar Eiríks skriðu á bæ Valþjófs á Valþjófsstöðum.	Then fell thralls Erik's landslide on farm Vallthjof at Vathjolfsstadr.	Then Erik's slaves caused a landslide to fall on the farm at Vallthjof at Vatnhjolfsstadr.
Eyjólfur saur frændi hans drap þrælana hjá Skeiðsbrekkum upp frá Vatnshorni.	Eyolf the-Foul, kinsman his, killed thralls beside Skeidsbrekkur up from Vatnshorn.	His kinsman Eyolf the Foul killed the slaves near Skeidsbrekkur above Vatnshorn.
Fyrir það vó Eiríkur Eyjólf saur.	For that slew Erik Eyolf the-Foul.	For that Erik killed Eyolf the Foul.

Old Icelandic	Literal	English
Hann vó og Hólmgöngu-Hrafn að Leikskálum.	He slew also Raven-the-Dueller at Leikskalar.	He also killed Raven the Dueller at Leikskalar.
Geirsteinn og Oddur á Jörva, frændur Eyjólfs, mæltu eftir hann.	Gerstein and Odd of Jorfi, kinsman Eyolf's, spoke after him.	Gerstein and Odd of Jorvi, Eyolf's kinsmen sought judgement for his killing.
Þá var Eiríkur ger á brott úr Haukadal.	Then was Erik made out from Haukadal.	Then Erik was outlawed from Haukadal.
Hann nam þá Brokey og Yxney og bjó að Tröðum í Suðurey hinn fyrsta vetur.	He took then Brokey and Oxney and settled at Tradir in Sudrey the first winter.	He took the islands Brokey and Oxney and settled at Tradir on Sudurey island that first winter.
Þá léði hann Þorgesti setstokka.	Then lent he Thorgest seat-posts.	Then he lent Thorgest bedstead boards.
Síðan fór Eiríkur í Yxney og bjó á Eiríksstöðum.	Afterwards travelled Erik to Oxney and settled at Eriksstadir.	Afterwards Erik travelled to Oxney and settled at Eriksstadir.
Þá heimti hann setstokkana og náði eigi.	Then claimed he seat-posts and got not.	Then he asked for the bedstead boards back, but did not get them.
Eiríkur sótti setstokkana á Breiðabólstað en Þorgestur fór eftir honum.	Erik took seat-posts from Breidabolstad, but Thorgest went after him.	Erik went to Breidabolstad and took the bedstead boards, but Thorgest went after him.
Þeir börðust skammt frá garði að Dröngum.	There fought short from garden at Drangar.	They fought a short distance from the farm at Drangar.
Þar féllu tveir synir Þorgests og nokkurir menn aðrir.	There fell two sons Thorgest's and some men other.	There Thorgest's two sons fell along with several other men.
Eftir það höfðu hvorirtveggju setu fjölmenna.	After that had either-side sitting many-men.	After that, both sides kept a large following of many men.
Styr veitti Eiríki og Eyjólfur úr Svíney, Þorbjörn Vífilsson og synir Þorbrands úr Álftafirði en Þorgesti veittu synir Þórðar gellis og Þorgeir úr Hítardal og Áslákur úr Langadal og Illugi son hans.	Styrr supported Erik and Eyolf of Sviney, Thorbjorn Vifilson and sons Thorbrand's from Alftafjord, but Thorgest supported sons Thord Gellir and Thorgeir of Hitardal, and Aslak of Langadal and Illugi, son his.	Erik had the support of Styrr, Eyolf of Sviney, Thorbjorn Vifilsson, and the sons of Thorbrand of Alftafjord, while Thorgest was supported by Thord Bellower, Thorgeir of Hitardal, Aslak of Langdal, and his son Illugi.
Þeir Eiríkur urðu sekir á Þórsnessþingi.	They and Erik became outlawed at Thorsnes-Thing.	Erik and his companions became outlawed at the Thorsnes Assembly.

Old Icelandic	Literal	English
Hann bjó skip í Eiríksvogi en Eyjólfur leyndi honum í Dímunarvogi meðan þeir Þorgestur leituðu hans um eyjarnar.	He prepared ship in Eriksvog, and Eyolf hid him in Dimunarvog, while they Thorgest sought him about islands.	He prepared a ship at Eriksvog, and Eyolf hid him in Dimunarvog while Thorgest and his men searched the islands for him.
Hann sagði þeim að hann ætlaði að leita lands þess er Gunnbjörn son Úlfs kráku sá, er hann rak vestur um haf og hann fann Gunnbjarnarsker.	He told them, that he intended to seek lands these, which Gunnbjorn, son-of Ulf Crow, saw, when he-was driven west about sea and he found Gunnbjarnarsker.	He said to them that he intended to search for the lands which Gunnbjorn son of Ulf Crow saw, when he was driven west at sea and found Gunnbjarbarsker.
Hann kveðst aftur mundu leita til vina sinna ef hann fyndi landið.	He said return would seek to friends his, if he found land.	He said that he would return to seek them out if he found land.
Þeir Þorbjörn og Styr og Eyjólfur fylgdu Eiríki út um eyjar og skildu með hinni mestu vináttu.	There Thorbjorn and Eyolf and Styrr followed Erik back around islands, and separated they with the most friendship.	Thorbjorn, Eyolf, and Styrr followed Erik through the islands, and they separated with the most friendship.
Kveðst Eiríkur þeim skyldu verða að þvílíku trausti sem hann mætti sér við koma ef þeir kynnu hans að þurfa.	Said Erik to-them should be to likewise trust, if he may them with come and circumstance they him to need.	Erik said to them that they should trust that he would help them in any way if they ever needed him.
Sigldi Eiríkur á haf undan Snæfellsjökli og kom utan að jökli þeim er Bláserkur heitir.	Sailed Erik to sea from Snaefellsjokli and came out of glacier that was Blaserkur named.	Erik sailed to sea from Snaefellsjolki and came out from a glacier that was named Blaserkur.
Hann fór þaðan suður að leita ef þar væri byggjanda.	He travelled from-there south to seek, if there was habitable.	He travelled south from there to see if there was any habitable land.
Hann var hinn fyrsta vetur í Eirikseyju, nær miðri hinni vestri byggðinni.	He was the first winter at Eriksey, near middle the western settlement.	For the first winter he was at Eriksey, near the middle of the Western Settlement.
Um vorið eftir fór hann til Eiríksfjarðar og tók sér þar bústað.	About spring after travelled he to Eriksfjord and took he there settlement.	After about spring he travelled to Eriksfjord and took settlement there.
Hann fór það sumar í hina vestri óbyggð og gaf víða örnefni.	He travelled that summer into the western settlement and gave widely place-names.	That summer he travelled into the Western Settlement and gave place names widely.
Hann var annan vetur í Eiríkshólmum við Hvarfsgnípu en hið þriðja sumar fór hann allt norður til Snæfells og inn í Hrafnsfjörð.	He was second winter at Eriksholmar off Hvarfsgnipu and the third summer went he altogether north to Snaefell and then into Hrafnsfjord.	The second winter he was at Eriksholmar near Hvarfsgnipu, and the third summer he travelled all the way north to Snaefell and into Hrafnsfjord.

Old Icelandic	Literal	English
Þá þóttist hann kominn fyrir botn Eiríksfjarðar.	Then thought he came before the-bottom-of Eriksfjord.	There he thought he had reached the head of Eriksfjord.
Hverfur hann þá aftur og var hinn þriðja vetur í Eiríkseyju fyrir mynni Eiríksfjarðar.	Turned he then back and was in third winter at Eriksey before the-mouth-of Eriksfjord.	Then he returned to winter at Eriksey at the mouth of Eriksfjord.
Eftir um sumarið fór hann til Íslands og kom í Breiðafjörð.	But afterwards about summer travelled he to Iceland and came to Breidafjord.	Then after about summer he travelled to Iceland and came to Breidafjord.
Hann var þann vetur með Ingólfi á Hólmlátri.	He was that winter with Ingolf at Holmlatr.	That winter he was with Ingolf at Holmlatr.
Um vorið börðust þeir Þorgestur og fékk Eiríkur ósigur.	About spring fought they Thorgest, and got Erik defeat.	About spring Erik and Thorgest fought, and Erik was defeated.
Eftir það voru þeir sættir.	After that were they reconciled.	After that they were reconciled.
Það sumar fór Eiríkur að byggja landið það er hann hafði fundið og hann kallaði Grænland því að hann kvað menn það mjög mundu fýsa þangað ef landið héti vel.	That summer went Erik to settle land that, which he had found and he called Greenland, because as he said people that much would desire there, if land named well.	That summer Erik went to settle the land that he had found, which he called Greenland, because as he said, people would be attracted if the land was named well.

3

Old Icelandic	Literal	English
Þorgeir Vífilsson kvongaðist og fékk Arnóru dóttur Einars frá Laugarbrekku, Sigmundarsonar, Ketilssonar þistils er numið hafði Þistilsfjörð.	Thorgeir Vifilson married and got Arnora, daughter Einar's from Laugarbrekka, son-of-Sigmund, son-of-Ketil Thistle who taken had Thistilsfjord.	Thorgeir Vifilson took as his wife Arnora, daughter of Einar from Laugarbrekk, the son of Sigmund, the son of Ketil Thistle who had taken Thistilsfjord.
Önnur dóttir Einars hét Hallveig.	Second daughter Einar's was-named Hallveig.	Einar's second daughter was named Hallveig.
Hennar fékk Þorbjörn Vífilsson og tók með land á Laugarbrekku á Hellisvöllum.	She married Thorbjorn Vifilson and took with land in Laugarbrekka, at Hellisvellir.	She married Thorbjorn Vifilson and took land at Laugarbrekku in Hellisvellir.
Réðst Þorbjörn þangað byggðum og gerðist göfugmenni mikið.	Moved Thorbjorn there settlement and became noble much.	Thorbjorn moved his settlement there and became a great nobleman.
Hann var goðorðsmaður og hafði rausnarbú.	He was a-good farmer and had great-estate.	He was a good farmer and had a great estate.
Guðríður hét dóttir Þorbjarnar.	Guthrid was-called daughter Thorbjorn's.	Thorbjorn's daughter was called Gudrid.
Hún var kvenna vænst og hinn mesti skörungur í öllu athæfi sínu.	She was woman fair and the most noble in all behaviour hers.	She was a fair woman and the most noble in all her behaviour.

The Saga of Erik the Red (Old Icelandic)

Old Icelandic	Literal	English
Maður hét Ormur er bjó að Arnarstapa.	A-man was-called Orm, who settled at Arnarstapi.	There was a man called Orm who settled at Arnarstapi.
Hann átti konu þá er Halldís hét.	He had a-wife, was Halldis named.	He had a wife who was named Halldis.
Ormur var góður bóndi og vinur Þorbjarnar mikill.	Orm was a-good farmer and friend-of Thorbjorn great.	Orm was a good farmer and a great friend of Thorbjorn.
Var Guðríður þar löngum að fóstri með honum.	Was Guthrid there long to foster with him.	Gudrid was fostered there and spent long periods of time with him.
Maður hét Þorgeir er bjó að Þorgeirsfelli.	A-man was-named Thorgeir who lived at Thorgeirsfell.	There was a man named Thorgeir who lived at Thorgeirsfell.
Hann var vellauðigur að fé og hafði verið leysingi.	He was wealthy in cattle and had-been made a-freed-man.	He was rich in cattle and had been made a free man.
Hann átti son er Einar hét.	He had a-son was Einar called.	He had a son who was named Einar.
Hann var vænn maður og vel mannaður og skartsmaður mikill.	He was a-fair man and well mannered and jewelled-man much.	He was a fair man and well mannered, and much bejewelled.
Einar var í siglingu landa í milli og tókst honum það vel.	Einar was among sailing between lands, and took him that well.	Einar was sailing between lands, and he took to it well.
Var hann jafnan sinn vetur hvort á Íslandi eða í Noregi.	Was he equally the winter either to Iceland or to Norway.	In winter he was equally in either Iceland or Norway.
Nú er frá því að segja eitt haust er Einar var út hér að hann fór með varning sinn út eftir Snæfellsnesi og skyldi selja.	Now is from that to say one autumn, then that Einar was in Iceland, as he came with wares his out along Snaefellstrond and wished to-sell.	From that is there now to say that one autumn when Einar was in Iceland, he came with goods to Snaefellstrond wishing to sell.
Hann kemur til Arnarstapa.	He came to Arnarstapi.	He came to Arnarstapi.
Ormur býður honum þar að vera og það þiggur Einar því að þar var vinátta við kjörin.	Orm invited him there to be, and that accepted Einar, because that there was friendship with chosen.	Orm invited him to be there, and Einar accepted, as friendship was also chosen.
Varningurinn Einars var borinn í eitthvert útibúr.	Were carried in wares his into an out-house.	His goods were carried into an outhouse.
Einar brýtur upp varninginn og sýndi Ormi og heimamönnum og bauð Ormi slíkt af að taka sem hann vildi.	Einar divided up wares his and showed Orm and housemen and invited him of to have such that he willed.	Einar divided up his goods and showed Orm and his housemen, inviting them to have whatever they wished.

Old Icelandic	Literal	English
Ormur þá þetta og taldi Einar vera góðan fardreng og auðnumann mikinn.	Orm then that also told Einar was good traveller-generous and fortune much.	Orm accepted and told Einar that he was a good merchant, generous, and of great fortune.
En er þeir héldu á varninginum gekk kona fyrir útibúrsdyrin.	When were they busy of wares, walked woman before outhouse-door.	While they were occupied with the goods, a woman walked in front of the outhouse door.
Einar spurði Orm hver sú hin fagra kona væri er þar gekk fyrir dyrnar "eg hefi hana eigi hér fyrr séð".	Einar asked Orm, who was that in fair woman, was there going before doorway, - "I have not her here before seen".	Einar asked Orm who that fair woman was who walked in front of the doorway: "I have not seen her here before".
Ormur segir: "Það er Guðríður fóstra mín, dóttir Þorbjarnar bónda frá Laugarbrekku".	Orm answered: "That is Guthrid, foster-child mine, daughter Thorbjorn's from Laugarbrekka".	Orm answered: "That is Gudrid, my foster child, daughter of Thorbjorn from Laugarbrekka".
Einar mælti: "Hún mun vera góður kostur.	Einar said: "She would be choice good.	Einar said: "She would be a good choice.
Eða hafa nokkurir menn til komið að biðja hennar?"	Or have some men towards come to propose her?"	Or have any men come forward to propose to her?"
Ormur svarar: "Beðið hefir hennar víst verið vinur og liggur eigi laust fyrir.	Orm answered: "Proposals have for-her made been friend and lies not less for.	Orm answered: "Proposals have been made to her, but without success.
Finnur það á að hún mun bæði vera mannvönd og faðir hennar".	Finding that of that she should choosing be husband and father hers".	She shall choose her husband, and so will her father".
"Svo fyrir það", kvað Einar, "að hún er sú kona er eg ætla mér að biðja og vildi eg að þessi mál kæmir þú fyrir mig við föður hennar og legðir á alendu að flytja því að eg skal þér fullkomna vináttu fyrir gjalda.	"So therefore that", said Einar, "That she is the woman that I intend me to propose and will I to this matter come you for me with father hers and lay all thoughts to carry because to I shall you full-come friendship for expenses.	"So be it", said Einar, "she's the woman I intend to propose to, and I would like you to seek the matter with her father Thorbjorn, and give it your thoughts, how this may be so. I will repay you with the fullest friendship, that I can say.
Má Þorbjörn bóndi á líta að okkur væru vel hentar tengdir því hann er sómamaður mikill og á staðfestu góða en lausafé hans er mér sagt að mjög sé á förum.	May Thorbjorn farmer that see, to ours would-be well suits joined, for to he is famous-man great and of established good, but liquidity his is to-me said rather to going.	Thorbjorn the farmer may see we would be well joined, as he is a man of high regard with a good farm, but it is said that his means are rather depleting".

Old Icelandic	Literal	English
En mig skortir hvorki land né lausafé og okkur feðga og mundi Þorbirni verða að því hinn mesti styrkur ef þessi ráð tækjust".	But my shortage neither land nor liquidity and us father-and-son, and should Thorbjorn be therefore this the most strength, if this takes".	But my father and I lack neither land or means, and would therefore give the most support, if this is concluded.
Ormur svarar: "Víst þykist eg vin þinn vera en þó er eg ekki fús að bera þessi mál upp því að Þorbjörn er skapstór og þó metnaðarmaður mikill".	Orm said: "Knowing think-us I friend yours be, but though am I not with my advice willing, of to bring this up, because that Thorbjorn is temperamental and though ambitious-man much".	Orm said: "Knowing that I consider myself your friend, I am though not willing to bring up this discussion, because Thorbjorn is temperamental and a very ambitious man".
Einar kveðst ekki vilja annað en upp væri borið bónorðið.	Einar said not willing another but up would-be carried proposal.	Einar said that he would not be satisfied unless the proposal was brought up.
Ormur kvað hann ráða skyldu.	Orm said his decision shall-be.	Orm said that his decision would be so.
Einar fór suður aftur uns hann kemur heim.	Travelled Einar south back, until he came home.	Einar travelled back south until he came home.
Nokkuru síðar hafði Þorbjörn haustboð sem hann átti vanda til því að hann var stórmenni mikið.	Sometime since had Thorbjorn harvest-feast, that he had accustomed to, because to him were great-men much.	Sometime after Thorbjorn had a harvest feast, that was his custom, as he was a great man.
Kom þar Ormur frá Arnarstapa og margir aðrir vinir Þorbjarnar.	Came there Orm from Arnarstapi and many other friends Thorbjorn's.	Orm came from Arnarstapi and many of Thorbjorn's other friends.
Ormur kemur að máli við Þorbjörn og segir að Einar var þar skömmu, frá Þorgeirsfelli, og gerðist efnilegur maður.	Orm came to speak with Thorbjorn and said, that Einar was there recently, from Thorgeirsfell, and became the promising man.	Orm came to speak with Thorbjorn and said, that Einar from Thorgeirsfell had been there recently, and he had become a promising man.
Hefur Ormur nú upp bónorðið fyrir hönd Einars og sagði að það væri vel hent fyrir sumra manna sakir að hluta "má þér bóndi að því verða styrkur mikill fyrir fjárkosta sakir".	Had Orm now upped proposal for hand Einar's and said to that would-be well joined for some people's sake to part "May to-you husband to therefore be steered much for financial-cost's sake".	Orm now brought up Einar's marriage proposal and said that it would be well joined on several accounts. "It may be to you be strong support in financial terms".
Þorbjörn svarar: "Eigi varði mig slíkra orða af þér að eg mundi þrælssyni gifta dóttur mína.	Thorbjorn answered: "Not expected I such words from you, that I should give thrall's-son daughter mine.	Thorbjorn answered: "I did not expect to hear such words from you, that I should give my daughter to a slave's son.

Old Icelandic	Literal	English
Og það finnið þér nú að fé mitt þverr er slík ráð gefið mér.	And that find you now, that wealth mine decreases, is such counsel given to-me.	As you now suggest, that my wealth is decreasing, to give such advice to me.
Og eigi skal hún fara með því ef þér þótti hún svo lítils gjaforðs verð".	And not shall she with you be longer, as you thought she such little marriage-offer deserve".	And no longer shall she be with you, as you thought she deserved such a lowly marriage offer".
Síðan fór Ormur heim og hver boðsmanna til sinna heimkynna.	Afterwards went Orm home and each other guests to their households.	Afterwards Orm went home an each of the other guests went to their homes.
Guðríður var eftir með föður sínum og var heima þann vetur.	Guthrid was remained with father hers and stayed home that winter.	Gudrid stayed behind with her father and spent that winter at home.
En að vori hafði Þorbjörn vinaboð og var veisla góð búin og kom þar margt manna og var veislan hin besta.	But in spring had Thorbjorn friend-invites, and came there many people, and was the best feast.	Then when spring came Thorbjorn invited his friends to come with many people, and there was the best feast.
Og að veislunni kvaddi Þorbjörn sér hljóðs og mælti: "Hér hefi eg búið langa ævi.	And at the-feast called Thorbjorn he be-heard and spoke: "Here have in lived long life.	During the feast, Thorbjorn asked to be heard and spoke: "Here I have lived a long life,
Hefi eg reynt góðvilja manna við mig og ástúð.	Have I experienced good-will men's to me and affection.	and I have enjoyed the good will and affection.
Kalla eg vel vor skipti farið hafa.	Call I well gone have been exchanges.	I call all our dealings well done.
En nú tekur fjárhagur minn að óhægjast fyrir lausafjár sakir en hefir kallað verið hingað til heldur virðingarráð.	But now take finances mine to maintain for liquidity's sake that have called have-been here to rather worthiness.	But now my benefit begins to be uneasy for the sake of means, though so far it has been called worthy.
Nú vil eg fyrr búi mínu bregða en sæmd minni týna, fyrr af landi fara en ætt mína svívirða.	Now will I for settlement mine foreclose than honour mine lose, for of land travel but-for lineage mine shame.	Now I wish to foreclose before I lose my honour. I intend to travel from this land, rather than shame my lineage,
Ætla eg nú að vitja um mál Eiríks rauða vinar míns er hann hafði þá er við skildum á Breiðafirði.	Intend I now to visit about matters Erik the-Red friend mine that he had then was with separated at Breidafjord.	and visit my friend Erik the Red who I was separated from at Breidafjord.
Ætla eg nú að fara til Grænlands í sumar ef svo fer sem eg vildi".	Intend I now to travel to Greenland in summer, if so goes as I wish".	I now intend to travel to Greenland I summer, if it goes as I wish".

The Vinland Sagas   *The Saga of Erik the Red (Old Icelandic)*

Old Icelandic	Literal	English
Mönnum þótti mikil tíðindi um þessa ráðagerð því að Þorbjörn hafði lengi vinsæll verið en þóttust vita að Þorbjörn mundi þetta hafa svo framt upp kveðið að hann mundi ekki stoða að letja.	People thought great this change, for that Thorbjorn was befriended man, but thought knowing, that Thorbjorn would so provide that up had declared, that not should avail to discourage.	People thought this was a great change, because Thorbjorn was a popular man, but they thought that once Thorbjorn had declared this, it would be to no avail to discourage him.
Gaf Þorbjörn mönnum gjafir og var veislu brugðið eftir þetta og fóru menn heim til heimkynna sinna.	Gave Thorbjorn people gifts and was feast brought-out after this and went people home to households theirs.	Thorbjorn gave people gifts and a feast was brought out, and afterwards everyone went to their homes.
Þorbjörn selur lendur sínar og kaupir skip er stóð uppi í Hraunhafnarósi.	Thorbjorn sold land his and bought himself ship, which up stood at Hraunhafnaros.	Thorbjorn sold his land and bought himself a ship, which stood at Hraunhafnaros.
Réðust til ferðar með honum þrír tigir manna.	Hired to travel with him three tens men.	He hired thirty men to travel with him.
Var þar Ormur frá Arnarstapa og kona hans og þeir vinir Þorbjarnar er eigi vildu við hann skilja.	Was there to travel Orm from Arnarstapi and wife his and other friends Thorbjorn's, they were not willing with him separate.	There to travel with him was Orm from Arnarstapi, and his wife, and Thorbjorn's other friends, they were not willing to separate with him.
Síðan létu þeir í haf.	Afterwards left they to sea.	Afterwards they put to sea.
Þá er þeir höfðu út látið var veður hagstætt en er þeir komu í haf tók af byri og fengu þeir mikil veður og fórst þeim ógreitt um sumarið.	Then when they had out left was weather favourable and when they came to sea taken of fair-wind and caught they much weather and went they not-without-obstacle about summer.	Then when had put to sea the weather was favourable, but when they came to sea, the fair wind disappeared, and they caught a storm and they were not without obstacles all summer.
Því næst kom sótt í lið þeirra og andaðist Ormur og Halldís kona hans og helmingur þeirra.	For next came sickness among team theirs, and died Orm and Halldis, wife his, and half team theirs.	Because next there came a sickness among their crew, and Orm died, and his wife Halldis, along with half of the crew.
Sjó tók að stæra og fengu þeir vos mikið og vesöld á marga vega og tóku þó Herjólfsnes á Grænlandi við veturnætur sjálfar.	Sea took to greatly, and endured men the most toil and misery in many ways, but took though Herjolfsnes to Greenland by winter itself.	The sea swelled, and people endured the most toil and misery in many ways, but they took land at Herjolfsnes in Greenland during the Winter Nights.
Sá maður bjó á Herjólfsnesi er Þorkell hét.	So a-man settled at Herjolfsnes was Thorkell called.	There was a man named Thorkell who lived at Herjolfsnes.
Hann var nytjumaður og hinn besti bóndi.	He was useful man the best farmer.	He was a useful man and the best farmer.

Old Icelandic	Literal	English
Hann tók við Þorbirni og öllum skipverjum hans um veturinn.	He took with Thorbjorn and all crew his about winter.	He took with Thorbjorn and all his crew for the winter.
Þorkell veitti þeim skörulega.	Thorkell provided-for them boldly.	Thorkell provided for them generously.
Líkaði Þorbirni vel og öllum skipverjum hans.	Liked Thorbjorn well and all crew his.	He was well liked by Thorbjorn and all his crew.
4	4	4
Í þenna tíma var hallæri mikið á Grænlandi.	In that time was famine much in Greenland.	At that time there was much famine in Greenland.
Höfðu menn fengið lítið, þeir sem í veiðiferð höfðu verið, en sumir eigi aftur komnir.	Had people caught little, they which to hunting had been, and some not after returning.	People that had been hunting had caught little, and some of them had not returned.
Sú kona var þar í byggð er Þorbjörg hét.	The woman was there in settlement, was Thorbjorg called.	There was a woman in the settlement who was named Thorbjorg.
Hún var spákona og var kölluð lítilvölva.	She was prophetess and was called Little-Prophetess.	She was a prophetess, and was called Little Prophetess.
Hún hafði átt sér níu systur og voru allar spákonur og var hún ein eftir á lífi.	She had descendents hers nine sisters, and were all prophetesses, and she alone was then yet living.	Among her family were nine sisters, and all were prophetesses, and she was the only one yet living.
Það var háttur Þorbjargar á vetrum að hún fór á veislur og buðu menn henni heim, mest þeir er forvitni var á um forlög sín eða árferð.	It was way Thorbjorg's about winter, that she went to feasts, and invited they people her most homes, that curious were for to know fortune theirs or season.	It was a custom of Thorbjorg's during winter, that she went to feasts, and to homes that people had invited her to, who were curious to know their fortune for the season.
Og með því að Þorkell var þar mestur bóndi þá þótti til hans koma að vita hvenær létta mundi óárani þessu sem yfir stóð.	And with because that Thorkell was there greatest landowner, then thought to him came to know, how near relieve should scarcity this, which over stood.	And with Thorkell being the greatest landowner, it was thought that he should come to know when the scarcity that stood over them would be relieved.
Þorkell býður spákonu þangað og er henni búin góð viðtaka sem siður var til þá er við þess háttar konu skyldi taka.	Invited Thorkell prophetess home, and was she there well welcomed, as custom was to, then was with this kind woman should take.	Thorkell invited the prophetess to his home, and she was well welcomed, as was the custom, when this kind of woman was received as a guest.
Búið var henni hásæti og lagt undir hægindi.	Was she prepared a-high-seat and laid under her a-cushion.	A high seat was prepared for her, and under it a cushion.

The Saga of Erik the Red (Old Icelandic)

Old Icelandic	Literal	English
Þar skyldi í vera hænsafiðri.	There should in be hen's-feathers.	This was to be filled with hen's feathers.
En er hún kom um kveldið og sá maður er í móti henni var sendur þá var hún svo búin að hún hafði yfir sér tuglamöttul blán og var settur steinum allt í skaut ofan.	Then when she came about evening and saw a-man, who meeting her was sent, then was she such ready, for she had over her mantle blue, and was set stones all in lap of.	Then when she arrived around evening, with the man who was sent to meet her when she was ready, she had over her a blue mantle, which was set with stones in the lap.
Hún hafði á hálsi sér glertölur.	She had on neck hers glass-beads.	She had glass beads on her neck.
Hún hafði á höfði lambskinnskofra svartan og við innan kattarskinn hvítt.	She had on head lamb-skin-hood black and with in cat-skin white.	She had on her head a hood of black lamb skin, lined with white cat skin.
Staf hafði hún í hendi og var á hnappur.	And she had staff in hand, and was on a-knob	And she had in her hand a staff, which had a knob on the top.
Hann var búinn messingu og settur steinum ofan um hnappinn.	It was set with brass and set stones on about knob.	It was set with brass and had stones set about the knob.
Hún hafði um sig hnjóskulinda og var þar á skjóðupungur mikill.	She had about herself a-girdle and was there on a-skin-purse great.	She wore a girdle with a large skin purse,
Varðveitti hún þar í töfur þau er hún þurfti til fróðleiks að hafa.	Kept she there in magic hers which she needed to knowledge of have.	She kept her magic in there, which she needed to have knowledge of.
Hún hafði kálfskinnsskó loðna á fótum og í þvengi langa og sterklega, látúnshnappar miklir á endunum.	She had on feet calf-skin-shoes fur and in tied long and in pewter-buttons great on ends.	She had calf skin shoes lined with fur, with long laces with pewter knobs on the ends.
Hún hafði á höndum sér kattskinnsglófa og voru hvítir innan og loðnir.	She had on hands hers cat-skin-gloves, and were white inside and furry.	She had cat skin gloves on her hands and they were white and furry inside.
En er hún kom inn þótti öllum mönnum skylt að velja henni sæmilegar kveðjur en hún tók því eftir sem henni voru menn skapfelldir til.	Then when she came in thought all people should to will her honourable greetings which she took according after which she was people agreeable to.	When she came in, everyone was supposed to give her honourable greetings. She responded to people according to how the person appealed to her.
Tók Þorkell bóndi í hönd vísindakonunni og leiddi hana til þess sætis er henni var búið.	Took Thorkell the-Farmer in hand hers and led her to this seat, which she was prepared.	Thorkell the Farmer took her hand and led her to the seat which was prepared for her.
Þorkell bað hana þá renna þar augum yfir hjörð og hjú og híbýli.	Thorkell asked her then run there eyes over herd and hearth and so settlement.	Thorkell asked her to run her eyes over the herd, the hearth, and the settlement.
Hún var fámálug um allt.	She was silent about all.	She was silent about all of it.

Old Icelandic	Literal	English
Borð voru upp tekin um kveldið og er frá því að segja að spákonunni var matbúið.	Tables were up taken about evening, and was from since to say, what prophetess was food-prepared.	That evening tables were set up, and afterwards it was to say, what food was prepared for the prophetess.
Henni var ger grautur af kiðjamjólk en til matar henni voru búin hjörtu úr alls konar kvikindum þeim sem þar voru til.	She was made porridge of kid's-milk and food-prepared hearts of all creatures, they that there were to.	She was made a porridge of kid's milk and hearts of all animals available there.
Hún hafði messingarspón og hníf tannskeftan, tvíhólkaðan af eiri, og var af brotinn oddurinn.	She had brass-spoon and knife walrus-tusk, two-ringed of bronze, and was broken of tip.	She had a brass spoon and a knife with a walrus tusk, two halves ringed with bronze, and the tip had been broken off.
En er borð voru upp tekin gengur Þorkell bóndi fyrir Þorbjörgu og spyr hversu henni virðist þar híbýli eða hættir manna eða hversu fljótlega hann mun þess vís verða er hann hefir spurt eftir og menn vildu vita.	Then when table was up taken, then went Thorkell farmer before Thorbjorg and asked, how she thought there about it looked or how agreeable to-her were there settlements or manner people's or how soon she could aware be this, that he had asked her and men were most curious to know.	And when the tables were taken up, then Thorkell the Farmer went before Thorbjorg and asked her what she thought of the conduct of the household, the manner of people, and how soon she would know what he had asked her, and what people were most curious to know.
Hún kveðst það ekki mundu upp bera fyrr en um morguninn þá er hún hefði sofið þar um nóttina.	She considered not would say before that about morning after, when she had after slept for night.	She said that she would not say before the following morning, when she had slept about the night.
En að áliðnum degi var henni veittur sá umbúningur sem hún skyldi til að fremja seiðinn.	Then from morning to following day was she given that clothing, which she needed to have for to perform enchantments.	Then the following morning she was given the clothing that she needed to have to perform her enchantments.
Bað hún fá sér konur þær sem kynnu fræði það er þyrfti til seiðinn að fremja og Varðlokur heita.	She asked also get the women there, who knew wisdom that, which for enchantments needed and warlock-songs called.	She asked for women who had the wisdom of the enchantments needed, which were called warlock songs.
En þær konur fundust eigi.	But those women were-found not.	But those women were not found.
Þá var að leitað um bæinn ef nokkur kynni.	They were to seek to about household, if anyone knew.	The people of the household searched for anyone who knew.

Old Icelandic	Literal	English
Þá svarar Guðríður: "Hvorki er eg fjölkunnig né vísindakona en þó kenndi Halldís fóstra mín mér á Íslandi það fræði er hún kallaði Varðlokur".	Then said Guthrid: "Neither am I of-magic nor fore-knowing-woman, but though taught Halldis, foster mine, to-me in Iceland that poem, that she called warlock-songs".	Then Gudrid said: "I am neither of magic nor prophecy, but my foster mother, Halldis, taught me chants that she called warlock songs.
Þorbjörg svaraði: "Þá ertu fróðari en eg ætlaði".	Thorbjorg answered: "Then are-you wiser than I supposed".	Thorbjorg answered: "Then you are wiser than I supposed".
Guðríður segir: "Þetta er þess konar fræði og atferli að eg ætla í öngvum atbeina að vera því að eg er kona kristin".	Guthrid said: "That is this kind-of wisdom and ceremony that I intend to nothing assist in being because that I am woman Christian".	Gudrid said: "That is the kind of wisdom and ceremony that I intend to be no assistance to, because I am a Christian woman".
Þorbjörg svarar: "Svo mætti verða að þú yrðir mönnum að liði hér um en þú værir þá kona ekki að verri.	Thorbjorg said: "So may be, that you become people to help here about, but you would-be then woman not worse than before.	Thorbjorg said: "So it may be that you may come to help here, but you would be no worse a woman than before.
En við Þorkel met eg að fá þá hluti hér til er þarf".	But with Thorkell should I evaluate to get the things for, which have need".	But I will appreciate getting the things from Thorkell that are needed".
Þorkell herðir nú að Guðríði en hún kveðst mundu gera sem hann vildi.	Thorkell hardened now to Guthrid, but she said do would as he wished.	Thorkell now hardened towards Gudrid, and said that she should do as he wished.
Slógu þá konur hring umhverfis en Þorbjörg sat uppi á seiðhjallinum.	Formed then women a-ring around the-platform, while Thorbjorg sat on up.	The women then formed a ring around the platform, while Thorbjorg sat above.
Kvað Guðríður þá kvæðið svo fagurt og vel að engi þóttist fyrr heyrt hafa með fegri raust kveðið sá er þar var.	Said Guthrid then recited so beautiful and well, that none thought heard had with more-beautiful voice poem sung, so as there was heard.	Gudrid then recited so beautifully and so well, that no one thought they had head a poem sung with more beautiful a voice, than that which they heard.
Spákona þakkar henni kvæðið.	Prophetess thanked her poem.	The prophetess thanked her for the poem.

The Vinland Sagas   *The Saga of Erik the Red (Old Icelandic)*

Old Icelandic	Literal	English
Hún hafði margar náttúrur hingað að sótt og þótti fagurt að heyra það er kveðið var "er áður vildu frá oss snúast og oss öngva hlýðni veita.	She had many spirits here to attended and think beautiful to hear that which poem was "Who before willed from us turn and us none homage grant.	She said that the many spirits have now attended who thought it beautiful to hear, as it was so well performed: "those who before turned their backs on us and refused to grant us assistance.
En mér eru nú margir þeir hlutir auðsýnir er áður var bæði eg og aðrir duldir.	And to-me are now many those things shown, which before were I hidden, and many others.	And there are now many things shown to me which before were hidden from me and others.
En eg kann það að segja að hallæri þetta mun ekki haldast lengur en í vetur og mun batna árangur sem vorar.	And I can to-you that to say to famine this should not hold longer than to winter, and should better harvest, then spring.	And I can now say to you, that this famine should not hold longer than to winter, and there should be a better harvest in the spring.
Sóttarfar það sem lengi hefir legið mun og batna vonum bráðara.	Sickness that, which to has laid, should also better-than hope sooner.	That sickness which has happened, should hopefully be better sooner.
En þér Guðríður skal eg launa í hönd liðsinni það sem oss hefir af staðið því að þín forlög eru mér nú öll glöggsæ.	And you, Guthrid, shall I reward in hand assistance that, for us have of you stood, because that your fortunes are to-me now clear.	And you, Gudrid, I shall reward in hand for the assistance that you placed, because to me your fortunes are now clear.
Það muntu gjaforð fá hér á Grænlandi er sæmilegast er til þó að þér verði það eigi til langæðar því að vegir þínir liggja út til Íslands og mun þar koma frá þér ættbogi bæði mikill og góður og yfir þínum ættkvíslum mun skína bjartur geisli.	You shall married be here in Greenland, that which honourable is, though for you will-be that not for long, because the way yours lies out to Iceland, and shall there come from you both great descendents and good, and over your family shine bright rays.	You shall be married here in Greenland, and honourably, though you will not be married for long, because your way lies out to Iceland, and there shall come from you good descendents, and bright rays will shine over your family.
Enda far nú vel og heil, dóttir mín".	End go you now whole and well, daughter".	After all, travel you now whole and well, daughter".
Síðan gengu menn að vísindakonunni og frétti hver eftir því sem mest forvitni var á.	Afterwards went people to wise-woman, and heard then each these, were most curious was of to know.	Afterwards people went to the wise woman, and then each heard that which they were most curious to know.
Var hún og góð af frásögnum. Gekk það og lítt í tauma er hún sagði.	She was also good of account. Went that also little of reins, that she said.	She gave a good answer. Things went little from the reins of what she had said.
Þessu næst var komið eftir henni af öðrum bæ og fór hún þá þangað.	This next were come after her from another farm and went she then from-there.	Following this, someone came from another farm, and she went from there.

Old Icelandic	Literal	English
Þá var sent eftir Þorbirni því að hann vildi eigi heima vera meðan slík heiðni var framin.	Then was sent after Thorbjorn for that she willed not home be while such heathenry was committed.	Then Thorbjorn was sent for, because she did not want to be home while such heathenry was committed.
Veðrátta batnaði skjótt þegar er vora tók sem Þorbjörg hafði sagt.	Weather bettered shortly, as Thorbjorg had said.	The weather soon bettered, as Thorbjorg had said.
Býr Þorbjörn skip sitt og fer uns hann kemur í Brattahlíð.	Prepared Thorbjorn ship his and travelled there to, that he came to Brattahlid.	Thorbjorn prepared his ship and travelled until he came to Brattahlid.
Tekur Eiríkur við honum báðum höndum og kvað það vel er hann var þar kominn.	Erik took well with him with friendliness and saying that well, that he was there coming.	Erik received him well with friendliness and said how good it was that he had come.
Var Þorbjörn með honum um veturinn og skuldalið hans.	Was Thorbjorn with him about winter and household his.	Thorbjorn was with him over the winter and his household.
Eftir um vorið gaf Eiríkur Þorbirni land á Stokkanesi og var þar ger sæmilegur bær og bjó hann þar síðan.	After about spring gave Erik Thorbjorn land in Stokkanes, and was there made honourable farm, and settled he there since.	After about spring, Erik gave Thorbjorn land in Stokkanes, and there was made an honourable farm, and he settled there since.
5	5	5
Eiríkur átti þá konu er Þjóðhildur hét og við henni tvo sonu.	Erik had then a-wife, was Thjodhild named, and with her two sons.	Erik had then a wife, who was named Thjodhild, and with her two sons.
Hét annar Þorsteinn en annar Leifur.	Was called-one Thorstein, and another Leif.	One was called Thorstein, and another Leif.
Þeir voru báðir efnilegir menn.	They were both promising men.	They were both promising men.
Var Þorsteinn heima með föður sínum og var eigi þá sá maður á Grænlandi er jafn mannvænn þótti sem hann.	Was Thorstein home with father his, and was not so a-man in Greenland, as equally-handsome thought as he.	Thorstein lived at home with his father, and there was no man in Greenland thought as equally handsome as him.
Leifur hafði siglt til Noregs.	Leif had sailed to Norway.	Leif had sailed to Norway.
Var hann þar með Ólafi konungi Tryggvasyni.	Was he there with Olaf king Tryggvason.	He was there with King Olaf Tryggvason.
En er Leifur sigldi af Grænlandi um sumarið urðu þeir sæhafa til Suðureyja.	But when Leif sailed from Greenland about summer, became they sea-scattered to Sudreyar.	But when Leif sailed from Greenland that summer, the ship was driven off course to Sudreyar.
Þaðan byrjaði þeim seint og dvöldust þar lengi um sumarið.	From-there began they late, and dwelled they there long about summer.	From there they began late, and they dwelled their a long time through the summer.

The Vinland Sagas   *The Saga of Erik the Red (Old Icelandic)*

Old Icelandic	Literal	English
Leifur lagði hug á konu þá er Þórgunna hét.	Leif laid thoughts to woman there was Thorgun called.	Leif fell in love with a woman there who was named Thorgun.
Hún var kona ættstór.	She was woman noble.	She was a noble woman.
Það sá Leifur að hún mundi kunna fleira en fátt eitt.	That saw Leif that she would-be knowing more than few alone.	Leif understood that she knew much.
En er Leifur sigldi á brott beiddist Þórgunna að fara með honum.	When was Leif prepared away, asked Thorgun to travel with him.	When Leif was preparing to leave, Thorgun asked to travel with him.
Leifur spurði hvort það væri nokkuð vilji frænda hennar.	Leif asked, if that was something wished kinsmen hers.	Leif asked if that was something her kinsmen would agree to.
Hún kveðst ekki að því fara.	She said that not consider.	She said that she did not care.
Leifur kveðst eigi kunna að gera hertekna svo stórættaða konu í ókunnu landi "en vér liðfáir".	Leif said not that know-how to make captive such noble woman in unknown land, - "as we-are few".	Leif said that he did not know how make a captive such a noble woman in an unknown land - "as we have few troops".
Þórgunna mælti: "Eigi er víst að þér þyki því betur ráðið".	Thorgun spoke: "Not is certain, that to-you seems therefore better decision".	Thorgun spoke: "I am not sure there is for you a better choice".
"Á það mun eg hætta", sagði Leifur.	"At that should I though stop", said Leif.	"I will stop at that", said Leif.
"Þá segi eg þér", sagði Þórgunna, "að eg fer eigi ein saman og mun eg vera með barni og segi eg það af þínum völdum.	"Then say I to-you", said Thorgun, "That I travel not alone together and should I be with child and say I that of your doing.	"Then I say to you", said Thorgun, "That I travel not alone, and I am with child, and I say that this is your doing.
Þess get eg og að eg muni svein fæða þá er þar kemur til.	This guess I also that I shall boy bear then is there coming to.	And I also guess that I shall give birth to a boy coming.
En þóttú viljir öngvan gaum að gefa þá mun eg upp fæða sveininn og þér senda til Grænlands þegar fara má með öðrum mönnum.	But though will-you no heed of give, then shall I up feed boy and to-you send to Greenland, when travel may with other people.	But though you will not heed him, I shall bring the boy up and send him to you in Greenland, when he may travel with other people.
En eg get að þér verði að þvílíkum nytjum sonareignin við mér sem nú verður skilnaður okkar til.	But I guess, that you will-be as for-like use son's-property as now worth parting ours to.	But I guess that he will serve you as well as you have served me with your departure.
En koma ætla eg mér til Grænlands áður en lýkur".	But come intend I myself to Greenland, before it-ends".	But I intend to come to Greenland myself, before it all ends".

Old Icelandic	Literal	English
Hann gaf henni fingurgull og möttul grænlenskan og tannbelti.	Leif gave her finger-gold and mantle Greenland-skin and tusk-belt.	He gave her gold for her finger and a mantle of Greenland-skin and a belt with ivory.
Þessi sveinn kom til Grænlands og nefndist Þorgils.	This boy came to Greenland and named Thorgils.	The boy came to Greenland and was named Thorgils.
Leifur tók við honum að faðerni.	Leif took with him to paternity.	Leif recognised him as his son.
Og er það sumra manna sögn að þessi Þorgils kæmi til Íslands fyrir Fróðárundur um sumarið.	And was that summer people said, that this Thorgils had come to Iceland before hauntings about summer.	And that summer people said that Thorgils had come to Iceland before the hauntings in summer.
En sjá Þorgils var síðan á Grænlandi og þótti enn eigi kynjalaust um verða áður lauk.	Then seen Thorgils was since in Greenland, and thought there yet not extraordinary about him to-be, before end.	Then Thorgils was seen afterwards in Greenland, and it was thought that there was something unusual about him before it ended.
Þeir Leifur sigldu í brott úr Suðureyjum og tóku Noreg um haustið.	There Leif sailed away from Sudreyar and took-to Norway about autumn.	There Leif sailed away from Sudreyar and took to land in Norway about autumn.
Réðst Leifur til hirðar Ólafs konungs Tryggvasonar og lagði konungur á hann góða virðing og þóttist sjá að Leifur mundi vera vel menntur maður.	Rode Leif to court Olaf king Tryggvason's and laid king to him good honour and thought he-saw that Leif would be well educated man.	Leif rode to the court of King Olaf Tryggvason and had good honour towards him, and thought that he was a well educated man.
Eitt sinn kom konungur að máli við Leif og spyr hann: "Ætlar þú til Grænlands í sumar að sigla?"	Once he came king to speak to Leif and asked he: "Intend you to Greenland in summer to sail?".	One time, the king came to speak to Leif and he asked: "Do you intend to sail to Greenland in summer?".
Leifur svarar: "Það ætla eg ef sá er yðvar vilji".	"That intend I", said Leif, "If that is your will".	"That I do intend", said Leif, "If that is your will".
Konungur svarar: "Eg get að svo muni vel vera.	King answered: "I guess that so shall well be.	The king answered: "I guess that shall be well.
Skaltu fara með erindum mínum að boða kristni á Grænlandi".	Shall-you travel with errand mine to preach Christianity to Greenland".	You shall travel with my purpose of preaching Christianity to Greenland.

The Saga of Erik the Red (Old Icelandic)

Old Icelandic	Literal	English
Leifur kvað hann ráða mundu en kveðst hyggja að það erindi mundi torflutt á Grænlandi en konungur kveðst eigi þann mann sjá er betur væri til þess fallinn en hann "og muntu giftu til bera".	Leif said he decide should but said thought it that errand would difficult-be in Greenland but king said none then man seen was better would-be to this fall than he "and should luck towards carry".	Leif said that the king should decide that, but that he thought the errand would be difficult in Greenland. The king said there was no one better for the task to fall to than him, "and luck shall carry you towards".
"Það mun því að eins", kvað Leifur, "að eg njóti yðvar við".	"That should therefore by likewise", said Leif, "If I benefit yours with".	"That it should be", said Leif, "if I travel with your luck also".
Leifur lét í haf þegar hann var búinn.	Leif put to sea when he was ready.	Leif put to sea when he was ready.
Leif velkti lengi úti og hitti hann á lönd þau er hann vissi áður öngva von í.	Leif drove long about and met he to lands those that he knew before none looked to.	Leif was driven about for a long time and met lands that he knew none had looked upon.
Voru þar hveitiakrar sjálfsánir og vínviður vaxinn.	Were there wheat-acres self-sowing and vine-trees growing.	There were acres of wheat that were self-sowing, and vine trees growing.
Þar voru og þau tré er mösur hétu og höfðu þeir af öllu þessu nokkur merki, sum tré svo mikil að í hús voru lögð.	There were there trees, were maple called, and had they from this all some imprint, some trees so great, that to houses were laid.	There were trees there known as burl, and they took some specimens of all of them, and some trees were so large that houses could be laid in them.
Leifur fann menn á skipflaki og flutti heim með sér og fékk öllum vist um veturinn.	Leif found people on shipwreck and brought home with him, and got all provisions about winter.	Leif found people on a shipwreck and brought them home with him, and gave them shelter and provisions over the winter.
Sýndi hann svo mikla stórmennsku og gæsku af sér.	Showed he so much greatness and goodness of him.	He showed so much greatness and goodness of himself.
Hann kom kristni á landið og hann bjargaði mönnunum.	He came Christianity to land and he saved people.	He brought Christianity to the land and saved people.
Var hann kallaður Leifur hinn heppni.	Was he called Leif the Lucky.	He was called Leif the Lucky.
Leifur tók land í Eiríksfirði og fer heim í Brattahlíð.	Leif took land in Eriksfjord and went home afterwards to Brattahlid.	Leif took land in Eriksfjord and went home afterwards to Brattahlid.
Tóku menn vel við honum.	Took there all people well with him.	People there all received him warmly.

The Vinland Sagas — *The Saga of Erik the Red (Old Icelandic)*

Old Icelandic	Literal	English
Hann boðaði brátt kristni um landið og almennilega trú og sýndi mönnum orðsendingar Ólafs konungs Tryggvasonar og sagði hversu mörg ágæti og mikil dýrð þessum sið fylgdi.	He preached soon Christianity about land and properly faith and showed people message Olaf king Tryggvason's and said, how much excellent and great glory followed this tradition.	He soon preached the faith of Christianity throughout the land and showed people the message that King Olaf Tryggvason who said how much excellence and glory followed this tradition.
Eiríkur tók því máli seint að láta sið sinn en Þjóðhildur gekk skjótt undir og lét gera kirkju eigi allnær húsunum.	Erik took since matter late, to leave tradition his, but Thjodhild went quickly behind and had made church not all-near the-house.	Erik was reluctant to take to it and leave his tradition, but Thjodhild was quick to follow and had a church made a distance away from the house.
Var það hús kallað Þjóðhildarkirkja.	Was that house called Thjodhildkirkja.	That house was called Thjodhildakirkja.
hafði hún þar fram bænir sínar og þeir menn sem við kristni tóku en þeir voru margir.	Had she there from prayers hers and they people since with Christianity took that there were many.	She held her prayers there, and with people who had since converted to Christianity, of which there were many.
Þjóðhildur vildi ekki halda samfarar við Eirík síðan er hún tók trú en honum var það mjög í móti skapi.	Thjodhild willed not intercourse with Erik, since she took faith, but he was that much against mood.	Thjodhild did not want to have intercourse with Erik since she had taken the faith, which went very much against his mood.
Af þessu gerðist orð mikið að menn mundu leita lands þess er Leifur hafði fundið.	Then therefore made words much, to people would search lands these, that Leif had found.	Then there were many words about people searching these lands that Leif had found.
Var þar formaður Þorsteinn Eiríksson, góður maður og fróður og vinsæll.	Was there chief to Thorstein Eriksson, good man and wise and popular.	Chief among them was Thorstein Eriksson, a good man, and a wise and popular man.
Eiríkur var og til beðinn og trúðu menn því að hans gæfa mundi framast vera og forsjá.	Erik was and to asked, and believed people his gifted foremost and foresight.	Erik was also asked, and people believed he was gifted and a man of foresight.
Hann var þá fyrir en kvað eigi nei við er vinir hans fýstu hann til.	He was then before that saying not no with when friends his urged him to.	He had been saying that he would not go, but his friends urged him to.
Bjuggu þeir skip það síðan er Þorbjörn hafði út haft og voru til ráðnir tuttugu menn.	Prepared they ship that since which Thorbjorn had out had and was to appointed twenty people.	There was a ship prepared, the one which Thorbjorn had sailed out on, and twenty men were hired.
Höfðu þeir fé lítið en meir vopn og vistir.	Had they cattle little but more weapons and provisions.	They had a little cattle, but more weapons and provisions.

Old Icelandic	Literal	English
Þann morgun er Eiríkur fór heiman tók hann kistil og var þar í gull og silfur.	That morning, was Erik riding home, took he one chest, and was there of gold and silver.	That morning, Erik was rode home, he took a chest, and therein was gold and silver.
Fal hann það fé og fór síðan leiðar sinnar.	Hid he that wealth and went afterwards way his.	He hid that and then travelled away afterwards.
Og er hann var skammt á leið kominn féll hann af baki og braut rif sín og lesti öxl sína og kvað við: "Ái, ái".	And when he was shortly on the-way coming fell he from back and broke ribs his and gripped shoulder his and said with: "Ai ái".	And when he had come a short distance, he fell back from the horse, and broke his ribs, and gripped his hand to his shoulder: "Ai! Ai!"
Af þessum atburð sendi hann konu sinni orð, að hún tæki féið á brott það er hann hafði fólgið, lét þess hafa að goldið er hann hafði féið fólgið.	Of these events said he Thjodhild, wife his, that she take treasure to away, should this have of gold, that he had wealth hidden.	He said to his wife Thjodhild what had happened, and asked her to take the treasure hidden away, and have this gold that he had hidden.
Síðan sigldu þeir út úr Eiríksfirði með gleði og þótti vænt um sitt ráð.	Since sailed they out from Eriksfjord with gladness and thought expected about their advice.	Afterwards they sailed out of Eriksfjord with much gladness. They thought expectantly about their prospects.
Þá velkti lengi úti í hafi og komu ekki á þær slóðir sem þeir vildu.	Then drove about long at sea, and came they not to those routes, which they willed.	Then they were driven about at sea for a long time, and did not come to those routes which they had wished.
Þeir komu í sýn við Ísland og svo höfðu þeir fugl af Írlandi.	They came it seemed to Iceland, and so had they birds of Ireland.	They came in sight of what seemed like Iceland they had birds of Ireland.
Reiddi þá skip þeirra um haf innan, fóru aftur um haustið og voru mæddir og mjög þrekaðir og komu við vetur sjálfan á Eiríksfjörð.	Driven then ship theirs about sea within, travelled back about autumn and were all-very worn and exhausted, came in winter itself to Eriksfjord.	Their ship was driven about the sea, and they travelled back about autumn, and all were very weary and exhausted, as winter was coming to Eriksfjord.
Þá mælti Eiríkur: "Kátari voruð þér í sumar er þér fóruð út úr firðinum en nú erum vér og eru nú þó mörg góð að".	Then said Erik: "Merrier sailed we this summer out from fjord than now are we, and are now though still many good to".	Then Erik said: "We sailed more merrily in the summer out of this fjord than we now return to it, but there is still much good".
Þorsteinn mælti: "Það er nú höfðinglegt bragð að sjá nokkuð ráð fyrir þeim mönnum sem nú eru ráðlausir og fá þeim vistir".	Thorstein answered: "That is now having-like solution to see some good proposal for those people all, which here are now disposed, and get they provisions to winter".	Thorstein answered: "Now we should propose that these people here are given provisions for the winter".

The Vinland Sagas — *The Saga of Erik the Red (Old Icelandic)*

Old Icelandic	Literal	English
Eiríkur svarar: "Skal þín orð um þetta fara".	Erik answered: "Shall your words about this go".	Erik answered: "Your words about this shall travel".
Fóru nú allir þeir er eigi höfðu áður vistir með þeim feðgum.	Went now all they, who not had other supplies, with they father-and-son.	All those who had no provisions with the father and son.
Síðan tóku þeir land og fóru heim.	Afterwards took they land and travelled home.	Afterwards they took land and travelled home.
6	6	6
Nú er frá því að segja að Þorsteinn Eiríksson vakti bónorð við Guðríði Þorbjarnardóttur.	Now is from accordingly to say that Thorstein Eriksson awoke proposal to Guthrid Thorbjornadottir.	Now following this is to say that Thorstein Eriksson brought up a marriage proposal to Gudrid Thorbjornadottir.
Var því máli vel svarað bæði af henni og svo af föður hennar og er þetta að ráðum gert að Þorsteinn gekk að eiga Guðríði og var brúðkaupið í Brattahlíð um haustið.	Was accordingly the-matter well answered both from her and so of father hers and was that the advice done that Thorstein went to marry Guthrid and was the-wedding in Brattahlid about autumn.	Accordingly the matter was well answered by both her and her father, and that which was planned was done, that Thorstein went to marry Gudrid and the wedding was in Brattahlid around autumn.
Fór sú veisla vel fram og var mjög fjölmenn.	Went seen the-feast well from, and were many-people.	The feast was well witnessed, and there were many people there.
Þorsteinn átti bú í Vestribyggð á bæ þeim er í Lýsufirði heitir.	Thorstein had a-farm in Vestribyggd in town theirs, was named it Lysufjord.	Thorstein had a farm in the Western Settlement in the worn, which was named Lysufjord.
Sá maður átti þar helming í búi er Þorsteinn hét.	But so a-man had there half a farm, was Thorstein called.	There was a man there that had a half share of a farm, who was named Thorstein.
Sigríður hét kona hans.	Sigrid was-called wife his.	His wife was named Sigrid.
Fóru þau Þorsteinn heim í Lýsufjörð og Guðríður bæði.	Went Thorstein to Lysufjord about autumn to namesake his and they Guthrid both.	They went to Lysufjord around autumn to both his namesake and Gudrid.
Var þar vel við þeim tekið.	Were there with them well taken.	They were well received by them.
Voru þau þar um veturinn.	Were they there about winter.	They were there around winter.
Það gerðist þar til tíðinda að sótt kom í bæ þeirra er lítið var af vetri.	That happened until news, that sickness came among settlement theirs, that little was from winter.	Then came the news, that sickness came among their settlement, shortly after the beginning of winter.

Old Icelandic	Literal	English
Garði hét þar verkstjóri.	Gardi was-called there a-foreman.	There was a foreman there who was named Gardi.
Hann var óvinsæll maður.	He was not popular a-man.	He was not a popular man.
Hann tók fyrst sótt og andaðist.	He took first sickness and died.	He was the first to become ill, and he died.
Síðan var skammt að bíða að hver tók sótt að öðrum og önduðust.	Since was short to wait, that each died the others.	It was not long after that, that each of the others died.
Þá tók sótt Þorsteinn Eiríksson og Sigríður kona Þorsteins.	Then took sickness Thorstein Eriksson and Sigrid, wife Thorstein's, namesake his.	Then the sickness took Thorstein Eriksson, and his namesake's wife Sigrid.
Og eitt kveld fýsist hún að ganga til garðs þess er stóð í gegnt útidyrum.	And one evening desired Sigrid to go to outhouse, which stood about opposite the-out-door.	And one evening, Sigrid wanted to go to the outhouse, which stood opposite the farmhouse door.
Guðríður fylgdi og sóttu þær í mót dyrunum.	Guthrid followed her, and looked they towards the-out-door.	Gudrid followed her, and they looked towards the farmhouse door.
Þá kvað Sigríður: "Ó".	Then cried-out she with loud, Sigrid "Oh!".	Then Sigrid cried out loudly "Oh!".
Guðríður mælti: "Við höfum farið óhyggilega og áttu öngvan stað við að kalt veður komi á og förum inn sem skjótast".	Guthrid said: "We have unwisely gone, and have-you none stand with, that cold comes to you, and go into home then quickly".	Gudrid said: "We have acted carelessly, you should not stand in the cold, and we must go inside quickly".
Sigríður svarar: "Eigi fer eg að svo búnu.	Sigrid answered: "Not am-i going-out as so are.	Sigrid answered: "I won't go out with things as they are.
Hér er liðið allt hið dauða fyrir dyrunum og þar í sveit kenni eg Þorstein bónda þinn og kenni eg mig og er slíkt hörmung að sjá".	Here is now company that all to death before the-door and Thorstein, husband yours, and there recognise I me. And is such horrible to see".	Here are now all the companions that died standing there before the door, and Thorstein your husband, and there I recognise myself. And it is such a horrible thing to see".
Og er þetta leið af mælti hún: "Förum við nú Guðríður.	And when that passed out-of, spoke she: "Gone known now, Guthrid.	And when it had passed, she spoke: "They are gone now Gudrid".
Nú sé ég eigi liðið".	Now see I not company".	Now I don't see those companions".

Old Icelandic	Literal	English
Var þá og verkstjórinn horfinn er henni þótti áður hafa svipu í hendi og vilja berja liðið.	Was then also the-foreman disappeared that she thought returned had whip in hand and willing to-bear-to company.	It was then that the foreman had disappeared. She thought he had returned with a whip in hand ready and willing to strike those companions.
Síðan gengu þær inn og áður morgunn kæmi var hún önduð og var ger kista að líkinu.	Afterwards went they in, and before morning came, then was she dead, and was made coffin for body.	Afterwards they went inside, and before the morning came, she was dead, and a coffin was made for her body.
Og þann sama dag ætluðu menn út að róa og leiddi Þorsteinn þá til vara og í annan lit fór hann að sjá um veiðiskap þeirra.	And then same day intended people out to row and led Thorstein they to wares and to accompany the-team went he to see about fishing there.	And then that same day people intended to row and go fishing, and they led Thorstein to where the goods were kept, and he went to see how the fishing was going.
Þá sendi Þorsteinn Eiríksson nafna sínum orð að hann kæmi til hans og sagði svo að þar var varla kyrrt og húsfreyja vildi færast á fætur og vildi undir klæðin hjá honum.	Then sent Thorstein Eriksson namesake his word, that he come to him, and said such, that there was hardly peace and housewife willed move to feet and willing under bedclothes by him.	Then Thorstein Eriksson sent his namesake his word to come to him, and said that there was no peace at home and his housewife was trying to rise up and get into bed with him.
Og er hann kom inn var hún komin á rekkjustokkinn hjá honum.	And when he came in, was she coming up to sideboards.	And when he came in, she had reached the sideboards of the bed.
Hann tók hana höndum og lagði bolöxi fyrir brjóstið.	Then took he her hand and laid a-pole-axe for breast hers.	Then he took her hand and drove an axe into her breast.
Þorsteinn Eiríksson andaðist nær dagsetri.	Thorstein Eriksson died near day-setting.	Thorstein Eriksson died close to sunset.
Þorsteinn bað Guðríði leggjast niður og sofa en hann kveðst vaka mundu um nóttina yfir líkunum.	Thorstein farmer asked Guthrid ti-lie down and sleep, and he said awake would-be about night over the-bodies.	Thorstein the Farmer told Gudrid to lie down and sleep, and he said that he would keep watch over the bodies.
Hún gerir svo.	She did so.	She did so.

The Saga of Erik the Red (Old Icelandic)

Old Icelandic	Literal	English
Guðríður sofnar brátt og er skammt leið á nóttina reistist hann upp Þorsteinn og kveðst vilja að Guðríður væri þangað kölluð og kveðst vilja mæla við hana: "Guð vill að þessi stund sé mér gefin til leyfis og umbóta míns ráðs".	Guthrid slept soon, and that short way in night, sat Thorstein Eriksson up and spoke, saying willed, that Guthrid was there called, and saying he-willed to-speak with her: "God wills, that this time so me given to leave and offer my plans".	Gudrid soon slept, and a short way into the night, Thorstein Eriksson sat up and spoke, saying that he wished for Gudrid to be called, as he willed to speak with her. "God wills that this time has been given to me to better my prospects".
Þorsteinn gengur á fund Guðríðar og vakti hana og bað hana signa sig og biðja sér guð hjálpa "Þorsteinn Eiríksson hefur mælt við mig að hann vill finna þig.	Thorstein went to find Guthrid and woke her and asked her to sign-herself and ask herself God's help, "Thorstein Eriksson had said to me that he wills find you.	Thorstein the Farmer went to find Gudrid and woke her, asking her to sign herself with the cross, and to ask for God's help, "Thorstein Eriksson has said to me that he wishes to meet you.
Sjá þú nú ráð fyrir, hvorgis kann eg fýsa".	See you now obliged for, neither know I desire".	Are you obliged to see what you will learn from this?, for I will not advise you either way".
Hún svarar: "Vera kann að þetta sé ætlað til nokkurra hluta þeirra sem síðan eru í minni hafðir, þessi hinn undarlegi hlutur, en eg vænti að guðs gæsla mun yfir mér standa.	She answered: "Be it possible that this intends to something part there which afterwards are to mine have, this the strange lot, but I expect that God's herding shall over me stand.	She answered: "Could it possibly be that there is some purpose to this, which afterwards will have consequences for me, this strange occurrence, but I hope that God will shepherd over me".
Mun eg á hætta með guðs miskunn að mæla við hann því að eg má nú ekki forðast mein til mín.	Should I to danger with God's mercy to speak with him because that I may now not avoid harm to mine.	I will to chance, with God's mercy, to speak with him, because I may not escape any threat to myself.
Vil eg síður að hann gangi víðara.	Will I less that he go far-and-wide.	I do not wish for him to have to go further and wider.
En mig grunar að það sé að öðrum kosti".	But I suspect that it so to other choice".	And I suspect that it would be the alternative choice".

The Vinland Sagas — *The Saga of Erik the Red (Old Icelandic)*

Old Icelandic	Literal	English
Nú fór Guðríður og hitti Þorstein og sýndist henni sem hann felldi tár og mælti í eyra henni nokkur orð hljótt svo að hún ein vissi og sagði að þeir menn væru sælir er trúna héldu vel og henni fylgdi miskunn og hjálp og sagði þó að margir héldu hana illa "er það engi háttur sem hér hefir verið á Grænlandi síðan kristni var hér að setja menn niður í óvígða mold við litla yfirsöngva.	Now came Guthrid and met Thorstein and seemed to-her that he shed tears and spoke in ear hers some words quietly so that she alone knew and said that they people were happy that faith held well and he followed mercy and help and said though that many held he badly "Is that no way which here has been in Greenland after Christianity was here to set people down among unconsecrated ground with little burial-service.	Now Gudrid came and met Thorstein. It seemed to her that he had shed tears. He spoke some words in her ear quietly, so that she alone knew, and he said that those men who had kept their faith well rejoiced as it brought them mercy and salvation, but he said that some had kept their faith badly though. "It is no way to set people down among unconsecrated dust with little burial service, which people have done here in Greenland since Christianity came here.
Vil eg mig láta flytja til kirkju og aðra þá menn sem hér hafa andast en Garða vil eg láta brenna á báli sem skjótast því að hann veldur öllum afturgöngum sem hér hafa orðið í vetur.	Will I me laid carried to church and others they people, which here have died, but Gardar will I burn let to fire that quickly, because that he caused all hauntings those, which here have been in winter".	I wish that I be carried to church, along with the other people who have died here, but Gardi should be burned on a pyre straight away, because he caused all those hauntings which were here in winter".
Hann sagði henni og um sína hagi og kvað hennar forlög mikil mundu verða en hann bað hana varast að giftast grænlenskum manni.	He told her and about his state and said her fortune great would be but he asked that avoid to marry Greenlander men.	He told her about his situation and said that her fortune would be great, but warned her against marrying a Greenlander.
Bað hann og að hún legði fé þeirra til kirkju eða gefa það fátækum mönnum.	Asked he also that she lay wealth theirs to church or give that-to poor people.	He also asked that she donate their wealth to the church, and to the poor.
Og þá hneig hann aftur í öðru.	And then knee he back second his.	And then he sank back down for the second time.
Sá hafði háttur verið á Grænlandi síðan kristni kom út þangað að menn voru grafnir þar á bæjum, er menn önduðust, í óvígðri moldu.	So had the-way been in Greenland, since Christianity came there, that people were buried in farms, there which died, in unconsecrated ground.	So had been the way in Greenland, since Christianity arrived there, that people were buried in farms where they died in unconsecrated ground.

The Vinland Sagas   *The Saga of Erik the Red (Old Icelandic)*

Old Icelandic	Literal	English
Skyldi setja staur upp af brjósti en síðan er kennimenn komu til þá skyldi kippa upp staurnum og hella þar í vígðu vatni og veita þar yfirsöngva þótt það væri miklu síðar.	As-should-be set poles up on breast in the-dead, then after, a priest came to, then should-be up pulled poles and flat-stones there among ground water and supplied there burial-service, though that was much later.	A pole was set up on the breast of each corpse, then afterwards there came a priest, then the poles were pulled up, and flat stones placed on the ground, and consecrated water poured into the hole with a burial service, even though this was done much later.
Líkin voru færð til kirkju í Eiríksfjörð og veittir yfirsöngvar af kennimönnum.	Body was taken to church in Eriksfjord and supplied burial-service from priests.	The body was taken to church in Eriksfjord and priests held burial services.
Eftir það andaðist Þorbjörn. Bar þá féið allt undir Guðríði.	After that died Thorbjorn. Bore then wealth all up-to Guthrid.	After that Thorbjorn died. All of his wealth was given up to Gudrid.
Tók Eiríkur við henni og sá vel um kost hennar.	Took Erik with her and saw well about costs hers.	Erik invited her to live with him and saw that she was well provided for.
7	7	7
Maður hét Þorfinnur karlsefni, son Þórðar hesthöfða, er bjó norður í Reyninesi í Skagafirði er nú er kallað.	A-man was-called Thorfin Karlsefni, son-of-Thord Horse-Head, who lived north in Reynines in Skagafjord as now is called.	There was a man called Thorfin Karlsefni, the son of Thord Horse-Head, who lived in the north in Reynines in Skagafjord, as it is now called.
Karlsefni var ættgóður maður og auðigur að fé.	Karlsefni was family-good man and wealthy in cattle.	Karlsefni was a man of good family and was wealthy in cattle.
Þórunn hét móðir hans. Hann var í kaupferðum og þótti fardrengur góður.	Thorun was-called mother his. He was on trading-journeys and thought travelling-companion good.	His mother was called Thorun. He went on trading journeys and was thought of as a good travelling companion.
Eitt sumar býr Karlsefni skip sitt og ætlaði til Grænlands.	One summer prepared Karlsefni ship his and intended to Greenland.	One summer Karlsefni intended to go to Greenland and prepared his ship.
Réðst til ferðar með honum Snorri Þorbrandsson úr Álftafirði og voru fjórir tigir manna með þeim.	Rode to travel with him Snorri Thorbrandson from Alftafjord and was four tens men with them.	Shorri Thorbrandson rode with him from Alftafjord and there were forty men with them.

Old Icelandic	Literal	English
Maður hét Bjarni Grímólfsson, breiðfirskur maður.	A-man was-called Bjarni Grimolfson, Breidafjord man.	There was a man called Bjarni Grimolfson, a man from Breidafjord.
Annar hét Þórhallur Gamlason, austfirskur maður.	Another was-called Thorhall Gamlason, east-fjords man.	Another was called Thorhall Gamlason, a man from the East Fjords.
Þeir bjuggu skip sitt samsumars sem Karlsefni og ætluðu til Grænlands.	There prepared ship theirs same-summer as Karlsefni and intended to Greenland.	There they prepared their ship that summer as Karlsefni intended to go to Greenland.
Þeir voru á skipi fjórir tigir manna.	They were to ship four tens men.	There were forty men on the ship.
Láta þeir í haf fram tvennum skipum þegar þeir eru búnir.	Had they to sea from two ships when they were ready.	They had the two ships put to sea as soon as they were ready.
Eigi var um það getið hversu langa útivist þeir höfðu, en frá því er að segja að bæði þessi skip komu í Eríksfjörð um haustið.	Not is about that told-of, how long out-journey they had, but from since was to say, that both these ships came to Eriksfjord about autumn.	Not much was said about how long a journey they had, but since was said that both these ships came to Eriksfjord about autumn.
Eiríkur reið til skips og aðrir landsmenn og tókst með þeim greiðleg kaupstefna.	Erik rode to ships and other landsmen and took with them promptly trading-posts.	Erik rode to the ships along with other men of the land, and they promptly took trading posts with them.
Buðu stýrimenn Eiríki að hafa slíkt af varninginum sem hann vildi.	Invited steersmen Erik to have such of wares that he willed.	The captains invited Erik to have whatever goods he wanted.
En Eiríkur sýni mikla stórmennsku af sér í móti því að hann bauð þessum skipverjunum báðum heim til sín til veturvistar í Brattahlíð.	Then Erik showed them great-man-ness of him among towards, for that he invited these two ships-ports to his home about winter to Brattahlid.	Erik then showed them great generosity, as he invited these two ships to his home for the winter at Brattahlid.
Þetta þágu kaupmenn og fóru með Eiríki.	This accepted trading-men and went with Erik.	The traders accepted this and travelled with Erik.
Síðan var fluttur heim varningur þeirra í Brattahlíð.	Then were transported home goods theirs to Brattahlid.	Later their goods were transported to Brattahlid.
Skorti þar eigi góð og stór útibúr að varðveita í.	Shortage there was-not good and great out-house of supplies to.	There was no shortage of good and large outhouses for their goods.
Líkaði kaupmönnum vel með Eiríki um veturinn.	Liked trading-men well with Erik about winter.	The traders very much enjoyed their winter with Erik.

The Saga of Erik the Red (Old Icelandic)

Old Icelandic	Literal	English
En er dró að jólum tók Eiríkur að verða óglaðari en hann átti vanda til.	But as drew to Yule, took Erik sadness much and was without-gladness that he had custom to.	But as it drew closer to Yule, Erik became sad and was without the cheerfulness that he usually had.
Eitt sinn kom Karlsefni að máli við Eirík og mælti: "Er þér þungt Eiríkur? Eg þykist finna að þú ert nokkuru fálátari en verið hefir, og þú veitir oss með mikilli rausn og erum vér skyldir að launa þér eftir því sem vér höfum föng á.	Along then came Karlsefni to speak with Erik and said: "Are you unhappy Erik I think find that you are somewhat withdrawn that been have, and you gave us with much generosity and are we obliged to repay you after because that we have possessions of.	Then along came Karlsefni to talk to Erik and said: "Are you unhappy, Erik the farmer? People seem to find that you are unhappier than usual. You have provided for us most generously, and we are obliged to repay you as best we can with everything we have.
Nú segðu hvað ógleði þinni veldur".	Now say, what sadness yours brought-about".	Now tell me, what is it that makes you sad?".
Eiríkur svarar: "Þér þiggið vel og góðmannlega.	Erik answered: "You accepted well and good-man-like.	Erik answered: "You have accepted with gratitude and respect.
Nú leikur mér það eigi í hug að á yður hallist um vor viðskipti.	Now like I that not in mind, that for you have-been inclined about what-was exchanged.	To my mind, you have not been lacking in our exchanges.
Hitt er heldur að mér þykir illt ef að er spurt að þér hafið engi jól verri haft en þessi er nú koma í hönd".	I find it rather ill if that are asked of you, have none Yule worse had than this is now coming in hand".	I find it rather bad, if you are asked, that you will have had no Yule worse than this one now approaching".
Karlsefni svarar: "Það mun ekki á þá leið.	Karlsefni answered: "That shall not so go".	Karlsefni answered: "It shall not be that way".
Vér höfum á skipum vorum malt og mjöl og korn og er yður heimilt að hafa af slíkt sem þér viljið og gerið veislu slíka sem stórmennsku ber til".	"We have in ships ours both malt and corn, have there of such that you will and make feast such great-man-ness as you like for according".	"We have malt and flour and grain aboard our ships, and you will have whatever you wish to make such a great feast according to your generosity".
Og það þiggur hann.	And that accepted he.	And he accepted this.
Var þá búið til jólaveislu og varð hún svo skörugleg að menn þóttust trautt slíka rausnarveislu séð hafa.	Were then preparations until Yule-feast and was it so honourable that people thought scarcely such generosity seen had.	There were then preparations for the Yule feast, and it was so honourable, and people thought that they had scarcely seen such generosity.

Old Icelandic	Literal	English
Og eftir jólin vekur Karlsefni við Eirík um ráðahag við Guðríði er honum leist sem það mundi á hans forræði en honum leist kona fríð og vel kunnandi.	And after Yule awoke Karlsefni to Erik about marriage-proposal to Guthrid was he impression that it could by him power and he liked woman peaceful and well knowing.	And after Yule, Karlsefni brought up a marriage proposal to Erik about Gudrid, as he was under the impression that he had protection of her, and peaceful and knowledgeable.
Eiríkur svarar, kveðst vel mundu undir taka hans mál en kvað hana góðs gjaforð verða "er það og líklegt að hún fylgi sínum forlögum" þó að hún væri honum gefin og kvað góða frétt af honum koma.	Erik answered, saying well would up-to take his matter then said he good given was "Is that also likely to her follow her fortune" though that she would him marry and said good news of him came.	Erik answered, saying that he would support him in this matter, and said that it was a good match, and said "It is also likely that she will follow her fortune" if she did marry him, and said that there came good news of him.
Nú er vakið mál við hana og lét hún það sitt ráð sem Eiríkur vildi fyrir sjá.	Now was awoken the-matter with her and allowed she that his advice which Erik wished for seen.	Now the matter was brought up with her, and she allowed herself to be guided by Erik's advice.
Og er nú ekki að lengja um það að þessi ráð tókust og var þá veisla aukin og gert brullaup.	And was now not that long about that of this advice took and was then the-feast increased and made wedding.	It was not long after this advice was taken that the feast increased and the wedding was made.
Gleði mikið var í Brattahlíð um veturinn.	Gladness much was in Brattahlid about winter.	There was much gladness in Brattahlid over the winter.
8	8	8
Á því léku miklar umræður um veturinn í Brattahlíð að þar voru mjög töfl uppi höfð og sagnaskemmtan og margt það er til híbýlabótar mátti vera.	Then since played much discussion about winter in Brattahlid that there were many table-games up taken and short-stories and many that were to living-space that-might be.	Then there played out much discussion over the winter in Brattahlid, and there were many table games set up and short stories, and many things that might be done to improve living space.
Ætluðu þeir Karlsefni og Snorri að leita Vínlands og töluðu menn margt um það.	Intended there Karlsefni and Snorri to seek Vinland and talked people many about that.	Karlsefni and Snorri intended to seek Vinland and many people talked about it.
En því lauk svo að þeir Karlsefni og Snorri bjuggu skip sitt og ætluðu að leita Vínlands um sumarið.	Then therefore concluded so that they Karlsefni and Snorri prepared ship theirs and intended to seek Vinland about summer.	Then it was settled that Karlsefni and Snorri prepared their ship and intended to seek Vinland during the summer.

The Saga of Erik the Red (Old Icelandic)

Old Icelandic	Literal	English
Til þeirrar ferðar réðust þeir Bjarni og Þórhallur með skip sitt og það föruneyti er þeim hafði fylgt.	To their travel appointed they Bjarni and Thorhall with ship theirs and that companions, that they had followed.	For their voyage, they hired Bjarni and Thorhall with their own ship, and their companions who followed them.
Maður hét Þorvarður.	A-man was-called Thorvard.	There was a man called Thorvard.
Hann átti Freydísi, dóttur Eiríks rauða laungetna.	He married Freydis, daughter Erik the-Red's, illegitimate.	He married Freydis, the illegitimate daughter of Erik the Red.
Hann fór með þeim og Þorvaldur son Eiríks og Þórhallur er var kallaður veiðimaður.	He went also with them and Thorvald, son Erik's, and Thorhall, who called was hunter.	He also travelled with them, along with Thorvald, Erik's son, and Thorhall, who was called the hunter.
Hann hafði lengi verið í veiðiförum með Eiríki um sumrum og hafði hann margar varðveislur.	He had long been to hunting with Erik around summer and had he much guarded.	He had long been hunting with Erik during the summer, and he had many times watched over him.
Þórhallur var mikill vexti, svartur og þurslegur.	Thorhall was large grown, dark and giant.	Thorhall was large grown, dark and giant.
Hann var heldur við aldur, ódæll í skapi, hljóðlyndur, fámálugur hversdaglega, undirförull og þó atmælasamur og fýstist jafnan hins verra.	He was held with age, unruly in mood, quiet, few-words always, scheming and though measured and desired equally the worst.	He was rather with age, unruly in mood, a man of few words, always scheming, usually desired to make trouble.
Hann hafði lítt við trú blandast síðan hún kom á Grænland.	He had little with faith mixed since it came to Greenland.	He had mixed little with the faith since it came to Greenland.
Þórhallur var lítt vinsældum horfinn en þó hafði Eiríkur lengi tal af honum haldið.	Thorhall was little-with popularity disappeared but though had Erik long talked of him staying.	Thorhall was not very popular with those around him, but Erik had long been in his confidence.
Hann var á skipi með þeim Þorvaldi því að honum var víða kunnigt í óbyggðum.	He was in ship with them Thorvald because that he was widely known to unsettled-land.	He was in the ship with Thorvald because he knew widely the unsettled land.
Þeir höfðu það skip er Þorbjörn hafði út þangað og réðust til ferðar með þeim Karlsefni og voru þar flestir grænlenskir menn á.	They had the ship that Thorbjorn had back there and appointed to travel with them Karlsefni and were there mostly Greenlander men on.	They had the ship that Thorbjorn had brought back there and Karlsefni hired people to travel with them, and they were mostly men from Greenland.
Á skipum þeirra voru fjórir tigir manna annars hundraðs.	On the-ship there were four tens men also hundred.	There were a hundred and forty men on their ships.
Sigldu þeir undan síðan til Vestribyggðar og til Bjarneyja.	Sailed they away since to Vestribyggd and to Bjarney.	They sailed away afterwards to the Western Settlement and to Bjarney.

Old Icelandic	Literal	English
Sigldu þeir þaðan undan Bjarneyjum norðan veður.	Sailed they from-there away-from Bjarney north winds.	They sailed away from Bjarney with the north winds.
Voru þeir úti tvö dægur.	Were they out two days.	They were out for two days.
Þá fundu þeir land og reru fyrir á bátum og könnuðu landið og fundu þar hellur margar og svo stórar að tveir menn máttu vel spyrnast í iljar.	Then found they land and rowed for in the-boat and explored land and found there slabs many and so large that two people may well touch of feet.	Then they found land and rowed towards in the boat, and explored the land, and found there many slabs, and they were so large that two people could lie across it touching feet.
Melrakkar voru þar margir.	Melrakka were there many.	There were many melrakka.
Þeir gáfu nafn landinu og kölluð Helluland.	They gave name to-the-land and called Helluland.	They gave a name to the land and called it Helluland.
Þá sigldu þeir norðan veður tvö dægur og var þá land fyrir þeim og var á skógur mikill og dýr mörg.	Then sailed they north winds two days and were then land for they and was of forest great and wild-animals many.	Then they sailed with a northerly wind for two days, and they were before land, and it was much forested and with many wild animals.
Ey lá í landsuður undan landinu og fundu þeir þar bjarndýr og kölluðu Bjarney en landið kölluðu þeir Markland.	An-island lay to south-east from land and found they there bear and called Bjarney and land called they Markland.	An island lay to the south east of the lane, and they found a bear there, and called it Bjarney, and called the land Markland.
Þar er skógurinn.	There were forests.	There were forests.
Þá er liðin voru tvö dægur sjá þeir land og þeir sigldu undir landið.	Then the teams were two days saw they land and they sailed near the-land.	Then the crew were sailing for two days when they saw land and sailed close by it.
Þar var nes er þeir komu að.	There was headland that they came to.	There was a headland which they came to.
Þeir beittu með landinu og létu landið á stjórnborða.	They applied with the-land and let land to starboard.	They kept the land to their starboard.
Þar var öræfi og strandir langar og sandar.	There was wilderness and beaches long and sands.	There was wilderness and long beaches and sands.
Fara þeir á bátum til lands og fundu þar á nesinu kjöl af skipi og köllu þar Kjalarnes.	Went they in the-boat to land and found there on the-headland a-keel from a-ship and called they Kjalarnes.	They went in the boat to land and found there on the headland a keel from a ship, and they called there Kjalarnes.
Þeir gáfu og nafn ströndunum og köllu Furðustrandir því að langt var með að sigla.	They called and beaches Furdustrandir, because by long was along to sail.	The called the beaches Furdustrandir because they were long to sail by.
Þá gerðist vogskorið landið og héldu þeir skipunum að vogunum.	Then became creek-indented land and held they ship to inlets.	Then the land became indented with creeks, and they kept their ship in an inlet.

The Saga of Erik the Red

Old Icelandic	Literal	English
Það var þá er Leifur var með Ólafi konungi Tryggvasyni og hann bað hann boða kristni á Grænlandi og þá gaf konungur honum tvo menn skoska.	That was then that Leif was with Olaf king Tryggvason and he asked him to-preach Christianity in Greenland and then gave king to-him two men Scottish.	When Leif was with King Olaf Tryggvason and he had asked him to preach Christianity in Greenland, the king then gave him two Scottish people.
Hét karlmaðurinn Haki en konan Hekja.	Called servants Haki, and woman Hekja.	The servants were called Haki, and a woman Hekja.
Konungur bað Leif taka til þessara manna ef hann þyrfti skjótleiks við því að þau voru dýrum skjótari.	The-king bid Leif take to these people if he needed speed with because that these were wild-animals faster-than.	The king offered Leif to take these people if he needed someone with speed, because they were faster than wild animals.
Þessa menn fengu þeir Leifur og Eiríkur til fylgdar við Karlsefni.	These people gathered they Leif and Erik to follow with Karlsefni.	Leif and Erik sent these people to follow with Karlsefni.
En er þeir höfðu siglt fyrir Furðustrandir þá létu þeir hina skosku menn á land og báðu þau hlaupa í suðurátt og leita landskosta og koma aftur áður þrjú dægur væru liðin.	Then when they had sailed for Furdustrandir, they let they the Scottish people to land and asked them run south of land to seek land-benefits and coming back, before three days would-be passed.	Then when they had sailed along Furdustrandir, the put the Scottish people on land and asked them to run southwards and explore the land and come back before three days were passed.
Þau voru svo búin að þau höfðu það klæði er þau kölluð kjafal.	They were so ready that they had the clothes that they called kjafal.	They were so prepared that they had the clothing that they called a kjafal.
Það var svo gert að hötturinn var á upp og opið að hliðum og engar ermar á og hneppt í milli fóta.	That was so made that hoods were for up and opened at sides and no sleeves of and fastened in between feet.	It was made with a hood at the top, with openings at the sides, and no sleeves, fastened between the feet.
Hélt þar saman hnappur og nesla en ber voru annars staðar.	Held they together fastening and nettle but bare were other places.	It was held together with a button and a loop, they were bare in other places.
Þeir köstuðu akkerum og lágu þar þessa stund.	They cast anchor and lay there this while.	They cast anchor and lay there awhile.
Og er þrír dagar voru liðnir hljópu þau af landi ofan og hafði annað þeirra í hendi vínber en annað hveiti sjálfsáið.	And when three days were passed ran they from land over and had one of-them in hand grapes and another wheat self-sowing.	And when three days were passed, they ran over from the land, and one of them had in hand grapes, and another self-sowing wheat.
Sagði Karlsefni að þau þóttust fundið hafa landskosti góða.	Said Karlsefni that they thought found had land-benefits good.	Karlsefni said that they thought they had found good benefit from the land.

The Vinland Sagas — The Saga of Erik the Red (Old Icelandic)

Old Icelandic	Literal	English
Tóku þeir þau á skip sitt og fóru leiðar sinnar þar til er varð fjarðskorið.	Took they these on ship theirs and travelled route theirs that towards then became fjords-carving.	They took these on their ship and travelled on their way until the land became a carved fjord.
Þeir lögðu skipunum inn á fjörðinn.	They put ship in to fjord.	They put the ship into the fjord.
Þar var ey ein út fyrir og voru þar straumar miklir og um eyna.	There was an-island alone out before and was there a-stream great and about island.	There was an island laying before it, and there were great streams surrounding the island.
Þeir kölluð hana Straumsey.	They called it Straumsey.	They called it Straumsey.
Fugl var þar svo margur að trautt mátti fæti niður koma í milli eggjanna.	Wild-birds were there so many that scarcely may feet down come in between eggs.	There were so many wild birds there that the could scarcely put down their feet between them.
Þeir héldu inn með firðinum og kölluðu hann Straumsfjörð og báru farminn af skipunum og bjuggust þar um.	They held in with fjord and called it Straumsfjord and carried cargo of ship and prepared there about.	They kept in the fjord and called it Straumsfjord, and carried their cargo out of the ship and settled thereabouts.
Þeir höfðu með sér alls konar fé og leituðu sér þar landsnytja.	They had with them all kinds cattle and sought they there land-benefits.	They had with them all kinds of livestock, and they sought the land's resources.
Fjöll voru þar og fagurt var þar um að litast.	Mountains were there and beautiful were they about to look.	The mountains there were beautiful to look upon.
Þeir gáðu einskis nema að kanna landið.	They looked only taken to exploring land.	They looked only to exploring the land.
Þar voru grös mikil.	There was grass great.	There was tall grass there.
Þar voru þeir um veturinn og gerðist vetur mikill en ekki fyrir unnið og gerðist illt til matarins og tókust af veiðarnar.	They were there about winter and happened winter much but nothing before working and becoming ill for food and taking of hunting.	They were there about winter, and the winter was harsh, and they had done nothing in preparation for it, and they became ill for want of food, and took they to hunting and fishing.
Þá fóru þeir út í eyna og væntu að þar mundi gefa nokkuð af veiðum eða rekum.	Then went they out to the-island and expected that there could give some of fishing or foraging.	They went out to the island and hoped to be given something of fishing or foraging.
Þar var þó lítið til matfanga en fé þeirra varð þar vel.	There was though little to hunt but cattle theirs was there well.	There was though little caught from hunting, but their livestock were well.
Síðan hétu þeir á guð að hann sendi þeim nokkuð til matfanga og var eigi svo brátt við látið sem þeim var annt til.	Afterwards pledged they to God that he send them something to hunt and was not so soon with left which they were wishing for.	Afterwards they prayed to God for him to send them something to hunt, but was not so soon anything left that they were wishing for.

The Vinland Sagas — *The Saga of Erik the Red (Old Icelandic)*

Old Icelandic	Literal	English
Þórhallur hvarf á brott og gengu menn að leita hans.	Thorhall disappeared to away and went people to seek him.	Thorhall disappeared away and people went to find him.
Stóð það yfir þrjú dægur í samt.	Was this over three days the same.	It was the same way for three days.
Á hinu fjórða dægri fundu þeir Karlsefni og Bjarni hann Þórhall á hamargnípu einni.	On the fourth day found they Karlsefni and Bjarni him Thorhall on cliff-top alone.	On the fourth day Karlsefni and Bjarni found Thorhall on a clip top alone.
Hann horfði í loft upp og gapti hann, bæði augum og munni og nösum, og klóraði sér og klípti sig og þuldi nokkuð.	He looked to sky up and agape he, both eyes and mouth and nose, and scratched himself and pinched himself and reciting something.	He was looking up to the sky, eyes, mouth, and nose agape, and scratched and pinched himself and he was reciting something.
Þeir spurðu hví hann væri þar kominn.	They asked why he was there come.	They asked why he had come there.
Hann kvað það öngu skipta.	He said that nothing of-exchange.	He said that it was nothing of any concern.
Bað hann þá ekki það undrast, kveðst svo lengst lifað hafa að þeir þurftu eigi ráð fyrir honum að gera.	Asked he then not that wonder, saying so long lived had that you need not advise for to-him to do.	He asked them not to wonder about it, saying that as long as he had lived, he had not needed their advice.
Þeir báðu hann fara heim með sér.	They asked him travel home with them.	They asked him to travel home with them.
Hann gerði svo.	He did so.	He did so.
Litlu síðar kom þar hvalur og drifu menn til og skáru hann en þó kenndu menn eigi hvað hval það var.	Little afterwards came there whale and drove men to and cut it and though knew people not what whale it was.	Shortly afterwards there came a whale, and men flocked to carve it up, though they did not know what kind of whale it was.
Karlsefni kunni mikla skyn á hvalnum og kenndi hann þó eigi.	Karlsefni knew much understanding of whales and knew he though not.	Karlsefni knew much about whales, though he did not know.
Þenna hval suðu matsveinar og átu af og varð þó öllum illt af.	This whale boiled ship's-cook and ate they and were though all ill from.	The ship's cook boiled the whale and they ate, and everyone was ill from it.
Þá gengur Þórhallur að og mælti: "Var eigi svo að hinn rauðskeggjaði varð drjúgari enn Kristur yðvar? Þetta hafði eg nú fyrir skáldskap minn er eg orti um Þór fulltrúann.	Then went Thorhall to and spoke: "Was not so that the Red-bearded was ample but Christ yours this have I now for poetry mine that I wrote about Thor patron.	Thorhall then spoke: "Ampler was the Red-Beard now than your Christ. I had this now for my poem, which I wrote about Thor, my guardian.
Sjaldan hefir hann mér brugðist".	Seldom has he me broken".	Seldom has he broken me".

The Vinland Sagas   *The Saga of Erik the Red (Old Icelandic)*

Old Icelandic	Literal	English
Og er menn vissu þetta vildu öngvir nýta og köstuðu fyrir björg ofan og sneru sínu máli til guðs miskunnar.	And when people knew this willed none take-advantage and cast before rocks over and turned their matter to God's mercy.	And when people knew this, they carried the whale to cast to sea, and threw themselves on God's mercy.
Gaf þeim þá út að róa og skorti þá eigi birgðir.	Gave they then back to row and shortage then not supplies.	They were then given back to rowing, and the found no shortage of supplies.
Um vorið fara þeir inn í Straumsfjörð og höfðu föng af hvorutveggja landinu, veiðar af meginlandinu, eggver og útróðra af sjónum.	About spring went they in to Straumsfjord and had provisions of either-way land, hunting of mainland, egg-gathering and fishing from sea.	About spring they went into Straumsfjord and had supplies from both shores, hunting on the mainland, gathering eggs and fishing from the sea.

9

Nú ræða þeir um ferð sína og hafa tilskipan.	Now discussed they about journey theirs and had decided.	Now they discussed about their journey and planned.
Vill Þórhallur veiðimaður fara norður um Furðustrandir og fyrir Kjalarnes og leita svo Vínlands en Karlsefni vill fara suður fyrir land og fyrir austan og þykir land því meira sem suður er meir og þykir honum það ráðlegra að kanna hvorttveggja.	Willed Thorhall the-Hunter go north about Furdustrandir and for Kjalarnes and seek so Vinland but Karlsefni willed to-travel south for land and for eastwards and thinking land for more which south was more and thought he that advisable to explore each-way.	Thorhall the Hunter wished to go north along Furdustrandir and Kjalarnes to seek Vinland, but Karlsefni wished to travel south along the land and east, thinking that the further south they went, the more the could explore either way.
Nú býst Þórhallur út undir eynni og urðu eigi meir í ferð með honum en níu menn.	Now prepared Thorhall out under island and became not more to travel with him but nine people.	Now Thorhall prepared his ship close to the island and there were not more than nine people to travel with him.
En með Karlsefni fór annað liðið þeirra.	And with Karlsefni went second group theirs.	And the second group went with Karlsefni.
Og einn dag er Þórhallur bar vatn á skip sitt þá drakk hann og kvað vísu þessa:	And one day was Thorhall carrying water to ship theirs then drank he and said verse this:	And one day when Thorhall was carrying water to their ship, he drank from it and said this verse:
Hafa kváðu mig meiðar málmþings, er kom eg hingað,	Shores sang me hurt metal-assemblied, when coming here,	The shores sang me hurt Metal assembled, when I came here,
mér samir láð fyr lýðum	To-me same invited for people	I have the same advice for the people
lasta, drykk hinn basta.	Load, drink the best.	Loaded, drink the best.
Bílds hattar verðr byttu	Axe hoods become replaced	Axe hoods will be replaced

Old Icelandic	Literal	English
beiði-Týr að reiða.	Bids-Tyr to ruling.	Asking for Tyr's ruling.
Heldr er svo að eg krýp að keldu,	Rather is so that I creep to the well,	It is rather that I creep to the well,
komat vín á grön mína.	Come wine to green mine.	Bring green wine to me.
Láta þeir út síðan og fylgir Karlsefni þeim undir eyna.	Put they out afterwards and followed Karlsefni they under the-island.	They put out to sea afterwards and Karlsefni followed the as far as the island.
Áður þeir drógu seglið upp kvað Þórhallur vísu:	Before they drew sails up said Thorhall verse:	Before they drew up the sails, Thorhall said this verse:
Förum aftr þar er órir	Travel-we back, there where others	We travel back to where the others
eru sandhimins landar,	are, sand-heaven's, land,	Are, the heavens of the sands, land,
látum kenni-Val kanna	let-us know-choose explore	Let us knowing choose to explore
knarrar skeið hin breiðu.	Ship sheathed-sword in wide,	Ship of swords in the wide,
Meðan bilstyggir byggja	while space settle	Among the space settle.
bellendr og hval vella	partakers and whale boil	Participants and boil the whale
Laufa veðrs, þeir er leyfa	leaf weathered, they have	Leaf weathered, they have
lönd, á Furðuströndum.	land, to Furdustrandir.	Land, in Furdustrandir.
Síðan skildu þeir og sigldu norður fyrir Furðustrandir og Kjalarnes og vildu beita þar fyrir vestan.	Then sailed they north along Furdustrandir and Kjalarnes and willed applied west for.	Then they sailed north along Furdustrandir and Kjalarnes, and wished to head for the west.
Kom þá veður á móti þeim og rak þá upp við Írland og voru þar mjög þjáðir og barðir.	Came then weather to meet them and drove then up to Ireland and were there very enslaved and beaten.	Then the west wind came towards them, and they were driven up to Ireland, and there they were beaten and enslaved.
Þá lét Þórhallur líf sitt.	Then laid Thorhall life his.	There Thorhall lost his life.
10	10	10
Karlsefni fór suður fyrir land og Snorri og Bjarni og annað lið þeirra.	Karlsefni came south along land and Snorri and Bjarni and another team theirs.	Now it is said of Karlsefni, that he went south along the land, with Snorri and Bjarni and the rest of their company.
Þeir fóru lengi og til þess er þeir komu að á þeirri er féll af landi ofan og í vatn og svo til sjóvar.	They travelled along and all there until, then they came to river one, which fell from land off and into lake single to sea.	They travelled along the land until they came to a river which fell from the land into a lake, and into the sea.
Eyrar voru þar miklar fyrir árósinum og mátti eigi komast inn í ána nema að háflæðum.	Islands were there great, and may not come in to river out of high-tide.	There were large islands there, and they could not come into the river outside of high tide.

The Vinland Sagas   *The Saga of Erik the Red (Old Icelandic)*

Old Icelandic	Literal	English
Sigldu þeir Karlsefni þá til áróssins og kölluðu í Hópi landið.	Sailed they Karlsefni then to river-mouth and called it Hop land.	There Karlsefni sailed them to the river mouth, and called the land Hop.
Þar fundu þeir sjálfsána hveitiakra þar sem lægðir voru en vínviður allt þar sem holta kenndi.	There found they of land self-sowing wheat-acres, there where low-ground was, and vines all there, which hills knew.	There they found acres of self-sowing wheat, where the low ground was, and vines growing on the hills.
Hver lækur var þar fullur af fiskum.	Every stream was there full of fish.	Every stream there was full of fish.
Þeir gerðu þar grafir sem landið mættist og flóðið gekk efst, og er út féll voru helgir fiskar í gröfunum.	They made trenches, there which may land and tide went highest, and then when back fell sea, were flat fish in trenches.	They made trenches in the land where the tide reached its highest, and then when the sea fell back, there were flat fish in the trenches.
Þar var mikill fjöldi dýra á skógi með öllu móti.	There were great many animals in forest with all met.	There were a great many wild animals of all kinds in the forest.
Þeir voru þar hálfan mánuð og skemmtu sér og urðu við ekki varir.	They were there half month and entertained themselves and became with nothing aware.	They were there half a month and entertained themselves and were not aware of anything unusual.
Fé sitt höfðu þeir með sér.	Cattle theirs had they with them.	They had their livestock with them.
Og einn morgunn snemma er þeir lituðust um sáu þeir níu húðkeipa og var veift trjánum af skipunum og lét því líkast í sem í hálmpústum og fer sólarsinnis.	And one morning early, when they looked about, saw they great many skin-boats, and were waving poles from boats, and had accordingly like as to straw-staves, and were waved sun-wise-motion.	And early one morning, when they looked about, they saw a great many hide-boats, and there were poles waving from the boats, which made a sound like a straw man, and they were waved in a sun-wise motion.
Þá mælti Karlsefni: "Hvað mun þetta tákna?"	Then spoke Karlsefni: "What could this have to betoken?"	Then spoke Karlsefni: "What could this mean?"
Snorri svarar honum: "Vera kann að þetta sé friðartákn og tökum skjöld hvítan og berum í mót".	Snorri Thorbrandson answered he: "Be-it can, that this so peace-mark, and take shield white and bear it towards".	Snorri Thorbrandson answered: "Maybe it can be a peace sign, and we should take a white shield and show it to them".
Og svo gerðu þeir. *Þá reru hinir í mót og undruðust þá og gengu þeir á land.*	And so did they. Then rowed they to meet and astonished they, as present were, and went to land up.	And so they did. Then they rowed to meet them, and they were astonished as they came up on land to meet them.

Old Icelandic	Literal	English
Þeir voru smáir menn og illilegir og illt höfðu þeir hár á höfði.	They were small men and ill-looking and disorderly heads their hair on heads.	They were small men, and looked threatening, with tangled hair on their heads.
Eygðir voru þeir mjög og breiðir í kinnunum og dvöldust þeir um stund og undruðust, reru síðan í brott og suður fyrir nesið.	Eyes were theirs large and broad in cheeks and dwelled they about awhile and marvelled, rowed then to away and south before headland.	They had large eyes and broad cheeks. They stayed around awhile and marvelled at those who were present, and then they rowed away and headed south around the headland.
Þeir höfðu gert byggðir sínar upp frá vatninu og voru sumir skálarnir nær vatninu en sumir firr.	They had made booths theirs up from lake and were some cabins near lake but some further.	They made their booths up from the lake, and there were some cabins near the lake, but some further inland.
Nú voru þeir þar þann vetur.	Now were they therefore then winter.	They were there for the winter.
Þar kom alls engi snjár og allur fénaður gekk þar úti sjálfala.	There came no snow, and all going cattle they themselves from.	There was no snow there, and all the livestock could fend for themselves outside.

11

En er vora tók geta þeir að líta einn morgun snemma að fjöldi húðkeipa reri sunnan fyrir nesið, svo margir sem kolum væri sáð og var þó veift á hverju skipi trjánum.	Then when spring took could they the company one morning early that many skin-boats rowing south before the-headland, so many as-if coal were sown and were though waving on each ship poles.	Then when spring came, early one morning they saw many hide boats rowing up from the south around the headland, so many that it looked like coal had been thrown across the water. They were also waving poles from each ship.
Þeir brugðu þá skjöldum upp og tóku kaupstefnu sín á milli og vildi það fólk helst kaupa rautt klæði.	They brought then shields up and took trading-posts theirs in between and willed that people preferably buy red cloth.	They brought up their shields and set up their trading posts between them and the people wanted to buy red cloth.
Þeir vildu og kaupa sverð og spjót en það bönnuðu þeir Karlsefni og Snorri.	They willed also purchase swords and spears but that banned they Karlsefni and Snorri.	They also wanted to purchase swords and spears, but Karlsefni and Snorri banned this.
Þeir höfðu ófölvan belg fyrir klæðið og tóku spannarlangt klæði fyrir belg og bundu um höfuð sér og fór svo um stund.	They had dark pelts and clothes and took spanning-long clothing for pelts and bound about heads theirs and went so about awhile.	They had dark pelts and clothes, and they took spans of cloth in exchange for pelts and tier the cloth around their heads, and so the trading went on in this way for a while.

Old Icelandic	Literal	English
En er minnka tók klæðið þá skáru þeir í sundur svo að eigi var breiðara en þvers fingrar breitt.	But as decreased took cloth then cut they to apart so that not was broader than across finger broad.	But as the amount of cloth decreased, they cut it so that it was not as broad, and only a finger width.
Gáfu þeir Skrælingjar jafnmikið fyrir eða meira.	Gave they Skraelings equal for or more.	The Skraelings exchanged for the same price or more.
Það bar til að griðungur hljóp úr skógi er þeir Karlsefni áttu og gall hátt við.	That bore towards that a-bull ran out-of woods which they Karlsefni owned and bellowed loudly with.	Then a bull which Karlsefni owned ran out of the woods towards them, bellowing loudly.
Þeir fælast við Skrælingjar og hlaupa út á keipana og reru suður fyrir land.	This frightened to Skraelings and ran out of trading and rowed south for land.	This frightened the Skraelings and they ran away from the trading posts and rowed away south around the headland.
Varð þá ekki vart við þá þrjár vikur í samt.	Were they not noticed by them three weeks at together.	They did not notice them again for another three weeks.
En er sjá stund var liðin sjá þeir sunnan fara mikinn fjölda skipa Skrælingja svo sem straumur stæði.	And when seen awhile was company, saw there travelling south great many Skraelings, so as stream steady.	Then after a while their company saw travelling from the south, a great many Skraelings, like a steady stream.
Var þá veift trjánum öllum rangsælis og ýla allir Skrælingjar hátt upp.	Were they waving poles all anti-sun-wise and howling all Skraelings loudly up.	They were all waving their poles anti-sunwise now, and all were howling very loudly.
Þá tóku þeir rauða skjöldu og báru í mót.	Then took they red shields and bore to meet.	Then Karlsefni's company took their red shields and carried them up to meet them.
Gengu þeir þá saman og börðust.	Went they then together and fought.	Then they went together to battle.
Varð þar skothríð hörð.	Were there launching hard.	They were launching hard.
Þeir höfðu og valslöngur Skrælingjar.	They had also war-slings Skraelings.	The Skraelings also had catapults.
Það sjá þeir Karlsefni og Snorri að þeir færðu upp á stöngum Skrælingjarnir knött mikinn og blán að lit og fló upp á land yfir liðið og lét illilega við þar er niður kom.	That saw they Karlsefni and Snorri that they went up to poles Skraelings balls great and blue that colour and flew up to land over team and lay badly with there that down came.	Karlsefni and Snorri saw that the Skraelings raised up poles, with large round objects on them, blue in colour, and they flew to the land where the company were, and the landed terribly wherever they fell.

The Vinland Sagas — *The Saga of Erik the Red (Old Icelandic)*

Old Icelandic	Literal	English
Við þetta sló ótta miklum yfir Karlsefni og á lið hans svo að þá fýsti einskis annars en halda undan og upp með ánni því að þeim þótti lið Skrælingja drífa að sér öllum megin og létta eigi fyrr en þeir koma til hamra nokkurra.	With that struck fear much over Karlsefni and to team his so that then desired nothing else than hold away and up along the-river because that they thought the-company-of Skraelings drove at them all ways and let not before that they came to crags some.	This struck great fear into Karlsefni and his men, so much so that they wanted nothing else but to flee up the river, since the Skraelings seemed to be attacking from all angles, and not stop until they reached a cliff.
Veittu þeir þar viðtöku harða.	Gave they there resistance hard.	They have a stiff resistance.
Freydís kom út og sá er þeir héldu undan.	Freydis came out and saw that they held ahead.	Freydis came out and saw that Karlsefni's company were fleeing,
Hún kallaði: "Hví rennið þér undan slíkum auvirðismönnum, svo gildir menn er mér þætti líklegt að þér mættuð drepa þá svo sem búfé? Og ef eg hefði vopn þætti mér sem eg mundi betur berjast en einnhver yðvar".	She called: "Why run you away such un-worthy-men, so thick men that to-me seems likely that you may kill them such as livestock and if I had weapon seems to-me that I would better fight than any-of you".	She called out: "Why are you running away from such unworthy opponents? such men that you are, who look to me like you could kill them as easily as livestock, and if I had a weapon I would fight them better than any of you".
Þeir gáfu öngvan gaum hvað sem hún sagði.	They gave no heed to-that which she said.	They paid no attention to what she said.
Freydís vildi fylgja þeim og varð hún heldur sein því að hún var eigi heil.	Freydis willed to-follow them and became she behind late because that she was not well.	Freydis wanted to follow them, and fell behind, because she was with child.
Gekk hún þá eftir þeim í skóginn en Skrælingjar sækja að henni.	Went she though after them into woods, but Skraelings sought towards her.	She went after them into the forest, but the Skraelings reached her.
Hún fann fyrir sér mann dauðan, Þorbrand Snorrason, og stóð hellusteinn í höfði honum.	She found ahead their man dead, Thorbrand Snorrason, and stood a-slab-stone in head his.	She found in front of her one of their men who had died. It was Thorbrand Snorrason, and a stone slab was buried in his head.
Sverðið lá hjá honum og hún tók það upp og býst að verja sig með.	Sword lay by him and she took that up and prepared to protect herself with.	A sword lay unsheathed next to him. She took that sword and prepared to protect herself.
Þá koma Skrælingjar að henni.	Then came the-Skraelings to her.	Then the Skraelings came to her.
Hún tekur brjóstið upp úr serkinum og slettir á sverðið.	She pulled then out breast from clothes and slapped on open sword.	She pulled out one of her breasts from her clothes, and slapped the sword against it.

Old Icelandic	Literal	English
Þeir fælast við og hlaupa undan og á skip sín og héldu á brottu.	With that feared Skraelings and ran away to ships theirs and rowed to away.	With that the Skraelings became afraid and they ran away to their ships and rowed away.
Þeir Karlsefni finna hana og lofa happ hennar.	There Karlsefni found her and praised zeal hers.	Here Karlsefni found her and praised her bravery.
Tveir menn féllu af Karlsefni en fjórir af Skrælingjum en þó urðu þeir Karlsefni ofurliði bornir.	Two men fell of Karlsefni but many of Skraelings but though became they Karlsefni outnumbered borne.	Two men from Karlsefni's company fell, and many of the Skraelings, but Karlsefni and his men were outnumbered.
Fara þeir nú til búða sinna og íhuga hvað fjölmenni það var er að þeim sótti á landinu.	Went they now to settlement theirs and thought what many that were that which they encountered on land.	They now went to their settlement and thought about what they had encountered on the land.
Sýnist þeim nú að það eina mun liðið hafa verið er á skipunum kom an annað liðið mun hafa verið þversýningar.	Seemed they now that the one could company at-sea have-been where the ships came but other company could have been illusions.	It seemed now that there could have been one team at sea where the ships came, but other people could have been illusions.
Þeir Skrælingjar fundu og mann dauðan og lá öx hjá honum.	There Skraelings found also a-man dead and lay an-axe by him.	The Skraelings also found a man dead, and an axe laying near to him.
Einn þeirra tók upp öxina og höggur með tré og þá hver að öðrum og þótti þeim vera gersemi og bíta vel.	One there took up the-axe and hewed with tree and then each to other and thought they it-was treasure and bit well.	One of them there took up the axe and hewed at a tree, and then each of them took turns trying it, and they thought it was a treasure that cut so well.
Síðan tók einn og hjó í stein og brotnaði öxin.	Then took one and struck at stone and broke the-axe.	Then one of them took up the axe and struck at stone with it, and the axe broke,
Þótti honum þá öngu nýt er eigi stóð við grjótinu og kastaði niður.	Thought he then no use that not withstood with stones and cast down.	and then they thought it was of no use, as it did not withstand stone, and they threw it down.
Þeir þóttust nú sjá þótt þar væru landskostir góðir að þar mundi jafnan ófriður og ótti á liggja af þeim er fyrir bjuggu.	There thought now looked thought there were land-benefits good that there could-be equal without-peace and fear to lay of them as before inhabitants.	There Karlsefni's company thought that although there were many benefits in that land, they would always be without peace, fearing attack by the inhabitants.

The Vinland Sagas — *The Saga of Erik the Red (Old Icelandic)*

Old Icelandic	Literal	English
Síðan bjuggust þeir á brottu og ætluðu til síns lands og sigldu norður fyrir landið og fundu fimm Skrælingja í skinnhjúpum, sofnaða, nær sjó.	Afterwards prepared they to leave and intended towards they land and sailed north along the land and found five Skraelings in skin-sacks, sleeping, near sea.	Afterwards they prepared to leave and intended to sail north around the land, and they found five Skraelings in skin sacks sleeping near the sea.
Þeir höfðu með sér stokka og í dýramerg, dreyra blandinn.	They had with them stock of in animal-marrow, blood mixed.	
Þóttust þeir Karlsefni það skilja að þessir menn myndu hafa verið gervir brott af landinu.	Thought they Karlsefni that separated which these people would have been made away from land.	Karlsefni's company thought that they must have been outlaws.
Þeir drápu þá.	They killed then.	They then killed them.
Síðan fundu þeir Karlsefni nes eitt og á fjölda dýra.	Afterwards found they Karlsefni headland one and of many animals.	Afterwards Karlsefni's company found a headland that had many wild animals.
Var nesið að sjá sem mykiskán væri af því að dýrin lágu þar um næturnar.	Was headland to see which muck-encrusted was of therefore were wild-animals laying there about night.	The headland looked like it was covered with dung, as the deer gathered there at night to sleep.
Nú koma þeir Karlsefni aftur í Straumsfjörð og voru þar fyrir alls gnóttir þess er þeir þurftu að hafa.	Now came they Karlsefni back to Straumfjord and were there before all abundance this as they needed to have.	Now Karlsefni's company came back to Straumfjord, where they found all in abundance, everything that they needed.
Það er sumra manna sögn að þau Bjarni og Guðríður hafi þar eftir verið og tíu tigir manna með þeim og hafi eigi farið lengra, en þeir Karlsefni og Snorri hafi suður farið og fjórir tigir manna með þeim og hafi eigi lengur verið í Hópi en vart tvo mánuði og hafi sama sumar aftur komið.	It was some men said that those Bjarni and Guthrid had there after been and ten tens men with them and have not travelled further, but there Karlsefni and Snorri had south travelled and four ten men with them and have no longer been in tidal-pool but hardly two months and had the-same summer returned come.	Some say that Bjarni and Gudrid had remained behind with a hundred men and had not travelled further, and that it was Karlsefni and Snorri who went further south with forty men, stayed at Hop for not longer than two months, and returned that same summer.
Karlsefni fór þá einu skipi að leita Þórhalls veiðimanns en annað liðið var eftir og fóru þeir norður fyrir Kjalarnes og ber þá fyrir vestan fram og var landið á bakborða þeim.	Karlsefni travelled then one ship to seek Thorhall the-Hunter but another team were remained and travelled they north for Kjalarnes and bore then for west from and was the-land to larboard-side theirs.	Karlsefni then travelled with one ship to find Thorhall the Hunter, while the other tem stayed behind, and they travelled north around Kjalarnes, and they then bore west, and the land was to their port side.

The Vinland Sagas   *The Saga of Erik the Red (Old Icelandic)*

Old Icelandic	Literal	English
Þar voru þá eyðimerkur einar allt að sjá fyrir þeim og nær hvergi rjóður í.	There was then deserted-forest only all to see before them and near neither clearing among.	There was then nothing to see except deserted forest before them, with no clearing among them.
Og er þeir höfðu lengi farið fellur á af landi ofan úr austri og í vestur.	And were they had long travelled, falls to out-of land above out east and to west.	And after they had travelled for a long time, they reached a river flowing from east to west.
Þeir lögðu inn í árósinn og lágu við hinn syðra bakkann.	They laid in to river-mouth and laid to in southern bank.	They sailed into the mouth of the river and lay to near the south bank.

12

Old Icelandic	Literal	English
Það var einn morgun er þeir Karlsefni sáu fyrir ofan rjóðrið flekk nokkurn sem glitraði við þeim og æptu þeir á það.	It was one morning, that they Karlsefni saw before above clearing speck certain, that glittered by them, and shouted they at that.	It was one morning that Karlsefni's company saw a clearing before them, and a speck of light that glittered before them, and they shouted at it.
Það hrærðist og var það einfætingur og skaust ofan á þann árbakkann sem þeir lágu við.	It stirred, and was it a-one-footer and launched down towards the river-bank, where they lay by.	It stirred, and it was a one legged creature, and it launched down towards the river bank there the ship was laid.
Þorvaldur Eiríksson rauða sat við stýri.	Thorvald son-of-Erik the-Red sat by steering.	Thorvald, son of Erik the Red, sat by the helm.
Þá mælti Þorvaldur: "Gott land höfum vér fengið".	Then spoke Thorvald: "Good land have we found".	Then Thorvald spoke: "Good land we have found here".
Þá hleypur einfætingurinn á brott og norður aftur og skaut áður í smáþarma á Þorvald.	Then ran one-footer to away and north back and shot back to small-intestine of Thorvald.	Then the one legged creature ran away back to the north and shot an arrow into Thorvald's intestine.
Hann dró út örina.	He dragged out the-arrow.	He dragged out the arrow.
Þá mælti Þorvaldur: "Feitt er um ístruna".	Then spoke Thorvald: "Bold is around the-belly".	Then Thorvald spoke: "Bold it is around the belly".
Þeir hljópu eftir einfætingi og sáu hann stundum og þótti sem hann leitaði undan.	They ran after one-footer and saw him sometimes and thought that he sought ahead.	They ran after the one legged creature and thought that they saw it ahead.
Hljóp hann út á vog einn.	Ran he out to inlet one.	He ran into an inlet.
Þá hurfu þeir aftur.	Then disappeared they returned.	Then he disappeared and they returned.
Þá kvað einn maður kviðling þenna:	Then said one man verse this:	Then one man said this verse:

The Vinland Sagas — *The Saga of Erik the Red (Old Icelandic)*

Old Icelandic	Literal	English
Eltu seggir, *allsátt var það,* *einn einfæting* *ofan til strandar* *en kynlegr maðr* *kostaði rásar* *hart of stopir,* *heyrðu, Karlsefni.*	"Pursued said, true was that, a one-footer down to shore, but uncanny man exerted rushed rough about stopped. Hear, Karlsefni".	"Pursued it was said true it was a one-footer down to the shore, but the uncanny man rushed away hard of stopping. Hear us, Karlsefni".
Þeir fóru þá í brott og norður aftur og þóttust sjá Einfætingaland.	They went then to away and north returning and thought saw One-Footer-Land.	Then they went away and headed back north and thought they saw One Footer Land.
Vildu þeir þá eigi lengur hætta liði sínu.	Willed they then not danger team theirs further.	They did not wish to put themselves in any further danger.
Þeir ætluðu öll ein fjöll, þau er í Hópi voru og þessi er nú fundu þeir, og það stæðist mjög svo á og væri jafnlangt úr Straumsfirði beggja vegna.	They supposed all same mountains, these, were among Hop was, and this, was now found they, and that place much so that also was equal-long from Straumfjord both ways.	They supposed that the mountains they saw were the same as the ones at Hop, and so that place was equally distant from Straumfjord.
Fóru þeir aftur og voru í Straumsfirði hinn þriðja vetur. *Gengu menn þá mjög sleitum.*	Went they again and were in Straumfjord the third winter. Went men then much fighting.	They went back and spent the third winter in Straumfjord. Then there was much fighting among the men.
Sóttu þeir er kvonlausir voru í hendur þeim er kvongaðir voru.	Sought they which unmarried were in hand that who married were.	Some of them who were not married sought the women who were married.
Þar kom til hið fyrsta haust Snorri son Karlsefnis og var hann þá þrívetur er þeir fóru á brott.	There came to the first autumn Snorri son Karlsefni's and was he then three-winters when they went out away.	Karlsefni's son Snorri was born there the first autumn, and he was three winters old when they left.
Höfðu þeir sunnanveður og hittu Markland og fundu Skrælingja fimm.	Had they southern-winds and met Markland and found Skraelings five.	They were taken by a southerly wind and reached Markland, and found there five Skraelings.
Var einn skeggjaður og tvær konur, börn tvö.	Was one bearded and two women, children two.	One of them was bearded, two were women, and two were children.
Tóku þeir Karlsefni til sveinanna en hitt komst undan og sukku í jörð niður.	Took they Karlsefni young-men, and others went away, and sank they Skraelings among land down.	Karlsefni's company took the two boys, and the others went away, and then the Skraelings disappeared into the earth.

Old Icelandic	Literal	English
En sveinana höfðu þeir með sér og kenndu þeim mál og voru skírðir.	Then young-men had they with them and taught them language and were baptised.	They kept the young men with them and taught them their language, and they were baptised.
Þeir nefndu móður sína Vethildi og föður Óvægi.	They named mother theirs Vethild and father Ovaegi.	Their mother was named Vethildi and their father Ovaegi.
Þeir sögðu að konungar stjórnuðu Skrælingjalandi.	They said that kings greatly-ruled-over Skraelings.	They said that there were great kings who ruled over the Skraelings,
Hét annar þeirra Avaldamon en annar hét Valdidida.	Called one theirs Avaldamon and another called Avaldidida.	one of them was called Avaldamon, and the other Valdidida.
Þeir kváðu þar engi hús og lágu menn í hellum eða holum.	They said there no houses and laid people in caves or holes.	They said that there were no houses there and people laid in caves or holes.
Þeir sögðu land þar öðrumegin gagnvart sínu landi og gengu menn þar í hvítum klæðum og æptu hátt og báru stangir og fóru með flíkur.	They said land there other-side going-from their land and went people there to white clothes and called-out loudly and bore poles and went with banners.	They said there was another land on the other side across from their land, and there people wore white clothes, and shouted loudly and carried poles fixed with banners.
Það ætla menn Hvítramannaland.	That supposed people White-man-land.	They supposed that this was White Man Land.
Nú komu þeir til Grænlands og eru með Eiríki rauða um veturinn.	Now came they to Greenland and were with Erik the-Red about winter.	Now they came to Greenland and were with Erik the Red by about winter.
13	13	13
Þá Bjarna Grímólfsson bar í Grænlandshaf og komu í maðksjá.	Then Bjarni Grimolfson carried to Greenland-Sea and came into ship-worms.	Then Bjarni Grimolfson was carried to the Greenland Sea and the ship was beset with ship worms.
Fundu þeir eigi fyrr en skipið gerist maðksmogið undir þeim.	Found they not before that ship was worm-eaten under them.	They found that the ship was eaten by worms underneath them.
Þá töluðu þeir um hvert ráð þeir skyldu taka.	Then talked they about what advice they should take.	Then they talked about what they should decision they should take.
Þeir höfðu eftirbát þann er bræddur var seltjöru.	They had boat then which spread was seal-fat.	They had a boat which had been spread with seal far.
Það segja menn að skelmaðkurinn smjúgi eigi það tré er seltjörunni er brætt.	That said people that shell-worms pierce not the beams that seal-fat are spread.	So people said that shell worms would not pierce the beams where seal fat was spread.

Old Icelandic	Literal	English
Var það flestra manna sögn og tillaga að skipa mönnum bátinn svo sem hann tæki upp.	Was that most people said and suggested to ships people boat so which he take up.	The majority of people said that they should fit as many people on the boat as they could.
En er það var reynt þá tók báturinn eigi meir upp en helming manna.	But was that was tried then took boat not more up than half the people.	But as they tried to board the boat, not more than half the people could fit on it.
Bjarni mælti þá að menn skyldu fara í bátinn og skyldi það fara að hlutföllum en eigi að mannvirðingum.	Bjarni said then that people should go to boat and should it go to lot-taking but not to rank.	Bjarni then said that people should go on to the boat according to drawing lots, not deciding it by rank.
En hver þeirra manna vildi fara í bátinn sem þar voru, þá mátti hann eigi við öllum taka.	Although each-of them men willed to-go among the-boat as they were, then may it not with all take.	Although each of the men wanted to go on to the boat, it would not take them all.
Fyrir því tóku þeir þetta ráð að hluta menn í bátinn og af kaupskipinu.	For therefore took they this advice that lots people to boat and of merchant-ship.	They therefore took this advice to draw lots to see who would board the boat from the merchant vessel.
Hlutaðist þar svo til að Bjarni hlaut að fara í bátinn og nær helmingur manna með honum.	Lots there so until that Bjarni lot to travel in the-boat and near half the-people with him.	The lots were drawn, and so it was Bjarni's lot to travel in the boat with nearly half the people with him.
Þá gengu þeir af skipinu og í bátinn er til þess höfðu hlotist.	Then went they out-of ship and to boat that to this had lots.	They went out of the ship and into the boat according to the lots they had drawn.
Þá er menn voru komnir í bátinn mælti einn ungur maður íslenskur sá er verið hafði förunautur Bjarna: "Ætlar þú Bjarni að skiljast hér við mig?"	Then spoke man was came to boat spoke one younger man Icelander so that been had crew Bjarni: "Intend you Bjarni to separate here with me?"	Then an Icelander who was in the ship spoke, who Bjarni had followed from Iceland: "Do you intend to separate with me now Bjarni?".
Bjarni svarar: "Svo verður nú að vera".	Bjarni answered: "So becomes now to be".	Bjarni answered: "So it has now come to be".
Hann segir: "Svo með því að þú hést mér eigi því þá er eg fór með þér frá Íslandi frá búi föður míns".	He said: "So with therefore that you promised to-me not for then that I went with you from Iceland from farm father mine".	He said: "So it goes not with what you promised me then, when I left my father's farm to follow you".
Bjarni segir: "Eigi sé eg hér þó annað ráð til eða hvað leggur þú hér til ráðs?"	Bjarni said: "Not see I here though other advice to but what have you here to advise?"	Bjarni said: "I do not see that here, but what other choice do we have?"

Old Icelandic	Literal	English
Hann segir: "Sé eg ráðið til að við skiptumst í rúmunum og farir þú hingað en eg mun þangað".	He said: "Say I advise to that with exchange of our-places and travel you here while I should there".	He said: "I say that we change places and you travel here while I should be there".
Bjarni svarar: "Svo skal vera og það sé eg að þú vinnur gjarna til lífs og þykir mikið fyrir að deyja".	Bjarni answered: "So shall be and that see I that you friend gladly to life and think much for to die".	Bjarni answered: "So it shall be, and I see that you my friend are glad in life, and think it too much to die".
Skiptust þeir þá í rúmunum.	Exchanged they then of places.	They then exchanged places.
Gekk þessi maður í bátinn en Bjarni upp í skipið og er það sögn manna að Bjarni létist þar í maðkahafinu og þeir menn sem í skipinu voru með honum.	Went this man to boat while Bjarni up to the-ship and was it said-of people that Bjarni perished there in the-worm-sea and they people which among the-ship were with him.	This man went on to the boat while Bjarni went up to the ship, and it was said by people that Bjarni perished there in the worm sea, and so did the people who were on the ship with him.
En báturinn og þeir er þar voru á fóru leiðar sinnar til þess er þeir tóku land og sögðu þessa sögu síðan.	But the-boat and they who there were in went route theirs until this that they took land and said this saga since.	Then the boat and they who were on board went on their way until they reached land and told this story since.

14

Old Icelandic	Literal	English
Annað sumar eftir fór Karlsefni til Íslands og Guðríður með honum og fór hann heim til bús síns í Reynines.	Next summer after went Karlsefni to Iceland and Guthrid with him and went he home to house his in Reynines.	The next summer Karlsefni went to Iceland with Gudrid and they went home to his house in Reynines.
Móður hans þótti sem hann hefði lítt til kostar tekið og var hún eigi heima þar hinn fyrsta vetur.	Mother his thought that he had little for choice taken and was she not home there the first winter.	His mother thought he had made a bad choice, and she did not stay with them for the first winter.
En er hún reyndi að Guðríður var skörungur mikill fór hún heim.	But when she experienced that Guthrid was noble much went she home.	But when she experienced that Gudrid was very noble, she went home.
Og voru samfarar þeirra góðar.	And was interaction theirs good.	And their relationship was good.
Dóttir Snorra Karlsefnissonar var Hallfríður móðir Þorláks byskups Runólfssonar.	Daughter-of Snorri Karlsefnison was Hallfrid, Mother Thorlak's the-Bishop son-of-Runolf.	Snorri Karlsefnison's daughter was Hallfrid, mother to Thorlak the Bishop, son of Runolf.
Þau áttu son er Þorbjörn hét.	They had a-son, was Thorbjorn named.	They had a son who was named Thorbjorn.

Old Icelandic	Literal	English
Hans dóttir hét Þórunn, móðir Bjarnar byskups.	His daughter was-called Thorun, mother Bjarn's the-Bishop.	His daughter was named Thorun, the mother of Bishop Bjarn.
Þorgeir hét sonur Snorra Karlsefnissonar, faðir Yngveldar, móður Brands byskups hins fyrra.	Thorgeir was-called son-of Snorri Karlsefnison, father-to Yngvild, mother-of Brand Bishop the first.	Snorri Karlsefnison's son was named Thorgeir, he was the father of Yngvild, the mother of the first Bishop Brand.
Og lýkur þar þessi sögu.	And ends here this saga.	And here ends this saga.

Word List *(Norse to English)*

Norse	English
A, a	
að	a OI, as OI, at OI, by OI, for OI, from OI, in OI, it OI, of OI, possible OI, that OI, the OI, to OI, towards OI, were OI, what OI, which OI
aðra	others ON, others OI
aðrar	other ON
aðrir	other OI, other ON, others ON, others OI
af	for OI, from OI, from OI, from ON, from ON, of OI, of ON, of ON, of OI, off OI, off ON, on ON, on OI, out OI, out-of ON, out-of OI, that OI, they OI
afkvæmi	offspring OI, offspring ON
afli	strength OI, strength ON
aftr	after ON, back ON, back OI, return ON, returned ON, returning ON
aftrgöngum	hauntings ON
aftur	after OI, again OI, back OI, return OI, returned OI, returning OI
afturgöngum	hauntings OI
akkeri	anchor OI, anchor ON
akkerum	anchor OI, anchor OI, anchor ON, anchor ON
albúið	all-prepared OI
albúinn	ready OI, ready ON
albúit	all-prepared ON
aldr	age ON
aldri	age OI, age ON
aldur	age OI
alendu	thoughts OI
algrá	grey ON
alla	all OI, all OI, all ON, all ON
allan	all OI, all ON
allar	all OI, all ON
allfjölmennt	many-people ON
allglöggsæ	clear ON
allill	evil OI, evil ON
allir	all OI, all OI, all ON, all ON
allmjök	all-very ON
allnær	all-near ON, near OI
allr	all ON
allra	every OI, every ON, everyone's OI, everyone's ON
alls	all OI, all OI, all ON, all ON
allsatt	true ON, true OI
allskonar	all-kinds ON
allt	all OI, all ON, altogether ON, altogether OI
allur	all OI, all OI
allvænt	expected ON
allvel	all-well OI, all-well ON
almennilega	properly OI
almenniliga	properly ON
an	but OI
andaðist	died OI, died OI, died ON, died ON
andaðr	dead ON
andaður	dead OI
andast	die OI, die ON, died OI
andazt	died ON
andist	died ON
andláti	death OI, death ON
andliti	face OI, face ON
andnesi	headland OI, headland ON
andsælis	anti-sun-wise ON
annað	another OI, else OI, next OI, one OI, other OI, second OI
annan	accompany OI, another OI, another ON, other OI, other ON, others ON, second OI, second ON
annar	another OI, one OI

175

Norse	English
annarr	another ON, called-one ON, other ON
annars	also OI, else ON, else OI, other ON, other OI, others' OI, others' ON, to-another ON
annat	another ON, another OI, else ON, next ON, one ON, other ON
annt	wish OI, wish ON, wishing OI
ari	Ari (name) ON
arnarstapa	Arnarstapa (place) ON, Arnarstapa (place) OI, Arnarstapi (place) ON, Arnarstapi (place) OI
arnlaugr	Arnlaug (name) ON
arnlaugsfjörð	Arnlaugsfjord (place) OI, Arnlaugsfjord (place) ON
arnlaugur	Arnlaug (name) OI
arnóru	Arnora (name) ON, Arnora (name) OI
at	a ON, as ON, at ON, but ON, by ON, for ON, from ON, in ON, it ON, man ON, of ON, that ON, the ON, therefore ON, to OI, to ON, towards ON, were ON, which ON
atbeina	assist OI, assistance ON
atburð	events OI, events ON
atburði	events OI, events ON
atburðum	events OI, events ON
atferli	ceremony ON, ceremony OI
athæfi	behaviour ON, behaviour OI
atmælasamur	measured OI
auðar	Aud (name) ON, Aud (name) OI
auðgara	richer OI, richer ON
auðið	fated OI
auðigr	wealthy ON
auðigur	wealthy OI
auðit	fated ON
auðnumann	fortune ON, fortune OI
auðr	Aud (name) ON
auðsýnir	shown ON, shown OI
auður	Aud (name) OI
augu	eyes OI, eyes ON
augum	eyes ON, eyes OI
augunum	eyes OI, eyes ON
aukin	increased ON, increased OI
austan	east OI, east ON, eastwards OI
austfirskur	East-Fjords (place) OI
austfirzkr	east-fjords ON
austfjörðum	Austfjord (place) OI, Austfjord (place) ON
austmaðr	eastern-man ON
austmaður	eastern-man OI
austmanns	The-Easterner (name) OI, the-easternman ON
austr	eastern ON
austri	east ON, east OI
austur	eastern OI
auvirðismönnum	un-worthy-men ON, un-worthy-men OI
avaldamon	Avaldamon (name) ON, Avaldamon (name) OI
avaldidida	Valdidida (name) ON
axlarliðnum	shoulder ON

Á, á

á	about OI, all OI, all ON, a-river OI, at OI, at ON, at-the OI, at-the ON, be ON, by ON, by OI, for OI, for ON, from ON, from OI, have OI, have ON, in OI, in ON, of OI, of ON, on OI, on ON, on-the ON, out OI, river ON, that ON, that OI, the OI, the ON, then OI, then ON, to OI, to ON, towards OI, towards ON, with OI, yet ON, yet OI
áðr	after ON, before ON, return ON, returned ON, until ON

The Vinland Sagas   *Word List (Norse to English)*

Norse	English
áður	back OI, before OI, return OI, returned OI, until OI
ágæti	excellent ON, excellent OI
ágæts	an-excellent OI, excellent ON
ágætt	fine OI, fine ON
ái	ai OI, ái OI
ákafast	fast OI, fast ON
ákaflega	extremely OI
ákafliga	extremely ON, very ON
ákveðin	agreed OI, agreed ON
álftafirði	Alftafjord (place) OI, Alftafjord (place) ON
álftafjörð	Alftafjord (place) OI, Alftafjord (place) ON
áliðnum	following ON, following OI
álna	cubits ON
ámæli	reproach OI, reproach OI, reproach ON, reproach ON
ána	river OI, river ON, river ON, river OI
ánauðgir	bondsmen ON, bondsmen OI
ánauðigr	bondsman ON
ánauðigur	bondsman OI
ánni	river OI, river ON, the-river OI
árangr	harvest ON
árangur	harvest OI
árbakkann	river-bank ON, river-bank OI
árferð	season ON, season OI
árósinn	river-mouth ON, river-mouth OI
árósinum	river-mouth OI
áróssins	river-mouth OI
áslákr	Aslak (name) ON
ásláksonar	Son-of-Aslak (name) ON
áslákur	Aslak (name) OI
ástúð	affection ON, affection OI
ásvalds	Asvald (name) OI, Asvald (name) ON, Asvald's (name) ON
átölur	reproaching OI, reproaching ON
átt	descendents ON, descendents OI, had OI, had ON, have ON
átta	eight OI, eight ON
átti	had OI, had ON, married OI, married ON
áttir	direction OI
áttu	had ON, had OI, have-you ON, have-you OI, owned ON, owned OI
átu	ate ON, ate OI

Æ, æ

Norse	English
æðr	eider-birds ON
æpðu	shouted ON
æptu	called-out OI, shouted OI
ætla	intend ON, intend OI, suppose OI, suppose ON, supposed OI, supposed ON
ætlað	intend OI, intended OI, intends OI
ætlaði	intended OI, intended ON, supposed OI, supposed ON
ætlaðr	intended ON
ætlaður	intended OI
ætlan	supposing ON
ætlar	intend ON, intend OI, intended ON
ætlat	intend ON, intended ON, purpose ON
ætluðu	intended OI, intended ON, supposed OI, supposed ON
ætt	ancestry ON, descendents ON, lineage ON, lineage OI
ættaðr	descended ON
ættaður	descended OI
ættbogi	descendents OI, descendents ON
ættgóður	family-good OI
ættir	direction ON

The Vinland Sagas   *Word List (Norse to English)*

Norse	English
ættkvíslum	family OI
ættstór	high-family OI, noble ON, noble OI
ættstórr	high-family ON
ævi	life ON, life OI

B, b

Norse	English
bað	asked OI, asked ON, bid OI, bid ON
báða	both ON
báðir	both ON, both OI
báðu	asked ON, asked OI
báðum	both OI, both ON
bæ	dwelling OI, dwelling ON, estate ON, estate OI, farm ON, farm OI, town ON, town OI
bæði	both OI, both ON, choosing OI
bæinn	dwellings ON, dwellings OI
bæjar	farm OI, farm ON
bæjum	farms ON, farms OI
bænahald	prayer-holdings ON, prayer-holdings OI
bænir	prayers ON, prayers OI
bænum	dwelling OI, dwelling ON
bær	farm ON, farm OI
bærist	bearing OI, bearing ON
bættu	repaired OI, repaired ON
bagga	bags OI, bags ON
bakborða	larboard-side OI, larboard-side ON
baki	back OI, back ON
bakkann	bank ON, bank OI
báli	fire ON, fire OI
bana	death OI, death ON
bannaði	banned OI, banned ON
bar	bear OI, bear ON, boar OI, bore OI, bore ON, carried ON, carried OI, carrying ON, carrying OI, was-carried ON
bardaga	battle OI, battle ON
bardagar	battle OI, battle ON
bardagi	battle OI, battle ON
bárðarson	Son-of-Bard (name) OI, Son-of-Bard (name) ON
barðir	beaten ON, beaten OI
barnæsku	childhood OI, childhood ON
barni	child ON, child OI
báru	bearing OI, bearing ON, bore OI, bore ON, brought OI, brought ON, carried ON, carried OI
báruð	carried OI, carried ON
bárust	bore OI, bore ON
basta	best OI
bát	boat ON
báti	boat OI, boat ON, boats OI, boats ON
bátinn	boat OI, boat ON, the-boat ON, the-boat OI
batna	better ON, better OI, better-than ON, better-than OI
batnaði	bettered ON, bettered OI
bátr	boat ON
bátrinn	boat ON
bátum	the-boat OI
báturinn	boat OI, the-boat OI
bauð	bid ON, invited OI, invited ON
bazta	best ON
beðið	proposals OI
beðinn	asked ON, asked OI
beðit	proposals ON
beggja	both ON, both OI
beið	waited OI, waited ON
beiddi	propose OI, propose ON
beiddist	asked ON, asked OI
beiði-týr	bids-tyr ON, Bids-Tyr (name) OI
beina	assist OI, assist ON
beita	applied ON, bid OI
beitim	apply ON
beittu	applied OI
beitum	apply OI
bekkinn	bench OI, bench ON

178

The Vinland Sagas — Word List (Norse to English)

Norse	English
bekknum	bench OI, bench ON
belg	pelts ON, pelts OI
belja	bellowing OI, bellowing ON
bellendr	partakers ON, partakers OI
ber	bare ON, bare OI, bore OI, carried OI
bera	bear OI, bear ON, bore OI, bore ON, bring OI, carry ON, carry OI, unload OI, unload ON
berim	bring ON
berja	to-bear ON, to-bear-to OI
berjast	fight ON, fight OI
berjum	berries OI, berries ON
berr	bore ON
bert	uncovered ON
beru	open ON
berum	bear ON, bear OI
best	best OI
besta	best OI
besti	best OI
betr	better ON
betra	better OI, better ON
betur	better OI
bezt	best ON
bezta	best ON
bezti	best ON
bið	bid OI
bíða	wait OI, wait ON
biðja	ask ON, ask OI, propose ON, propose OI
biðk	bid ON
biðr	asked ON
biðuðu	settled ON
bílds	blood-letting ON, blood-letting OI
bilstyggir	space OI
bilstyggvir	space ON
birgðir	supplies OI
birni	Bjorn (name) ON, Bjorn (name) OI
biskup	bishop OI, bishop ON
biskups	the-bishop OI, the-bishop ON
biskupsstóll	bishop's-seat OI, bishop's-seat ON
bíta	bit ON, bit OI
bjarg	rock OI, rock ON
bjargaði	saved OI
bjarna	Bjarni (name) OI, Bjarni (name) ON
bjarnar	Bear's (name) OI, Bear's (name) ON, Bjarn (name) ON, Bjarn (name) OI, Bjarn's (name) ON
bjarnarhöfn	Bjarnarhofn (place) ON, Bjarnarhofn (place) OI
bjarnarsonar	Son-of-Bjorn (name) ON, Son-Of-Bjorn (name) OI
bjarndýr	bear OI
bjarney	Bjarney (place) ON, Bjarney (place) OI
bjarneyja	Bjarney (place) OI
bjarneyjar	Bjarney (place) ON
bjarneyjum	Bjarney (place) OI
bjarni	Bjarni (name) OI, Bjarni (name) ON
bjart	bright OI, bright ON
bjartari	bright ON
bjartur	bright OI
bjó	dwelt OI, dwelt ON, lived OI, lived ON, prepared OI, prepared ON, settled ON
bjóða	bid OI, bid ON, invite OI, invite ON
björg	rocks OI
björn	bear ON, Bjorn (name) OI, Bjorn (name) ON
bjóst	prepared OI, prepared OI, prepared ON, prepared ON
bjuggu	dwelt OI, dwelt ON, inhabitants ON, inhabitants OI, lived OI, lived ON, prepared OI, prepared ON, settled OI, settled ON, settles OI
bjuggust	prepared OI, prepared ON, settled ON

179

The Vinland Sagas — Word List (Norse to English)

Norse	English
blán	blue ON, blue OI
blandast	mixed OI
blandinn	mixed ON, mixed OI
bláserkr	Blaserkur (place) ON
bláserkur	Blaserkur (place) OI
blíðu	friendliness ON
boða	preach ON, preach OI, to-preach OI
boðaði	preached ON, preached OI
boðið	bid OI
boðit	bid ON
boðsmanna	guests ON, guests OI
böggunum	bags OI, bags ON
bolöxi	a-pole-axe ON, a-pole-axe OI
bönd	binding OI, binding ON
bónda	farmer OI, hunsband's ON, husband OI, husband ON, husband's OI, the-Farmer OI, the-farmer ON
bóndi	Farmer ON, farmer OI, Farmer (a nickname) OI, husband OI, husband ON, landowner ON, landowner OI, the-Farmer OI, the-Farmer ON, The-Farmer (name) OI
bóndum	farms ON
bönnuðu	banned ON, banned OI
bónorð	proposal ON, proposal OI
bónorðið	proposal OI
bónorðit	proposal ON
borð	board OI, board ON, table ON, table OI, tables ON, tables OI
börðu	beat OI, beat ON
börðust	battled ON, fought ON, fought OI
borgarfirði	Borgafjord (place) OI, Borgafjord (place) ON
borið	bore OI, carried OI
borinn	carried ON, carried OI
borit	bore ON, carried ON
börn	children OI, children ON
bornir	borne ON, borne OI
botn	bottom-of OI, bottom-of ON, the-bottom-of ON, the-bottom-of OI
brá	drew OI, drew ON, prepared OI, prepared ON
bráðara	sooner ON, sooner OI
bræddr	spread ON
bræddur	spread OI
bræðr	brothers ON
bræðra	brothers OI, brothers ON
bræðrum	brothers OI, brothers ON
bræður	brothers OI
brætt	spread OI
bragð	solution ON, solution OI
brakaði	creaked OI, creaked ON
brands	Brand (name) OI, Brand (name) ON, Brand's (name) ON
brátt	soon OI, soon ON
brattahlíð	Brattahlid (place) OI, Brattahlid (place) ON
brattahlíð]	Brattahlid (place) ON
brattahlíðar	Brattahlid (place) OI, Brattahlid (place) ON
brattleitr	steep-looking ON
brattleitur	steep-looking OI
braut	away OI, away ON, away ON, broke OI, divided ON
bregða	foreclose ON, foreclose OI
breiðabólstað	Breidabolstad (place) ON, Breidabolstad (place) OI, upholstery OI, upholstery ON
breiðafirði	Breidafjord (place) OI, Breidafjord (place) ON
breiðafjarðar	Breidafjord (place) OI, Breidafjord (place) ON
breiðafjörð	Breidafjord (place) OI, Breidafjord (place) ON
breiðara	broad ON, broader OI
breiðfirskur	Breidafjord (place) OI

The Vinland Sagas   Word List (Norse to English)

Norse	English
breiðfirzkr	Breidafjord (place) ON
breiðir	broad ON, broad OI
breiðu	wide ON, wide OI
breitt	broad OI
brenna	burn ON, let OI
brest	crash OI, crash ON
brimum	Bremen (place) OI, Bremen (place) ON
brjóst	breast ON
brjósti	breast ON, breast OI
brjóstið	breast OI, the-breast OI
brjóstit	breast ON
bróðir	brother OI, brother ON
bróður	brother OI, brother ON
brokey	Brokey (place) ON, Brokey (place) OI
brot	away ON
brotinn	broken ON, broken OI
brotna	broke ON
brotnaði	broke ON, broke OI
brott	away OI, away ON, out ON, out OI
brottu	away OI, gone OI, gone ON, leave ON, leave OI
brúðhlaup	wedding OI
brúðkaup	wedding ON
brúðkaupið	the-wedding OI
brúðlaup	wedding ON
brugðið	brought-out OI
brugðist	broken OI
brugðit	brought-out ON
brugðizt	broken ON
brugðu	brought OI, brought ON
brullaup	wedding ON, wedding OI
brutu	broke OI, broke ON
bryggjum	bridge OI, bridge ON
bryggjunum	bridge OI, bridge ON
bryti	steward ON
brýtur	divided OI
bú	a-farm ON, farm OI, settlement OI, settlement ON
búa	dwell OI, dwell ON, laid OI, laid ON, prepare OI, prepare ON, prepared OI, prepared ON
búast	prepared OI, prepared ON, stay OI, stay ON
búða	settlement ON, settlement OI
búðir	booths OI, booths ON
buðu	invited ON, invited OI, offered OI, offered ON
búfé	livestock ON, livestock OI
búi	dwelling OI, farm OI, farm ON, settled OI, settled ON, settlement OI, settlement ON
búið	dwelt OI, preparations OI, prepare OI, prepare ON, prepared OI, settlement OI
búin	prepared OI, ready OI, ready ON
búinn	prepared ON, prepared-with OI, ready OI, ready ON
búinu	dwelling ON
búit	dwelt ON, preparations ON, prepared ON, settlement ON
bundinn	bound OI, bound ON
bundu	bound ON, bound OI
búnir	prepared OI, prepared ON, ready OI, ready ON
bunu	Buna (name) ON, Buna (name) OI
búnu	are ON, are OI
búnyt	milk-products OI, milk-products ON
burt	away OI, away ON
bús	home OI, home ON, house OI, settlement OI, settlement ON
bústað	abode OI, abode ON, dwelling ON, dwelling OI, dwellings OI
bústaði	dwellings ON
búsvarðveislu	farming OI
búsvarðveizlu	farming ON
býðr	invited ON

Norse	English	Norse	English
býður	invited OI	daga	days OI, days ON
byggð	settlement OI, settlement ON	dagar	days OI
		dagmála	morning ON
byggðinni	settlement OI	dagmálastað	morning OI
byggðir	booths OI, dwellings OI, dwellings ON	dags	day ON
		dagsetri	day-setting ON, day-setting OI
byggðu	settled ON		
byggðum	settlement ON, settlement OI	dalalönd	dale-land ON, Dale-Land (place) OI
byggilegast	dwelling OI	dauð	dead OI, dead ON
byggiligast	dwelling ON	dauða	dead OI, death ON, the-dead ON
byggja	settle OI, settle ON		
byggjanda	habitable ON, habitable OI	dauðan	dead ON, dead OI
		dauðr	dead ON
byggjandi	habitable OI	dauðum	dead OI, dead ON
byggjum	inhabit OI, inhabit ON	dauður	dead OI
byggt	settled OI, settled ON	degi	day ON, day OI
byggva	settle ON	deila	share OI, share ON
byr	fair-wind OI, fair-wind ON, wind ON	deilur	disputes OI, disputes ON
býr	prepared OI, prepared ON	deyja	die OI
		dímunarvági	Dimunarvog (place) ON
byrðar	burdens OI, burdens ON		
byrðusmjörs	Byrdusmjors (name) ON	dímunarvogi	Dimunarvog (place) OI
		djúpúðgu	the-deep-minded ON, The-Deep-Minded (name) OI
byri	fair-wind OI, fair-wind ON		
byrina	fair-wind OI, fair-wind ON	dó	died ON
		dögg	dew OI, dew ON
byrjaði	began ON, began OI	döggina	dew OI, dew ON
byrjar	begin OI, begin ON, fair-wind OI, fair-wind ON	dögurðarár	Dogurdara (place) ON, Dogurdara (place) OI
byskups	bishop ON, Bishop (name) OI, Bishop'S (name) OI, the-bishop ON	dóttir	daughter OI, daughter ON, daughter-of ON, daughter-of OI
		dóttur	daughter ON, daughter OI, daughter-of OI, daughter-of ON
býst	prepared ON, prepared OI		
byttu	buckets ON, buckets OI	drakk	drank ON, drank OI
		drap	killed ON, killed OI
		drápu	killed ON, killed OI
		dregil	pulled OI, pulled ON
		drengiliga	bravely ON
		drengskap	honour ON

D, d

Norse	English	Norse	English
dægr	days ON	drepa	kill ON, kill OI, killed OI, killed ON
dægri	day OI		
dægrum	days OI, days ON	drepnir	killed OI, killed ON
dægur	days OI		
dag	day OI, day ON	drepr	failed ON

Norse	English
drepstokki	Drepstokk (place) OI, Drepstokk (place) ON
drepur	failed OI
dreyra	blood ON, blood OI
drífa	drove ON, drove OI
drifu	drove OI
drjúgari	ample ON, ample OI
drjúgum	greatly ON
dró	dragged ON, dragged OI, drew ON, drew OI, pulled ON
drógu	drew OI
dröngum	Drangar (place) OI, Drangar (place) ON
drottinn	master OI
dróttinn	master ON
drukkit	drink ON
drykk	drink ON, drink OI
duga	help OI, help ON
duldið	hidden ON
duldir	hidden OI
dura	door ON
durum	doorway ON
durunum	the-door ON
dvöl	dwelled OI, dwelled ON
dvöldust	dwelled OI
dvölðust	dwelled ON
dyflinnar	Dublin (place) ON
dyflinnarskíri	Dublinshire (place) ON, Dublinshire (place) OI
dyflinni	Dublin (place) ON, Dublin (place) OI
dygði	enough OI, enough ON
dýr	wild-animals ON, wild-animals OI
dyra	door OI
dýra	animals OI, animals ON
dýramerg	animal-marrow ON, animal-marrow OI
dýraveiðr	animal-hunting ON
dýrð	glory ON, glory OI
dyrin	doorway OI
dýrin	wild-animals ON, wild-animals OI
dyrnar	doors OI, doorway OI
dyrrin	doorway ON
dyrrnar	doors ON
dyrum	doorway OI
dýrum	wild-animals ON, wild-animals OI
dyrunum	out-door OI, the-door OI

E, e

Norse	English
eða	but OI, but ON, or OI, or ON
eðr	or ON
ef	if OI, if ON
efndi	kept OI, kept ON
efni	prospects ON
efnilegir	promising OI
efnilegsti	promising OI
efnilegur	promising OI
efniligir	promising ON
efniligsti	promising ON
efra	over OI, over ON
efst	highest OI
eftir	after OI, after ON, afterwards ON, afterwards OI, along ON, along OI, behind OI, behind ON, left OI, left ON, remained OI, remained ON
eftirbát	boat OI
eftirbátr	boat ON, boats ON
eftirbátur	boat OI, boats OI
eg	I OI, in OI
eggjaði	urged ON
eggjanna	eggs OI
eggjum	eggs ON
eggver	egg-gathering OI, eggs ON
eiga	marry ON, marry OI
eigi	no ON, no OI, none ON, none OI, not OI, not ON, not-be OI, not-be ON, was-not ON, was-not OI
eigum	own OI, own ON

Norse	English	Norse	English
ein	a OI, a ON, alone OI, alone ON, along OI, an ON, one OI, one ON, same ON, same OI	eiríks	Erik (name) OI, Erik (name) ON, Erik's (name) ON, Erik'S (name) OI
eina	one OI, one ON, only ON	eiríksdóttir	Eriksdottir (name) OI, Eriksdottir (name) ON
einar	Einar (name) ON, Einar (name) OI, only ON, only OI	eiríksey	Eriksey (place) OI, Eriksey (place) ON
		eiríkseyju	Eriksey (place) OI
einarr	Einar (name) ON	eiríksfirði	Eriksfjord (place) OI, Eriksfjord (place) ON
einars	einar's ON, Einar's (name) ON, Einar'S (name) OI	eiríksfjarðar	Eriksfjord (place) OI, Eriksfjord (place) ON
einarsfjörð	Einarsfjord (place) ON	eiríksfjörð	Eriksfjord (place) OI, Eriksfjord (place) ON
einfæting	one-footer ON, one-footer OI	eiríkshólmum	Eriksholmar (place) ON, Eriksholmar (place) OI
einfætingaland	One-Footer-Land (place) ON, One-Footer-Land (place) OI	eiríksson	Eriksson (name) ON, Eriksson (name) OI, Son-of-Erik (name) OI, Son-of-Erik (name) ON
einfætingi	one-footer OI		
einfætingr	a-one-footer ON, one-footer ON, the-one-footer ON	eiríkssonar	Son-of-Erik (name) OI, Son-of-Erik (name) ON
einfætingur	a-one-footer OI	eiríksstöðum	Eriksstadir (place) OI, Eriksstadir (place) ON
einfætingurinn	one-footer OI		
einhverju	one-such OI, one-such ON, some ON	eirikssyni	Eriksson (name) OI, Eriksson (name) ON
einn	a ON, a OI, one OI, one ON	eiríksvági	Eriksvog (place) ON
einnhver	any-of OI	eiríksvogi	Eriksvog (place) OI
einnhverr	any-of ON	eiríkur	Erik (name) OI
einni	alone ON, alone OI, one OI, one ON	eitt	alone OI, along OI, along ON, an ON, once ON, once OI, one OI, one ON, single ON
eins	likewise ON, likewise OI		
einsetukona	recluse OI, recluse ON	eitthvert	some OI
einskis	nothing ON, nothing OI, only OI	ek	I ON
		ekki	not OI, not ON, nothing OI, nothing ON
einþykkr	solitary ON		
einþykkur	solitary OI	elnaði	attacked OI, attacked ON
einu	one OI, one ON		
einum	any OI, any ON, one OI, one ON	elskað	loved OI
		elskat	loved ON
eiri	bronze ON, bronze OI	eltu	pursued ON, pursued OI
eirík	Erik (name) OI, Erik (name) ON	em	am ON
eiríki	Erik (name) OI, Erik (name) ON		
eiríkr	Erik (name) ON		

The Vinland Sagas — Word List (Norse to English)

Norse	English
en	and ᴏɪ, and ᴏɴ, as ᴏɪ, as ᴏɴ, before ᴏɴ, but ᴏɪ, but ᴏɴ, but-for ᴏɴ, but-for ᴏɪ, than ᴏɪ, than ᴏɴ, that ᴏɪ, that ᴏɴ, then ᴏɪ, then ᴏɴ, when ᴏɴ, when ᴏɪ, which ᴏɪ, while ᴏɪ, while ᴏɴ
enda	end ᴏɴ, end ᴏɪ
endunum	ends ᴏɴ, ends ᴏɪ
enga	any ᴏɴ, none ᴏɴ
engan	no ᴏɴ, none ᴏɴ
engar	no ᴏɴ, no ᴏɪ, none ᴏɴ
engi	no ᴏɪ, no ᴏɴ, none ᴏɪ, none ᴏɴ, no-one ᴏɴ, not ᴏɪ, not ᴏɴ, nothing ᴏɪ, nothing ᴏɴ
engin	no ᴏɴ
enginn	no ᴏɴ
engu	none ᴏɴ, nothing ᴏɴ
engum	no ᴏɴ, none ᴏɴ
enn	but ᴏɪ, but ᴏɴ, still ᴏɪ, still ᴏɴ, was ᴏɪ, was ᴏɴ, yet ᴏɪ, yet ᴏɴ
er	a ᴏɪ, a ᴏɴ, am ᴏɪ, am-i ᴏɴ, are ᴏɪ, are ᴏɴ, as ᴏɪ, as ᴏɴ, at ᴏɪ, at ᴏɴ, for ᴏɴ, is ᴏɪ, is ᴏɴ, spoke ᴏɪ, that ᴏɪ, that ᴏɴ, the ᴏɪ, then ᴏɪ, then ᴏɴ, to ᴏɴ, to ᴏɪ, was ᴏɪ, was ᴏɴ, were ᴏɪ, were ᴏɴ, when ᴏɪ, when ᴏɴ, where ᴏɪ, where ᴏɴ, which ᴏɪ, which ᴏɴ, who ᴏɪ, who ᴏɴ, who-was ᴏɴ
erendi	errand ᴏɴ
erendum	errand ᴏɴ
eríksfjörð	Eriksfjord (place) ᴏɴ, Eriksfjord (place) ᴏɪ
erindi	errand ᴏɪ
erindum	errand ᴏɪ
ermar	sleeves ᴏɴ, sleeves ᴏɪ
ert	are ᴏɴ, are ᴏɪ
ertu	are-you ᴏɪ, are-you ᴏɴ
eru	are ᴏɪ, are ᴏɴ, were ᴏɪ, were ᴏɴ
eruð	are ᴏɪ, are ᴏɴ
erum	are ᴏɴ, are ᴏɪ, we-are ᴏɪ, we-are ᴏɴ
es	where ᴏɴ, which ᴏɴ
ey	an-island ᴏɪ, island ᴏɪ, island ᴏɴ
eyðimerkr	deserted-forest ᴏɴ
eyðimerkur	deserted-forest ᴏɪ
eygð	eyed ᴏɪ, eyed ᴏɴ
eygðir	eyed ᴏɴ, eyes ᴏɪ
eyjar	islands ᴏɪ, the-island ᴏɪ, the-island ᴏɴ
eyjarinnar	island ᴏɪ, island ᴏɴ
eyjarnar	islands ᴏɴ, islands ᴏɪ
eyjólf	Eyolf (name) ᴏɴ, Eyolf (name) ᴏɪ
eyjólfr	Eyjolf (name) ᴏɴ, Eyolf (name) ᴏɴ
eyjólfs	Eyolf's (name) ᴏɪ, Eyolf's (name) ᴏɴ
eyjólfur	Eyjolf (name) ᴏɪ, Eyolf (name) ᴏɪ
eyjótt	islands ᴏɪ, islands ᴏɴ
eyju	island ᴏɪ, island ᴏɴ
eyki	animals ᴏɪ, animals ᴏɴ
eyktar	mid-afternoon ᴏɴ
eyktarstað	mid-afternoon ᴏɪ
eyland	island ᴏɪ, island ᴏɴ
eyna	island ᴏɪ, the-island ᴏɪ
eynni	island ᴏɴ, island ᴏɪ
eyra	ear ᴏɴ, ear ᴏɪ
eyrar	islands ᴏɪ, islands ᴏɴ, Islands (place) ᴏɪ
eysteins	Eystein (name) ᴏɴ, Eystein (name) ᴏɪ
eystri	eastern ᴏɪ, eastern ᴏɴ
eyvindar	Eyvind (name) ᴏɴ, Eyvind (name) ᴏɪ

É, é

Norse	English
ég	I ᴏɪ

F, f

The Vinland Sagas — Word List (Norse to English)

Norse	English
fá	be ON, be OI, get OI, get ON
faðerni	paternity ON, paternity OI
faðir	father OI, father ON, father-of OI, father-of ON, father-to OI
fæð	sadness ON
fæða	bear OI, feed ON, feed OI
fæddi	bore OI, bore ON
fæddr	fathered ON
fæddur	fathered OI
fæðist	born ON
fælast	frightened ON, frightened OI
fær	go ON
færa	bring OI, bring ON, brought OI, brought ON
færast	move ON, move OI
færð	taken ON, taken OI
færði	took OI, took ON
færðu	travelled OI, travelled ON, went ON, went OI
færi	travel ON
fært	going-out ON, taken OI, taken ON
færu	travel OI
fæti	feet OI, feet ON
fætr	feet ON
fættast	carry ON
fætur	feet OI
fagnað	welcomed OI
fagnat	welcomed ON
fagra	fair ON, fair OI
fagrt	beautiful ON
fagurt	beautiful OI
fái	give OI, give ON
fal	hid ON, hid OI
fala	bargain OI, bargain ON
falar	bargained-for OI, bargained-for ON
fálátari	withdrawn OI
fall	fall ON, fall OI
fallin	fallen OI, fallen ON
fallinn	fall ON, fall OI
fámálug	silent ON, silent OI
fámálugur	few-words OI
fang	grasp OI, grasp ON, provisions ON
fann	found OI, found ON
fannst	found OI, found ON
far	go OI, go ON
fara	go OI, go ON, to-go OI, to-travel OI, travel OI, travel ON, travelled OI, travelled ON, travelling ON, travelling OI, went OI
farar	travel OI, travel ON, voyages OI, voyages ON
fardreng	traveller-generous ON, traveller-generous OI
fardrengr	travelling-companion ON
fardrengur	travelling-companion OI
fari	go OI, go ON, travel OI, travel ON
farið	going OI, gone OI, travel OI, travelled OI
farir	travel OI
farit	going ON, gone ON, travel ON, travelled ON
farkost	vessel OI, vessel ON
farm	from ON
farmi	cargo OI, cargo ON
farminn	cargo OI, cargo ON
farmr	cargo ON
farmur	cargo OI
fásinni	remote OI, remote ON
fátæku	poor ON
fátækum	poor ON, poor OI
fátt	few OI
fé	cattle OI, cattle ON, wealth ON, wealth OI
feðga	father-and-son ON, father-and-son OI
feðgar	father-and-son ON, father-and-son OI
feðgum	father-and-son OI, father-and-son ON
feðr	father ON
fegri	more-beautiful ON, more-beautiful OI
féið	treasure OI, wealth OI
féit	treasure ON, wealth ON

The Vinland Sagas   Word List (Norse to English)

Norse	English
feitt	bold ON, bold OI
fekk	gave ON, got ON, married OI, married ON
fékk	gave OI, got OI, married OI
félaga	companion OI, companion ON, companions ON
félagar	comrades OI, comrades ON
fell	fell ON, mountain ON
féll	fell OI, mountain OI
fella	fell OI, fell ON
felldi	fell OI, fell ON, shed ON, shed OI
felldu	fell ON, fell OI
felli	rising ON
félli	rising OI
fellr	falls ON
fellu	fell ON
féllu	fell OI
fellur	falls OI
félögum	companions OI, companions ON
fémunum	goods OI, goods ON
fénað	cattle OI, cattle ON
fénaðr	cattle ON
fénaður	cattle OI
feng	gifts OI, gifts ON
fengi	got ON
fengið	caught OI, found OI, got OI
fengist	caught ON
fengit	caught ON, found ON, got ON
fengju	got OI
fengjust	caught OI
fengu	caught ON, caught OI, gathered OI, gathered ON, got OI
fer	goes OI, going OI, travel OI, travelled OI, went OI
ferð	journey OI, journey ON, travel OI, travel ON, voyage OI, voyage ON
ferðar	go OI, go ON, journey OI, journey ON, travel ON, travel OI, voyage OI, voyage ON
ferðum	voyages OI, voyages ON
ferr	goes ON, journeyed ON, travelled ON
festar	fixed ON
festi	joined ON
fimm	five OI, five ON
fimmtán	fifteen OI, fifteen ON
fingrar	finger ON, finger OI
fingrgull	finger-gold ON
fingurgull	finger-gold OI
finna	find OI, find ON, found ON, found OI
finnboga	Finnbogi (name) OI, Finnbogi (name) ON
finnbogi	Finnbogi (name) OI, Finnbogi (name) ON
finnið	find ON, find OI
finnst	finding ON
finnur	finding OI
firðinum	fjord ON, fjord OI, Fjord (place) OI, Fjord (place) ON
firr	further OI, further ON
fiska	fish OI, fish ON
fiskar	fish ON, fish OI
fiski	fishing ON
fiskum	fish ON, fish OI
fjár	wealth OI, wealth ON
fjarðarkjafta	Fjord-Mouth (place) OI, Fjord-Mouth (place) ON
fjarðskorið	fjords-carving OI
fjárhagur	finances OI
fjárkosta	financial-cost's ON, financial-cost's OI
fjóði	fourth OI
fjögr	four ON
fjögur	four OI
fjöl	plank OI, plank ON
fjölda	many OI
fjölða	many ON
fjöldi	many OI
fjölði	many ON

187

Word List (Norse to English)

Norse	English
fjölkunnig	full-knowing ON, full-knowing OI
fjöll	mountains OI, mountains ON
fjöllótt	mountainous OI, mountainous ON
fjölmenn	many-people OI
fjölmenna	many-men ON, many-men OI
fjölmenni	many OI, many ON
fjóra	forty ON
fjörð	fjord ON
fjórða	fourth OI, fourth ON
fjórði	fourth OI, fourth ON
fjörðinn	fjord OI, Fjord (place) OI, Fjord (place) ON
fjórir	four ON, four OI, many OI
fjörsins	live ON
fjórtán	fourteen OI, fourteen ON
fjöru	tide OI, tide ON
flatnefs	Flat-Nose (name) ON, Flat-Nose (name) OI
fleira	more OI, more ON
fleiri	more OI, more ON
flekk	a-speck OI, speck ON
flestir	mostly OI
flestra	most ON, most OI
fleygðu	flew ON
flíkr	banners ON
flíkur	banners OI
fljótast	immediately OI, immediately ON, quickly OI, quickly ON
fljótlega	soon OI
fljótliga	soon ON
fló	fled OI, fled ON, flew OI
flóðið	tide OI
flóðit	tide ON
flokkr	group ON
flokkur	group OI
flutt	performed ON
flutti	brought ON, brought OI
fluttr	transferred ON
fluttu	floated OI, floated ON
fluttur	transferred OI
flýja	fled OI, fled ON, fleeing ON
flytist	flows ON
flytja	carried ON, carried OI, carry OI, carry ON
fóðr	fodder ON
fóður	fodder OI
föður	father OI, father ON, father's ON, father-of OI, father-of ON
foldar	folds OI, folds ON
fólgið	hidden OI
fólgit	hidden ON
fólk	folk OI, folk ON, people ON, people OI
fólki	folk ON
fólkit	people ON
fölleit	pale OI, pale ON
föng	possessions OI, possessions ON, provisions OI, supplies ON
fór	came ON, came OI, journeyed OI, returned ON, returned OI, travelled OI, travelled ON, travelling OI, went ON, went OI
forðast	avoid ON, avoid OI
förinni	voyage OI, voyage ON
forlög	fortune OI, fortune ON, fortunes ON, fortunes OI
forlögum	fortune ON, fortune OI
formaðr	chief ON
formaður	chief OI
forræði	power ON, power OI
forsjá	foresight ON, foresight OI
fórst	travelled OI, travelled ON, went ON, went OI
fóru	travelled OI, travelled ON, went ON, went OI
fóruð	travelled OI
fórum	travelling ON

The Vinland Sagas   *Word List (Norse to English)*

Norse	English
förum	go ON, go OI, going ON, going OI, gone ON, gone OI, travel OI, travel ON, travelling OI, travel-we ON, travel-we OI
förunauta	companions OI, companions ON
förunautar	companions OI, companions ON
förunautum	travelling-men OI, travelling-men ON
förunautur	ship's-company OI
föruneyti	companions OI, companions ON
föruneytinu	companions OI, companions ON
forvitni	curiosity OI, curiosity ON, curious ON, curious OI
föstnuð	betrothed OI, betrothed ON
fóstra	foster ON, foster OI, foster-child ON, foster-child OI, foster-father OI, foster-father ON
fóstri	foster OI, foster ON
fóta	feet ON, feet OI
fótr	foot ON
fótum	feet OI, feet ON
fótur	foot OI
frá	from OI, from ON, time ON, time OI
fræði	knowledge OI, wisdom ON, wisdom OI
frænda	kinsmen ON, kinsmen OI
frændi	kinsman OI, kinsman ON
frændum	kinsmen OI, kinsmen ON
frændur	kinsman OI
fram	from OI, from OI, from ON, from ON
framar	from OI, from ON
framast	foremost ON, foremost OI
framgengt	from-going ON
framið	committed ON
framin	committed OI
frammi	from OI, from ON
framstafn	prow OI, prow ON
framt	provide OI
framúr	from OI
fráskili	separated OI, separated ON
frásögn	said OI, said ON
frásögnum	account ON, account OI
fremi	provide ON
fremja	perform ON, perform OI
frétt	news ON, news OI
frétti	heard ON, heard OI
freydís	Freydis (name) OI, Freydis (name) ON
freydísar	Freydis (name) OI, Freydis (name) ON
freydísi	Freydis (name) OI, Freydis (name) ON
fríð	peaceful OI
friðarmark	peace-mark ON
friðartákn	peace-mark OI
friðgerðar	Fridgerdar (name) ON
friðmenn	peaceful-men OI, peaceful-men ON
friðrekr	Fridrek (name) ON
friðrekur	Fridrek (name) OI
frjálsa	free ON, free OI
fróðari	wiser OI
fróðárundr	hauntings ON
fróðárundur	hauntings OI
fróðir	wise OI, wise ON
fróðleiks	knowledge ON, knowledge OI
fróðr	wise ON
fróður	wise OI
frost	frost OI, frost ON
fugl	birds ON, birds OI, wild-birds OI
fullkomna	full-come ON, full-come OI
fullr	full ON
fulltrúann	patron ON, patron OI
fullur	full OI
fund	find ON, find OI, meet OI, meet ON, visit OI, visit ON
fundar	meet OI, meet ON
fundi	meet OI, meet ON

The Vinland Sagas — Word List (Norse to English)

Norse	English
fundið	found OI
fundit	found ON
fundr	battle ON
fundu	found OI, found ON
fundur	battle OI
fundust	found OI, met ON, were-found ON
furðustrandir	Furdustrandir (place) ON, Furdustrandir (place) OI
furðuströndum	Furdustrandir (place) ON, Furdustrandir (place) OI
fús	willing OI
fúss	willing ON
fylgd	follow OI
fylgð	follow ON
fylgdar	follow OI
fylgdi	followed OI
fylgði	followed ON
fylgdu	followed OI
fylgðu	followed ON
fylgi	follow OI
fylgir	followed OI
fylgja	follow OI, follow ON, to-follow OI
fylgt	followed ON, followed OI
fylldr	filled ON
fylltur	filled OI
fyndi	found OI, found ON
fyr	for ON, for OI
fyrir	ahead ON, ahead OI, ahead-of OI, ahead-of ON, along ON, along OI, and OI, at-hand OI, at-hand ON, because-of ON, because-of OI, because-of-a OI, because-of-a ON, before OI, before ON, for OI, for ON, for-the OI, for-the ON, present OI, present ON, therefore OI, to ON before OI, before ON, for ON, for OI
fyrr	before OI, before ON, for ON, for OI
fyrra	first OI, first ON
fyrri	before OI, before ON
fyrst	first OI, first ON
fyrsta	first OI, first ON
fýsa	attract OI, attract ON, desire ON, desire OI
fýsist	desired OI
fýsti	desired ON, desired OI
fýstist	desired OI, desired ON
fýstu	urged OI, urged ON

G, g

Norse	English
gáðu	heeded ON, looked OI
gæða	quality OI, quality ON
gæðalaust	without-quality OI, without-quality ON
gæði	quality OI, quality ON
gæðum	quality OI, quality ON
gæfa	gift OI
gæfi	gave ON, gave OI, give OI, give ON
gæfu	gifted ON
gæsku	goodness OI
gæsla	herding OI
gæzla	herding ON
gaf	gave OI, gave ON
gáfu	gave ON, gave OI
gagnvart	going-from ON, going-from OI
gakk	go ON
gall	bellowed OI
gamlason	Gamlason (name) ON, Gamlason (name) OI
ganga	go OI, go ON, walk ON, went OI, went ON
gangast	go OI, go ON
gangi	go ON, go OI
gangir	go OI, go ON
gapði	gaping ON
gapti	agape OI
garða	Gardar (place) OI
garðar	Gardar (place) ON
garðarr	Gardi (name) ON
garði	garden ON, garden OI, Gardi (name) OI
garðs	garden OI

Word List (Norse to English)

Norse	English
gáttum	doorway OI, doorway ON
gaum	heed ON, heed OI
geðjaðir	agreeable ON
gefa	give OI, give ON
gefið	given ON, given OI
gefin	given ON, given OI, married OI, married ON, marry OI
gefit	given ON
gegnt	opposite OI, opposite ON
geirsteinn	Gerstein (name) ON, Gerstein (name) OI
geislar	rays ON
geisli	rays OI
gekk	going OI, going ON, walked ON, walked OI, went OI, went ON
gellis	Gellir (name) OI, Gellir (name) ON, Gellis (name) ON
gellr	bellowed ON
gengið	go OI, gone OI
gengin	gone OI, gone ON
genginn	going OI, going ON
gengit	go ON, gone ON
gengr	went ON
gengu	went OI, went ON
gengur	went OI
ger	made ON, made OI
gera	did OI, did ON, do OI, do ON, made OI, made ON, make OI, make ON
gerði	did OI, did ON, made OI, made ON, was OI, was ON
gerðist	became OI, became ON, became-a ON, becoming OI, happened ON, happened OI, made OI, made ON
gerðu	did OI, did ON, made OI, made ON, make OI, make ON
gerður	made OI
gerðust	did OI, did ON, made OI, made ON
gerið	make ON, make OI
gerir	did OI, did ON, made OI, made ON
gerist	was OI
gerr	made ON
gersemi	treasure OI
gersimi	treasure ON
gerst	made OI, made ON
gert	done OI, done ON, made ON, made OI, was OI, was ON, was-done ON
gervir	made ON, made OI
gerzt	made ON
get	can ON, do ON, guess ON, guess OI
geta	can ON, could OI
getið	told-of OI
getit	told-of ON
gift	married OI, married ON
gifta	give ON, give OI
giftast	marry ON, marry OI
gifti	gave ON, gave OI
giftu	luck ON, luck OI
gildir	thick ON, thick OI
gjafar	gifts ON
gjafir	gifts OI
gjaforð	given OI, married ON, married OI
gjaforðs	marriage-offer ON, marriage-offer OI
gjalda	expenses ON, expenses OI
gjalla	snorting OI, snorting ON
gjarna	gladly OI
glaumbæ	Glaumbaer (place) OI
glaumbæjarland	Glaumbaer (place) OI, Glaumbaer (place) ON
glaunbæ	Glaumbaer (place) ON
gleði	gladness ON, gladness OI
glertölur	glass-beads ON, glass-beads OI
glitraði	glittered ON, glittered OI
glöggsæ	clear OI
glóra	The-Sensible (name) ON

The Vinland Sagas — Word List (Norse to English)

Norse	English
glumru	Glumra (name) ON, Glumra (name) OI
gnóttir	abundance ON, abundance OI
góð	good OI, good ON
góða	good ON, good OI
góðan	good ON, good OI
góðar	good ON, good OI
góðir	good ON, good OI
góðmannlega	good-man-like OI
góðmannliga	good-man-like ON
goðorðsmaður	good-words-man OI
góðr	a-good ON, good ON
góðra	good OI, good ON
góðs	good OI
góðu	good OI, good ON
góður	a-good OI, good OI
góðvilja	good-will ON, good-will OI
göfgan	esteemed ON, esteemed OI
göfgasti	respectable OI, respectable ON
göfgir	noble ON, noble OI
göfgustum	respectable OI, respectable ON
göfugmenni	greatest OI, greatest ON, noble ON, noble OI
goldið	gold OI
goldit	gold ON
gólfið	floor OI
gólfit	floor ON
görðum	Gardar (place) OI, Gardar (place) ON
gott	benefit OI, benefit ON, benefited ON, benefitted OI, good OI, good ON
graðfé	cattle OI, cattle ON
graðungr	bull ON
graðungur	bull OI
grænland	Greenland (place) OI, Greenland (place) ON
grænlandi	Greenland (place) OI, Greenland (place) ON
grænlands	Greenland (place) OI, Greenland (place) ON
grænlandsferðar	Greenland-voyage OI, Greenland-voyage ON
grænlandshaf	Greenland-Sea (place) OI, Greenland-Sea (place) ON
grænlenskan	Greenland-Skin (place) OI
grænlenskir	Greenlander (place) OI
grænlenskum	Greenlander (place) OI
grænlenzkan	greenland-skin ON
grænlenzkum	Greenlander (place) ON
grafa	engrave OI, engrave ON
grafar	trenches ON
grafir	trenches OI
grafnir	buried ON, buried OI
gras	grass OI, grass ON
grasinu	grass OI, grass ON
grautr	porridge ON
grautur	porridge OI
grávara	grey-skins OI, grey-skins ON
greiðleg	smoothly OI
greiðlig	smoothly ON
grélaðar	Grelod (name) ON, Grelod (name) OI
gretti	frowned OI, frowned ON
griðung	bull OI, bull ON
griðungr	bull ON
griðungur	a-bull OI
grímhildar	Grimhild's OI
grímhildr	Grimhild (name) ON
grímhildur	Grimhild (name) OI
grímólfsson	Grimolfson (name) ON, Grimolfson (name) OI
grjótinu	stones OI
grjótit	stones ON
gró	Gro (name) ON, Groa (name) OI
gröfunum	trenches ON, trenches OI
grön	green ON, green OI
grös	grass OI, grass ON
grunar	suspect ON, suspect OI
grunnsævi	shallows OI, shallows ON

Norse	English	Norse	English
guð	god ON, God (name) OI, God's (name) ON, God'S (name) OI	hafgrímr	Hafgrim (name) ON
		hafgrímsfjörð	Hafgrimsfjord (place) OI, Hafgrimsfjord (place) ON
guðríðar	Guthrid (name) OI, Guthrid (name) ON	hafgrímur	Hafgrim (name) OI
guðríði	Guthrid (name) OI, Guthrid (name) ON	hafi	had ON, had OI, have OI, have ON, sea ON, sea OI
guðríðr	Guthrid (name) ON	hafið	have OI, have ON
guðríður	Guthrid (name) OI	hafim	have ON
guðröðarsonar	Son-of-Gudrod (name) ON, Son-Of-Gudrod (name) OI	háflæðum	high-tide ON, high-tide OI
guðs	god ON, God's (name) ON, God'S (name) OI	hafs	sea OI, sea ON
		haft	had OI, had ON
gull	gold ON, gold OI	hafvillur	open-sea ON
gulls	gold OI, gold ON	hagi	state ON, state OI
gunnbjarnarsker	Gunnbjarnarsker (place) OI, Gunnbjarnarsker (place) ON	hagleik	sports OI, sports ON
		hagr	benefits ON
		hagstætt	favourable OI
gunnbjörn	Gunnbjorn (name) OI, Gunnbjorn (name) ON	haki	Haki (name) ON, Haki (name) OI
		halda	have OI, held OI, held ON, hold OI, hold ON, holding ON, keep OI, keep ON

H, h

Norse	English	Norse	English
hæðir	heights OI, heights ON	haldast	hold OI, hold ON
hægendi	a-cushion ON	haldi	hold OI, hold ON
hægindi	pillows OI	haldið	staying OI
hænsafiðri	hen's-feathers ON, hen's-feathers OI	haldinorðir	held-words OI, held-words ON
hætta	danger ON, danger OI, leave ON, leave OI	hálfa	half OI, half ON
		hálfan	half OI, half ON
hætti	stop OI, stop ON, way OI, way ON	hálfdanarsonar	Son-of-Halfdan (name) ON, Son-Of-Halfdan (name) OI
hættir	gave-up ON, manner ON, mannered OI	hálfr	half ON, half-of ON
haf	sea OI, sea ON	hálft	half-of ON, half-of OI
hafa	at-sea ON, at-sea OI, had ON, had OI, have OI, have ON, have-been OI, having OI, having ON, sea OI, sea ON	hálfur	half OI, half-of OI
		hallæri	famine ON, famine OI
		hallar	hall OI, hall ON
		hallat	inclined ON
		halldís	Halldis (name) ON, Halldis (name) OI
hafði	had OI, had ON, had-been OI, had-been ON, have OI, married ON	hallfríðr	Hallfrid (name) ON
		hallfríður	Hallfrid (name) OI
hafðir	have ON, have OI	hallist	will-be OI
hafgerðingadrápu	sea-poem OI, sea-poem ON	hallveig	Hallveig (name) ON, Hallveig (name) OI

The Vinland Sagas   Word List (Norse to English)

Norse	English	Norse	English
hálmþúst	straw-staves ON	hausti	autumn OI, autumn ON
hálmþústum	straw-staves OI	haustið	autumn OI
hálsi	neck ON, neck OI	haustit	autumn ON
hamargnípu	cliff-top ON, cliff-top OI	heðan	hence ON
hamra	crags ON, crags OI	héðan	hence OI
han	he ON	hef	have OI
hana	he OI, her OI, her ON, him OI, him ON, it ON, it OI, she OI, she ON, that OI	hefða	had ON
		hefði	had ON, had OI, have ON
		hefðu	had OI
hann	[she] ON, he OI, he ON, he-was ON, him OI, him ON, himself ON, it OI, it ON, she OI	hefi	have OI, have ON
		hefir	had ON, had OI, has OI, has ON, have OI, have ON
hans	he OI, he ON, him OI, him ON, his OI, his ON, to-him ON	hefnir	avenge OI, avenge ON
		hefr	had ON
		hefur	had OI
happ	zeal ON, zeal OI	heiðið	heathen OI
happfróð	lucky-wise ON	heiðis	heath OI, heath ON
hár	hair OI, hair ON	heiðit	heathen ON
hárar	high ON	heiðni	heathenry OI
harða	hard ON, hard OI	heil	well ON, well OI, whole ON, whole OI
hárrar	high OI		
hart	rough ON, rough OI	heill	luck OI, luck ON
hásæti	a-high-seat ON, a-high-seat OI	heilu	whole OI, whole ON
háseta	men OI, men ON	heim	home OI, home ON, homes ON
hásetar	sailors OI, sailors ON	heima	home OI, home ON, homes ON
hásetum	sailors OI, sailors ON		
hátt	high OI, high ON, loud ON, loudly OI, loudly ON	heimamönnum	housemen ON, housemen OI
háttað	the-way OI	heiman	home OI, home ON
hattar	customs ON, customs OI	heimilis	households ON
		heimilt	may OI
háttar	kind ON, kind OI	heimkynna	households OI
háttat	the-way ON	heimti	claimed ON, claimed OI
háttr	the-way ON, way ON	heita	called ON, named OI, named ON
háttur	the-way OI, way OI		
haukadal	Haukadal (place) OI, Haukadal (place) ON	heiti	am-named ON, name OI, name ON, named OI, named ON
haukdælski	Haukadal (place) OI, Haukadal (place) ON		
		heitið	pledged OI
hausakljúfr	Scull-Cleaver (name) ON	heitir	called ON, is-named OI, is-named ON, named OI, named ON
hausakljúfur	Scull-Cleaver (name) OI		
haust	autumn ON, autumn OI	heitit	called ON, pledged ON
haustboð	harvest-feast ON, harvest-feast OI	hekja	Hekja (name) ON, Hekja (name) OI

194

The Vinland Sagas — Word List (Norse to English)

Norse	English
heldi	held ON
heldr	behold ON, held ON, Heldr'S (name) OI, rather ON
heldr's	Heldr's (name) ON
heldu	busy ON, held ON
héldu	busy OI, held OI
heldur	behind OI, behold OI, held OI, rather OI
helga	Helga (name) OI, Helga (name) ON, Helgi (name) OI
helgasonar	Helgason (name) OI, Son-of-Helga (name) ON
helgi	Helgi (name) OI, Helgi (name) ON
helgir	flat ON, flat OI
hella	flat-stones ON, flat-stones OI, stone-slab OI, stone-slab ON
hellisvöllum	Hellisvellir (place) ON, Hellisvellir (place) OI
helluland	Helluland (place) OI, Helluland (place) ON
hellum	caves ON, caves OI
hellur	slabs ON, slabs OI
hellusteinn	a-slab-stone OI, slab-stone ON
helming	half OI, half ON
helmingr	half ON
helmingur	half OI
helst	preferably OI
helt	held ON
hélt	held OI
helzt	preferably ON, rather ON
hendi	arm OI, arm ON, hand ON, hand OI
hendr	caught ON, hand ON
hendur	caught OI, hand OI
hennar	for-her ON, for-her OI, her OI, her ON, hers OI, hers ON, she ON, she OI
henni	he OI, he ON, her OI, her ON, hers ON, hers OI, him ON, she ON, she OI, to-her ON, to-her OI
hent	joined ON, joined OI
hentar	suits ON, suits OI
heppni	lucky OI, lucky ON
hér	here OI, here ON, she ON
herðir	hardened ON, hardened OI
herjaði	harried ON, harried OI
herjólfi	Herjolf (name) ON
herjólfr	Herjolf (name) ON
herjólfsfjörð	Herjolfsfjord (place) OI, Herjolfsfjord (place) ON
herjólfsnes	Herjolfsnes (place) ON, Herjolfsnes (place) OI
herjólfsnesi	Herjolfsnes (place) OI, Herjolfsnes (place) ON
herjólfsson	Son-of-Herjolf (name) ON
herjólfssonar	Son-of-Herjolf (name) ON
herjólfur	Herjolf (name) OI
herjúlfi	Herjolf (name) OI
herjúlfsnesi	Herjolfsness (place) OI
herjúlfsson	Son-of-Herjolf OI
herjúlfssonar	Son-of-Herjolf OI
herjúlfur	Herjolf (name) OI
herkonungr	warrior-king ON
herkonungur	a-warrior-king OI
hertekinn	war-taken ON, war-taken OI
hertekna	captive ON, captive OI
herteknir	war-taken ON, war-taken OI
hést	promised OI
hesthöfða	Horse-Head (name) OI, Horse-Head (name) ON
hesthöfði	Horse-Head (name) ON
hestrinn	horse's ON
hesturinn	horse's OI
hét	called ON, named OI, named ON, was ON, was-called ON, was-named OI, was-named ON

The Vinland Sagas — Word List (Norse to English)

Norse	English
héti	named ON, named OI, was-named OI, was-named ON
hétu	called ON, named OI, pledged OI
heyr	hear ON
heyra	hear ON, hear OI
heyrði	heard OI, heard ON
heyrðu	hear OI, heard ON
heyrt	heard ON, heard OI
hézt	promised ON
híbýlabótar	living-space OI
híbýli	dwelling OI, dwelling ON, dwellings ON, dwellings OI
hið	the OI
hímu	aunt ON
hin	in OI, that OI, the OI
hina	the OI, the ON
hindrvitni	hindered-knowledge ON
hingað	here OI
hingat	here ON
hinir	others ON, others OI
hinn	a OI, he OI, in OI, of OI, the OI
hinni	of-the OI, the OI
hins	the OI
hinu	the OI
hinum	the OI
hirða	consider ON
hirðar	court ON, court OI
hirðmaðr	court-man ON
hirðmaður	court-man OI
hítardal	Hitardal (place) OI, Hitardal (place) ON
hitt	encounter ON, encounter OI, other ON, they OI
hitti	met ON, met OI
hittir	met ON
hittu	met OI, met ON
hjá	beside ON, beside OI, by ON, by OI, heard ON, near OI, near ON
hjallinn	the-platform ON
hjálp	help ON, help OI
hjálpa	help OI
hjálpar	help ON
hjó	struck OI, struck ON
hjón	couple OI, couple ON
hjónum	couple OI
hjónunum	couple ON
hjörð	hearth ON, herd OI
hjörtu	hearts ON, hearts OI
hjú	hearth OI, herd ON
hlaupa	ran ON, ran OI, run ON, run OI
hlaut	lot ON, lot OI
hleypr	ran ON
hleypur	ran OI
hliðum	sides OI
hliðunum	sides ON
hljóðlyndr	quiet ON
hljóðlyndur	quiet OI
hljóðs	be-heard ON, be-heard OI
hljóp	ran ON, ran OI
hljópu	ran ON, ran OI
hljótt	quietly ON, quietly OI
hlotist	lots OI
hlupu	running ON
hluta	lot ON, lots OI, part OI, Part's (name) ON
hlutaðir	lots ON
hlutaðist	lots OI
hlutföllum	lot-taking OI
hluti	part-of OI, part-of ON, things OI, things ON
hlutir	things ON, things OI
hlutr	lot ON
hlutuðu	lots ON
hlutur	lot OI
hlýðni	homage ON, homage OI
hnappinn	knob OI
hnappur	a-knob OI, fastening OI
hné	knee ON
hneig	knee OI
hneppt	fastened OI
hníf	knife ON, knife OI
hniginn	declining OI, declining ON
hnígr	fell ON
hnígur	fell OI

Norse	English	Norse	English
hnjóskulinda	a-girdle ON, a-girdle OI	höndum	hand ON, hand OI, handed OI, handed ON, hands OI, hands ON
höfð	have OI, have ON, taken OI, taken ON	honum	he OI, he ON, her OI, him OI, him ON, his OI, his ON, to-him OI, to-him ON
höfða	headland OI, headland ON, Hofda (place) ON		
höfðann	headland OI, headland ON	hópi	Hop (place) ON, Hop (place) OI, tidal-pool ON, tidal-pool OI
höfðanum	headland OI, headland ON		
höfðaströnd	Hofdastrond (place) ON	hópit	group ON
höfði	head OI, head ON, heads ON, heads OI	hörð	hard ON, hard OI
höfðingi	leader OI, leader ON	horfa	turn OI, turn ON
höfðinglegt	having-like OI	horfði	looked OI, looking ON
höfðingligt	having-like ON	horfðu	looked ON
höfðu	had OI, had ON, heads OI	horfin	disappeared OI, disappeared ON
höfga	heaviness OI, heaviness ON	horfinn	disappeared ON, disappeared OI
hófsmaðr	moderate-man ON	hörmung	horrible ON, horrible OI
hófsmaður	moderate-man OI	hornströndum	Hornstrandir (place) OI, Hornstrandir (place) ON
höfuð	head OI, head ON, heads ON, heads OI		
höfum	have OI, have ON	höttr	hood ON
hófust	began ON	hötturinn	hoods OI
hogginn	cut-down OI	hræddust	frightened OI, frightened ON
höggr	hewed ON		
höggur	hewed OI	hrærðist	stirred ON, stirred OI
höggva	fell OI, fell ON, strike OI, strike ON	hrafn	Hrafn (name) OI, Hrafn (name) ON
höggvinn	cut-down ON	hrafnsfjörð	Hrafnsfjord (place) OI, Hrafnsfjord (place) ON
höldnu	safe OI, safe ON		
hólmgöngu-hrafn	Raven-the-Dueller (name) ON, Raven-The-Dueller (name) OI	hraunhafnarósi	Hraunhafnaros (place) ON, Hraunhafnaros (place) OI
hólmgöngu-hrafns	Raven-The-Dueller (name) OI, Raven-The-Dueller (name) ON		
		hríð	awhile ON, time OI, time ON
hólmlátri	Holmlatr (place) ON, Holmlatr (place) OI	hring	a-ring ON, a-ring OI
		hróaldssonar	Roaldsson (name) ON
hólmum	Holm (place) OI, Holm (place) ON	hryggs	the-sad ON
		húðföt	skin-cots OI, skin-cots ON
holta	hills ON, hills OI	húðkeipa	skin-boats OI, skin-boats ON
holum	holes ON, holes OI		
hon	it ON, she ON	hug	mind ON, mind OI, thoughts OI, thoughts ON
hönd	arm OI, arm ON, hand OI, hand ON		
höndina	hand ON	hugðum	thought OI, thought ON

The Vinland Sagas — Word List (Norse to English)

Norse	English
huggaði	comforted OI, comforted ON
hugganar	comfort ON
huggunar	comfort OI
hún	her OI, it OI, she OI, she ON
hundrað	hundred ON
hundraðs	hundred OI
hurð	door OI, door ON
hurðinni	door OI, door ON
hurfu	disappeared ON, disappeared OI
hús	house ON, house OI, houses OI, houses ON
húsa	houses OI, houses ON
húsanna	houses OI, houses ON
húsasnotru	house-besom OI, house-besom ON
húsasnotruna	house-besom OI, house-besom ON
húsfreyja	housewife OI, housewife ON
húsfreyju	housewife OI, housewife ON
húsgerð	house-building OI, house-building ON
húsin	house ON, houses OI, houses ON
húskarli	houseman OI, houseman ON
húss	houses OI, houses ON
húsunum	the-house ON, the-house OI
hvað	to-that OI, what OI, what ON
hval	whale ON, whale OI
hvala	whale ON
hvalinn	whale OI, whale ON
hvalnum	whales OI
hvalr	a-whale ON
hvalur	whale OI
hvammi	Hvamm (place) ON, Hvamm (place) OI
hvar	where OI, where ON
hvarf	disappeared OI, disappeared ON
hvarfsgnípu	Hvarfsgnipu (place) OI, Hvarfsgnipu (place) ON
hvárigir	neither ON
hvárir	each ON
hvárirtveggju	either-side ON
hvárki	neither ON
hvárkis	neither ON
hvárt	either ON, how ON, if ON, whether ON
hvasst	stormy OI, stormy ON
hvat	what ON
hvé	how ON
hveiti	wheat OI
hveitiakra	wheat-acres ON, wheat-acres OI
hveitiakrar	wheat-acres ON, wheat-acres OI
hveitiax	wheat ON
hvenær	when OI
hver	each OI, each-of OI, every OI, who OI, who ON
hverfr	turned ON
hverfur	turned OI
hvergi	neither OI, neither ON
hverju	each OI, each ON
hverjum	each OI, each ON
hvern	each OI, each ON
hverr	each ON, every ON, who ON
hversdaglega	always OI
hversu	how OI, how ON
hvert	what OI, where OI, where ON, which OI, which ON
hví	why OI, why ON
hvíldarstaða	resting-place OI
hvíldastaða	resting-place ON
hvílu	bed OI, bed ON
hvít	white ON
hvítan	white ON, white OI
hvítbeins	White-Leg (name) ON, White-Leg (name) OI
hvíti	the-White (name) ON, The-White (name) OI
hvítir	white OI, white ON
hvítramannaland	White-Man-Land (place) ON, White-Man-Land (place) OI
hvítt	white OI

198

Norse	English
hvítum	white ON, white OI
hvorgis	neither OI
hvorigir	neither OI
hvorir	each OI
hvorirtveggju	either-side OI
hvorki	neither OI
hvort	either OI, how OI, if OI, whether OI
hvorttveggja	each-way OI
hvorutveggja	either-way OI
hýbýli	dwelling ON
hygg	think OI, think ON
hyggja	thought OI, thought ON

I, i

Norse	English
i	to ON
iljar	feet OI
illa	a-bad ON, bad OI, bad ON, badly ON, badly OI, evil OI, evil ON
illilega	badly OI
illilegir	ill-looking OI
illiliga	badly ON
illiligir	ill-looking ON
illorðr	difficult-of-words ON
illr	ill ON
ills	ill OI, ill ON
illsku	ill-will OI, ill-will ON
illt	disorderly ON, disorderly OI, ill ON, ill OI
illugi	Illugi (name) ON, Illugi (name) OI
illur	ill OI
ilmað	favoured OI
ilmat	favoured ON
in	in ON, the ON
ina	the ON
ingjalds	Ingjald's (name) ON, Ingjald'S (name) OI
ingólfi	Ingolf (name) ON, Ingolf (name) OI
ingólfr	Ingolf (name) ON
ingólfs	Ingolf's (name) OI, Ingolf's (name) ON
ingólfur	Ingolf (name) OI
inn	a ON, he ON, in OI, in ON, inside OI, of ON, that OI, that ON, the OI, the ON, then OI, then ON
innan	in ON, in OI, inside ON, inside OI, within OI, within ON
inni	in OI, in ON, of-the ON, the ON
innstr	inside ON
innstur	inside OI
ins	the ON
inu	the ON
inum	in ON, the ON
it	the ON, to ON

Í, í

Norse	English
í	a ON, a OI, about ON, about OI, among OI, among ON, at OI, at ON, ay ON, in OI, in ON, into OI, into ON, is OI, is ON, it OI, it ON, of ON, of OI, on OI, on ON, the OI, this ON, to OI, to ON
íhuga	thought ON, thought OI
írakonungs	Ireland-King (name) ON
írland	Ireland (place) ON, Ireland (place) OI
írlandi	Ireland (place) ON, Ireland (place) OI
írlandshaf	the-Irish-Sea (place) ON
ísland	Iceland (place) OI, Iceland (place) ON
íslandi	Iceland (place) OI, Iceland (place) ON
íslands	Iceland (place) OI, Iceland (place) ON
íslenskir	Icelanders OI
íslenskum	Icelander OI
íslenskur	Icelander (place) OI
íslenzkir	Icelanders ON
íslenzkr	Icelander (place) ON
íslenzkum	Icelander ON

Norse	English
ístruna	belly-fat ON, the belly OI
íþróttamaðr	excellent ON
íþróttamaður	excellent OI

J, j

Norse	English
jaðri	Jaeren (place) OI, Jaeren (place) ON
jafn	equal OI
jafna	equal ON
jafnan	equal ON, equal OI, equally ON, equally OI, ever OI, ever ON
jafndægri	equal-day OI, equal-day ON
jafnlangt	equal-long ON, equal-long OI
jafnmannvænn	equally-handsome ON
jafnmikið	equal OI
jafnmikil	equal OI, equal ON
jafnmikit	equal ON
jafnsætt	as-sweet OI, as-sweet ON
jafnsaman	equally OI, equally ON
jarl	earl OI, earl ON, Earl (name) ON, Earl (name) OI
jarli	Earl (name) ON, Earl (name) OI
jarls	earl OI, earl ON, earl's OI, earl's ON
járnsíðu	Ironside (name) ON
játar	accepted OI, accepted ON
játtu	agreed OI, agreed ON
jöfnum	even OI, even ON
jöklanna	mountains OI, mountains ON
jöklar	glaciers OI, glaciers ON
jökli	glacier ON, glacier OI
jöklum	glaciers OI, glaciers ON
jökull	glaciers OI, glaciers ON
jól	Yule (name) ON, Yule (name) OI
jólaveislu	Yule-Feast (name) OI
jólaveizlu	yule-feast ON
jólin	Yule (name) ON, Yule (name) OI
jólum	Yule (name) ON, Yule (name) OI
jörð	land OI, land ON, the-earth OI
jörðuð	buried OI, buried ON
jörundar	Jorund (name) OI, Jorund (name) ON
jörva	Jorfi (name) ON, Jorfi (place) OI

K, k

Norse	English
kæmi	came OI, came ON, come ON, come OI
kæmir	come OI
kaf	submerge ON
kálfskinnsskó	calf-skin-shoes OI
kálfskinnsskúa	calf-skin-shoes ON
kall	shout OI, shout ON
kalla	call OI, call ON
kallað	called OI
kallaði	called OI, called ON
kallaðir	called ON, called OI
kallaðr	called ON
kallaður	called OI
kallast	considered ON
kallat	called ON
kallið	call OI, call ON
kallim	call ON
kallit	call ON
kalt	cold ON, cold OI
kann	can ON, can OI, can-it ON, it OI, know OI, know ON, known ON
kanna	explore OI, explore ON, exploring OI
kannað	explored OI
kannat	explored ON
kápu	cape OI, cape ON
karla	men OI, men ON
karlar	men OI, men ON
karlmaðrinn	menservants ON
karlmaðurinn	servants OI
karlsefni	Karlsefni (name) OI, Karlsefni (name) ON

The Vinland Sagas   Word List (Norse to English)

Norse	English
karlsefnis	Karlsefni's (name) OI, Karlsefni's (name) ON
karlsefnissonar	Karlsefnison (name) ON, Karlsefnison (name) OI, Son-of-Karlesfni (name) OI, Son-of-Karlesfni (name) ON, Son-of-Karlsefni (name) ON
kasta	cast OI, cast ON
kastaði	cast OI
katanes	Caithness (place) ON, Caithness (place) OI
katanesi	Caithness (place) ON, Caithness (place) OI
kátari	merrier ON, merrier OI
kattarskinn	cat-skin ON, cat-skin OI
kattskinnsglófa	cat-skin-gloves ON, cat-skin-gloves OI
kaupa	buy OI, buy ON, purchase ON, purchase OI
kaupferðum	trading-journeys ON, trading-journeys OI
kaupför	purchases OI, purchases ON
kaupir	bought ON, bought OI
kaupmenn	trading-men ON, trading-men OI
kaupmönnum	trading-men ON, trading-men OI
kaupskipið	merchant-ship OI
kaupskipinu	merchant-ship OI
kaupskipit	merchant-ship ON
kaupstefna	trading-posts ON, trading-posts OI
kaupstefnu	trading-posts ON, trading-posts OI
keip	canoe OI, canoe ON
keipana	trading ON, trading OI
keldu	wellspring ON, wellspring OI
kemr	came ON, come ON
kemur	came OI, come OI, coming OI
kenndi	knew ON, knew OI, taught ON, taught OI
kenndu	knew OI, taught ON, taught OI
kenni	recognise ON, recognise OI
kennimenn	priest ON, priests OI
kennimönnum	priests ON, priests OI
kenni-val	know-choose ON, know-choose OI
kennt	known OI, known ON
ketill	Ketil (name) OI, Ketil (name) ON
ketils	Ketil (name) OI, Ketil's (name) ON
ketilsfjörð	Ketilsfjord (place) OI, Ketilsfjord (place) ON
ketilssonar	Son-of-Ketil (name) ON, Son-Of-Ketil (name) OI
keypti	bought OI, bought ON
keyptu	sold OI, sold ON
kiðjamjólk	kid's-milk ON, kid's-milk OI
kinnum	cheeks ON
kinnunum	cheeks OI
kippa	pulled ON, pulled OI
kirkja	church OI, church ON
kirkju	church OI, church ON, the-church ON
kista	coffin ON, coffin OI
kistil	chest ON, chest OI
kistu	coffin OI, coffin ON
kistur	coffins OI, coffins ON
kjafal	kjafal ON, kjafal OI
kjalarnes	Kjalarnes (place) OI, Kjalarnes (place) ON
kjarvals	Kjarval (name) ON
kjöl	a-keel OI, keel ON
kjölinn	keel OI, keel ON
kjörin	chosen OI
klæddist	dressed OI, dressed ON
klæði	cloth OI, clothes ON, clothes OI, clothing OI, clothing ON
klæðið	cloth OI, clothes OI
klæðin	bed-clothes ON, bed-clothes OI
klæðum	clothes ON, clothes OI
klæðunum	clothes ON
klípti	pinched OI

The Vinland Sagas   Word List (Norse to English)

Norse	English
klofa	gap OI, gap ON
klóraði	scratched OI
knappi	fastening ON
knappinn	knob ON
knappr	a-knob ON
knarrar	merchant-ship ON, ship OI
knarrarbringu	Knarrarbringu (name) OI, Knarrarbringu (name) ON
kneppt	fastened ON
knjám	knees OI, knees ON
knörr	ship ON, ship OI
knött	balls ON, balls OI
koðránsson	Son-of-Kodran (name) OI, Son-of-Kodran (name) ON
köld	cold OI, cold ON
köldum	cold OI, cold ON
köllu	called OI
kölluð	called ON, called OI
kölluðu	called ON, called OI
köllum	call OI
kolum	coal ON, coal OI
kom	came OI, came ON, come OI
koma	came OI, came ON, come OI, come ON, coming ON, coming OI
komast	come ON, come OI
komat	come ON, come OI
komi	come OI, come ON, comes ON
komið	came OI, come OI, come ON
komin	coming ON, coming OI
kominn	came ON, came OI, come OI, come ON, coming OI, coming ON
komit	came ON, come ON
komk	come ON
komnir	came ON, came OI, coming OI, coming ON, returning OI
komst	came OI, came ON
komu	came OI
kómu	came ON
komur	come OI

Norse	English
komust	arrived OI
kómust	arrived ON, went ON
kona	as-a-woman ON, wife OI, wife ON, woman OI, woman ON
konan	the-woman OI, woman OI, woman ON
konar	all-kinds OI, kind-of OI, kinds OI, kinds ON, kinds-of OI, kinds-of ON
könnuðu	explore ON, explored OI
konu	a-wife ON, a-wife OI, a-woman ON, a-woman OI, wife OI, wife ON, woman OI, woman ON
konum	woman ON, women OI, women ON
konungar	kings ON, kings OI
konungi	king ON, king OI
konungr	king ON, King (name) ON, the-king ON
konungs	king ON, king OI, the-King (name) ON, The-King (name) OI
konungur	king OI, King (name) OI, The-King (name) OI
konur	women OI, women ON
körin	chosen ON
korn	corn ON, corn OI
kornhjálm	corn-shed OI, corn-shed ON
kost	advantage OI, advantage ON, choice OI, choice ON, costs OI, provided ON
kostaði	exerted ON, exerted OI
kostar	choice ON, choice OI
kosti	benefits OI
kostr	choice ON
köstuðu	cast OI, cast ON, threw ON
kostum	benefit OI, benefit ON, benefit ON
kostur	choice OI
krafði	called ON
kráku	crow ON, Crow (name) OI, Crow (name) ON

202

Word List (Norse to English)

Norse	English
kristin	Christian (name) ON, Christian (name) OI
kristinn	christian OI, christian ON, Christian (name) ON
kristnað	Christian OI
kristnat	Christian ON
kristni	christianity OI, christianity ON, Christianity (name) ON, Christianity (name) OI
kristr	Christ (name) ON
kristur	Christ (name) OI
krossa	cross OI, cross ON, crosses ON, crosses OI
krossanes	Krossanes (place) OI, Krossanes (place) ON
krosshólum	Krossholar (place) ON, Krossholar (place) OI
krýp	creep OI
krýpk	creep ON
kunna	know-how ON, know-how OI, knowing OI
kunnandi	knowing OI
kunni	could OI, could ON, knew OI, knew ON
kunnigt	known ON, known OI
kunnu	known OI, known ON
kvað	called OI, cried-out ON, cried-out OI, said OI, said ON, saying ON, saying OI
kvaddi	called OI
kvaðst	said OI, said ON
kváðu	said OI, said ON
kváðust	said OI, said ON
kvæði	poem ON
kvæðið	poem OI
kvæðit	poem ON, recited ON
kvæntir	married ON
kvámur	come ON
kvángaðist	married ON
kvángaðr	married ON
kvángazt	married ON
kveðið	declaring OI, poem OI, sung OI
kveðit	declared ON, sung ON
kveðjur	greetings ON, greetings OI
kveðr	said ON
kveðst	said OI, said ON, saying OI, saying ON
kveður	said OI
kveld	evening ON, evening OI
kveldi	evening OI, evening ON
kveldið	evening OI
kveldit	evening ON
kvenna	woman ON, woman OI
kvenskörungr	noble ON
kviðling	verse ON, verse OI
kvikfé	livestock OI, livestock ON
kvikindum	creatures OI
kvongaðir	married OI
kvongaðist	married OI
kvongaður	married OI
kvongast	married OI
kvonlausir	unmarried OI
kykvendum	creatures ON
kyni	kin OI, kin ON
kynjalaust	extraordinary ON, extraordinary OI
kynkvíslum	family ON
kynlegr	wonderful OI
kynligr	wonderful ON
kynni	circumstance ON, knew ON, knew OI
kynnu	circumstance OI, knew OI
kynsæll	kin-blessed OI, kin-blessed ON
kyrrt	peace ON, peace OI, still OI, still ON

L, l

Norse	English
lá	lay OI, lay ON, laying ON
láð	invited ON, invited OI
lægðir	low-ground ON, low-ground OI
lægðu	lowered OI, lowered ON
lægi	lay OI, lay ON

The Vinland Sagas — Word List (Norse to English)

Norse	English
lækr	stream ON
lækur	stream OI
lætr	laid ON, let ON
lætur	laid OI
lág	low OI, low ON
lagði	laid ON, laid OI, lay OI, lay ON
lagðist	lay OI, lay ON
lags	position ON, position OI
lagt	laid ON, laid OI
lágu	laid OI, laid ON, lay OI, lay ON, laying ON, laying OI
lambskinnskofra	lamb-skin-hood ON, lamb-skin-hood OI
land	land OI, land ON
landa	lands ON, lands OI
landaleitan	land-exploring OI, land-exploring ON
landar	land ON, land OI
landi	land OI, land ON
landið	land OI, lands OI, the-land OI, the-land OI
landinu	land OI, land ON, the-land OI, to-the-land OI
landit	land ON, lands ON, the-land ON
landkosta	land-benefits ON
landkostr	land-benefits ON
landkostum	land-benefits OI, land-benefits ON
landnámamanns	land-taking-man OI, land-taking-man ON
landnyrðingsveðr	North-East-Wind ON
landnyrðingsveður	North-East-Wind OI
lands	land OI, land ON, lands OI, lands ON
landsins	land OI, land ON, lands ON
landskosta	land-benefits ON, land-benefits OI
landskosti	land-benefits OI
landskostir	land-benefits ON, land-benefits OI
landskostr	land-benefits ON
landskostur	land-benefits OI
landsleg	landscape ON
landsmenn	landsmen ON, landsmen OI
landsnytja	land-benefits OI
landsuðr	south-east ON
landsuðrs	south-east ON
landsuður	south-east OI
landsýn	land-sight OI, land-sight ON
langa	long OI, long ON, long ON, long OI
langadal	Langadal (place) ON, Langadal (place) OI
langæðar	long ON, long OI
langar	long OI, long ON
langt	long OI, long ON
lasta	blamed ON, blamed OI
láta	burn OI, laid ON, lay OI, lay ON, leave ON, leave OI, let OI, let ON, put OI, put ON
látið	laid OI, left OI, let OI
látin	dead ON
látit	laid ON, let ON
látizt	died ON
látum	let-us ON, let-us OI
látúnshnappar	brass-buttons OI
laufa	leaf ON, leaf OI
laugarbrekku	Laugarbrekka (place) ON, Laugarbrekka (place) OI
lauk	closed OI, closed ON, end ON, end OI, ended ON, ended OI
laun	hired ON, hired OI
launa	loan ON, loan OI, repay ON, repay OI
laungetna	illegitimate ON, illegitimate OI
lausafé	liquidity ON, liquidity OI
lausafjár	liquidity's ON, liquidity's OI
lauseygr	loose-eyed ON
lauseygur	loose-eyed OI
laust	less ON, less OI
lax	salmon OI, salmon ON
léði	lent OI, lent ON
legði	lay OI, leave ON
legðir	lay ON, lay OI
leggja	lay OI, lay ON, let OI, let ON

204

The Vinland Sagas — Word List (Norse to English)

Norse	English
leggjast	to-lie ON, to-lie OI
leggur	have OI
legið	laid OI
legit	laid ON
leið	during OI, journey OI, journey ON, laid OI, laid ON, lay OI, passed ON, passed OI, the-way OI, way OI, way ON
leiða	lead OI, lead ON
leiðar	route ON, route OI, way ON, way OI
leiddi	led ON, led OI
leiddu	lead OI, lead ON
leif	Leif (name) OI, Leif (name) ON
leifi	Leif (name) OI, Leif (name) ON
leifr	Leif (name) ON
leifs	Leif (name) OI, Leif (name) ON, Leif's OI, Leif's ON
leifsbúða	Leif's-Camp (place) OI, Leif's-Camp (place) ON
leifur	Leif (name) OI
leikar	sports OI, sports ON
leikr	like ON
leikskálum	Leikskalar (place) ON, Leikskalar (place) OI
leikur	like OI
leist	impression OI, liked OI
leit	looked OI, looked ON
leita	search OI, search ON, seek OI, seek ON
leitað	seek OI
leitaði	sought OI, sought ON
leitaðir	seek ON
leitar	sought OI, sought ON
leitat	seek ON
leituðu	sought ON, sought OI
leizt	looked-like ON
léku	played OI, played ON
lendur	land OI
lengi	along ON, along OI, long OI, long ON
lengja	long OI
lengr	longer ON
lengra	further OI, further ON
lengst	long OI, long ON
lengur	longer OI
lesa	gather OI, gather ON
lesti	gripped ON, gripped OI
lestist	injured OI, injured ON
lét	allowed OI, allowed ON, laid OI, laid ON, lay ON, lay OI, let OI, let ON, lost ON
létist	perished OI
letja	discourage ON, discourage OI
létta	let ON, let OI, relieve ON, relieve OI
létu	laid OI, laid ON, left OI, left ON, let OI, let ON
leyfa	allow ON, allow OI
leyfis	leave ON, leave OI
leyna	conceal OI, conceal ON
leyndi	concealed OI, concealed ON
leysingi	a-freed-man ON, a-freed-man OI
leysti	released ON, released OI
leystu	loosened OI, loosened ON
lézt	died ON, should ON
lið	company OI, company ON, team OI, team ON, the-company-of OI
liðfáir	few ON, few OI
liði	company OI, company ON, help ON, help OI, team ON, team OI
liðið	company OI, team OI
liðin	a-company OI, company ON, passed ON, passed OI, teams OI
liðit	company ON, team ON, the-company ON
liðnir	passed OI
liðs	company OI, company ON, team ON
liðsinni	assistance ON, assistance OI

Norse	English
líf	life ON, life OI, lives OI, lives ON
lifa	live OI, live ON
lifað	lived OI
lifði	lived OI, lived ON
lífi	life OI, life ON, living ON, living OI
lífs	life OI
liggja	lay ON, lay OI, lies ON, lies OI, lying ON, the-alternative ON
liggr	lies ON
liggur	lies OI
lík	body OI, body ON
líkaði	liked ON, liked OI
líkar	like OI, like ON
líkast	like OI, like ON
líki	body OI, body ON
líkið	body OI
líkin	bodies OI, bodies ON, body OI
líkinu	body ON, body OI, the-bodies ON
líkit	body ON
líklegt	likely OI
líkum	bodies OI, bodies ON
líkunum	the-bodies OI
líst	appears OI
lit	around ON, colour OI, the-team ON, the-team OI
líta	company OI, look OI
litast	look OI
lítast	looked ON
lítið	little OI
lítill	little OI, little ON
lítilmenni	little-man OI, little-man ON
lítils	little ON, little OI
lítilvölva	Little-Prophetess (name) ON, Little-Prophetess (name) OI
lítit	little ON
litla	little OI, little ON
litlu	a-little ON, little OI, little ON, Little (name) OI
litlum	little OI, little ON
lítt	little OI, little ON, little-with OI
lituðust	looked ON, looked OI
lízt	appears ON
ljá	loan OI, loan ON
ljósjörp	bright-chestnut OI, bright-chestnut ON
loðbrókar	Lothbrok (name) ON
loðna	fur ON, hair OI
loðnir	furry ON, furry OI
lofa	praised ON, praised OI
loft	sky ON, sky OI
lög	law ON
lögð	laid ON, laid OI
lögðu	laid OI, laid ON, lay OI, lay ON
lögtekin	law-taken OI, law-taken ON
lokið	ended OI, left OI
lokit	ended ON, left ON
lönd	land OI, land ON, lands ON, lands OI
löndum	lands OI, lands ON
löngum	long ON, long OI
lutu	lent OI, lent ON
lýðum	people ON, people OI
lýkr	ended ON, ends ON, it-ends ON
lýkur	ended OI, ends OI
lýsir	declared OI, declared ON
lýsufirði	Lysufjord (place) OI, Lysufjord (place) ON
lýsufjörð	Lysufjord (place) ON, Lysufjord (place) OI

M, m

Norse	English
má	may OI, may ON
maðkahafinu	The-Worm-Sea (place) OI
maðksjá	ship-worms OI
maðksjó	ship-worms ON
maðksjónum	the-worm-sea ON
maðksmogið	worm-eaten OI
maðr	a-man ON, man ON, man OI

The Vinland Sagas

Word List (Norse to English)

Norse	English
maður	a-man OI, man OI
mæddir	wearied OI
mæla	speak ON, speak OI, to-speak OI
mælt	said OI, said ON
mælti	said OI, said ON, spoke OI, spoke ON, talked OI, talked ON
mæltu	spoke ON, spoke OI
mætti	may ON, may OI
mættið	may ON
mættist	may ON, may OI
mættu	may OI
mættuð	may OI
magra	Lean (name) ON, Lean (name) OI
mál	language OI, language ON, matter OI, matters OI, said OI, said ON, the-matter OI
mála	matter ON
máldaga	agreement OI, agreement ON
máldagi	matters OI, matters ON
máli	matter ON, matter OI, speak ON, speak OI, speech OI, speech ON, the-matter ON, the-matter OI
malmþings	metal-assemblies ON
málmþings	metal-assemblies OI
máls	speak OI, speak ON
malt	malt ON, malt OI
málum	the-matter OI, the-matter ON
mann	a-man OI, man ON, man OI, men OI, men ON
manna	man OI, man ON, man's OI, men OI, men ON, men's ON, men's OI, Men's (name) ON, people ON, people OI, people's ON, people's ON, people's OI, the people OI, the-men ON, the-people OI
mannaðr	attended ON
mannaður	attended OI
mannaverk	men's-work OI, men's-work ON
mannavistir	habitation OI
manni	a-man OI, a-man ON, man OI, man ON, men OI
manns	man OI, man ON
mannshausi	men's-heads OI, men's-heads ON
mannvænn	handsome OI
mannvirðingar	man-worthiness OI, man-worthiness ON, worthiness OI, worthiness ON
mannvirðingu	rank ON
mannvirðingum	rank OI
mannvönd	husband ON, husband OI
mánuð	month ON, month OI
mánuði	months ON, months OI
marga	many OI, many ON
margar	as-much-as ON, many ON, many OI
margir	many OI, many ON
margkunnig	many-knowing ON
margt	many ON, many OI
margur	many OI
markland	Markland (place) OI, Markland (place) ON
mart	many OI
mat	food OI, food ON
matar	food OI, food ON
matarins	food OI
matbúið	food-prepared OI
matbúin	food-prepared ON
matbúit	food-prepared ON
matfanga	hunt OI
matsveinar	ship's-cook ON, ship's-cook OI
mátti	as-may OI, as-may ON, may OI, may ON, that-might OI
máttu	could OI, could ON, may OI, may ON
með	along OI, along ON, between OI, between ON, well ON, with OI, with ON
meðal	between ON

207

The Vinland Sagas — Word List (Norse to English)

Norse	English
meðan	awhile OI, awhile ON, long-as OI, long-as ON, meantime ON, while OI, while ON
mega	able OI, able ON, be-able ON
megin	most ON, side OI, side ON, ways ON, ways OI
meginlandinu	mainland OI
megum	may ON
meiðar	hurt ON, hurt OI
mein	harm ON, harm OI
meinalausan	harmlessly OI, harmlessly ON
meir	more ON, more OI
meira	greater OI, greater ON, more OI, more ON
melrakka	melrakka ON
melrakkar	melrakka OI
menn	man OI, men OI, men ON, people ON, people OI
mennina	men ON
menntr	well-educated ON
menntur	educated OI
mér	i ON, i OI, me OI, me ON, mine OI, mine ON, more OI, myself ON, myself OI, to-me OI, to-me ON
meræfi	Moray (place) ON, Moray (place) OI
merki	imprint ON, imprint OI
messingarspón	brass-spoon ON, brass-spoon OI
messingu	brass ON, brass OI
mest	most ON, most OI
mesta	most OI, most ON
mesti	most ON, most OI
mestr	greatest ON
mestri	most OI, most ON
mestu	most ON, most OI
mestur	greatest OI
met	evaluate OI
meta	evaluate ON
metnaðarmaðr	ambitious-man ON
metnaðarmaður	ambitious-man OI
miðjan	middle OI, middle ON
miðjökul	Midjokul (place) OI, Midjokul (place) ON
miðri	middle OI, middle ON, the-middle ON
mig	i OI, me OI, my OI
mik	i ON, me ON, my ON
mikið	great OI, greatly OI, much OI, very OI
mikil	great OI, great ON, large OI, large ON, much OI, much ON
mikill	big OI, big ON, great OI, great ON, large OI, large ON, much OI, much ON, very OI, very ON
mikilli	much ON, much OI
mikinn	a-great OI, as-big ON, great OI, great ON, much ON, much OI
mikit	great ON, greatly ON, much ON, very ON
mikla	great ON, much ON, much OI
miklar	great ON, great OI, much ON, much OI
mikli	large OI, large ON
miklir	great OI, great ON, large OI, large ON
miklu	much OI, much ON
miklum	much OI, much ON
milli	between OI, between ON
millum	between OI
mín	mine OI, mine ON
mína	mine OI, mine ON
mínar	my OI, my ON
minn	mine OI, mine ON
minna	less OI, less ON
minnar	my OI, my ON
minni	less OI, less ON, mind ON, mine OI
minnka	decreased OI
míns	mine OI, mine ON, my ON, my OI
mínu	mine OI, mine ON
mínum	mine ON, mine OI
miskunn	mercy ON, mercy OI
miskunnar	mercy OI

The Vinland Sagas   Word List (Norse to English)

Norse	English
mitt	mine OI, mine ON, my OI, my ON
mjög	large OI, many OI, much OI, very OI
mjök	much ON, very ON
mjöl	meal OI
móðir	mother ON, mother OI, mother-of ON, mother-of OI, mother-to OI
móður	mother ON, mother OI, mother-of OI, mother-of ON
mögum	stomachs OI, stomachs ON
mold	dust ON, ground OI
moldu	ground ON, ground OI
mönnum	men OI, men ON, people ON, people OI
mönnunum	people OI
mörg	many OI, many ON
morgin	morning ON
morgininn	morning ON
morginn	morning ON
mörgu	many ON
mörgum	many OI, many ON
morgun	morning OI
morguninn	morning OI, morning ON
morgunn	morning OI
mörk	mark OI, mark ON
mörkina	trees OI, trees ON
mösur	maple OI
mösurr	maple ON
mót	against OI, against ON, meet OI, meet ON, towards OI
móti	against ON, against OI, meet ON, meet OI, meeting ON, met ON, met OI, towards OI, towards ON
móts	meet OI, meet ON
möttul	mantle OI
mun	could OI, could ON, shall OI, shall ON, should OI, should ON, will OI, will ON, would OI, would ON, would-be OI, would-be ON
mundi	could OI, could ON, could-be OI, should OI, would OI, would ON, would-be OI
mundu	should OI, would OI, would ON, would-be ON, would-be OI
muni	shall OI, shall ON, should OI, should ON, would OI
munka	monks OI, monks ON
munn	mouth OI, mouth ON, mouths OI, mouths ON
munni	mouth ON, mouth OI
munr	difference ON
munt	shall OI, shall ON
muntu	shall OI, shall ON, should ON, should OI
munu	shall OI, shall ON
munuð	shall OI, shall ON
munum	should OI, should ON
munur	difference OI
mykiskán	muck-encrusted ON, muck-encrusted OI
mynda	should ON
myndi	should ON, would ON
myndu	would OI
mynni	the-inlet OI, the-inlet ON, the-mouth-of ON, the-mouth-of OI
myrgin	morning ON

N, n

Norse	English
ná	near OI, near ON
náðahúss	outhouse ON
náði	got OI, got ON
nær	near OI, near ON, nearly ON, near-the OI, near-the ON
næst	next OI, next ON
næstir	nearest OI, nearest ON
nætr	nights ON
nætrnar	night ON
nætur	nights OI
næturnar	night OI

Norse	English	Norse	English
nafn	name OI, name ON, named ON, named OI	nökkur	some ON, something ON
nafna	namesake ON, namesake OI	nokkurar	some OI
nafni	namesake OI, namesake ON	nökkurar	some ON
		nokkurir	some OI
náim	near ON	nökkurir	some ON
nálguðust	approached OI, approached ON	nokkurn	certain OI
		nökkurn	certain ON, some ON
nam	took ON, took OI	nökkurr	anyone ON
námkyrtli	gown OI, gown ON	nokkurra	some OI, something OI
námu	took OI, took ON	nökkurra	some ON, something ON
nánd	close OI, close ON		
náttúrur	spirits ON, spirits OI	nokkuru	sometime OI, somewhat OI
nauðsyn	necessity OI, necessity ON	nökkuru	sometime ON
náum	near OI	nökkut	any ON, few ON, some ON, something ON
nautfé	cattle OI, cattle ON	norænn	Nordic OI
né	nor OI, nor ON	norðan	north OI, north ON, northwards OI, northwards ON
nefndist	named ON, named OI		
nefndu	named ON, named OI	norðr	north ON
nei	no ON, no OI	norður	North OI
nema	taken OI, taken ON, taking OI, taking ON	noreg	Norway (place) OI
		nóreg	Norway (place) ON
nenni	bother OI, bother ON	noregi	Norway OI, Norway (place) OI
nenntu	bothered OI, bothered ON	nóregi	Norway (place) ON
nes	headland OI, headland ON	noregs	Norway OI, Norway (place) OI
nesi	headland ON	nóregs	Norway (place) ON
nesið	headland OI, the-headland OI	norrænn	Nordic ON
nesinu	headland OI, headland ON, the-headland OI	norrænu	norse OI, norse ON
		norrænur	north-wind OI, north-wind ON
nesit	headland ON		
nesla	nettle OI	nösum	nose ON, nose OI
ness	headland OI, headland ON	nótt	night OI, night ON
		nóttina	night ON, night OI
nezlu	nettle ON	nú	now OI, now ON
niðr	down ON	numið	taken OI
niður	down OI	numit	taken ON
níu	nine ON, nine OI	nunna	a-nun OI, a-nun ON
njóta	enjoy ON	nunnuvígslu	nun's-vows OI, nun's-vows ON
njóti	benefit OI		
nokkuð	any OI, few OI, some OI, something OI	nýju	again OI, again ON
		nýnæmi	new OI, new ON
nokkur	anyone OI, some OI, something OI	nyrðra	north OI, north ON

Norse	English
nýt	benefit ON, use ON, use OI
nýta	take-advantage OI
nytjum	use ON, use OI
nytjumaður	useful OI

O, o

Norse	English
oddr	Odd (name) ON
oddrinn	tip ON
oddur	Odd (name) OI
oddurinn	tip OI
of	about ON, about OI, of OI, of ON
ofan	above ON, above OI, down ON, down OI, of ON, of OI, off OI, off ON, on OI, on ON, over OI
ofast	highest ON
ofrliði	outnumbered ON
ofurliði	outnumbered OI
og	also OI, and OI, and ON, but OI, man OI, of OI
ok	also ON, and OI, and ON, of ON
okkar	ours OI
okkarr	ours ON
okkr	ours ON, us ON, we ON
okkur	our OI, us OI, we OI
opið	opened OI
opit	opened ON
orð	word OI, word ON, words ON, words OI
orða	words ON, words OI
orði	words OI, words ON
orðið	become OI, word OI
orðinn	become OI, become ON
orðit	word ON
orðsending	message ON
orðsendingar	message OI
orðum	words ON
orkneyjar	Orkney (place) ON, Orkney (place) OI
orm	Orm (name) ON, Orm (name) OI
ormi	Orm (name) ON, Orm (name) OI
ormr	Orm (name) ON
ormur	Orm (name) OI
orrostu	battle ON
orta	wrote ON
orti	wrote OI, wrote ON
orustu	battle OI
oss	us OI, us ON, we OI, we ON

Ó, ó

Norse	English
ó	oh OI
óárani	scarcity ON, scarcity OI
óbirgir	without-supplies OI, without-supplies ON
óbyggð	settlement OI, settlement ON
óbyggðum	unsettled-land ON, unsettled-land OI
ódáðum	dishonour OI, dishonour ON
ódæll	unruly OI
ófjöllótt	without-mountains OI, without-mountains ON
ófölvan	dark ON, dark OI
óforvitinn	no-curiosity OI, no-curiosity ON
ófriði	warlike OI, warlike ON
ófriðr	without-peace ON
ófriður	without-peace OI
ógagnvænlegt	uninviting OI
ógagnvænligt	uninviting ON
óglaðari	un-glad ON, without-gladness ON, without-gladness OI
ógleði	sadness ON, sadness OI
ógreitt	not-without-obstacle ON, not-without-obstacle OI
óhægjast	maintain ON, maintain OI
óhyggilega	unwisely OI
ókunnu	unknown ON, unknown OI
ókunnugum	strangers OI

The Vinland Sagas — Word List (Norse to English)

Norse	English
ókunnum	strangers ON
ókvæntir	unmarried ON
ólafi	Olaf (name) OI
óláfi	Olaf (name) ON
óláfr	Olaf (name) ON
ólafs	Olaf (name) OI
óláfs	Olaf (name) ON
ólafssonar	Son-Of-Olaf (name) OI
óláfssonar	Son-of-Olaf (name) ON
óleifur	Olaf (name) OI
ór	from ON, of ON, out ON, out-of ON
órir	others ON, others OI
óró	uneasiness ON
ósæbratt	unbroken-sea OI, unbroken-sea ON
ósigr	defeat ON
ósigur	defeat OI
ósinn	inlet ON
óskatt	uninjured OI, uninjured ON
ótal	countless OI, countless ON
ótta	fear ON, fear OI
óttast	feared ON
ótti	fear ON, fear OI
óvægi	Ovaegi (name) ON, Ovaegi (name) OI
óvarliga	unwisely ON
óvíða	little-wide OI, little-wide ON
óvígða	un-consecrated ON, un-consecrated OI
óvígðri	unconsecrated ON, unconsecrated OI
óvinsæll	not-popular OI
óvitrlig	unwise ON
óviturleg	unwisely OI
óx	grew OI, grew ON
óxu	grew ON, grew OI

Ö, ö

Norse	English
öðru	other OI, other ON, otherwise ON
öðrum	another ON, another OI, next OI, next ON, other OI, other ON, others ON, others OI
öðrumegin	other-side OI
öll	all OI, all ON
öllu	all OI, all ON
öllum	all OI, all ON
ölnboga	elbows OI, elbows ON
önduð	dead OI
önduðust	died OI, died ON
öndverðum	beginning OI, beginning ON
öngar	none OI
öngu	no OI, nothing OI
öngum	none OI
öngva	any OI, none OI
öngvan	no OI, none OI
öngvir	none OI
öngvum	nothing OI
önnur	second ON, second OI
ör	arrow OI, arrow ON
öræfi	wilderness OI
örglast	rises OI, rises ON
örin	arrow OI, arrow ON
örina	arrow ON, the-arrow OI
örnefni	place-names OI, place-names ON
öx	an-axe OI, axe ON
öxi	axe OI, axe ON
öxin	axe ON, the-axe OI
öxina	axe ON, the-axe OI
öxinni	axe OI, axe ON
öxl	shoulder OI
öxna-þórissonar	Son-of-Oxna-Thori (name) OI, Son-of-Oxna-Thori (name) ON, Son-of-Ox-Thorir (name) ON
öxney	Oxney (place) OI, Oxney (place) ON

P, p

Norse	English
píndi	tortured OI, tortured ON

The Vinland Sagas — Word List (Norse to English)

Norse	English

R, r

Norse	English
ráð	advice OI, advice ON, advise OI, advised OI, advised ON, counsel OI, counsel ON, obliged ON, obliged OI, plan OI, plan ON, proposal ON, proposal OI
ráða	advise ON, advise OI, decide OI, decide ON, plan OI, plan ON, rule OI, rule ON
ráðabreytni	important ON
ráðagerð	important OI
ráðahag	marriage-proposal OI
ráði	advice ON, advised ON
ráðið	advice OI, advise OI, resolved OI
ráðin	agreed OI, agreed ON
ráðit	advice ON, resolved ON
ráðlausir	disposed OI
ráðlegra	advisable OI
ráðnir	appointed ON, appointed OI
ráðs	advise OI, counsel OI, counsel ON, plans ON, plans OI
ráðstafalausir	disposed ON
ráðum	advice OI, counsel OI, counsel ON
ræð	advise OI, advise ON
ræða	discussed OI
ræddu	advised OI, advised ON, discussed OI, discussed ON
ragnarssonar	Son-of-Ragnar (name) ON
rak	driven OI, driven ON, drove OI
rammlegan	strong OI
rammligan	strong ON
rangsælis	anti-sun-wise OI
rásar	rushed ON, rushed OI
rauða	red OI, Red (name) ON, the-Red OI, the-Red ON, the-Red (name) ON, The-Red (name) OI, the-Red's (name) ON, The-Red'S (name) OI
rauðan	Red (name) ON
rauði	red ON, Red (name) OI, Red (name) ON, the-Red OI, the-red ON, the-Red (name) ON, The-Red (name) OI
rauðr	the-Red (name) ON
rauðs	The-Red'S (name) OI, the-Red's (name) ON
rauðskeggjaði	Redbeard (name) ON, red-bearded OI
rauður	The-Red (name) OI
rausn	generosity ON, generosity OI, generous ON
rausnarbú	great-estate OI
rausnarráð	great-estate ON
rausnarveislu	generosity OI
raust	voice OI
rautt	red ON, red OI
réð	appointed OI, appointed ON, hired OI, hired ON
réði	leader OI, leader ON
réðst	appointed ON, appointed OI, moved ON, moved OI, rode OI, rode ON, went OI, went ON
réðust	appointed ON, appointed OI
reið	riding OI, riding ON, rode ON, rode OI
reiða	advice ON, advice OI, decided OI, decided ON
reiddi	aimed OI, aimed ON, driven OI
reiðfara	voyage OI, voyage ON
reisa	raise OI, raise ON, raised OI
reisim	raise ON

The Vinland Sagas — Word List (Norse to English)

Norse	English
reist	raised OI, raised ON
reistist	rose OI
reisum	raise OI
reka	expel OI, expel ON
rekin	driven OI, driven ON
rekkjustokkinn	sideboards ON, sideboards OI
rekum	foraging OI
renna	run ON, run OI
rennið	run ON, run OI
rénuðu	receded OI, receded ON
reri	rowing ON, rowing OI
reru	rowed ON, rowed OI
réru	rowed OI
rétti	extended OI, extended ON
reyðr	rorqual ON
reyður	rorqual OI
reykjaness	Reykjanes (place) OI, Reykjanes (place) ON
reyndi	experienced ON, experienced OI
reyni	tester OI, tester ON
reynines	Reynines (place) ON, Reynines (place) OI
reyninesi	Reynines (place) OI
reynt	experienced ON, experienced OI, tried OI
riðr	rode ON
ríður	rode OI
rif	ribs OI
rífastr	demanded ON
rífastur	demanded OI
rifin	rib ON
ríka	rich OI, Rich (name) ON
rjóðr	clearing ON
rjóðrið	clearing OI
rjóðrit	clearing ON
rjóður	clearing OI
rjúpu	Rjupa (name) ON
róa	row ON, row OI
rödd	voice ON
ross	Ross (place) ON, Ross (place) OI
ruddi	cleared ON, cleared OI
rúmi	room OI, room ON
rúmið	room OI
rúmit	room ON
rúmunum	our-places OI, places OI
runnu	ran OI, ran ON
runólfs	Runolf'S (name) OI, Runolf'S (name) ON
runólfssonar	Runolfsson (name) OI, Son-of-Runolf (name) ON
ryðja	cleared OI, cleared ON

S, s

Norse	English
sá	saw OI, saw ON, so OI, so ON, that OI, that ON, the OI, the ON, this OI, this ON
sáð	sown OI
sæhafa	sea-scattered ON, sea-scattered OI
sækja	seek ON, sought OI, sought ON
sælir	happy ON, happy OI
sæmd	honour OI
sæmðinni	honour ON
sæmilegar	honourable OI
sæmilegast	honourable OI
sæmilegur	honourable OI
sæmiligar	honourable ON
sæmiligast	honourable ON
sæmiligr	honourable ON
sæmiligsta	honourable ON
sæti	sit OI, sit ON
sætis	seat ON, seat OI
sætt	settled OI, settled ON
sætti	agreed OI, agreed ON
sættir	reconciled ON, reconciled OI
safali	sables OI, sables ON
saga	story OI, story ON
sagði	said OI, said OI, said ON, said ON, told OI, told ON
sagðir	said OI, said ON
sagna	say OI, say ON

The Vinland Sagas   Word List (Norse to English)

Norse	English
sagnaskemmtan	short-stories OI
sagt	said OI, said ON
sáit	seen ON
sakar	conviction ON, sake ON
sakir	conviction OI, conviction ON, sake OI
sama	same OI, same ON, the-same ON, the-same OI
saman	together OI, together ON
samfarar	interaction ON, interaction OI, intercourse OI
samfarir	together OI, together ON
samflota	together OI, together ON
samir	same ON, same OI
samræði	intercourse ON
samsumars	same-summer OI
samt	same OI, together OI, together ON
sandar	sands OI, sands ON, sandy ON
sandhimins	sand-heaven's ON, sand-heaven's OI
sandinum	sands OI, sands ON
sár	wound OI, wound ON, wounds ON
sári	wound ON
sárir	wounded OI, wounded ON, wounds OI, wounds ON
sárlega	woundingly OI
sárliga	woundingly ON
sást	looked ON
sat	sat OI, sat ON
satt	true OI, true ON
sátu	sat OI, sat ON
sáu	saw OI, saw OI
sauðarvömb	sheep's-stomach ON
saur	the-Foul (name) ON, The-Foul (name) OI
saurr	the-Foul (name) ON
saurs	the-Foul OI, the-foul ON
sáust	looked OI
saxlandi	Saxony (place) OI, Saxony (place) ON
sé	say OI, see OI, see ON, so ON, so OI, this OI, which ON
séð	seen OI
segðu	say ON, say OI
seggir	said ON, said OI
segi	say ON, say OI
segir	answered OI, said OI, said ON, say OI, say ON, says OI, says ON
segja	said OI, said ON, say OI, say ON
segl	sails OI, sails ON
seglið	sails OI
seiðhjallinum	spell-platform OI
seiðinn	enchantments ON, enchantments OI
seiðsins	enchantments ON
sein	late OI
seinn	late OI, late ON
seinni	behind ON
seint	late ON, late OI
sekir	outlawed ON, outlawed OI
sekr	outlawed ON
sekur	outlawed OI
seldi	sold OI, sold ON
selja	sell OI, sell ON, to-sell ON, to-sell OI
selr	sold ON
seltjöru	seal-fat ON, seal-fat OI
seltjörunni	seal-fat OI
selur	sold OI
sem	as OI, as ON, as-if OI, if OI, since OI, since ON, so ON, that OI, that ON, then ON, then OI, where ON, where OI, wherever ON, wherever OI, which OI, which ON, while ON, while OI, who OI, who ON
senda	send ON, send OI
sendi	send OI, sent ON, sent OI
sendr	sent ON
sendur	sent OI
senn	same OI, same ON

215

The Vinland Sagas — Word List (Norse to English)

Norse	English
sent	sent ON, sent OI
sér	he OI, he ON, her ON, her OI, hers ON, hers OI, herself ON, herself OI, him OI, him ON, himself ON, himself OI, his OI, his ON, the ON, the OI, their ON, their OI, theirs OI, theirs ON, them OI, them ON, themselves ON, themselves OI, they OI, they ON
serkinum	shirt OI
sét	seen ON
setið	sat OI
setit	sat ON
setja	set OI, set ON
setstokka	seat-posts OI, seat-posts ON
setstokkana	seat-posts ON, seat-posts OI
sett	set OI, set ON
settist	sat OI, sat ON
settr	set ON
settu	sat OI, sat ON, set OI, set ON, turned OI, turned ON
settur	set OI
settust	sat OI, sat ON
setu	sitting ON, sitting OI
séu	so OI
sex	six OI, six ON
sið	tradition OI, tradition ON
síðan	after OI, after ON, afterwards OI, afterwards ON, since OI, since ON, then OI, then ON
síðar	afterwards ON, afterwards OI, later ON, later OI, since ON, since OI
síðast	last OI, last ON
síðasta	last OI, last ON
síðir	eventually OI, eventually ON
siðr	custom ON
síðr	less ON
síðunni	his ON
siður	custom OI
síður	less OI
siðvenju	custom OI, custom ON
sig	herself OI, himself OI, sign-herself OI, themselves OI
sigla	sail OI, sail ON, sailed OI, sailed ON, sailing OI, sailing ON
sigldi	sailed OI, sailed ON
sigldu	sailed OI, sailed ON
sigldum	sailed ON
siglingu	sailing OI
siglingum	sailing ON
siglir	sailed OI, sailed ON
siglt	sailed OI, sailed ON
siglufjörð	Siglefjord (place) ON
sigmundarsonar	Son-of-Sigmund (name) ON, Son-Of-Sigmund (name) OI
signa	to OI, to-sign ON
sigríðr	Sigrid (name) ON
sigríður	Sigrid (name) OI
sigurði	Sigurd (name) ON, Sigurd (name) OI
sik	herself ON, himself ON, themselves ON
sildu	sailed ON
silfr	silver ON
silfur	silver OI
silgdu	sailed ON
sín	hers OI, hers ON, his ON, his OI, theirs OI, theirs ON, them OI, them ON
sína	hers OI, hers ON, his OI, his ON, theirs OI, theirs ON
sínar	hers ON, hers OI, his OI, theirs OI, theirs ON
sinn	he OI, he ON, his OI, his ON, the OI, the ON, their OI, their ON, theirs OI, theirs ON, then ON, then OI, they ON

Norse	English	Norse	English
sinna	hers OI, hers ON, his OI, his ON, their OI, theirs ON, theirs OI	sjónum	sea OI, sea ON, the-sea OI, the-sea ON
		sjór	sea OI, sea ON
sinnar	his OI, his ON, theirs ON, theirs OI	sjórinn	sea ON
		sjóvar	sea OI, sea ON
sinni	his OI, his ON, theirs OI, theirs ON, they OI	skagafirði	Skagafjord (place) OI
		skagafjörð	Skagafjord (place) OI, Skagafjord (place) ON
sins	their ON		
síns	hers OI, hers ON, his OI, his ON, their ON, theirs OI, theirs ON, they ON, they OI	skal	shall OI, shall ON
		skála	cabin OI, cabin ON
		skálanna	cabins OI, cabins ON
		skálanum	cabin OI, cabin ON
		skálarnir	cabins ON, cabins OI
sínu	her ON, hers OI, hers ON, his OI, his ON, their ON, their OI, theirs OI, theirs ON, they ON	skálavegginum	cabins OI, cabins ON
		skáldskap	poetry ON, poetry OI
		skalt	shall OI, shall ON
		skaltu	shall-you ON, shall-you OI
sínum	her ON, her OI, hers OI, hers ON, his OI, his ON, theirs OI, theirs ON	skammar	shame OI, shame ON
		skammdegi	short-time-of-day OI, short-time-of-day ON
sitr	sat ON		
sitt	his OI, his ON, their ON, their OI, theirs OI, theirs ON, these OI, these ON	skammt	short OI, short ON, shortly OI
		skapfelld	agreeable ON
		skapfelldir	agreeable OI
situr	sat OI	skapgott	well-tempered OI, well-tempered ON
sjá	he-saw OI, looked OI, looked ON, saw OI, saw ON, see OI, see ON, seen ON, seen OI, they-saw OI	skapi	mood ON, mood OI
		skapstór	temperamental OI
		skapstórr	temperamental ON
		skartsmaðr	jewelled-man ON
sjáið	see OI, see ON	skartsmaður	jewelled-man OI
sjaldan	seldom ON, seldom OI	skáru	cut OI, cut ON
sjálfala	themselves ON, themselves OI	skaust	launched OI
sjálfan	itself ON, itself OI	skaut	lap ON, lap OI, shot OI, shot ON, stern OI, stern ON
sjálfar	itself OI		
sjálfsáið	self-sowing OI	skauzt	launched ON
sjálfsáit	self-sowing ON	skeggjaðr	bearded ON
sjálfsána	self-sowing ON, self-sowing OI	skeggjaður	bearded OI
sjálfsánir	self-sowing ON, self-sowing OI	skeið	sheathed-sword ON, sheathed-sword OI
		skeiðsbrekkum	Skeidsbrekkur (place) ON, Skeidsbrekkur (place) OI
sjást	looked OI, looked ON		
sjávar	sea ON		
sjó	sea ON, sea OI, the-sea OI	skelmaðkurinn	shell-worms OI
sjóinn	sea OI, sea ON	skemmtan	amusement OI, amusement ON
sjómaðkr	sea-worms ON		
sjónhverfingar	illusions ON		

The Vinland Sagas — Word List (Norse to English)

Norse	English
skemmtanar	entertain OI, entertain ON
skemmtu	entertained OI
skemmtuðu	entertained ON
sker	rock OI, rock ON
skerið	rock OI
skerinu	rock OI, rock ON
skerit	rock ON
skíðgarð	fence OI, fence ON
skíðgarðinn	fence OI, fence ON
skilði	understood ON
skildu	knew OI, left OI, separated OI
skilðu	knew ON
skildum	separated OI
skilðum	separated ON
skilðust	separated ON
skilist	separate ON
skilja	separate ON, separate OI, separated OI, separated ON
skiljast	separate ON, separate OI
skiljist	separate OI
skilnað	separate OI, separate ON
skilnaðr	parting ON
skilnaður	parting OI
skína	shine ON, shine OI
skinn	skins ON
skinnavara	furs OI, furs ON
skinnavöru	skin-wares OI, skin-wares ON
skinnhjúpum	skin-sacks ON, skin-sacks OI
skinnvöru	skin-wares ON
skip	ship OI, ship ON, ships ON, ships OI, then ON
skipa	ships OI, ships ON
skipborðsins	ship's-berth OI, ship's-berth ON
skipflaki	shipwreck ON, shipwreck OI
skipi	a-ship OI, ship OI, ship ON, ships OI, ships ON, the-ship ON
skipið	ship OI, the-ship OI
skipinu	ship OI, ship ON, the-ship OI, the-ship ON
skipit	ship ON
skips	ship OI, ship ON, ships OI, ships ON
skipshöfnum	ships-ports ON
skipsins	ship OI, ship ON, ship's OI, ship's ON, ships-his ON
skipta	change ON, change OI, divide OI, divide ON, of-exchange OI
skipti	exchanged ON, exchanges ON, exchanges OI, time OI, time ON
skiptu	divided OI, divided ON
skiptumst	exchange OI
skiptust	exchanged OI
skipum	ship OI, ship ON, ships ON, ships OI, the-ship OI
skipunum	boats ON, boats OI, ship ON, ship OI, ships ON, ships OI
skipverja	crew OI, crew ON
skipverjum	ship's-company ON, ship's-company OI
skipverjunum	ships-ports OI
skírð	baptised ON, baptised OI
skírðir	baptised ON, baptised OI
skjaldarins	shield OI, shield ON
skjóðupungr	skin-purse ON
skjóðupungur	a-skin-purse OI
skjöld	shield ON, shield OI, shields ON
skjöldu	shields OI
skjöldum	shields ON, shields OI
skjóta	launched OI, launched ON
skjótari	faster-than ON, faster-than OI
skjótast	quickly OI, quickly ON
skjótleiks	speed OI
skjótt	quickly ON, quickly OI, shortly ON, shortly OI
skkutu	launched ON
skóg	forest OI, forest ON
skógar	forests OI, forests ON

Word List (Norse to English)

Norse	English
skógi	forest OI, forest ON, forests OI, forests ON, woods ON, woods OI
skóginn	the-woods OI, woods OI, woods ON
skóginum	forest OI, forest ON
skógótt	forested OI, forested ON
skógr	forest ON
skógur	forest OI
skógurinn	forests OI
skógvaxit	forest-grown ON
skóklæðin	shoes OI, shoes ON
skömmu	recently ON, recently OI
skorti	shortage OI, shortage ON
skortir	shortage OI, shortage ON
sköruleg	honourable OI, strong OI
skörulega	boldly OI
skörulegastur	striking OI
skörulig	strong ON
sköruliga	boldly ON
sköruligastr	striking ON
skörungr	noble ON
skörungur	noble OI
skoska	Scottish (place) OI
skosku	Scottish (place) OI
skotar	Scots (name) ON, Scots (place) OI
skothríð	launching ON, launching OI
skotland	Scotland (place) ON, Scotland (place) OI
skozka	Scottish (place) ON
skozku	Scottish (place) ON
skrælinga	skraelings ON, Skraelings (name) ON
skrælingar	skraelings ON, Skraelings (name) ON
skrælingaskipa	Skraelings (name) ON
skrælingi	Skraeling OI
skrælingja	Skraelings OI, Skraelings (name) OI
skrælingjalandi	Skraelings (place) OI
skrælingjar	Skraelings OI, Skraelings (name) OI, The-Skraelings (name) OI
skrælingjarnir	Skraelings (name) OI
skrælingjum	Skraelings (name) OI
skrælingr	skraeling ON
skrælingum	Skraelings (name) ON
skraumuhlaupsár	Skraumuhlaupsa (place) ON, Skraumuhlaupsa (place) OI
skriðu	landslide ON, landslide OI
skrúð	cloth ON
skrúðit	cloth ON
skúa	shoes OI, shoes ON
skugga	shadow OI, shadow ON
skuldalið	indebted ON, indebted-to OI
skuluð	should OI, should ON
skulum	shall OI, shall ON, should OI, should ON
skutu	launched OI, launched ON
skylda	should ON
skyldi	as-should-be ON, as-should-be OI, should OI, should ON, should-be ON, should-be OI, wished OI
skyldir	obliged ON, obliged OI
skyldu	should OI, should ON, would ON, would OI
skylt	should ON, should OI
skyn	understanding OI
sleitum	slighting OI
slétt	flat OI, flat ON
slettir	slapped ON, slapped OI
slík	such OI, such ON
slíka	such OI
slíkan	such OI, such ON
slíkra	such ON, such OI
slikt	such ON
slíkt	such ON, such OI
slíku	such ON
slíkum	such OI
sló	struck OI, struck ON

The Vinland Sagas — Word List (Norse to English)

Norse	English
slóðir	routes ON, routes OI
slógu	struck ON, struck OI
smáir	small OI
smár	small OI, small ON
smáskitlegr	dirty ON
smáskitlegur	dirty OI
smáþarma	small-intestine ON, small-intestine OI
smátt	small ON
smjúgi	pierce OI
snæfells	Snaefell (place) OI, Snaefell (place) ON
snæfellsjökli	Snaefellsjokli (place) OI, Snaefellsjokli (place) ON
snæfellsnesi	Snaefellstrond (place) OI
snæfellströnd	Snaefellstrond (place) ON
snemma	early OI, early ON
sneru	turned OI
snjár	snow OI
snjór	snow ON
snorra	Snorri (name) OI, Snorri (name) ON, Snorri'S (name) OI
snorrason	Snorrason (name) ON, Snorrason (name) OI
snorrasonar	Son-of-Snorri (name) OI, Son-of-Snorri (name) ON
snorri	Snorri (name) OI, Snorri (name) ON
snúa	turned OI, turned ON
snúast	turn OI
sofa	sleep ON, sleep OI
sofið	slept OI
sofit	slept ON
sofna	slept OI, slept ON
sofnaða	sleeping ON, sleeping OI
sofnar	slept OI
soföndum	sleeping ON
sofundum	sleeping OI
sögðu	said OI, said ON, told ON
sögn	said ON, said OI, said-of OI, story OI, story ON
sögu	saga OI, saga ON
sökk	sank ON
sól	sun OI, sun ON, the-sun OI, the-sun ON
sólarsinnis	sun-wise-motion ON, sun-wise-motion OI
sölvadal	Solvadal (place) OI, Solvadal (place) ON
sölvi	Sölvi (name) OI, Sölvi (name) ON
sómamaðr	famous-man ON
sómamaður	famous-man OI
son	a-son ON, a-son OI, son OI, son ON, son-of OI, Son-Of (name) OI
sonar	son OI, son ON
sonareignin	son's-property ON, son's-property OI
sonr	of ON, son ON, son-of ON, Son-of (name) ON
sonu	sons ON, sons OI
sonur	son OI, son-of OI, Son-Of (name) OI
sótt	attended ON, attended OI, sickness OI, sickness ON
sóttarfar	sickness ON, sickness OI
sótti	encountered ON, encountered OI, took ON, took OI
sóttin	sickness OI, sickness ON
sóttina	sickness OI, sickness ON
sóttu	looked OI, sought OI
spá	prophecy OI, prophecy ON
spákona	prophetess ON, prophetess OI, Prophetess (name) OI
spákonan	prophetess ON
spákonu	prophetess OI
spákonunni	prophetess ON, prophetess OI
spákonur	prophetesses ON, prophetesses OI
spannarlangt	long-spanning ON, spanning-long OI
spjót	spears ON, spears OI

The Vinland Sagas — Word List (Norse to English)

Norse	English
spurði	asked OI, asked ON, heard-of ON, heard-of OI
spurðist	heard ON
spurðu	asked OI, asked ON
spurt	asked ON, asked OI
spyr	asked OI, asks OI
spyrja	asked OI, asked ON
spyrnast	touch OI
spyrr	asked ON, asks ON
stað	place OI, place ON, stand ON, stand OI, stood ON
staðar	place ON, places ON, places OI
staðfestu	established ON, established OI
staði	parts OI, parts ON
staðið	stood OI
staðit	stood ON
stæði	steady ON, steady OI
stæðist	place ON, place OI
stæra	greatly ON, greatly OI
stærra	larger OI, larger ON
staf	staff ON, staff OI
stafn	stern OI, stern ON
stalli	altar OI, altar ON
standa	stand OI, stand ON
standir	stand OI, stand ON
stangir	poles ON, poles OI
staur	poles ON, poles OI
staurinum	poles ON
staurnum	poles OI
stef	stave OI, stave ON
stefndu	steered OI, steered ON
stein	stone ON, stone OI
steinum	stones ON, stones OI
sterk	strong OI, strong ON
sterklega	strongly OI
sterkr	strong ON
sterkur	strong OI
stígr	climbed ON
stígur	climbed OI
stjórn	steering OI, steering ON, stern ON
stjórnborða	starboard OI
stjórnuðu	greatly-ruled-over ON, greatly-ruled-over OI
stóð	stood OI, stood ON, was OI, withstood OI
stoða	stand OI
stóðst	stood OI, stood ON, withstood ON
stofunni	room OI, room ON
stokka	stock ON, stock OI
stokkanesi	Stokkanes (place) ON, Stokkanes (place) OI
stokki	bed OI, bed ON
stóli	stool OI, stool ON
stólinn	stool OI, stool ON
stólinum	stool OI, stool ON
stöng	poles ON
stönginni	poles ON
stöngum	poles OI
stopir	stopped ON, stopped OI
stór	great ON, great OI
stórættaða	noble ON, noble OI
stórar	large ON, large OI
stórauðigr	wealthy ON
stórauðigur	wealthy OI
stórilla	greatly OI, greatly ON
stórmannliga	great-man-ness ON
stórmenni	great-men ON, great-men OI
stórmennsku	great-man-ness ON, great-man-ness OI, greatness ON, greatness OI
strandar	shore ON, shore OI
strandir	beaches ON, beaches OI
strandirnar	beaches ON
straumar	a-stream OI, streams ON
straumey	Straumey (place) ON
straumfirði	Straumfjord (place) ON
straumfjörð	Straumfjord (place) ON
straumr	stream ON
straumsey	Straumsey (place) OI
straumsfirði	Straumfjord (place) OI
straumsfjörð	Straumfjord (place) OI, Straumsfjord (place) OI
straumur	a-stream OI

The Vinland Sagas — Word List (Norse to English)

Norse	English
ströndunum	beaches OI
stund	awhile OI, awhile ON, time ON, time OI, while OI, while ON
stundar	around ON
stundum	sometimes ON, sometimes OI
styr	Styrr (name) OI
stýra	steer OI, steer ON
stýrði	steered OI, steered ON
stýrðu	steered OI, steered ON
stýri	steering ON, steering OI
stýrimenn	steersmen ON, steersmen OI
stýrir	steer OI, steer ON
styrkr	strength ON
styrkur	steered OI, strength OI
styrr	Styrr (name) OI, Styrr (name) ON
sú	seen OI, that ON, the ON, the OI, their OI, their ON, was OI
suðr	south ON
suðræn	southern ON
suðrey	Sudrey (place) ON
suðreyja	Sudreyar (place) ON
suðreyjar	Sudreyar (place) ON
suðreyjum	Sudreyar (place) ON
suðreyskr	south-islander ON
suðri	south ON
suðrland	Sutherland (place) ON
suðrmaðr	southern-man ON
suðu	boiled ON, boiled OI
suður	south OI
suðurátt	south OI
suðurey	Sudrey (place) OI
suðureyja	Sudreyar (place) OI
suðureyjar	Sudreyar (place) OI
suðureyjum	Sudreyar (place) OI
suðureyskur	south-islander OI
suðurland	Sutherland (place) OI
suðurmaður	southern-man OI
sukku	sank ON, sank OI
sum	some OI, some ON
sumar	summer OI, summer ON
sumarið	summer OI
sumarit	summer ON
sumars	summer OI, summer ON
sumir	some OI, some ON
sumra	some ON, some OI, summer ON, summer OI
sumri	summer OI, summer ON
sumrum	summer ON, summer OI
sumt	some ON
sund	strait OI, strait ON
sundr	distribute ON
sundrþykki	discord ON
sundur	apart OI
sundurþykki	discord OI
sunnan	from-the-south OI, south ON, south OI
sunnanveður	southern-winds OI
svá	so ON, such ON
sváfu	slept OI, slept ON
svara	answer OI, answer ON
svarað	answered OI
svaraði	answered OI, answered ON
svarar	answered OI, answered ON
svarat	answered ON
svarri	haughty OI, haughty ON
svarta	the-Black ON, the-Black (name) OI, the-Black's ON
svartan	black ON, black OI
svarti	the-Black (name) OI, The-Black (name) ON
svartir	dark ON
svartr	dark ON, the-Black ON
svartur	dark OI, the-Black (name) OI
svát	so ON
svein	boy OI
sveina	young-men ON
sveinana	young-men ON, young-men OI
sveinanna	young-men OI
sveinbarn	baby-boy OI, baby-boy ON, boy ON
sveininn	boy ON, boy OI

The Vinland Sagas — Word List (Norse to English)

Norse	English
sveinn	boy OI, boy ON
sveit	company OI
sveitir	areas ON
sverð	swords ON, swords OI
sverðið	sword OI, the-sword OI
sverðinu	sword ON
sverðit	sword ON
sviku	betrayed ON, betrayed OI
svíney	Sviney (place) OI, Sviney (place) ON
svipta	shorten OI, shorten ON
svipu	whip ON, whip OI
svívirða	shame ON, shame OI
svo	so OI, south OI, such OI
svör	answer OI, answer ON
svörtum	dark OI, dark ON
svörum	answer OI, answer ON
syðra	southern ON, southern OI
sýn	seemed ON, seemed OI
sýndi	showed ON, showed OI
sýndist	seemed OI, seemed ON
syni	Son-of (name) ON, Son-Of (name) OI
sýni	show OI, show ON, showed OI
synir	sons OI, sons ON
sýnir	showed ON
sýnist	seemed ON, seemed OI
sýslur	pursuits OI, pursuits ON
systr	sisters ON
systur	sister OI, sister ON, sister-of ON, sister-of OI, sisters OI

T, t

Norse	English
táðit	say ON
tæki	take ON, take OI
tækist	takes ON
tækjust	takes OI
taka	take OI, take ON, taken OI, took ON
takast	take OI, take ON
tákna	betoken OI
tal	talked OI
tala	say ON, talk OI, talk ON, to-speak ON
talaði	talked OI, talked ON
talat	told ON
taldi	talked OI, told OI, told ON
talði	talked ON, told ON
taldist	told OI
talðist	told ON
tannbelti	tusk-belt ON, tusk-belt OI
tannskeftan	walrus-tusk ON, walrus-tusk OI
tár	tears ON, tears OI
tauma	reins ON, reins OI
teikna	betoken ON
tekið	taken OI
tekin	taken ON, taken OI
tekit	taken ON
tekr	take ON, takes ON, took ON
tekst	took OI, took ON
tekur	pulled OI, take OI, took OI
telgja	told OI, told ON
tengdir	joined OI
tengðir	joined ON
tíðast	swiftly OI, swiftly ON
tíðenda	news ON
tíðendi	tidings ON
tíðinda	news OI
tíðindi	news OI, tidings OI
tíðindum	news OI, news ON
tigi	tens OI
tigir	ten ON, ten OI, tens ON, tens OI
tigu	ten ON, tens ON
til	for OI, for ON, to OI, to ON, towards OI, towards ON, until OI, until ON
tillaga	suggested OI
tilskipan	decided OI
tíma	time OI, time ON, times OI, times ON

The Vinland Sagas — Word List (Norse to English)

Norse	English
tinknappar	tin-buttons ON
tíu	ten OI, ten ON
tjaldi	tent OI, tent ON
tjaldinu	tent OI, tent ON
tjóa	avail ON
töfl	table-games OI
töfr	magic ON
töfur	magic OI
tög	twenty ON
tögr	twenty ON
tók	received ON, taken ON, taken OI, took OI, took ON
tókst	took ON, took OI
tóku	taken ON, took OI, took ON, took-to ON, took-to OI
tökum	take ON, take OI
tókust	taken ON, taking OI, took OI, took ON, took OI
tólf	twelve OI, twelve ON
töluðu	spoke OI, told OI, told ON
torflutt	difficult-be ON, difficult-be OI
trausti	trust ON, trust OI
trautt	scarcely ON, scarcely OI
tré	beam OI, beam ON, beams OI, tree OI, tree ON, trees ON, trees OI, wood OI, wood ON
trjám	poles ON
trjánum	poles ON, poles OI
tröðum	Tradir (place) ON, Tradir (place) OI
trú	faith ON, faith OI
trúðu	believed ON, believed OI
trúna	faith ON, faith OI
trúuð	religious ON, religious OI
tryggvason	Tryggvason (name) ON
tryggvasonar	Tryggvason'S (name) OI, Tryggvason's (name) ON, Tryggvason'S (name) OI
tryggvasyni	Tryggvason (name) ON, Tryggvason (name) OI
tug	twenty OI
tuglamöttul	mantle ON, mantle OI
tugur	twenty OI
tuttugu	twenty ON, twenty OI
tvá	two ON
tvær	two ON, two OI
tvau	two ON
tveim	two ON
tveir	two OI, two ON
tvennar	two OI, two ON
tvennum	two OI
tvíhólkaðan	two-ringed ON, two-ringed OI
tvo	two OI
tvö	two OI
týna	lose ON, lose OI
týndust	lost OI, lost ON
tyrkir	Tyrkir (name) OI, Tyrkir (name) ON

Þ, þ

Norse	English
þá	the ON, them OI, them ON, then OI, then ON, there OI, there ON, they OI, they ON, to-them ON, when OI, when ON
það	it OI, than OI, that OI, that-to OI, the OI, they OI, this OI
þaðan	from-there OI, from-there ON, there OI, there ON
þær	there ON, there OI, they OI, they ON, those ON, those OI
þætti	seems ON, seems OI
þagði	silent OI, silent OI, silent ON, silent ON
þágu	accepted OI, accepted ON
þakkaði	thanked OI, thanked ON
þakkar	thanked ON, thanked OI

The Vinland Sagas   Word List (Norse to English)

Norse	English	Norse	English
þangað	from-there OI, there OI, there OI	þeira	of-them ON, the ON, their ON, theirs ON, them ON, there ON, they ON, this ON
þangat	from-there ON, there ON, there ON		
þann	that OI, that ON, that ON, that OI, the OI, the ON, the ON, the OI, then OI, then ON, they OI, they ON, this OI, this ON	þeirar	their ON, there ON
		þeirra	of-them OI, the OI, their OI, theirs OI, them OI, there OI
		þeirrar	their OI, there OI
		þeirri	there OI
þar	here OI, that OI, their OI, their ON, there OI, there ON, therefore OI, they OI, they ON, where ON, where OI	þeirs	they ON
		þenna	that OI, then ON, these OI, these ON, this ON, this OI
þarf	need ON, needed ON, needed OI	þér	to-you OI, to-you ON, you OI, you ON
þat	it ON, ship ON, than ON, that ON, that ON, the ON, they ON, this ON, this ON	þess	these OI, these ON, this OI, this ON
		þessa	these ON, these OI, this OI, this ON
þau	hers OI, them OI, them ON, them ON, them OI, there ON, there OI, these OI, these ON, they OI, they ON, those OI, those ON	þessar	these OI, these ON
		þessara	these OI
		þessi	these OI, these ON, this OI, this ON
		þessir	these OI, these ON
þegar	already OI, already ON, as-soon-as ON, straightaway OI, straightaway ON, then OI, then ON, when OI, when ON	þessu	his ON, this OI, this ON
		þessum	these OI, these ON, this ON, this OI
		þetta	that OI, that ON, this OI, this ON, thus OI, thus ON
		þette	this ON
þegði	silence ON	þið	you OI, you-two OI
þegðu	silence OI	þig	you OI
þeim	that OI, that ON, theirs ON, theirs OI, them OI, them ON, these OI, these ON, they OI, they ON, those ON, those OI, to ON, to-them OI, to-them ON	þiggið	accepted ON, accepted OI
		þiggja	receive OI, receive ON
		þiggr	accepted ON
		þiggur	accepted OI
		þik	you ON, yours ON
		þín	your ON, your OI, yours ON
þeir	the ON, their ON, their OI, theirs OI, them OI, them ON, then ON, there OI, there ON, they OI, they ON, this OI, those OI, those ON, you OI	þínir	yours OI, yours ON
		þinn	you OI, you ON, yours ON, yours OI
		þinnar	yours OI, yours ON
		þinni	yours ON, yours OI
		þíns	yours OI, yours ON
		þínum	your ON, your OI

Norse	English	Norse	English
þistils	Thistle (name) ON, Thistle (name) OI	þorbjörg	Thorbjorg (name) ON, Thorbjorg (name) OI
þistilsfjörð	Thistilsfjord (place) ON, Thistilsfjord (place) OI	þorbjörgu	Thorbjorg (name) ON, Thorbjorg (name) OI
þit	you ON, you-two ON	þorbjörn	Thorbjorn (name) OI, Thorbjorn (name) ON
þitt	your OI, your ON, yours OI, yours ON	þorbrand	Thorbrand (name) OI
þjáðir	enslaved ON, enslaved OI	þorbrandr	Thorbrand (name) ON
þjóðhildar	Thjodhild (name) OI, Thjodhild (name) ON	þorbrands	Thorbrand (name) OI, Thorbrand (name) ON, Thorbrand's (name) ON, Thorbrand'S (name) OI
þjóðhildarkirkja	Thjodhildakirkja (place) ON, Thjodhildkirkja (place) OI	þorbrandsson	Son-of-Thorbrand (name) OI, Son-of-Thorbrand (name) ON, Thorbrandson (name) ON, Thorbrandson (name) OI
þjóðhildi	Thjodhild (name) ON		
þjóðhildr	Thjodhild (name) ON		
þjóðhildur	Thjodhild (name) OI		
þjósti	vehemence OI, vehemence ON	þórðar	Son-of-Thord (name) OI, Son-of-Thord (name) ON, Thord (name) ON, Thord (name) OI
þó	though OI, though ON, thought OI, yet OI, yet ON		
þokar	stretches OI, stretches ON	þórðarsonar	Son-of-Thord (name) OI, Son-of-Thord (name) ON
þokka	thoughts ON		
þökkuðu	thanked ON	þórðr	Thord (name) ON
þokur	fog OI, fog ON	þorfinnr	Thorfin (name) ON
þolðu	endured ON	þorfinns	Thorfin's (name) ON
þór	Thor (name) ON, Thor (name) OI	þorfinnur	Thorfin (name) OI
þorbirni	Thorbjorn (name) ON, Thorbjorn (name) OI	þorgeir	Thorgeir (name) OI
		þorgeirr	Thorgeir (name) ON
þorbjargar	thorbjorg ON, Thorbjorg (name) OI, Thorbjorg (name) ON, Thorbjorg's (name) ON, Thorjborn'S (name) OI	þorgeirsfelli	Thorgeirsfell (place) ON, Thorgeirsfell (place) OI
		þorgerði	Thorgerd (name) ON
		þorgerðr	Thorgerd (name) ON
		þorgerður	Thorgerd (name) OI
þorbjarnar	Thorbjorn (name) OI, Thorbjorn's (name) ON, Thorjborn'S (name) OI	þorgesti	Thorgest (name) OI, Thorgest (name) ON
		þorgestlingum	Thorgest's-Sons (name) OI, Thorgest's-Sons (name) ON
þorbjarnardóttur	Thorbjarnardottur (name) OI, Thorbjarnardottur (name) ON, Thorbjornadottir (name) OI	þorgestr	Thorgest (name) ON
		þorgests	Thorgest's (name) ON, Thorgest'S (name) OI
		þorgestur	Thorgest (name) OI

Norse	English	Norse	English
þorgils	Thorgils (name) ON, Thorgils (name) OI	þórunnar	Thorun (name) OI, Thorun (name) ON
þorgilsson	Thorgilson (name) ON	þorvald	Thorvald (name) OI, Thorvald (name) ON
þorgrímsson	Son-of-Thorgrim (name) OI, Son-of-Thorgrim (name) ON	þorvaldi	Thorvald (name) OI, Thorvald (name) ON
þórgunna	Thorgun (name) ON, Thorgun (name) OI	þorvaldr	Thorvald (name) ON
þórhall	Thorhall (name) OI	þorvalds	Thorvald's (name) OI, Thorvald's (name) ON
þórhallr	Thorhall (name) ON	þorvaldur	Thorvald (name) OI
þórhalls	Thorhall (name) ON, Thorhall (name) OI	þorvarði	Thorvard (name) ON
þórhallur	Thorhall (name) OI	þorvarðr	Thorvald (name) ON, Thorvard (name) ON
þórhildi	Thorhild (name) ON	þorvarður	Thorvard (name) OI
þóri	Thori (name) OI, Thori (name) ON	þótt	though ON, though OI, thought ON, thought OI
þórir	Thorir (name) OI, Thorir (name) ON	þótti	think OI, thinks OI, thinks ON, thought OI, thought ON
þóris	Thori (name) OI, Thori (name) ON, Thori's (name) ON	þóttist	thought OI, thought ON
þorkel	Thorkell (name) ON, Thorkell (name) OI	þóttu	thought OI, thought ON
þorkell	Thorkell (name) ON, Thorkell (name) OI	þóttú	though ON, though OI
þorláks	Thorlak (name) OI, Thorlak (name) ON, Thorlak's (name) ON	þóttust	thought OI, thought ON
		þrælana	thralls ON, thralls OI
		þrælar	thralls ON, thralls OI
		þrælssyni	thrall's-son ON, thrall's-son OI
þórsnessþingi	Thorsnes-Assembly (name) OI, Thorsnes-Assembly (name) ON, Thorsnes-Thing (name) ON, Thorsnes-Thing (place) OI	þreifar	feels OI, feels ON
		þrekaðir	exhausted ON, exhausted OI
		þrem	three OI
		þremr	three ON
		þrévetr	three-winters ON
þorstein	Thorstein (name) OI, Thorstein (name) ON	þriði	thirty OI, thirty ON, thirty-and ON
þorsteini	Thorstein (name) OI, Thorstein (name) ON	þriðja	third OI, third ON
þorsteinn	Thorstein (name) OI, Thorstein (name) ON	þrifum	thriving OI, thriving ON
		þrír	three ON, three OI
þorsteins	Thorstein (name) OI, Thorstein (name) ON, Thorstein's OI, Thorstein's ON, Thorstein's (name) ON, Thorstein'S (name) OI	þrívetur	three-winters OI
		þrjá	three OI, three ON
		þrjár	three OI, three ON
		þrjóta	exhausted OI, exhausted ON
		þrjú	three OI, three ON
		þroskasamt	developed OI, developed ON
þórunn	Thorun (name) ON, Thorun (name) OI	þú	you OI, you ON
		þuldi	reciting OI

227

The Vinland Sagas — Word List (Norse to English)

Norse	English
þulði	rattling-off ON
þungt	unhappy ON, unhappy OI
þurfa	need OI, need ON, needed OI, needed ON
þurfti	needed OI, needed ON
þurftu	need OI, needed ON, needed OI
þurftugir	in-need OI, in-need ON
þuríðar	Thorid (name) ON, Thorid (name) OI
þurrkanar	dry OI
þurrkunar	dry ON
þurslegur	giant OI
þursligr	giant ON
þústr	discord ON
þústur	discord OI
þvengi	tied ON, tied OI
þverr	decreases ON, decreases OI
þvers	across ON, across OI
þversýningar	illusions OI
því	according OI, according ON, accordingly OI, accordingly ON, as ON, because OI, because ON, before OI, before ON, for OI, for ON, since OI, since ON, that OI, that ON, therefore OI, therefore ON
þvílíka	spectacular ON
þvílíku	likewise ON, likewise OI
þvílíkum	for-like ON, for-like OI
þyki	think OI
þykir	seemed OI, seems OI, think OI, thinking OI, thought OI
þykist	think OI
þykja	seem OI, valued OI
þykki	think ON, thought ON
þykkir	seemed ON, seems ON
þykkja	seem ON, think ON, valued ON
þykkjast	think ON
þykkjumst	think-us ON
þyrfti	needed OI
þýsku	German OI
þýzku	german ON

U, u

Norse	English
uggligt	fearful ON
um	about OI, about ON, among OI, among ON, around ON, around OI, at OI, at ON, for OI, for ON, from ON, inclined OI
umbóta	about-further OI
umbótar	about-further ON
umbúningr	clothing ON
umbúningur	clothing OI
umfram	about-from OI
umhverfis	around OI
umráði	counsel OI, counsel ON
umræða	discussed OI, discussed ON, discussion OI, discussion ON, talk OI, talk ON
umræði	discussion OI, discussion ON
umræður	discussion ON, discussion OI
undan	ahead ON, ahead OI, away OI, away ON, away-from OI, from OI, from ON, under ON
undarlegi	strange OI
undarlegum	strange OI
undarligi	strange ON
undarligum	strange ON
undir	behind ON, behind OI, near OI, near ON, under OI, under ON, up-to OI, up-to ON
undirförull	scheming OI
undrast	wonder OI
undruðust	astonished ON, astonished OI, marvelled ON, marvelled OI
undu	hoisted ON
ung	young OI, young ON

Norse	English
unga	young OI, young ON
ungur	younger OI
unnið	working OI
unnit	spared ON
unnu	won ON, won OI
uns	until OI
unz	until ON
upp	up OI, up ON, upped ON, upped OI
uppi	up OI, up ON
upplendingakonungs	Opplands-King (name) ON, Opplands-King (name) OI
urðu	became OI, became ON
utan	except-for OI, out OI, out-of OI, out-travel OI

Ú, ú

Norse	English
úlfs	ulf ON, Ulf (name) OI, Ulf (name) ON
úlfssonar	Son-of-Ulf (name) OI, Son-of-Ulf (name) ON, Ulfson (name) ON, Ulfson (name) OI
úr	from OI, of OI, out OI, out-of OI
úrigt	irritable OI, irritable ON
út	back ON, back OI, back-from ON, back-from OI, from ON, out OI, out ON, out-of OI, out-of ON
útan	except-for ON, out ON, out-of ON, outside-of ON, out-travel ON
úti	about OI, about ON, out OI, out ON
útibú	out-houses ON
útibúr	out-house ON, out-house OI
útibúrsdyrin	out-house-door OI
útibúrsdyrrin	out-house-door ON
útidurum	the-out-door ON
útidurunum	the-out-door ON
útidyrum	out-door OI

Norse	English
útivist	out-journey ON, out-journey OI
útróðra	fishing OI, out-rowing ON
útsynnings	South-West (place) ON
útsynningsbyr	south-west-wind OI

V, v

Norse	English
vá	slew ON
vaðmálsmöttul	mantle ON
vænn	a-fair ON, a-fair OI, handsome OI, handsome ON
vænst	fair ON, fair OI
vænt	expected OI
vænti	expect OI, wait ON
væntu	expected OI
væri	had ON, was OI, was ON, were OI, were ON, would OI, would ON, would-be ON, would-be OI
værir	would-be ON, would-be OI
væru	being OI, had OI, were OI, would-be ON, would-be OI
væstir	worn ON
vág	inlet ON
vágs	Vog (place) ON
vágskorit	creek-indented ON
vaka	awake ON, awake OI
vakði	awoke ON, woke ON
vaki	wake OI, wake ON
vakið	awoken OI
vaknar	awoke OI, awoke ON
vakti	awoke OI, woke OI
valdi	chose OI
valði	chose ON
valdidida	Avaldidida (name) OI
valslöngur	war-slings ON, war-slings OI
valþjófs	Vallthjof (place) ON, Vallthjof (place) OI

The Vinland Sagas — Word List (Norse to English)

Norse	English
valþjófsstöðum	Vathjolfsstadr (place) ON, Vathjolfsstadr (place) OI
ván	looked ON
vana	custom ON
vanda	accustomed OI, custom OI
vanða	accustomed ON
vandliga	closely ON
vann	won ON, won OI
vant	missing OI, missing ON
vánu	hope ON
vápn	weapon ON, weapons ON
vápnin	weapons ON
var	stayed ON, stayed OI, was OI, was ON, were OI, were ON
vár	been ON, our ON, sprung ON, what-was ON, will ON
vara	wares ON, wares OI
vára	going ON, spring ON
várar	spring ON
varast	avoid ON, avoid OI
varð	became ON, became OI, was OI, was ON, were OI, were ON
varða	concerned ON
varði	expected ON, expected OI
varðlokur	warlock-songs ON, warlock-songs OI
varðveislur	preservation OI
varðveita	supplies ON, supplies OI
varðveitti	preserved ON, preserved OI
vári	spring ON
varir	aware OI, aware ON, foreseen OI, foreseen ON
várit	spring ON
varla	barely ON, hardly ON, hardly OI, rarely ON
várn	ours ON
varnað	wares OI, wares ON
varning	goods OI, goods ON, wares OI, wares ON
varningi	wares ON
varninginn	wares OI
varninginum	wares ON, wares OI
varningr	goods ON, wares ON
varningur	goods OI
varningurinn	wares OI
varp	threw OI, threw ON
várra	ours ON
varstu	was OI, was ON
vart	hardly ON, hardly OI, noticed ON, noticed OI
várt	ours ON
váru	ours ON, was ON, were ON
várum	we ON
vas	was ON
vás	toil ON
vási	cold-and-wet ON
vaskasti	valiant OI, valiant ON
vát	wet ON
vatn	lake ON, lake OI, water OI, water ON
vatnað	water-taken OI
vatnahverfi	Vatnahverfi (place) OI, Vatnahverfi (place) ON
vatnat	water-taken ON
vatni	river OI, river ON, water ON, water OI
vatnið	lake OI
vatninu	lake OI, lake ON
vatnit	lake ON
vatnshorni	Vatnshorn (place) OI, Vatnshorn (place) ON
vatnsströndu	beach OI, beach ON
vaxið	growing OI, grown OI
vaxin	grown OI
vaxinn	growing ON, growing OI, grown ON
vaxit	growing ON, grown ON
veðr	weather ON, wind ON, winds ON
veðrátta	weather ON, weather OI
veðri	weather OI, weather ON
veðrið	wind OI
veðrit	wind ON

The Vinland Sagas — Word List (Norse to English)

Norse	English
veðrs	weathered ON, weathered OI
veður	weather OI, winds OI
veg	way OI, way ON
vega	fight OI, fight ON, ways OI, ways ON
veginn	away OI, away ON
vegir	way ON, way OI
vegna	ways ON, ways OI
vegr	slayed ON
vegur	slayed OI
veiðar	hunting OI
veiðarnar	fishing ON, hunting OI
veiddu	caught OI, caught ON
veiðiferð	hunting OI
veiðiferðir	hunting ON
veiðiförum	hunting OI
veiðimaðr	hunter ON, the-hunter ON
veiðimaður	hunter OI, the-hunter OI
veiðimanns	the-hunter ON, the-hunter OI
veiðiskap	fishing ON, fishing OI
veiðum	fishing OI, hunting OI, hunting ON
veift	waved ON, waving ON, waving OI
veik	referred OI, referred ON
veisla	feast OI, the-feast OI
veislan	feast OI
veislu	feast OI
veislunni	the-feast OI
veislur	feasts OI
veit	know OI, know ON
veita	grant ON, grant OI, know OI, know ON, lead OI, lead ON, supplied ON, supplied OI, supply OI, supply ON
veitir	gave OI
veitt	given ON
veitti	provided-for ON, provided-for OI, supported OI, supported ON
veittir	supplied ON, supplied OI
veittr	given ON
veittu	gave ON, gave OI, supported OI, supported ON
veittur	given OI
veizla	feast ON, the-feast ON
veizlan	the-feast ON
veizlu	feast ON
veizlum	feasts ON
veizlunni	feast ON, the-feast ON
vekr	awoke ON
vekur	awoke OI
vel	a ON, well OI, well ON
veldr	brought-about ON, caused ON
veldur	brought-about OI, caused OI
velja	will ON, will OI
velkði	drove ON
velkti	drove OI
vella	boil ON, boil OI
vellauðigur	wealthy OI
vér	we OI, we ON, we-are ON, we-are OI
vera	be OI, be ON, being OI, being ON, it-was OI, shall-be OI, shall-be ON, to-be ON, to-be OI, was OI, was ON, were OI, were ON
verð	deserve OI, deserve ON
verða	be OI, be ON, being OI, to-be ON, to-be OI, was OI, were ON
verði	be OI, be ON, will-be ON, will-be OI
verðr	become ON, become OI, becomes ON, were ON, worth ON
verður	becomes OI, worth OI
verið	been OI, had-been OI, have-been OI, made OI
verit	been ON, had-been ON, have-been ON, made ON
verja	protect ON, protect OI, protection OI, protection ON

Norse	English	Norse	English
verjast	defend OI, defend ON	veturnætur	winter OI
verk	work OI, work ON	veturvist	winter OI
verkstjóri	a-foreman ON, a-foreman OI	veturvistar	winter OI
verkstjórinn	the-foreman OI	vexti	grown OI, grown ON, well-built OI, well-built ON
verra	worse OI, worse ON, worst OI	við	by ON, by OI, in OI, in ON, off ON, off OI, to OI, to ON, we OI, with OI, with ON, wood OI, wood ON
verri	worse ON, worse OI		
vert	worthy OI, worthy ON		
vertu	be OI, be ON		
vesæll	wretched OI		
vesall	wretched ON	víða	many OI, many ON, widely OI, widely ON
vesallegr	poor-wretch ON	víðar	wide ON
vesallegur	poor-wretch OI	víðara	far-and-wide ON, far-and-wide OI
vesöld	misery OI		
vesölð	misery ON	viði	wood OI, wood ON, woods OI, woods ON
vestan	west ON, west OI, western OI, western ON	viðinn	trees OI, trees ON
		viðskipti	exchanged OI
vestanveðr	west-wind ON	viðskiptum	dealings OI, dealings ON
vestarlega	westward OI		
vestarliga	westward ON	viðtaka	taken OI
vestr	west ON	viðtöku	resistance ON, resistance OI
vestrætt	westwards ON		
vestri	western OI, western ON	viðu	wood OI, wood ON
vestribyggð	Vestribyggd (place) ON, Vestribyggd (place) OI	vífill	Vifil (name) ON, Vifil (name) OI
		vífilsdal	Vifilsdal (place) ON, Vifilsdal (place) OI
vestribyggðar	Vestribyggd (place) OI, Vestribyggd (place) ON	vífilsson	Son-of-Vifil (name) OI, Son-of-Vifil (name) ON, Vifilson (name) ON, Vifilson (name) OI
vestrvíking	west-raiding ON		
vestur	west OI	víg	killing-of OI, killing-of ON
vesturátt	westwards OI		
vesturvíking	west-raiding OI	víga	killing OI, killing ON
vethildi	Vethild (name) ON, Vethild (name) OI	vígðu	ground ON, ground OI
		vígfleka	battle OI, battle ON
vetr	winter ON, wintered ON	vígra	fighting OI, fighting ON
vetra	winter OI, winter ON	vika	week OI, week ON
vetrar	winter OI, winter ON	vikur	weeks ON, weeks OI
vetri	winter OI, winter ON	vil	will OI, will ON
vetrinn	winter ON	vilda	will ON, wish ON, wished ON
vetrum	winter OI, winter ON, winters OI, winters ON	vildi	will OI, will ON, willed OI, willed ON, willing ON, wish OI, wished ON, wished OI
vetrvist	winter ON		
vetur	winter OI, wintered OI		
veturinn	winter OI		

The Vinland Sagas   Word List (Norse to English)

Norse	English
vildu	willed OI, willed ON, willing ON, willing OI, would ON
vili	will ON, wished ON
vilið	will ON
vilir	will-you ON
vilja	he-willed ON, will OI, will ON, willed OI, willed ON, willing ON, willing OI, would OI, would ON
viljað	willed OI
viljat	willed ON
vilji	will OI, wished OI
viljið	will OI
viljir	will OI
vill	will ON, will OI, willed OI, willed ON, wills ON, wills OI, wished OI, wished ON
villtu	will-you ON
vilt	will OI
viltu	will-you OI, will-you ON
vin	friend OI
vín	wine ON, wine OI
vina	friends OI, friends ON
vinaboð	friend-invites ON, friend-invites OI
vinar	friend ON, friend OI
vinátta	friendship ON, friendship OI
vináttu	friendship ON, friendship OI
vínbejaköngul	grape-vines ON
vínber	grapes OI, grapes ON
vínberjum	grapes OI, grapes ON
vinda	wind OI, wind ON
vinir	friends ON, friends OI
vínland	Vinland (place) OI, Vinland (place) ON
vínlandi	Vinland (place) OI, Vinland (place) ON
vínlands	Vinland (place) OI, Vinland (place) ON
vínlandsferð	Vinland-voyage OI, vinland-voyage ON
vínlandsför	Vinland-voyage OI, Vinland-voyage ON

Norse	English
vinnast	go-on ON
vinnur	friend OI
vinr	friend ON
vinsældum	popularity OI
vinsæll	befriended ON, befriended OI, popular ON, popular OI
vinur	friend OI, friend-of OI
vínvið	vines OI, vines ON
vínviði	vines OI, vines ON
vínviðr	vine-trees ON
vínviður	vines OI, vine-trees OI
virðing	honour ON, honour OI
virðingar	worthiness OI, worthiness ON
virðingarráð	worthiness ON, worthiness OI
virðingu	worthiness OI, worthiness ON
virðist	seemed OI
vís	aware ON, aware OI
vísendakona	fore-knowing-woman ON
vísendakonunni	wise-woman ON
vísindakona	fore-knowing-woman OI
vísindakonunni	prophetess OI, wise-woman OI
vissi	knew OI, knew ON
vissu	knew OI, knew ON
vist	provisions OI, provisions ON
víst	certain ON, certain OI, made ON, made OI, wise ON, wise OI
vistar	lodge OI, lodge ON, lodging OI, lodging ON, stay OI, stay ON
vistir	lodging ON, lodgings OI, provisions OI, provisions ON, supplies ON
vistlaus	homeless OI
vistlauss	homeless ON
vistuðu	saved ON
vísu	know OI, know ON, verse ON, verse OI
vit	into ON, known ON, to ON, we ON, with ON

233

Norse	English
vita	know ON, know OI, knowing ON, knowing OI
vitja	visit OI, visit ON
vitr	wise ON
vitur	wise OI
vó	slew OI
vog	inlet OI
vöggu	cradle OI, cradle ON
vogs	Vogs (place) OI
vogskorið	creek-indented OI
vogunum	inlets OI
vöknuðu	awoke OI, awoke ON
vöku	awake OI, awake ON
völdum	doing ON, doing OI
von	looked OI
vonum	hope OI
vopn	weapon OI, weapons OI
vopnin	weapons OI
vor	been OI, gone OI, our OI, sprung OI, what-was OI, will OI
vora	going OI, spring OI
vorar	spring OI
vori	spring OI
vorið	spring OI
vorn	ours OI
vort	ours OI
voru	ours OI, was OI, were OI
voruð	were OI
vorum	ours OI
vos	toil OI
vosi	cold-and-wet OI
vot	wet OI

Y, y

Norse	English
yðr	you ON
yðra	depart OI, depart ON
yður	you OI, yours OI, yours ON
yðvar	you ON, you OI, your OI, yours ON, yours OI
yðvarr	your ON, yours ON
yfir	over OI, over ON
yfirlæti	respectable OI, respectable ON
yfirsöngva	burial-service ON, burial-service OI
yfirsöngvar	burial-service ON, burial-service OI
ykkar	you OI
ykkr	you ON
ykkrar	you ON
ykkur	you OI, you ON, your OI
yngveldar	Yngvild (name) OI
yngvildar	Yngvild (name) ON
yrðir	become ON, become OI
yxna-þórissonar	Son-Of-Ox-Thorir (name) OI
yxney	Oxney (place) OI

Ý, ý

Norse	English
ýla	howling ON, howling OI
ýmisst	either ON
ýmist	either OI

Word List (English to Norse)

English	Norse

A, a

English	Norse
a	að OI, at ON, ein OI, ein ON, einn OI, einn ON, er OI, er ON, hinn OI, í OI, í ON, inn ON, vel ON
a-bad	illa ON
able	mega OI, mega ON
abode	bústað OI, bústað ON
about	á OI, í OI, í ON, of OI, of ON, um OI, um ON, úti OI, úti ON
about-from	umfram OI
about-further	umbóta OI, umbótar ON
above	ofan OI, ofan ON
a-bull	griðungur OI
abundance	gnóttir OI, gnóttir ON
accepted	játar OI, játar ON, þágu OI, þágu ON, þiggið OI, þiggið ON, þiggr ON, þiggur OI
accompany	annan OI
according	því OI, því ON
accordingly	því OI, því ON
account	frásögnum OI, frásögnum ON
accustomed	vanda OI, vanða ON
a-company	liðin OI
across	þvers OI, þvers ON
a-cushion	hægendi ON
advantage	kost OI, kost ON
advice	ráð OI, ráð ON, ráði ON, ráðið OI, ráðit ON, ráðum OI, reiða OI, reiða ON
advisable	ráðlegra OI
advise	ráð OI, ráða OI, ráða ON, ráðið OI, ráðs OI, ræð OI, ræð ON
advised	ráð OI, ráð ON, ráði ON, ræddu OI, ræddu ON
a-fair	vænn OI, vænn ON
a-farm	bú ON
affection	ástúð OI, ástúð ON
a-foreman	verkstjóri OI, verkstjóri ON
a-freed-man	leysingi OI, leysingi ON
after	áðr ON, aftr ON, aftur OI, eftir OI, eftir ON, síðan OI, síðan ON
afterwards	eftir OI, eftir ON, síðan OI, síðan ON, síðar OI, síðar ON
again	aftur OI, nýju OI, nýju ON
against	mót OI, mót ON, móti OI, móti ON
agape	gapti OI
age	aldr ON, aldri OI, aldri ON, aldur OI
a-girdle	hnjóskulinda OI, hnjóskulinda ON
a-good	góðr ON, góður OI
a-great	mikinn OI
agreeable	geðjaðir ON, skapfelld ON, skapfelldir OI
agreed	ákveðin OI, ákveðin ON, játtu OI, játtu ON, ráðin OI, ráðin ON, sætti OI, sætti ON
agreement	máldaga OI, máldaga ON
ahead	fyrir OI, fyrir ON, undan OI, undan ON
ahead-of	fyrir OI, fyrir ON
a-high-seat	hásæti OI, hásæti ON
ai	ái OI
aimed	reiddi OI, reiddi ON
a-keel	kjöl OI
a-knob	hnappur OI, knappr ON
Alftafjord (place)	álftafirði OI, álftafirði ON, álftafjörð OI, álftafjörð ON
a-little	litlu ON

The Vinland Sagas — Word List (English to Norse)

English	Norse
all	á OI, á ON, alla OI, alla OI, alla ON, alla ON, allan OI, allan ON, allar OI, allar ON, allir OI, allir OI, allir ON, allir ON, allr ON, alls OI, alls OI, alls ON, alls ON, allt OI, allt ON, allur OI, öll OI, öll ON, öllu OI, öllu ON, öllum OI, öllum ON
all-kinds	allskonar ON, konar OI
all-near	allnær ON
allow	leyfa OI, leyfa ON
allowed	lét OI, lét ON
all-prepared	albúið OI, albúit ON
all-very	allmjök ON
all-well	allvel OI, allvel ON
alone	ein OI, ein ON, einni OI, einni ON, eitt OI
along	eftir OI, eftir ON, ein OI, eitt OI, eitt ON, fyrir OI, fyrir ON, lengi OI, lengi ON, með OI, með ON
already	þegar OI, þegar ON
also	annars OI, og OI, ok ON
altar	stalli OI, stalli ON
altogether	allt OI, allt ON
always	hversdaglega OI
am	em ON, er OI
a-man	maðr ON, maður OI, mann OI, manni OI, manni ON
ambitious-man	metnaðarmaðr ON, metnaðarmaður OI
am-i	er ON
am-named	heiti ON
among	í OI, í ON, um OI, um ON
ample	drjúgari OI, drjúgari ON
amusement	skemmtan OI, skemmtan ON
an	ein ON, eitt ON
an-axe	öx OI
ancestry	ætt ON
anchor	akkeri OI, akkeri ON, akkerum OI, akkerum ON
and	en OI, en ON, fyrir OI, og OI, og ON, ok OI, ok ON
an-excellent	ágæts OI
animal-hunting	dýraveiðr ON
animal-marrow	dýramerg OI, dýramerg ON
animals	dýra OI, dýra ON, eyki OI, eyki ON
an-island	ey OI
another	annað OI, annan OI, annan ON, annar OI, annarr ON, annat ON, öðrum OI, öðrum ON
answer	svara OI, svara ON, svör OI, svör ON, svörum OI, svörum ON
answered	segir OI, svarað OI, svaraði OI, svaraði ON, svarar OI, svarar ON, svarat ON
anti-sun-wise	andsælis ON, rangsælis OI
a-nun	nunna OI, nunna ON
any	einum OI, einum ON, enga ON, nokkuð OI, nökkut ON, öngva OI
any-of	einnhver OI, einnhverr ON
anyone	nokkur OI, nökkurr ON
a-one-footer	einfætingr ON, einfætingur OI
apart	sundur OI
a-pole-axe	bolöxi OI, bolöxi ON
appears	líst OI, lízt ON
applied	beita ON, beittu OI
apply	beitim ON, beitum OI
appointed	ráðnir OI, ráðnir ON, réð OI, réð ON, réðst OI, réðst ON, réðust OI, réðust ON
approached	nálguðust OI, nálguðust ON
are	búnu OI, búnu ON, er OI, er ON, ert OI, ert ON, eru OI, eru ON, eruð OI, eruð ON, erum OI, erum ON
areas	sveitir ON
are-you	ertu OI, ertu ON
Ari (name)	ari ON
a-ring	hring OI, hring ON

The Vinland Sagas — Word List (English to Norse)

English	Norse
a-river	á OI
arm	hendi OI, hendi ON, hönd OI, hönd ON
Arnarstapa (place)	arnarstapa OI, arnarstapa ON
Arnarstapi (place)	arnarstapa OI, arnarstapa ON
Arnlaug (name)	arnlaugr ON, arnlaugur OI
Arnlaugsfjord (place)	arnlaugsfjörð OI, arnlaugsfjörð ON
Arnora (name)	arnóru OI, arnóru ON
around	lit ON, stundar ON, um OI, um ON, umhverfis OI
arrived	komust OI, kómust ON
arrow	ör OI, ör ON, örin OI, örin ON, örina ON
as	að OI, at ON, en OI, en ON, er OI, er ON, sem OI, sem ON, því ON
as-a-woman	kona ON
as-big	mikinn ON
a-ship	skipi OI
as-if	sem OI
ask	biðja OI, biðja ON
asked	bað OI, bað ON, báðu OI, báðu ON, beðinn OI, beðinn ON, beiddist OI, beiddist ON, biðr ON, spurði OI, spurði ON, spurðu OI, spurðu ON, spurt OI, spurt ON, spyr OI, spyrja OI, spyrja ON, spyrr ON
a-skin-purse	skjóðupungur OI
asks	spyr OI, spyrr ON
a-slab-stone	hellusteinn OI
Aslak (name)	áslákr ON, áslákur OI
as-may	mátti OI, mátti ON
as-much-as	margar ON
a-son	son OI, son ON
a-speck	flekk OI
as-should-be	skyldi OI, skyldi ON
assist	atbeina OI, beina OI, beina ON
assistance	atbeina ON, liðsinni OI, liðsinni ON
as-soon-as	þegar ON
as-sweet	jafnsætt OI, jafnsætt ON
astonished	undruðust OI, undruðust ON
a-stream	straumar OI, straumur OI
Asvald (name)	ásvalds OI, ásvalds ON
Asvald's (name)	ásvalds ON
at	á OI, á ON, að OI, at ON, er OI, er ON, í OI, í ON, um OI, um ON
ate	átu OI, átu ON
at-hand	fyrir OI, fyrir ON
at-sea	hafa OI, hafa ON
attacked	elnaði OI, elnaði ON
attended	mannaðr ON, mannaður OI, sótt OI, sótt ON
at-the	á OI, á ON
attract	fýsa OI, fýsa ON
Aud (name)	auðar OI, auðar ON, auðr ON, auður OI
aunt	hímu ON
Austfjord (place)	austfjörðum OI, austfjörðum ON
autumn	haust OI, haust ON, hausti OI, hausti ON, haustið OI, haustit ON
avail	tjóa ON
Avaldamon (name)	avaldamon OI, avaldamon ON
Avaldidida (name)	valdidida OI
avenge	hefnir OI, hefnir ON
avoid	forðast OI, forðast ON, varast OI, varast ON
awake	vaka OI, vaka ON, vöku OI, vöku ON
aware	varir OI, varir ON, vís OI, vís ON
a-warrior-king	herkonungur OI
away	braut OI, braut ON, brot ON, brott OI, brott ON, brottu OI, burt OI, burt ON, undan OI, undan ON, veginn OI, veginn ON
away-from	undan OI
a-whale	hvalr ON

The Vinland Sagas — Word List (English to Norse)

English	Norse
awhile	hríð ON, meðan OI, meðan ON, stund OI, stund ON
a-wife	konu OI, konu ON
awoke	vakði ON, vaknar OI, vaknar ON, vakti OI, vekr ON, vekur OI, vöknuðu OI, vöknuðu ON
awoken	vakið OI
a-woman	konu OI, konu ON
axe	öx ON, öxi OI, öxi ON, öxin ON, öxina ON, öxinni OI, öxinni ON
ay	í ON

Á, á

English	Norse
ái	ái OI

B, b

English	Norse
baby-boy	sveinbarn OI, sveinbarn ON
back	áður OI, aftr OI, aftr ON, aftur OI, baki OI, baki ON, út OI, út ON
back-from	út OI, út ON
bad	illa OI, illa ON
badly	illa OI, illa ON, illilega OI, ílliliga ON
bags	bagga OI, bagga ON, böggunum OI, böggunum ON
balls	knött OI, knött ON
bank	bakkann OI, bakkann ON
banned	bannaði OI, bannaði ON, bönnuðu OI, bönnuðu ON
banners	flíkr ON, flíkur OI
baptised	skírð OI, skírð ON, skírðir OI, skírðir ON
bare	ber OI, ber ON
barely	varla ON
bargain	fala OI, fala ON
bargained-for	falar OI, falar ON
battle	bardaga OI, bardaga ON, bardagar OI, bardagar ON, bardagi OI, bardagi ON, fundr ON, fundur OI, orrostu ON, orustu OI, vígfleka OI, vígfleka ON
battled	börðust ON
be	á ON, fá OI, fá ON, vera OI, vera ON, verða OI, verða ON, verði OI, verði ON, vertu OI, vertu ON
be-able	mega ON
beach	vatnsströndu OI, vatnsströndu ON
beaches	strandir OI, strandir ON, strandirnar ON, ströndunum OI
beam	tré OI, tré ON
beams	tré OI
bear	bar OI, bar ON, bera OI, bera ON, berum OI, berum ON, bjarndýr OI, björn ON, fæða OI
bearded	skeggjaðr ON, skeggjaður OI
bearing	bærist OI, bærist ON, báru OI, báru ON
Bear's (name)	bjarnar OI, bjarnar ON
beat	börðu OI, börðu ON
beaten	barðir OI, barðir ON
beautiful	fagrt ON, fagurt OI
became	gerðist OI, gerðist ON, urðu OI, urðu ON, varð OI, varð ON
became-a	gerðist ON
because	því OI, því ON
because-of	fyrir OI, fyrir ON
because-of-a	fyrir OI, fyrir ON
become	orðið OI, orðinn OI, orðinn ON, verðr OI, verðr ON, yrðir OI, yrðir ON
becomes	verðr ON, verður OI
becoming	gerðist OI
bed	hvílu OI, hvílu ON, stokki OI, stokki ON
bed-clothes	klæðin OI, klæðin ON

The Vinland Sagas — Word List (English to Norse)

English	Norse	English	Norse
been	vár ON, verið OI, verit ON, vor OI	between	með OI, með ON, meðal ON, milli OI, milli ON, millum OI
before	áðr ON, áður OI, en ON, fyrir OI, fyrir ON, fyrr OI, fyrr ON, fyrri OI, fyrri ON, því OI, því ON	bid	bað OI, bað ON, bauð ON, beita OI, bið OI, biðk ON, bjóða OI, bjóða ON, boðið OI, boðit ON
befriended	vinsæll OI, vinsæll ON	bids-tyr	beiði-týr ON
began	byrjaði OI, byrjaði ON, hófust ON	Bids-Tyr (name)	beiði-týr OI
begin	byrjar OI, byrjar ON	big	mikill OI, mikill ON
beginning	öndverðum OI, öndverðum ON	binding	bönd OI, bönd ON
behaviour	athæfi OI, athæfi ON	birds	fugl OI, fugl ON
be-heard	hljóðs OI, hljóðs ON	bishop	biskup OI, biskup ON, byskups ON
behind	eftir OI, eftir ON, heldur OI, seinni ON, undir OI, undir ON	Bishop (name)	byskups OI
behold	heldr ON, heldur OI	Bishop'S (name)	byskups OI
being	væru OI, vera OI, vera ON, verða OI	bishop's-seat	biskupsstóll OI, biskupsstóll ON
believed	trúðu OI, trúðu ON	bit	bíta OI, bíta ON
bellowed	gall OI, gellr ON	Bjarn (name)	bjarnar OI, bjarnar ON
bellowing	belja OI, belja ON	Bjarnarhofn (place)	bjarnarhöfn OI, bjarnarhöfn ON
belly-fat	ístruna ON	Bjarney (place)	bjarney OI, bjarney ON, bjarneyja OI, bjarneyjar ON, bjarneyjum OI
bench	bekkinn OI, bekkinn ON, bekknum OI, bekknum ON	Bjarni (name)	bjarna OI, bjarna ON, bjarni OI, bjarni ON
benefit	gott OI, gott ON, kostum OI, kostum ON, njóti OI, nýt ON	Bjarn's (name)	bjarnar ON
benefited	gott ON	Bjorn (name)	birni OI, birni ON, björn OI, björn ON
benefits	hagr ON, kosti OI	black	svartan OI, svartan ON
benefitted	gott OI	blamed	lasta OI, lasta ON
berries	berjum OI, berjum ON	Blaserkur (place)	bláserkr ON, bláserkur OI
beside	hjá OI, hjá ON	blood	dreyra OI, dreyra ON
best	basta OI, bazta ON, best OI, besta OI, besti OI, bezt ON, bezta ON, bezti ON	blood-letting	bílds OI, bílds ON
		blue	blán OI, blán ON
betoken	tákna OI, teikna ON	boar	bar OI
betrayed	sviku OI, sviku ON	board	borð OI, borð ON
betrothed	föstnuð OI, föstnuð ON	boat	bát ON, báti OI, báti ON, bátinn OI, bátinn ON, bátr ON, bátrinn ON, báturinn OI, eftirbát OI, eftirbátr ON, eftirbátur OI
better	batna OI, batna ON, betr ON, betra OI, betra ON, betur OI		
bettered	batnaði OI, batnaði ON		
better-than	batna OI, batna ON		

The Vinland Sagas   Word List (English to Norse)

English	Norse	English	Norse
boats	báti OI, báti ON, eftirbátr ON, eftirbátur OI, skipunum OI, skipunum ON	brass	messingu OI, messingu ON
		brass-buttons	látúnshnappar OI
bodies	líkin OI, líkin ON, líkum OI, líkum ON	brass-spoon	messingarspón OI, messingarspón ON
body	lík OI, lík ON, líki OI, líki ON, líkið OI, líkin OI, líkinu OI, líkinu ON, líkit ON	Brattahlid (place)	brattahlíð OI, brattahlíð ON, brattahlíð] ON, brattahlíðar OI, brattahlíðar ON
boil	vella OI, vella ON	bravely	drengiliga ON
boiled	suðu OI, suðu ON	breast	brjóst ON, brjósti OI, brjósti ON, brjóstið OI, brjóstit ON
bold	feitt OI, feitt ON		
boldly	skörulega OI, sköruliga ON	Breidabolstad (place)	breiðabólstað OI, breiðabólstað ON
bondsman	ánauðigr ON, ánauðigur OI	Breidafjord (place)	breiðafirði OI, breiðafirði ON, breiðafjarðar OI, breiðafjarðar ON, breiðafjörð OI, breiðafjörð ON, breiðfirskur OI, breiðfirzkr ON
bondsmen	ánauðgir OI, ánauðgir ON		
booths	búðir OI, búðir ON, byggðir OI		
bore	bar OI, bar ON, báru OI, báru ON, bárust OI, bárust ON, ber OI, bera OI, bera ON, berr ON, borið OI, borit ON, fæddi OI, fæddi ON		
		Bremen (place)	brimum OI, brimum ON
		bridge	bryggjum OI, bryggjum ON, bryggjunum OI, bryggjunum ON
Borgafjord (place)	borgarfirði OI, borgarfirði ON	bright	bjart OI, bjart ON, bjartari ON, bjartur OI
born	fæðist ON	bright-chestnut	ljósjörp OI, ljósjörp ON
borne	bornir OI, bornir ON	bring	bera OI, berim ON, færa OI, færa ON
both	báða ON, báðir OI, báðir ON, báðum OI, báðum ON, bæði OI, bæði ON, beggja OI, beggja ON	broad	breiðara ON, breiðir OI, breiðir ON, breitt OI
		broader	breiðara OI
bother	nenni OI, nenni ON	broke	braut OI, brotna ON, brotnaði OI, brotnaði ON, brutu OI, brutu ON
bothered	nenntu OI, nenntu ON		
bottom-of	botn OI, botn ON	broken	brotinn OI, brotinn ON, brugðist OI, brugðizt ON
bought	kaupir OI, kaupir ON, keypti OI, keypti ON		
bound	bundinn OI, bundinn ON, bundu OI, bundu ON	Brokey (place)	brokey OI, brokey ON
		bronze	eiri OI, eiri ON
boy	svein OI, sveinbarn ON, sveininn OI, sveininn ON, sveinn OI, sveinn ON	brother	bróðir OI, bróðir ON, bróður OI, bróður ON
		brothers	bræðr ON, bræðra OI, bræðra ON, bræðrum OI, bræðrum ON, bræður OI
Brand (name)	brands OI, brands ON		
Brand's (name)	brands ON		

The Vinland Sagas *Word List (English to Norse)*

English	Norse
brought	báru OI, báru ON, brugðu OI, brugðu ON, færa OI, færa ON, flutti OI, flutti ON
brought-about	veldr ON, veldur OI
brought-out	brugðið OI, brugðit ON
buckets	byttu OI, byttu ON
bull	graðungr ON, graðungur OI, griðung OI, griðung ON, griðungr ON
Buna (name)	bunu OI, bunu ON
burdens	byrðar OI, byrðar ON
burial-service	yfirsöngva OI, yfirsöngva ON, yfirsöngvar OI, yfirsöngvar ON
buried	grafnir OI, grafnir ON, jörðuð OI, jörðuð ON
burn	brenna ON, láta OI
busy	héldu OI, heldu ON
but	an OI, at ON, eða OI, eða ON, en OI, en ON, enn OI, enn ON, og OI
but-for	en OI, en ON
buy	kaupa OI, kaupa ON
by	á OI, á ON, að OI, at ON, hjá OI, hjá ON, við OI, við ON
Byrdusmjors (name)	byrðusmjörs ON

C, c

English	Norse
cabin	skála OI, skála ON, skálanum OI, skálanum ON
cabins	skálanna OI, skálanna ON, skálarnir OI, skálarnir ON, skálavegginum OI, skálavegginum ON
Caithness (place)	katanes OI, katanes ON, katanesi OI, katanesi ON
calf-skin-shoes	kálfskinnsskó OI, kálfskinnsskúa ON
call	kalla OI, kalla ON, kallið OI, kallið ON, kallim ON, kallit ON, köllum OI
called	heita ON, heitir ON, heitit ON, hét ON, hétu ON, kallað OI, kallaði OI, kallaði ON, kallaðir OI, kallaðir ON, kallaðr ON, kallaður OI, kallat ON, köllu OI, kölluð OI, kölluð ON, kölluðu OI, kölluðu ON, krafði ON, kvað OI, kvaddi OI
called-one	annarr ON
called-out	æptu OI
came	fór OI, fór ON, kæmi OI, kæmi ON, kemr ON, kemur OI, kom OI, kom ON, koma OI, koma ON, komið OI, kominn OI, kominn ON, komit ON, komnir OI, komnir ON, komst OI, komst ON, komu OI, kómu ON
can	get ON, geta ON, kann OI, kann ON
can-it	kann ON
canoe	keip OI, keip ON
cape	kápu OI, kápu ON
captive	hertekna OI, hertekna ON
cargo	farmi OI, farmi ON, farminn OI, farminn ON, farmr ON, farmur OI
carried	bar OI, bar ON, báru OI, báru ON, báruð OI, báruð ON, ber OI, borið OI, borinn OI, borinn ON, borit ON, flytja OI, flytja ON
carry	bera OI, bera ON, fættast ON, flytja OI, flytja ON
carrying	bar OI, bar ON
cast	kasta OI, kasta ON, kastaði OI, köstuðu OI, köstuðu ON
cat-skin	kattarskinn OI, kattarskinn ON

The Vinland Sagas   *Word List (English to Norse)*

English	Norse	English	Norse
cat-skin-gloves	kattskinnsglófa OI, kattskinnsglófa ON	cliff-top	hamargnípu OI, hamargnípu ON
cattle	fé OI, fé ON, fénað OI, fénað ON, fénaðr ON, fénaður OI, graðfé OI, graðfé ON, nautfé OI, nautfé ON	climbed	stígr ON, stígur OI
		close	nánd OI, nánd ON
		closed	lauk OI, lauk ON
		closely	vandliga ON
		cloth	klæði OI, klæðið OI, skrúð ON, skrúðit ON
caught	fengið OI, fengist ON, fengit ON, fengjust OI, fengu OI, fengu ON, hendr ON, hendur OI, veiddu OI, veiddu ON	clothes	klæði OI, klæði ON, klæðið OI, klæðum OI, klæðum ON, klæðunum ON
caused	veldr ON, veldur OI	clothing	klæði OI, klæði ON, umbúningr ON, umbúningur OI
caves	hellum OI, hellum ON		
ceremony	atferli OI, atferli ON		
certain	nokkurn OI, nökkurn ON, víst OI, víst ON	coal	kolum OI, kolum ON
		coffin	kista OI, kista ON, kistu OI, kistu ON
change	skipta OI, skipta ON		
cheeks	kinnum ON, kinnunum OI	coffins	kistur OI, kistur ON
chest	kistil OI, kistil ON	cold	kalt OI, kalt ON, köld OI, köld ON, köldum OI, köldum ON
chief	formaðr ON, formaður OI		
child	barni OI, barni ON	cold-and-wet	vási ON, vosi OI
childhood	barnæsku OI, barnæsku ON	colour	lit OI
children	börn OI, börn ON	come	kæmi OI, kæmi ON, kæmir OI, kemr ON, kemur OI, kom OI, koma OI, koma ON, komast OI, komast ON, komat OI, komat ON, komi OI, komi ON, komið OI, komið ON, kominn OI, kominn ON, komit ON, komk ON, komur OI, kvámur ON
choice	kost OI, kost ON, kostar OI, kostar ON, kostr ON, kostur OI		
choosing	bæði OI		
chose	valdi OI, valði ON		
chosen	kjörin OI, körin ON		
Christ (name)	kristr ON, kristur OI		
christian	kristinn OI, kristinn ON, kristnað OI, kristnat ON		
Christian (name)	kristin OI, kristin ON, kristinn ON	comes	komi ON
		comfort	hugganar ON, huggunar OI
christianity	kristni OI, kristni ON	comforted	huggaði OI, huggaði ON
Christianity (name)	kristni OI, kristni ON	coming	kemur OI, koma OI, koma ON, komin OI, komin ON, kominn OI, kominn ON, komnir OI, komnir ON
church	kirkja OI, kirkja ON, kirkju OI, kirkju ON		
circumstance	kynni ON, kynnu OI		
claimed	heimti OI, heimti ON		
clear	allglöggsæ ON, glöggsæ OI	committed	framið ON, framin OI
cleared	ruddi OI, ruddi ON, ryðja OI, ryðja ON	companion	félaga OI, félaga ON
clearing	rjóðr ON, rjóðrið OI, rjóðrit ON, rjóður OI		

The Vinland Sagas   *Word List (English to Norse)*

English	Norse
companions	félaga ON, félögum OI, félögum ON, förunauta OI, förunauta ON, förunautar OI, förunautar ON, föruneyti OI, föruneyti ON, föruneytinu OI, föruneytinu ON
company	lið OI, lið ON, liði OI, liði ON, liðið OI, liðin ON, liðit ON, liðs OI, liðs ON, líta OI, sveit OI
comrades	félagar OI, félagar ON
conceal	leyna OI, leyna ON
concealed	leyndi OI, leyndi ON
concerned	varða ON
consider	hirða ON
considered	kallast ON
conviction	sakar ON, sakir OI, sakir ON
corn	korn OI, korn ON
corn-shed	kornhjálm OI, kornhjálm ON
costs	kost OI
could	geta OI, kunni OI, kunni ON, máttu OI, máttu ON, mun OI, mun ON, mundi OI, mundi ON
could-be	mundi OI
counsel	ráð OI, ráð ON, ráðs OI, ráðs ON, ráðum OI, ráðum ON, umráði OI, umráði ON
countless	ótal OI, ótal ON
couple	hjón OI, hjón ON, hjónum OI, hjónunum ON
court	hirðar OI, hirðar ON
court-man	hirðmaðr ON, hirðmaður OI
cradle	vöggu OI, vöggu ON
crags	hamra OI, hamra ON
crash	brest OI, brest ON
creaked	brakaði OI, brakaði ON
creatures	kvikindum OI, kykvendum ON
creek-indented	vágskorit ON, vogskorið OI

English	Norse
creep	krýp OI, krýpk ON
crew	skipverja OI, skipverja ON
cried-out	kvað OI, kvað ON
cross	krossa OI, krossa ON
crosses	krossa OI, krossa ON
crow	kráku ON
Crow (name)	kráku OI, kráku ON
cubits	álna ON
curiosity	forvitni OI, forvitni ON
curious	forvitni OI, forvitni ON
custom	siðr ON, siður OI, siðvenju OI, siðvenju ON, vana ON, vanda OI
customs	hattar OI, hattar ON
cut	skáru OI, skáru ON
cut-down	hogginn OI, höggvinn ON

D, d

English	Norse
dale-land	dalalönd ON
Dale-Land (place)	dalalönd OI
danger	hætta OI, hætta ON
dark	ófölvan OI, ófölvan ON, svartir ON, svartr ON, svartur OI, svörtum OI, svörtum ON
daughter	dóttir OI, dóttir ON, dóttur OI, dóttur ON
daughter-of	dóttir OI, dóttir ON, dóttur OI, dóttur ON
day	dægri OI, dag OI, dag ON, dags ON, degi OI, degi ON
days	dægr ON, dægrum OI, dægrum ON, dægur OI, daga OI, daga ON, dagar OI
day-setting	dagsetri OI, dagsetri ON
dead	andaðr ON, andaður OI, dauð OI, dauð ON, dauða OI, dauðan OI, dauðan ON, dauðr ON, dauðum OI, dauðum ON, dauður OI, látin ON, önduð OI

The Vinland Sagas   *Word List (English to Norse)*

English	Norse	English	Norse
dealings	viðskiptum OI, viðskiptum ON	Dimunarvog (place)	dímunarvági ON, dímunarvogi OI
death	andláti OI, andláti ON, bana OI, bana ON, dauða ON	direction	ættir ON, áttir OI
		dirty	smáskitlegr ON, smáskitlegur OI
decide	ráða OI, ráða ON	disappeared	horfin OI, horfin ON, horfinn OI, horfinn ON, hurfu OI, hurfu ON, hvarf OI, hvarf ON
decided	reiða OI, reiða ON, tilskipan OI		
declared	kveðit ON, lýsir OI, lýsir ON		
declaring	kveðið OI	discord	sundrþykki ON, sundurþykki OI, þústr ON, þústur OI
declining	hniginn OI, hniginn ON		
decreased	minnka OI	discourage	letja OI, letja ON
decreases	þverr OI, þverr ON	discussed	ræða OI, ræddu OI, ræddu ON, umræða OI, umræða ON
defeat	ósigr ON, ósigur OI		
defend	verjast OI, verjast ON		
demanded	rífastr ON, rífastur OI	discussion	umræða OI, umræða ON, umræði OI, umræði ON, umræður OI, umræður ON
depart	yðra OI, yðra ON		
descended	ættaðr ON, ættaður OI		
descendents	ætt ON, ættbogi OI, ættbogi ON, átt OI, átt ON	dishonour	ódáðum OI, ódáðum ON
		disorderly	illt OI, illt ON
deserted-forest	eyðimerkr ON, eyðimerkur OI	disposed	ráðlausir OI, ráðstafalausir ON
deserve	verð OI, verð ON	disputes	deilur OI, deilur ON
desire	fýsa OI, fýsa ON	distribute	sundr ON
desired	fýsist OI, fýsti OI, fýsti ON, fýstist OI, fýstist ON	divide	skipta OI, skipta ON
		divided	braut ON, brýtur OI, skiptu OI, skiptu ON
developed	þroskasamt OI, þroskasamt ON	do	gera OI, gera ON, get ON
dew	dögg OI, dögg ON, döggina OI, döggina ON	Dogurdara (place)	dögurðarár OI, dögurðarár ON
did	gera OI, gera ON, gerði OI, gerði ON, gerðu OI, gerðu ON, gerðust OI, gerðust ON, gerir OI, gerir ON	doing	völdum OI, völdum ON
		done	gert OI, gert ON
		door	dura ON, dyra OI, hurð OI, hurð ON, hurðinni OI, hurðinni ON
die	andast OI, andast ON, deyja OI	doors	dyrnar OI, dyrrnar ON
died	andaðist OI, andaðist ON, andast OI, andazt ON, andist ON, dó ON, látizt ON, lézt ON, önduðust OI, önduðust ON	doorway	durum ON, dyrin OI, dyrnar OI, dyrrin ON, dyrum OI, gáttum OI, gáttum ON
		down	niðr ON, niður OI, ofan OI, ofan ON
difference	munr ON, munur OI	dragged	dró OI, dró ON
difficult-be	torflutt OI, torflutt ON	Drangar (place)	dröngum OI, dröngum ON
difficult-of-words	illorðr ON	drank	drakk OI, drakk ON

The Vinland Sagas — *Word List (English to Norse)*

English	Norse
Drepstokk (place)	drepstokki OI, drepstokki ON
dressed	klæddist OI, klæddist ON
drew	brá OI, brá ON, dró OI, dró ON, drógu OI
drink	drukkit ON, drykk OI, drykk ON
driven	rak OI, rak ON, reiddi OI, rekin OI, rekin ON
drove	drífa OI, drífa ON, drifu OI, rak OI, velkði ON, velkti OI
dry	þurrkanar OI, þurrkunar ON
Dublin (place)	dyflinnar ON, dyflinni OI, dyflinni ON
Dublinshire (place)	dyflinnarskíri OI, dyflinnarskíri ON
during	leið OI
dust	mold ON
dwell	búa OI, búa ON
dwelled	dvöl OI, dvöl ON, dvöldust OI, dvölðust ON
dwelling	bæ OI, bæ ON, bænum OI, bænum ON, búi OI, búinu ON, bústað OI, bústað ON, byggilegast OI, byggiligast ON, híbýli OI, híbýli ON, hýbýli ON
dwellings	bæinn OI, bæinn ON, bústað OI, bústaði ON, byggðir OI, byggðir ON, híbýli OI, híbýli ON
dwelt	bjó OI, bjó ON, bjuggu OI, bjuggu ON, búið OI, búit ON

E, e

English	Norse
each	hvárir ON, hver OI, hverju OI, hverju ON, hverjum OI, hverjum ON, hvern OI, hvern ON, hverr ON, hvorir OI
each-of	hver OI
each-way	hvorttveggja OI
ear	eyra OI, eyra ON
earl	jarl OI, jarl ON, jarls OI, jarls ON
Earl (name)	jarl OI, jarl ON, jarli OI, jarli ON
earl's	jarls OI, jarls ON
early	snemma OI, snemma ON
east	austan OI, austan ON, austri OI, austri ON
eastern	austr ON, austur OI, eystri OI, eystri ON
eastern-man	austmaðr ON, austmaður OI
east-fjords	austfirzkr ON
East-Fjords (place)	austfirskur OI
eastwards	austan OI
educated	menntur OI
egg-gathering	eggver OI
eggs	eggjanna OI, eggjum ON, eggver ON
eider-birds	æðr ON
eight	átta OI, átta ON
Einar (name)	einar OI, einar ON, einarr ON
einar's	einars ON
Einar'S (name)	einars OI, einars ON
Einarsfjord (place)	einarsfjörð ON
either	hvárt ON, hvort OI, ýmisst ON, ýmist OI
either-side	hvárirtveggju ON, hvorirtveggju OI
either-way	hvorutveggja OI
elbows	ölnboga OI, ölnboga ON
else	annað OI, annars OI, annars ON, annat ON
enchantments	seiðinn OI, seiðinn ON, seiðsins ON
encounter	hitt OI, hitt ON
encountered	sótti OI, sótti ON
end	enda OI, enda ON, lauk OI, lauk ON
ended	lauk OI, lauk ON, lokið OI, lokit ON, lýkr ON, lýkur OI
ends	endunum OI, endunum ON, lýkr ON, lýkur OI

245

The Vinland Sagas   *Word List (English to Norse)*

English	Norse	English	Norse
endured	þolðu ON	*established*	staðfestu OI, staðfestu ON
engrave	grafa OI, grafa ON	*estate*	bæ OI, bæ ON
enjoy	njóta ON	*esteemed*	göfgan OI, göfgan ON
enough	dygði OI, dygði ON	*evaluate*	met OI, meta ON
enslaved	þjáðir OI, þjáðir ON	*even*	jöfnum OI, jöfnum ON
entertain	skemmtanar OI, skemmtanar ON	*evening*	kveld OI, kveld ON, kveldi OI, kveldi ON, kveldið OI, kveldit ON
entertained	skemmtu OI, skemmtuðu ON	*events*	atburð OI, atburð ON, atburði OI, atburði ON, atburðum OI, atburðum ON
equal	jafn OI, jafna ON, jafnan OI, jafnan ON, jafnmikið OI, jafnmikil OI, jafnmikil ON, jafnmikit ON		
		eventually	síðir OI, síðir ON
equal-day	jafndægri OI, jafndægri ON	*ever*	jafnan OI, jafnan ON
		every	allra OI, allra ON, hver OI, hverr ON
equal-long	jafnlangt OI, jafnlangt ON		
equally	jafnan OI, jafnan ON, jafnsaman OI, jafnsaman ON	*everyone's*	allra OI, allra ON
		evil	allill OI, allill ON, illa OI, illa ON
equally-handsome	jafnmannvænn ON	*excellent*	ágæti OI, ágæti ON, ágæts ON, íþróttamaðr ON, íþróttamaður OI
Erik (name)	eirík OI, eirík ON, eiríki OI, eiríki ON, eiríkr ON, eiríks OI, eiríks ON, eiríkur OI		
		except-for	utan OI, útan ON
		exchange	skiptumst OI
Erik'S (name)	eiríks OI, eiríks ON	*exchanged*	skipti ON, skiptust OI, viðskipti OI
Eriksdottir (name)	eiríksdóttir OI, eiríksdóttir ON		
		exchanges	skipti OI, skipti ON
Eriksey (place)	eiríksey OI, eiríksey ON, eiríkseyju OI	*exerted*	kostaði OI, kostaði ON
		exhausted	þrekaðir OI, þrekaðir ON, þrjóta OI, þrjóta ON
Eriksfjord (place)	eiríksfirði OI, eiríksfirði ON, eiríksfjarðar OI, eiríksfjarðar ON, eiríksfjörð OI, eiríksfjörð ON, eríksfjörð OI, eríksfjörð ON		
		expect	vænti OI
		expected	allvænt ON, vænt OI, væntu OI, varði OI, varði ON
		expel	reka OI, reka ON
		expenses	gjalda OI, gjalda ON
Eriksholmar (place)	eiríkshólmum OI, eiríkshólmum ON	*experienced*	reyndi OI, reyndi ON, reynt OI, reynt ON
Eriksson (name)	eiríksson OI, eiríksson ON, eiríkssyni OI, eiríkssyni ON	*explore*	kanna OI, kanna ON, könnuðu ON
		explored	kannað OI, kannat ON, könnuðu OI
Eriksstadir (place)	eiríksstöðum OI, eiríksstöðum ON	*exploring*	kanna OI
Eriksvog (place)	eiríksvági ON, eiríksvogi OI	*extended*	rétti OI, rétti ON
		extraordinary	kynjalaust OI, kynjalaust ON
errand	erendi ON, erendum ON, erindi OI, erindum OI	*extremely*	ákaflega OI, ákafliga ON

The Vinland Sagas   Word List (English to Norse)

English	Norse
eyed	eygð OI, eygð ON, eygðir ON
eyes	augu OI, augu ON, augum OI, augum ON, augunum OI, augunum ON, eygðir OI
Eyjolf (name)	eyjólfr ON, eyjólfur OI
Eyolf (name)	eyjólf OI, eyjólf ON, eyjólfr ON, eyjólfur OI
Eyolf's (name)	eyjólfs OI, eyjólfs ON
Eystein (name)	eysteins OI, eysteins ON
Eyvind (name)	eyvindar OI, eyvindar ON

F, f

English	Norse
face	andliti OI, andliti ON
failed	drepr ON, drepur OI
fair	fagra OI, fagra ON, vænst OI, vænst ON
fair-wind	byr OI, byr ON, byri OI, byri ON, byrina OI, byrina ON, byrjar OI, byrjar ON
faith	trú OI, trú ON, trúna OI, trúna ON
fall	fall OI, fall ON, fallinn OI, fallinn ON
fallen	fallin OI, fallin ON
falls	fellr ON, fellur OI
family	ættkvíslum OI, kynkvíslum ON
family-good	ættgóður OI
famine	hallæri OI, hallæri ON
famous-man	sómamaðr ON, sómamaður OI
far-and-wide	víðara OI, víðara ON
farm	bæ OI, bæ ON, bæjar OI, bæjar ON, bær OI, bær ON, bú OI, búi OI, búi ON
farmer	bónda OI, bóndi OI, bóndi ON
Farmer (a nickname)	bóndi OI
farming	búsvarðveislu OI, búsvarðveizlu ON
farms	bæjum OI, bæjum ON, bóndum ON
fast	ákafast OI, ákafast ON
fastened	hneppt OI, kneppt ON
fastening	hnappur OI, knappi ON
faster-than	skjótari OI, skjótari ON
fated	auðið OI, auðit ON
father	faðir OI, faðir ON, feðr ON, föður OI, föður ON
father's	föður ON
father-and-son	feðga OI, feðga ON, feðgar OI, feðgar ON, feðgum OI, feðgum ON
fathered	fæddr ON, fæddur OI
father-of	faðir OI, faðir ON, föður OI, föður ON
father-to	faðir OI
favourable	hagstætt OI
favoured	ilmað OI, ilmat ON
fear	ótta OI, ótta ON, ótti OI, ótti ON
feared	óttast ON
fearful	uggligt ON
feast	veisla OI, veislan OI, veislu OI, veizla ON, veizlu ON, veizlunni ON
feasts	veislur OI, veizlum ON
feed	fæða OI, fæða ON
feels	þreifar OI, þreifar ON
feet	fæti OI, fæti ON, fætr ON, fætur OI, fóta OI, fóta ON, fótum OI, fótum ON, iljar OI
fell	féll OI, fell ON, fella OI, fella ON, felldi OI, felldi ON, felldu OI, felldu ON, féllu OI, fellu ON, hnígr ON, hnígur OI, höggva OI, höggva ON
fence	skíðgarð OI, skíðgarð ON, skíðgarðinn OI, skíðgarðinn ON
few	fátt OI, liðfáir OI, liðfáir ON, nokkuð OI, nökkut ON
few-words	fámálugur OI
fifteen	fimmtán OI, fimmtán ON
fight	berjast OI, berjast ON, vega OI, vega ON
fighting	vígra OI, vígra ON

247

The Vinland Sagas   Word List (English to Norse)

English	Norse
filled	fylldr ON, fylltur OI
finances	fjárhagur OI
financial-cost's	fjárkosta OI, fjárkosta ON
find	finna OI, finna ON, finnið OI, finnið ON, fund OI, fund ON
finding	finnst ON, finnur OI
fine	ágætt OI, ágætt ON
finger	fingrar OI, fingrar ON
finger-gold	fingrgull ON, fingurgull OI
Finnbogi (name)	finnboga OI, finnboga ON, finnbogi OI, finnbogi ON
fire	báli OI, báli ON
first	fyrra OI, fyrra ON, fyrst OI, fyrst ON, fyrsta OI, fyrsta ON
fish	fiska OI, fiska ON, fiskar OI, fiskar ON, fiskum OI, fiskum ON
fishing	fiski ON, útróðra OI, veiðarnar ON, veiðiskap OI, veiðiskap ON, veiðum OI
five	fimm OI, fimm ON
fixed	festar ON
fjord	firðinum OI, firðinum ON, fjörð ON, fjörðinn OI
Fjord (place)	firðinum OI, firðinum ON, fjörðinn OI, fjörðinn ON
Fjord-Mouth (place)	fjarðarkjafta OI, fjarðarkjafta ON
fjords-carving	fjarðskorið OI
flat	helgir OI, helgir ON, slétt OI, slétt ON
Flat-Nose (name)	flatnefs OI, flatnefs ON
flat-stones	hella OI, hella ON
fled	fló OI, fló ON, flýja OI, flýja ON
fleeing	flýja ON
flew	fleygðu ON, fló OI
floated	fluttu OI, fluttu ON
floor	gólfið OI, gólfit ON
flows	flytist ON
fodder	fóðr ON, fóður OI
fog	þokur OI, þokur ON

English	Norse
folds	foldar OI, foldar ON
folk	fólk OI, fólk ON, fólki ON
follow	fylgd OI, fylgð ON, fylgdar OI, fylgi OI, fylgja OI, fylgja ON
followed	fylgdi OI, fylgði ON, fylgdu OI, fylgðu ON, fylgir OI, fylgt OI, fylgt ON
following	áliðnum OI, áliðnum ON
food	mat OI, mat ON, matar OI, matar ON, matarins OI
food-prepared	matbúið OI, matbúin ON, matbúit ON
foot	fótr ON, fótur OI
for	á OI, á ON, að OI, af OI, at ON, er ON, fyr OI, fyr ON, fyrir OI, fyrir ON, fyrr OI, fyrr ON, því OI, því ON, til OI, til ON, um OI, um ON
foraging	rekum OI
foreclose	bregða OI, bregða ON
fore-knowing-woman	vísendakona ON, vísindakona OI
foremost	framast OI, framast ON
foreseen	varir OI, varir ON
foresight	forsjá OI, forsjá ON
forest	skóg OI, skóg ON, skógi OI, skógi ON, skóginum OI, skóginum ON, skógr ON, skógur OI
forested	skógótt OI, skógótt ON
forest-grown	skógvaxit ON
forests	skógar OI, skógar ON, skógi OI, skógi ON, skógurinn OI
for-her	hennar OI, hennar ON
for-like	þvílíkum OI, þvílíkum ON
for-the	fyrir OI, fyrir ON
fortune	auðnumann OI, auðnumann ON, forlög OI, forlög ON, forlögum OI, forlögum ON
fortunes	forlög OI, forlög ON
forty	fjóra ON

English	Norse	English	Norse
foster	fóstra OI, fóstra ON, fóstri OI, fóstri ON	from-there	þaðan OI, þaðan ON, þangað OI, þangat ON
foster-child	fóstra OI, fóstra ON	from-the-south	sunnan OI
foster-father	fóstra OI, fóstra ON	frost	frost OI, frost ON
fought	börðust OI, börðust ON	frowned	gretti OI, gretti ON
found	fann OI, fann ON, fannst OI, fannst ON, fengið OI, fengit ON, finna OI, finna ON, fundið OI, fundit ON, fundu OI, fundu ON, fundust OI, fyndi OI, fyndi ON	full	fullr ON, fullur OI
		full-come	fullkomna OI, fullkomna ON
		full-knowing	fjölkunnig OI, fjölkunnig ON
		fur	loðna ON
		Furdustrandir (place)	furðustrandir OI, furðustrandir ON, furðuströndum OI, furðuströndum ON
four	fjögr ON, fjögur OI, fjórir OI, fjórir ON	furry	loðnir OI, loðnir ON
fourteen	fjórtán OI, fjórtán ON	furs	skinnavara OI, skinnavara ON
fourth	fjóði OI, fjórða OI, fjórða ON, fjórði OI, fjórði ON	further	firr OI, firr ON, lengra OI, lengra ON
free	frjálsa OI, frjálsa ON		
Freydis (name)	freydís OI, freydís ON, freydísar OI, freydísar ON, freydísi OI, freydísi ON		

G, g

English	Norse
Fridgerdar (name)	friðgerðar ON
Fridrek (name)	friðrekr ON, friðrekur OI
friend	vin OI, vinar OI, vinar ON, vinnur OI, vinr ON, vinur OI
friend-invites	vinaboð OI, vinaboð ON
friendliness	blíðu ON
friend-of	vinur OI
friends	vina OI, vina ON, vinir OI, vinir ON
friendship	vinátta OI, vinátta ON, vináttu OI, vináttu ON
frightened	fælast OI, fælast ON, hræddust OI, hræddust ON
from	á OI, á ON, að OI, af OI, af ON, at ON, farm ON, frá OI, frá ON, fram OI, fram ON, framar OI, framar ON, frammi OI, frammi ON, framúr OI, ór ON, um ON, undan OI, undan ON, úr OI, út ON
from-going	framgengt ON

English	Norse
Gamlason (name)	gamlason OI, gamlason ON
gap	klofa OI, klofa ON
gaping	gapði ON
Gardar (place)	garða OI, garðar ON, görðum OI, görðum ON
garden	garði OI, garði ON, garðs OI
Gardi (name)	garðarr ON, garði OI
gather	lesa OI, lesa ON
gathered	fengu OI, fengu ON
gave	fékk OI, fekk ON, gæfi OI, gæfi ON, gaf OI, gaf ON, gáfu OI, gáfu ON, gifti OI, gifti ON, veitir OI, veittu OI, veittu ON
gave-up	hættir ON
Gellir (name)	gellis OI, gellis ON
Gellis (name)	gellis ON
generosity	rausn OI, rausn ON, rausnarveislu OI
generous	rausn ON
German	þýsku OI, þýzku ON
Gerstein (name)	geirsteinn OI, geirsteinn ON

The Vinland Sagas — Word List (English to Norse)

English	Norse
get	fá OI, fá ON
giant	þurslegur OI, þursligr ON
gift	gæfa OI
gifted	gæfu ON
gifts	feng OI, feng ON, gjafar ON, gjafir OI
give	fái OI, fái ON, gæfi OI, gæfi ON, gefa OI, gefa ON, gifta OI, gifta ON
given	gefið OI, gefið ON, gefin OI, gefin ON, gefit ON, gjaforð OI, veitt ON, veittr ON, veittur OI
glacier	jökli OI, jökli ON
glaciers	jöklar OI, jöklar ON, jöklum OI, jöklum ON, jökull OI, jökull ON
gladly	gjarna OI
gladness	gleði OI, gleði ON
glass-beads	glertölur OI, glertölur ON
Glaumbaer (place)	glaumbæ OI, glaumbæjarland OI, glaumbæjarland ON, glaunbæ ON
glittered	glitraði OI, glitraði ON
glory	dýrð OI, dýrð ON
Glumra (name)	glumru OI, glumru ON
go	fær ON, far OI, far ON, fara OI, fara ON, fari OI, fari ON, ferðar OI, ferðar ON, förum OI, förum ON, gakk ON, ganga OI, ganga ON, gangast OI, gangast ON, gangi OI, gangi ON, gangir OI, gangir ON, gengið OI, gengit ON
god	guð ON, guðs ON
God (name)	guð OI
God'S (name)	guð OI, guð ON, guðs OI, guðs ON
goes	fer OI, ferr ON
going	farið OI, farit ON, fer OI, förum OI, förum ON, gekk OI, gekk ON, genginn OI, genginn ON, vára ON, vora OI
going-from	gagnvart OI, gagnvart ON
going-out	fært ON
gold	goldið OI, goldit ON, gull OI, gull ON, gulls OI, gulls ON
gone	brottu OI, brottu ON, farið OI, farit ON, förum OI, förum ON, gengið OI, gengin OI, gengin ON, gengit ON, vor OI
good	góð OI, góð ON, góða OI, góða ON, góðan OI, góðan ON, góðar OI, góðar ON, góðir OI, góðir ON, góðr ON, góðra OI, góðra ON, góðs OI, góðu OI, góðu ON, góður OI, gott OI, gott ON
good-man-like	góðmannlega OI, góðmannliga ON
goodness	gæsku OI
goods	fémunum OI, fémunum ON, varning OI, varning ON, varningr ON, varningur OI
good-will	góðvilja OI, góðvilja ON
good-words-man	goðorðsmaður OI
go-on	vinnast ON
got	fékk OI, fekk ON, fengi ON, fengið OI, fengit ON, fengju OI, fengu OI, náði OI, náði ON
gown	námkyrtli OI, námkyrtli ON
grant	veita OI, veita ON
grapes	vínber OI, vínber ON, vínberjum OI, vínberjum ON
grape-vines	vínbejaköngul ON
grasp	fang OI, fang ON
grass	gras OI, gras ON, grasinu OI, grasinu ON, grös OI, grös ON

The Vinland Sagas — Word List (English to Norse)

English	Norse
great	mikið OI, mikil OI, mikil ON, mikill OI, mikill ON, mikinn OI, mikinn ON, mikit ON, mikla ON, miklar OI, miklar ON, miklir OI, miklir ON, stór OI, stór ON
greater	meira OI, meira ON
greatest	göfugmenni OI, göfugmenni ON, mestr ON, mestur OI
great-estate	rausnarbú OI, rausnarráð ON
greatly	drjúgum ON, mikið OI, mikit ON, stæra OI, stæra ON, stórilla OI, stórilla ON
greatly-ruled-over	stjórnuðu OI, stjórnuðu ON
great-man-ness	stórmannliga ON, stórmennsku OI, stórmennsku ON
great-men	stórmenni OI, stórmenni ON
greatness	stórmennsku OI, stórmennsku ON
green	grön OI, grön ON
Greenland (place)	grænland OI, grænland ON, grænlandi OI, grænlandi ON, grænlands OI, grænlands ON
Greenlander (place)	grænlenskir OI, grænlenskum OI, grænlenzkum ON
Greenland-Sea (place)	grænlandshaf OI, grænlandshaf ON
greenland-skin	grænlenzkan ON
Greenland-Skin (place)	grænlenskan OI
Greenland-voyage	grænlandsferðar OI, grænlandsferðar ON
greetings	kveðjur OI, kveðjur ON
Grelod (name)	grélaðar OI, grélaðar ON
grew	óx OI, óx ON, óxu OI, óxu ON
grey	algrá ON
grey-skins	grávara OI, grávara ON
Grimhild (name)	grímhildr ON, grímhildur OI
Grimhild's	grímhildar OI
Grimolfson (name)	grímólfsson OI, grímólfsson ON
gripped	lesti OI, lesti ON
Gro (name)	gró ON
Groa (name)	gró OI
ground	mold OI, moldu OI, moldu ON, vígðu OI, vígðu ON
group	flokkr ON, flokkur OI, hópit ON
growing	vaxið OI, vaxinn OI, vaxinn ON, vaxit ON
grown	vaxið OI, vaxin OI, vaxinn ON, vaxit ON, vexti OI, vexti ON
guess	get OI, get ON
guests	boðsmanna OI, boðsmanna ON
Gunnbjarnarsker (place)	gunnbjarnarsker OI, gunnbjarnarsker ON
Gunnbjorn (name)	gunnbjörn OI, gunnbjörn ON
Guthrid (name)	guðríðar OI, guðríðar ON, guðríði OI, guðríði ON, guðríðr ON, guðríður OI

H, h

English	Norse
habitable	byggjanda OI, byggjanda ON, byggjandi OI
habitation	mannavistir OI
had	átt OI, átt ON, átti OI, átti ON, áttu OI, áttu ON, hafa OI, hafa ON, hafði OI, hafði ON, hafi OI, hafi ON, haft OI, haft ON, hefða ON, hefði OI, hefði ON, hefðu OI, hefir OI, hefir ON, hefr ON, hefur OI, höfðu OI, höfðu ON, væri ON, væru OI
had-been	hafði OI, hafði ON, verið OI, verit ON

The Vinland Sagas Word List (English to Norse)

English	Norse	English	Norse
Hafgrim (name)	hafgrímr ON, hafgrímur OI	hauntings	aftrgöngum ON, afturgöngum OI, fróðárundr ON, fróðárundur OI
Hafgrimsfjord (place)	hafgrímsfjörð OI, hafgrímsfjörð ON		
hair	hár OI, hár ON, loðna OI	have	á OI, á ON, átt ON, hafa OI, hafa ON, hafði OI, hafðir OI, hafðir ON, hafi OI, hafi ON, hafið OI, hafið ON, hafim ON, halda OI, hef OI, hefði ON, hefi OI, hefi ON, hefir OI, hefir ON, höfð OI, höfð ON, höfum OI, höfum ON, leggur OI
Haki (name)	haki OI, haki ON		
half	hálfa OI, hálfa ON, hálfan OI, hálfan ON, hálfr, hálfur OI, helming OI, helming ON, helmingr ON, helmingur OI		
half-of	hálfr ON, hálft OI, hálft ON, hálfur OI	have-been	hafa OI, verið OI, verit ON
hall	hallar OI, hallar ON	have-you	áttu OI, áttu ON
Halldis (name)	halldís OI, halldís ON	having	hafa OI, hafa ON
Hallfrid (name)	hallfríðr ON, hallfríður OI	having-like	höfðinglegt OI, höfðingligt ON
Hallveig (name)	hallveig OI, hallveig ON		
hand	hendi OI, hendi ON, hendr ON, hendur OI, hönd OI, hönd ON, höndina ON, höndum OI, höndum ON	he	han ON, hana OI, hann OI, hann ON, hans OI, hans ON, henni OI, henni ON, hinn OI, honum OI, honum ON, inn ON, sér OI, sér ON, sinn OI, sinn ON
handed	höndum OI, höndum ON		
hands	höndum OI, höndum ON	head	höfði OI, höfði ON, höfuð OI, höfuð ON
handsome	mannvænn OI, vænn OI, vænn ON	headland	andnesi OI, andnesi ON, höfða OI, höfða ON, höfðann OI, höfðann ON, höfðanum OI, höfðanum ON, nes OI, nes ON, nesi ON, nesið OI, nesinu OI, nesinu ON, nesit ON, ness OI, ness ON
happened	gerðist OI, gerðist ON		
happy	sælir OI, sælir ON		
hard	harða OI, harða ON, hörð OI, hörð ON		
hardened	herðir OI, herðir ON		
hardly	varla OI, varla ON, vart OI, vart ON		
harm	mein OI, mein ON		
harmlessly	meinalausan OI, meinalausan ON	heads	höfði OI, höfði ON, höfðu OI, höfuð OI, höfuð ON
harried	herjaði OI, herjaði ON		
harvest	árangr ON, árangur OI	hear	heyr ON, heyra OI, heyra ON, heyrðu OI
harvest-feast	haustboð OI, haustboð ON	heard	frétti OI, frétti ON, heyrði OI, heyrði ON, heyrðu ON, heyrt OI, heyrt ON, hjá ON, spurðist ON
has	hefir OI, hefir ON		
haughty	svarri OI, svarri ON		
Haukadal (place)	haukadal OI, haukadal ON, haukdælski OI, haukdælski ON		
		heard-of	spurði OI, spurði ON
		hearth	hjörð ON, hjú OI

The Vinland Sagas — Word List (English to Norse)

English	Norse	English	Norse
hearts	hjörtu OI, hjörtu ON	Herjolfsnes (place)	herjólfsnes OI, herjólfsnes ON, herjólfsnesi OI, herjólfsnesi ON
heath	heiðis OI, heiðis ON		
heathen	heiðið OI, heiðit ON		
heathenry	heiðni OI	Herjolfsness (place)	herjúlfsnesi OI
heaviness	höfga OI, höfga ON	hers	hennar OI, hennar ON, henni OI, henni ON, sér OI, sér ON, sín OI, sín ON, sína OI, sína ON, sínar OI, sínar ON, sinna OI, sinna ON, síns OI, síns ON, sínu OI, sínu ON, sínum OI, sínum ON, þau OI
heed	gaum OI, gaum ON		
heeded	gáðu ON		
heights	hæðir OI, hæðir ON		
Hekja (name)	hekja OI, hekja ON		
held	halda OI, halda ON, heldi ON, heldr ON, héldu OI, heldu ON, heldur OI, hélt OI, helt ON		
		herself	sér OI, sér ON, sig OI, sik ON
Heldr'S (name)	heldr OI, heldr's ON	he-saw	sjá OI
held-words	haldinorðir OI, haldinorðir ON	he-was	hann ON
		hewed	höggr ON, höggur OI
Helga (name)	helga OI, helga ON	he-willed	vilja ON
Helgason (name)	helgasonar OI	hid	fal OI, fal ON
Helgi (name)	helga OI, helgi OI, helgi ON	hidden	duldið ON, duldir OI, fólgið OI, fólgit ON
Hellisvellir (place)	hellisvöllum OI, hellisvöllum ON	high	hárar ON, hárrar OI, hátt OI, hátt ON
Helluland (place)	helluland OI, helluland ON	highest	efst OI, ofast ON
		high-family	ættstór OI, ættstórr ON
help	duga OI, duga ON, hjálp OI, hjálp ON, hjálpa OI, hjálpar ON, liði OI, liði ON	high-tide	háflæðum OI, háflæðum ON
		hills	holta OI, holta ON
hence	héðan OI, heðan ON	him	hana OI, hana ON, hann OI, hann ON, hans OI, hans ON, henni ON, honum OI, honum ON, sér OI, sér ON
hen's-feathers	hænsafiðri OI, hænsafiðri ON		
her	hana OI, hana ON, hennar OI, hennar ON, henni OI, henni ON, honum OI, hún OI, sér OI, sér ON, sínu ON, sínum OI, sínum ON		
		himself	hann ON, sér OI, sér ON, sig OI, sik ON
herd	hjörð OI, hjú ON	hindered-knowledge	hindrvitni ON
herding	gæsla OI, gæzla ON	hired	laun OI, laun ON, réð OI, réð ON
here	hér OI, hér ON, hingað OI, hingat ON, þar OI		
Herjolf (name)	herjólfi ON, herjólfr ON, herjólfur OI, herjúlfi OI, herjúlfur OI		
Herjolfsfjord (place)	herjólfsfjörð OI, herjólfsfjörð ON		

253

The Vinland Sagas   *Word List (English to Norse)*

English	Norse
his	hans OI, hans ON, honum OI, honum ON, sér OI, sér ON, síðunni ON, sín OI, sín ON, sína OI, sína ON, sínar OI, sinn OI, sinn ON, sinna OI, sinna ON, sinnar OI, sinnar ON, sinni OI, sinni ON, síns OI, síns ON, sínu OI, sínu ON, sínum OI, sínum ON, sitt OI, sitt ON, þessu ON
Hitardal (place)	hítardal OI, hítardal ON
Hofda (place)	höfða ON
Hofdastrond (place)	höfðaströnd ON
hoisted	undu ON
hold	halda OI, halda ON, haldast OI, haldast ON, haldi OI, haldi ON
holding	halda ON
holes	holum OI, holum ON
Holm (place)	hólmum OI, hólmum ON
Holmlatr (place)	hólmlátri OI, hólmlátri ON
homage	hlýðni OI, hlýðni ON
home	bús OI, bús ON, heim OI, heim ON, heima OI, heima ON, heiman OI, heiman ON
homeless	vistlaus OI, vistlauss ON
homes	heim ON, heima ON
honour	drengskap ON, sæmd OI, sæmðinni ON, virðing OI, virðing ON
honourable	sæmilegar OI, sæmilegast OI, sæmilegur OI, sæmiligar ON, sæmiligast ON, sæmiligr ON, sæmiligsta ON, sköruleg OI
hood	höttr ON
hoods	hötturinn OI
Hop (place)	hópi OI, hópi ON
hope	vánu ON, vonum OI
Hornstrandir (place)	hornströndum OI, hornströndum ON
horrible	hörmung OI, hörmung ON
Horse-Head (name)	hesthöfða OI, hesthöfða ON, hesthöfði ON
horse's	hestrinn ON, hesturinn OI
house	bús OI, hús OI, hús ON, húsin ON
house-besom	húsasnotru OI, húsasnotru ON, húsasnotruna OI, húsasnotruna ON
house-building	húsgerð OI, húsgerð ON
households	heimilis ON, heimkynna OI
houseman	húskarli OI, húskarli ON
housemen	heimamönnum OI, heimamönnum ON
houses	hús OI, hús ON, húsa OI, húsa ON, húsanna OI, húsanna ON, húsin OI, húsin ON, húss OI, húss ON
housewife	húsfreyja OI, húsfreyja ON, húsfreyju OI, húsfreyju ON
how	hvárt ON, hvé ON, hversu OI, hversu ON, hvort OI
howling	ýla OI, ýla ON
Hrafn (name)	hrafn OI, hrafn ON
Hrafnsfjord (place)	hrafnsfjörð OI, hrafnsfjörð ON
Hraunhafnaros (place)	hraunhafnarósi OI, hraunhafnarósi ON
hundred	hundrað ON, hundraðs OI
hunsband's	bónda ON
hunt	matfanga OI
hunter	veiðimaðr ON, veiðimaður OI
hunting	veiðar OI, veiðarnar OI, veiðiferð OI, veiðiferðir ON, veiðiförum OI, veiðum OI, veiðum ON
hurt	meiðar OI, meiðar ON

English	Norse	English	Norse
husband	bónda OI, bónda ON, bóndi OI, bóndi ON, mannvönd OI, mannvönd ON	indebted-to	skuldalið OI
		Ingjald'S (name)	ingjalds OI, ingjalds ON
		Ingolf (name)	ingólfi OI, ingólfi ON, ingólfr ON, ingólfur OI
husband's	bónda OI	Ingolf's (name)	ingólfs OI, ingólfs ON
Hvamm (place)	hvammi OI, hvammi ON	inhabit	byggjum OI, byggjum ON
Hvarfsgnipu (place)	hvarfsgnípu OI, hvarfsgnípu ON	inhabitants	bjuggu OI, bjuggu ON
		injured	lestist OI, lestist ON
		inlet	ósinn ON, vág ON, vog OI

I, i

English	Norse	English	Norse
		inlets	vogunum OI
		in-need	þurftugir OI, þurftugir ON
I	eg OI, ég OI, ek ON, mér OI, mér ON, mig OI, mik ON	inside	inn OI, innan OI, innan ON, innstr ON, innstur OI
Iceland (place)	ísland OI, ísland ON, íslandi OI, íslandi ON, íslands OI, íslands ON	intend	ætla OI, ætla ON, ætlað OI, ætlar OI, ætlar ON, ætlat ON
Icelander	íslenskum OI, íslenzkum ON	intended	ætlað OI, ætlaði OI, ætlaði ON, ætlaðr ON, ætlaður OI, ætlar ON, ætlat ON, ætluðu OI, ætluðu ON
Icelander (place)	íslenskur OI, íslenzkr ON		
Icelanders	íslenskir OI, íslenzkir ON		
if	ef OI, ef ON, hvárt ON, hvort OI, sem OI	intends	ætlað OI
		interaction	samfarar OI, samfarar ON
ill	illr ON, ills OI, ills ON, illt OI, illt ON, illur OI	intercourse	samfarar OI, samræði ON
illegitimate	laungetna OI, laungetna ON	into	í OI, í ON, vit ON
		invite	bjóða OI, bjóða ON
ill-looking	illilegir OI, illiligir ON	invited	bauð OI, bauð ON, buðu OI, buðu ON, býðr ON, býður OI, láð OI, láð ON
Illugi (name)	illugi OI, illugi ON		
illusions	sjónhverfingar ON, þversýningar OI		
		Ireland (place)	írland OI, írland ON, írlandi OI, írlandi ON
ill-will	illsku OI, illsku ON	Ireland-King (name)	írakonungs ON
immediately	fljótast OI, fljótast ON	Ironside (name)	járnsíðu ON
important	ráðabreytni ON, ráðagerð OI	irritable	úrigt OI, úrigt ON
impression	leist OI	is	er OI, er ON, í OI, í ON
imprint	merki OI, merki ON	island	ey OI, ey ON, eyjarinnar OI, eyjarinnar ON, eyju OI, eyju ON, eyland OI, eyland ON, eyna OI, eynni OI, eynni ON
in	á OI, á ON, að OI, at ON, eg OI, hin OI, hinn OI, í OI, í ON, in ON, inn OI, inn ON, innan OI, innan ON, inni OI, inni ON, inum ON, við OI, við ON		
inclined	hallat ON, um OI		
increased	aukin OI, aukin ON		
indebted	skuldalið ON		

The Vinland Sagas   Word List (English to Norse)

English	Norse	English	Norse
islands	eyjar OI, eyjarnar OI, eyjarnar ON, eyjótt OI, eyjótt ON, eyrar OI, eyrar ON	Ketilsfjord (place)	ketilsfjörð OI, ketilsfjörð ON
Islands (place)	eyrar OI	kid's-milk	kiðjamjólk OI, kiðjamjólk ON
is-named	heitir OI, heitir ON	kill	drepa OI, drepa ON
it	að OI, at ON, hana OI, hana ON, hann OI, hann ON, hon ON, hún OI, í OI, í ON, kann OI, það OI, þat ON	killed	drap OI, drap ON, drápu OI, drápu ON, drepa OI, drepa ON, drepnir OI, drepnir ON
		killing	víga OI, víga ON
it-ends	lýkr ON	killing-of	víg OI, víg ON
itself	sjálfan OI, sjálfan ON, sjálfar OI	kin	kyni OI, kyni ON
		kin-blessed	kynsæll OI, kynsæll ON
it-was	vera OI	kind	háttar OI, háttar ON

J, j

		kind-of	konar OI
		kinds	konar OI, konar ON
		kinds-of	konar OI, konar ON
		king	konungi OI, konungi ON, konungr ON, konungs OI, konungs ON, konungur OI
Jaeren (place)	jaðri OI, jaðri ON		
jewelled-man	skartsmaðr ON, skartsmaður OI		
joined	festi ON, hent OI, hent ON, tengdir OI, tengðir ON	King (name)	konungr ON, konungur OI
		kings	konungar OI, konungar ON
Jorfi (name)	jörva ON	kinsman	frændi OI, frændi ON, frændur OI
Jorfi (place)	jörva OI		
Jorund (name)	jörundar OI, jörundar ON	kinsmen	frænda OI, frænda ON, frændum OI, frændum ON
journey	ferð OI, ferð ON, ferðar OI, ferðar ON, leið OI, leið ON	kjafal	kjafal OI, kjafal ON
		Kjalarnes (place)	kjalarnes OI, kjalarnes ON
journeyed	ferr ON, fór OI	Kjarval (name)	kjarvals ON
		Knarrarbringu (name)	knarrarbringu OI, knarrarbringu ON

K, k

		knee	hné ON, hneig OI
		knees	knjám OI, knjám ON
Karlsefni (name)	karlsefni OI, karlsefni ON	knew	kenndi OI, kenndi ON, kenndu OI, kunni OI, kunni ON, kynni OI, kynni ON, kynnu OI, skildu OI, skilðu ON, vissi OI, vissi ON, vissu OI, vissu ON
Karlsefni's (name)	karlsefnis OI, karlsefnis ON		
Karlsefnison (name)	karlsefnissonar OI, karlsefnissonar ON		
keel	kjöl ON, kjölinn OI, kjölinn ON		
keep	halda OI, halda ON	knife	hníf OI, hníf ON
kept	efndi OI, efndi ON	knob	hnappinn OI, knappinn ON
Ketil (name)	ketill OI, ketill ON, ketils OI		
Ketil's (name)	ketils ON		

Word List (English to Norse)

English	Norse
know	kann OI, kann ON, veit OI, veit ON, veita OI, veita ON, vísu OI, vísu ON, vita OI, vita ON
know-choose	kenni-val OI, kenni-val ON
know-how	kunna OI, kunna ON
knowing	kunna OI, kunnandi OI, vita OI, vita ON
knowledge	fræði OI, fróðleiks OI, fróðleiks ON
known	kann ON, kennt OI, kennt ON, kunnigt OI, kunnigt ON, kunnu OI, kunnu ON, vit ON
Krossanes (place)	krossanes OI, krossanes ON
Krossholar (place)	krosshólum OI, krosshólum ON

L, l

English	Norse
laid	búa OI, búa ON, lætr ON, lætur OI, lagði OI, lagði ON, lagt OI, lagt ON, lágu OI, lágu ON, láta ON, látið OI, látit ON, legið OI, legit ON, leið OI, leið ON, lét OI, lét ON, létu OI, létu ON, lögð OI, lögð ON, lögðu OI, lögðu ON
lake	vatn OI, vatn ON, vatnið OI, vatninu OI, vatninu ON, vatnit ON
lamb-skin-hood	lambskinnskofra OI, lambskinnskofra ON
land	jörð OI, jörð ON, land OI, land ON, landar OI, landar ON, landi OI, landi ON, landið OI, landinu OI, landinu ON, landit ON, lands OI, lands ON, landsins OI, landsins ON, lendur OI, lönd OI, lönd ON
land-benefits	landkosta ON, landkostr ON, landkostum OI, landkostum ON, landskosta OI, landskosta ON, landskosti OI, landskostir OI, landskostir ON, landskostr ON, landskostur OI, landsnytja OI
land-exploring	landaleitan OI, landaleitan ON
landowner	bóndi OI, bóndi ON
lands	landa OI, landa ON, landið OI, landit ON, lands OI, lands ON, landsins ON, lönd OI, lönd ON, löndum OI, löndum ON
landscape	landsleg ON
land-sight	landsýn OI, landsýn ON
landslide	skriðu OI, skriðu ON
landsmen	landsmenn OI, landsmenn ON
land-taking-man	landnámamanns OI, landnámamanns ON
Langadal (place)	langadal OI, langadal ON
language	mál OI, mál ON
lap	skaut OI, skaut ON
larboard-side	bakborða OI, bakborða ON
large	mikil OI, mikil ON, mikill OI, mikill ON, mikli OI, mikli ON, miklir OI, miklir ON, mjög OI, stórar OI, stórar ON
larger	stærra OI, stærra ON
last	síðast OI, síðast ON, síðasta OI, síðasta ON
late	sein OI, seinn OI, seinn ON, seint OI, seint ON
later	síðar OI, síðar ON
Laugarbrekka (place)	laugarbrekku OI, laugarbrekku ON

The Vinland Sagas   Word List (English to Norse)

English	Norse
launched	skaust OI, skauzt ON, skjóta OI, skjóta ON, skkutu ON, skutu OI, skutu ON
launching	skothríð OI, skothríð ON
law	lög ON
law-taken	lögtekin OI, lögtekin ON
lay	lá OI, lá ON, lægi OI, lægi ON, lagði OI, lagði ON, lagðist OI, lagðist ON, lágu OI, lágu ON, láta OI, láta ON, legði OI, legðir OI, legðir ON, leggja OI, leggja ON, leið OI, lét OI, lét ON, liggja OI, liggja ON, lögðu OI, lögðu ON
laying	lá ON, lágu OI, lágu ON
lead	leiða OI, leiða ON, leiddu OI, leiddu ON, veita OI, veita ON
leader	höfðingi OI, höfðingi ON, réði OI, réði ON
leaf	laufa OI, laufa ON
Lean (name)	magra OI, magra ON
leave	brottu OI, brottu ON, hætta OI, hætta ON, láta OI, láta ON, legði ON, leyfis OI, leyfis ON
led	leiddi OI, leiddi ON
left	eftir OI, eftir ON, látið OI, létu OI, létu ON, lokið OI, lokit ON, skildu OI
Leif (name)	leif OI, leif ON, leifi OI, leifi ON, leifr ON, leifs OI, leifs ON, leifur OI
Leif's	leifs OI, leifs ON
Leif's-Camp (place)	leifsbúða OI, leifsbúða ON
Leikskalar (place)	leikskálum OI, leikskálum ON
lent	léði OI, léði ON, lutu OI, lutu ON
less	laust OI, laust ON, minna OI, minna ON, minni OI, minni ON, síðr ON, síður OI
let	brenna OI, lætr ON, láta OI, láta ON, látið OI, látit ON, leggja OI, leggja ON, lét OI, lét ON, létta OI, létta ON, létu OI, létu ON
let-us	látum OI, látum ON
lies	liggja OI, liggja ON, liggr ON, liggur OI
life	ævi OI, ævi ON, líf OI, líf ON, lífi OI, lífi ON, lífs OI
like	leikr ON, leikur OI, líkar OI, líkar ON, líkast OI, líkast ON
liked	leist OI, líkaði OI, líkaði ON
likely	líklegt OI
likewise	eins OI, eins ON, þvílíku OI, þvílíku ON
lineage	ætt OI, ætt ON
liquidity	lausafé OI, lausafé ON
liquidity's	lausafjár OI, lausafjár ON
little	lítið OI, lítill OI, lítill ON, lítils OI, lítils ON, lítit ON, litla OI, litla ON, litlu OI, litlu ON, litlum OI, litlum ON, lítt OI, lítt ON
Little (name)	litlu OI
little-man	lítilmenni OI, lítilmenni ON
Little-Prophetess (name)	lítilvölva OI, lítilvölva ON
little-wide	óvíða OI, óvíða ON
little-with	lítt OI
live	fjörsins ON, lifa OI, lifa ON
lived	bjó OI, bjó ON, bjuggu OI, bjuggu ON, lifað OI, lifði OI, lifði ON
lives	líf OI, líf ON
livestock	búfé OI, búfé ON, kvikfé OI, kvikfé ON
living	lífi OI, lífi ON
living-space	híbýlabótar OI
loan	launa OI, launa ON, ljá OI, ljá ON
lodge	vistar OI, vistar ON
lodging	vistar OI, vistar ON, vistir ON

The Vinland Sagas — Word List (English to Norse)

English	Norse
lodgings	vistir OI
long	langa OI, langa ON, langæðar OI, langæðar ON, langar OI, langar ON, langt OI, langt ON, lengi OI, lengi ON, lengja OI, lengst OI, lengst ON, löngum OI, löngum ON
long-as	meðan OI, meðan ON
longer	lengr ON, lengur OI
long-spanning	spannarlangt ON
look	líta OI, litast OI
looked	gáðu OI, horfði OI, horfðu ON, leit OI, leit ON, lítast ON, lituðust OI, lituðust ON, sást ON, sáust OI, sjá OI, sjá ON, sjást OI, sjást ON, sóttu OI, ván ON, von OI
looked-like	leizt ON
looking	horfði ON
loose-eyed	lauseygr ON, lauseygur OI
loosened	leystu OI, leystu ON
lose	týna OI, týna ON
lost	lét ON, týndust OI, týndust ON
lot	hlaut OI, hlaut ON, hluta ON, hlutr ON, hlutur OI
Lothbrok (name)	loðbrókar ON
lots	hlotist OI, hluta OI, hlutaðir ON, hlutaðist OI, hlutuðu ON
lot-taking	hlutföllum OI
loud	hátt ON
loudly	hátt OI, hátt ON
loved	elskað OI, elskat ON
low	lág OI, lág ON
lowered	lægðu OI, lægðu ON
low-ground	lægðir OI, lægðir ON
luck	giftu OI, giftu ON, heill OI, heill ON
lucky	heppni OI, heppni ON
lucky-wise	happfróð ON
lying	liggja ON
Lysufjord (place)	lýsufirði OI, lýsufirði ON, lýsufjörð OI, lýsufjörð ON

M, m

English	Norse
made	ger OI, ger ON, gera OI, gera ON, gerði OI, gerði ON, gerðist OI, gerðist ON, gerðu OI, gerðu ON, gerður OI, gerðust OI, gerðust ON, gerir OI, gerir ON, gerr ON, gerst OI, gerst ON, gert OI, gert ON, gervir OI, gervir ON, gerzt ON, verið OI, verit ON, víst OI, víst ON
magic	töfr ON, töfur OI
mainland	meginlandinu OI
maintain	óhægjast OI, óhægjast ON
make	gera OI, gera ON, gerðu OI, gerðu ON, gerið OI, gerið ON
malt	malt OI, malt ON
man	at ON, maðr OI, maðr ON, maður OI, mann OI, mann ON, manna OI, manna ON, manni OI, manni ON, manns OI, manns ON, menn OI, og OI
manner	hættir ON
mannered	hættir OI
man's	manna OI
mantle	möttul OI, tuglamöttul OI, tuglamöttul ON, vaðmálsmöttul ON
man-worthiness	mannvirðingar OI, mannvirðingar ON

259

The Vinland Sagas — Word List (English to Norse)

English	Norse
many	fjölda OI, fjölða ON, fjöldi OI, fjöldi ON, fjölmenni OI, fjölmenni ON, fjórir OI, marga OI, marga ON, margar OI, margar ON, margir OI, margir ON, margt OI, margt ON, margur OI, mart OI, mjög OI, mörg OI, mörg ON, mörgu ON, mörgum OI, mörgum ON, víða OI, víða ON
many-knowing	margkunnig ON
many-men	fjölmenna OI, fjölmenna ON
many-people	allfjölmennt ON, fjölmenn OI
maple	mösur OI, mösurr ON
mark	mörk OI, mörk ON
Markland (place)	markland OI, markland ON
marriage-offer	gjaforðs OI, gjaforðs ON
marriage-proposal	ráðahag OI
married	átti OI, átti ON, fekk OI, fékk OI, fekk ON, gefin OI, gefin ON, gift OI, gift ON, gjaforð OI, gjaforð ON, hafði ON, kvæntir ON, kvángaðist ON, kvángaðr ON, kvángazt ON, kvongaðir OI, kvongaðist OI, kvongaður OI, kvongast OI
marry	eiga OI, eiga ON, gefin OI, giftast OI, giftast ON
marvelled	undruðust OI, undruðust ON
master	drottinn OI, dróttinn ON
matter	mál OI, mála ON, máli OI, máli ON
matters	mál OI, máldagi OI, máldagi ON
may	heimilt OI, má OI, má ON, mætti OI, mætti ON, mættið ON, mættist OI, mættist ON, mættu OI, mættuð OI, mátti OI, mátti ON, máttu OI, máttu ON, megum ON
me	mér OI, mér ON, mig OI, mik ON
meal	mjöl OI
meantime	meðan ON
measured	atmælasamur OI
meet	fund OI, fund ON, fundar OI, fundar ON, fundi OI, fundi ON, mót OI, mót ON, móti OI, móti ON, móts OI, móts ON
meeting	móti ON
melrakka	melrakka ON, melrakkar OI
men	háseta OI, háseta ON, karla OI, karla ON, karlar OI, karlar ON, mann OI, mann ON, manna OI, manna ON, manni OI, menn OI, menn ON, mennina ON, mönnum OI, mönnum ON
men's	manna OI, manna ON
Men's (name)	manna ON
menservants	karlmaðrinn ON
men's-heads	mannshausi OI, mannshausi ON
men's-work	mannaverk OI, mannaverk ON
merchant-ship	kaupskipið OI, kaupskipinu OI, kaupskipit ON, knarrar ON
mercy	miskunn OI, miskunn ON, miskunnar OI
merrier	kátari OI, kátari ON
message	orðsending ON, orðsendingar OI

The Vinland Sagas — Word List (English to Norse)

English	Norse
met	fundust ON, hitti OI, hitti ON, hittir ON, hittu OI, hittu ON, móti OI, móti ON
metal-assemblies	málmþings OI, malmþings ON
mid-afternoon	eyktar ON, eyktarstað OI
middle	miðjan OI, miðjan ON, miðri OI, miðri ON
Midjokul (place)	miðjökul OI, miðjökul ON
milk-products	búnyt OI, búnyt ON
mind	hug OI, hug ON, minni ON
mine	mér OI, mér ON, mín OI, mín ON, mína OI, mína ON, minn OI, minn ON, minni OI, míns OI, míns ON, mínu OI, mínu ON, mínum OI, mínum ON, mitt OI, mitt ON
misery	vesöld OI, vesölð ON
missing	vant OI, vant ON
mixed	blandast OI, blandinn OI, blandinn ON
moderate-man	hófsmaðr ON, hófsmaður OI
monks	munka OI, munka ON
month	mánuð OI, mánuð ON
months	mánuði OI, mánuði ON
mood	skapi OI, skapi ON
Moray (place)	meræfi OI, meræfi ON
more	fleira OI, fleira ON, fleiri OI, fleiri ON, meir OI, meir ON, meira OI, meira ON, mér OI
more-beautiful	fegri OI, fegri ON
morning	dagmála ON, dagmálastað OI, morgin ON, morgininn ON, morginn ON, morgun OI, morguninn OI, morguninn ON, morgunn OI, myrgin ON
most	flestra OI, flestra ON, megin ON, mest OI, mest ON, mesta OI, mesta ON, mesti OI, mesti ON, mestri OI, mestri ON, mestu OI, mestu ON
mostly	flestir OI
mother	móðir OI, móðir ON, móður OI, móður ON
mother-of	móðir OI, móðir ON, móður OI, móður ON
mother-to	móðir OI
mountain	féll OI, fell ON
mountainous	fjöllótt OI, fjöllótt ON
mountains	fjöll OI, fjöll ON, jöklanna OI, jöklanna ON
mouth	munn OI, munn ON, munni OI, munni ON
mouths	munn OI, munn ON
move	færast OI, færast ON
moved	réðst OI, réðst ON
much	mikið OI, mikil OI, mikil ON, mikill OI, mikill ON, mikilli OI, mikilli ON, mikinn OI, mikinn ON, mikit ON, mikla OI, mikla ON, miklar OI, miklar ON, miklu OI, miklu ON, miklum OI, miklum ON, mjög OI, mjök ON
muck-encrusted	mykiskán OI, mykiskán ON
my	mig OI, mik ON, mínar OI, mínar ON, minnar OI, minnar ON, míns OI, míns ON, mitt OI, mitt ON
myself	mér OI, mér ON

N, n

English	Norse
name	heiti OI, heiti ON, nafn OI, nafn ON

261

The Vinland Sagas   Word List (English to Norse)

English	Norse
named	heita OI, heita ON, heiti OI, heiti ON, heitir OI, heitir ON, hét OI, hét ON, héti OI, héti ON, hétu OI, nafn OI, nafn ON, nefndist OI, nefndist ON, nefndu OI, nefndu ON
namesake	nafna OI, nafna ON, nafni OI, nafni ON
near	allnær OI, hjá OI, hjá ON, ná OI, ná ON, nær OI, nær ON, náim ON, náum OI, undir OI, undir ON
nearest	næstir OI, næstir ON
nearly	nær ON
near-the	nær OI, nær ON
necessity	nauðsyn OI, nauðsyn ON
neck	hálsi OI, hálsi ON
need	þarf ON, þurfa OI, þurfa ON, þurftu OI
needed	þarf OI, þarf ON, þurfa OI, þurfa ON, þurfti OI, þurfti ON, þurftu OI, þurftu ON, þyrfti OI
neither	hvárigir ON, hvárki ON, hvárkis ON, hvergi OI, hvergi ON, hvorgis OI, hvorigir OI, hvorki OI
nettle	nesla OI, nezlu ON
new	nýnæmi OI, nýnæmi ON
news	frétt OI, frétt ON, tíðenda ON, tíðinda OI, tíðindi OI, tíðindum OI, tíðindum ON
next	annað OI, annat ON, næst OI, næst ON, öðrum OI, öðrum ON
night	nætrnar ON, næturnar OI, nótt OI, nótt ON, nóttina OI, nóttina ON
nights	nætr ON, nætur OI
nine	níu OI, níu ON
no	eigi OI, eigi ON, engan ON, engar OI, engar ON, engi OI, engi ON, engin ON, enginn ON, engum ON, nei OI, nei ON, öngu OI, öngvan OI
noble	ættstór OI, ættstór ON, göfgir OI, göfgir ON, göfugmenni OI, göfugmenni ON, kvenskörungr ON, skörungr ON, skörungur OI, stórættaða OI, stórættaða ON
no-curiosity	óforvitinn OI, óforvitinn ON
none	eigi OI, eigi ON, enga ON, engan ON, engar ON, engi OI, engi ON, engu ON, engum ON, öngar OI, öngum OI, öngva OI, öngvan OI, öngvir OI
no-one	engi ON
nor	né OI, né ON
Nordic	norænn OI, norænn ON
norse	norrænu OI, norrænu ON
north	norðan OI, norðan ON, norðr ON, norður OI, nyrðra OI, nyrðra ON
North-East-Wind	landnyrðingsveðr ON, landnyrðingsveður OI
northwards	norðan OI, norðan ON
north-wind	norrænur OI, norrænur ON
Norway	noregi OI, noregs OI
Norway (place)	noreg OI, nóreg ON, noregi OI, nóregi ON, noregs OI, nóregs ON
nose	nösum OI, nösum ON
not	eigi OI, eigi ON, ekki OI, ekki ON, engi OI, engi ON
not-be	eigi OI, eigi ON
nothing	einskis OI, einskis ON, ekki OI, ekki ON, engi OI, engi ON, engu ON, öngu OI, öngvum OI

262

The Vinland Sagas

English	Norse
noticed	vart OI, vart ON
not-popular	óvinsæll OI
not-without-obstacle	ógreitt OI, ógreitt ON
now	nú OI, nú ON
nun's-vows	nunnuvígslu OI, nunnuvígslu ON

O, o

English	Norse
obliged	ráð OI, ráð ON, skyldir OI, skyldir ON
Odd (name)	oddr ON, oddur OI
of	á OI, á ON, að OI, af OI, af ON, at ON, hinn OI, í OI, í ON, inn ON, of OI, of ON, ofan OI, ofan ON, og OI, ok ON, ór ON, sonr ON, úr OI
of-exchange	skipta OI
off	af OI, af ON, ofan OI, ofan ON, við OI, við ON
offered	buðu OI, buðu ON
offspring	afkvæmi OI, afkvæmi ON
of-the	hinni OI, inni ON
of-them	þeira ON, þeirra OI
oh	ó OI
Olaf (name)	ólafi OI, ólafi ON, ólafr ON, ólafs OI, ólafs ON, óleifur OI
on	á OI, á ON, af OI, af ON, í OI, í ON, ofan OI, ofan ON
once	eitt OI, eitt ON
one	annað OI, annar OI, annat ON, ein OI, ein ON, eina OI, eina ON, einn OI, einn ON, einni OI, einni ON, einu OI, einu ON, einum OI, einum ON, eitt OI, eitt ON
one-footer	einfæting OI, einfæting ON, einfætingi OI, einfætingr ON, einfætingurinn OI
One-Footer-Land (place)	einfætingaland OI, einfætingaland ON

Word List (English to Norse)

English	Norse
one-such	einhverju OI, einhverju ON
only	eina ON, einar OI, einar ON, einskis OI
on-the	á ON
open	beru ON
opened	opið OI, opit ON
open-sea	hafvillur ON
Opplands-King (name)	upplendingakonungs OI, upplendingakonungs ON
opposite	gegnt OI, gegnt ON
or	eða OI, eða ON, eðr ON
Orkney (place)	orkneyjar OI, orkneyjar ON
Orm (name)	orm OI, orm ON, ormi OI, ormi ON, ormr ON, ormur OI
other	aðrar ON, aðrir OI, aðrir ON, annað OI, annan OI, annan ON, annarr ON, annars OI, annars ON, annat ON, hitt ON, öðru OI, öðru ON, öðrum OI, öðrum ON
others	aðra OI, aðra ON, aðrir OI, aðrir ON, annan ON, hinir OI, hinir ON, öðrum OI, öðrum ON, órir OI, órir ON
others'	annars OI, annars ON
other-side	öðrumegin OI
otherwise	öðru ON
our	okkur OI, vár ON, vor OI
our-places	rúmunum OI
ours	okkar OI, okkarr ON, okkr ON, várn ON, várra ON, várt ON, váru ON, vorn OI, vort OI, voru OI, vorum OI
out	á OI, af OI, brott OI, brott ON, ór ON, úr OI, út OI, út ON, utan OI, utan ON, úti OI, úti ON
out-door	dyrunum OI, útidyrum OI
outhouse	náðahúss ON
out-house	útibúr OI, útibúr ON

English	Norse	English	Norse
out-house-door	útibúrsdyrin OI, útibúrsdyrrin ON	people	fólk OI, fólk ON, fólkit ON, lýðum OI, lýðum ON, manna OI, manna ON, menn OI, menn ON, mönnum OI, mönnum ON, mönnunum OI
out-houses	útibú ON		
out-journey	útivist OI, útivist ON		
outlawed	sekir OI, sekir ON, sekr ON, sekur OI		
outnumbered	ofrliði ON, ofurliði OI		
out-of	af OI, af ON, ór ON, úr OI, út OI, út ON, utan OI, útan ON	people's	manna ON
		people's	manna OI, manna ON
		perform	fremja OI, fremja ON
out-rowing	útróðra ON	performed	flutt ON
outside-of	útan ON	perished	létist OI
out-travel	utan OI, útan ON	pierce	smjúgi OI
Ovaegi (name)	óvægi OI, óvægi ON	pillows	hægindi OI
over	efra OI, efra ON, ofan OI, yfir OI, yfir ON	pinched	klípti OI
		place	stað OI, stað ON, staðar ON, stæðist OI, stæðist ON
own	eigum OI, eigum ON		
owned	áttu OI, áttu ON		
Oxney (place)	öxney OI, öxney ON, yxney OI	place-names	örnefni OI, örnefni ON
		places	rúmunum OI, staðar OI, staðar ON

P, p

English	Norse	English	Norse
		plan	ráð OI, ráð ON, ráða OI, ráða ON
pale	fölleit OI, fölleit ON	plank	fjöl OI, fjöl ON
part	hluta OI	plans	ráðs OI, ráðs ON
partakers	bellendr OI, bellendr ON	played	léku OI, léku ON
parting	skilnaðr ON, skilnaður OI	pledged	heitið OI, heitit ON, hétu OI
part-of	hluti OI, hluti ON	poem	kvæði ON, kvæðið OI, kvæðit ON, kveðið OI
parts	staði OI, staði ON	poetry	skáldskap OI, skáldskap ON
Part's (name)	hluta ON		
passed	leið OI, leið ON, liðin OI, liðin ON, liðnir OI	poles	stangir OI, stangir ON, staur OI, staur ON, staurinum ON, staurnum OI, stöng ON, stönginni ON, stöngum OI, trjám ON, trjánum OI, trjánum ON
paternity	faðerni OI, faðerni ON		
patron	fulltrúann OI, fulltrúann ON		
peace	kyrrt OI, kyrrt ON		
peaceful	fríð OI	poor	fátæku ON, fátækum OI, fátækum ON
peaceful-men	friðmenn OI, friðmenn ON	poor-wretch	vesallegr ON, vesallegur OI
peace-mark	friðarmark ON, friðartákn OI	popular	vinsæll OI, vinsæll ON
pelts	belg OI, belg ON	popularity	vinsældum OI
		porridge	grautr ON, grautur OI
		position	lags OI, lags ON
		possessions	föng OI, föng ON
		possible	að OI

English	Norse
power	forræði OI, forræði ON
praised	lofa OI, lofa ON
prayer-holdings	bænahald OI, bænahald ON
prayers	bænir OI, bænir ON
preach	boða OI, boða ON
preached	boðaði OI, boðaði ON
preferably	helst OI, helzt ON
preparations	búið OI, búit ON
prepare	búa OI, búa ON, búið OI, búið ON
prepared	bjó OI, bjó ON, bjóst OI, bjóst ON, bjuggu OI, bjuggu ON, bjuggust OI, bjuggust ON, brá OI, brá ON, búa OI, búa ON, búast OI, búast ON, búið OI, búin OI, búinn ON, búit ON, búnir OI, búnir ON, býr OI, býr ON, býst OI, býst ON
prepared-with	búinn OI
present	fyrir OI, fyrir ON
preservation	varðveislur OI
preserved	varðveitti OI, varðveitti ON
priest	kennimenn ON
priests	kennimenn OI, kennimönnum OI, kennimönnum ON
promised	hést OI, hézt ON
promising	efnilegir OI, efnilegsti OI, efnilegur OI, efniligir ON, efniligsti ON
properly	almennilega OI, almenniliga ON
prophecy	spá OI, spá ON
prophetess	spákona OI, spákona ON, spákonan ON, spákonu OI, spákonunni OI, spákonunni ON, vísindakonunni OI
Prophetess (name)	spákona OI
prophetesses	spákonur OI, spákonur ON
proposal	bónorð OI, bónorð ON, bónorðið OI, bónorðit ON, ráð OI, ráð ON

English	Norse
proposals	beðið OI, beðit ON
propose	beiddi OI, beiddi ON, biðja OI, biðja ON
prospects	efni ON
protect	verja OI, verja ON
protection	verja OI, verja ON
provide	framt OI, fremi ON
provided	kost ON
provided-for	veitti OI, veitti ON
provisions	fang ON, föng OI, vist OI, vist ON, vistir OI, vistir ON
prow	framstafn OI, framstafn ON
pulled	dregil OI, dregil ON, dró ON, kippa OI, kippa ON, tekur OI
purchase	kaupa OI, kaupa ON
purchases	kaupför OI, kaupför ON
purpose	ætlat ON
pursued	eltu OI, eltu ON
pursuits	sýslur OI, sýslur ON
put	láta OI, láta ON

Q, q

English	Norse
quality	gæða OI, gæða ON, gæði OI, gæði ON, gæðum OI, gæðum ON
quickly	fljótast OI, fljótast ON, skjótast OI, skjótast ON, skjótt OI, skjótt ON
quiet	hljóðlyndr ON, hljóðlyndur OI
quietly	hljótt OI, hljótt ON

R, r

English	Norse
raise	reisa OI, reisa ON, reisim ON, reisum OI
raised	reisa OI, reist OI, reist ON
ran	hlaupa OI, hlaupa ON, hleypr ON, hleypur OI, hljóp OI, hljóp ON, hljópu OI, hljópu ON, runnu OI, runnu ON

The Vinland Sagas   Word List (English to Norse)

English	Norse	English	Norse
rank	mannvirðingu ON, mannvirðingum OI	respectable	göfgasti OI, göfgasti ON, göfgustum OI, göfgustum ON, yfirlæti OI, yfirlæti ON
rarely	varla ON		
rather	heldr ON, heldur OI, helzt ON	resting-place	hvíldarstaða OI, hvíldastaða ON
rattling-off	þuldi ON	return	áðr ON, áður OI, aftr ON, aftur OI
Raven-The-Dueller (name)	hólmgöngu-hrafn OI, hólmgöngu-hrafn ON, hólmgöngu-hrafns OI, hólmgöngu-hrafns ON	returned	áðr ON, áður OI, aftr ON, aftur OI, fór OI, fór ON
rays	geislar ON, geisli OI	returning	aftr ON, aftur OI, komnir OI
ready	albúinn OI, albúinn ON, búin OI, búin ON, búinn OI, búinn ON, búnir OI, búnir ON	Reykjanes (place)	reykjaness OI, reykjaness ON
		Reynines (place)	reynines OI, reynines ON, reyninesi OI
receded	rénuðu OI, rénuðu ON	rib	rifin ON
receive	þiggja OI, þiggja ON	ribs	rif OI
received	tók ON	rich	ríka OI
recently	skömmu OI, skömmu ON	Rich (name)	ríka ON
recited	kvæðit ON	richer	auðgara OI, auðgara ON
reciting	þuldi OI	riding	reið OI, reið ON
recluse	einsetukona OI, einsetukona ON	rises	örglast OI, örglast ON
recognise	kenni OI, kenni ON	rising	félli OI, felli ON
reconciled	sættir OI, sættir ON	river	á ON, ána OI, ána ON, ánni OI, ánni ON, vatni OI, vatni ON
red	rauða OI, rauði ON, rautt OI, rautt ON	river-bank	árbakkann OI, árbakkann ON
Red (name)	rauða ON, rauðan ON, rauði OI, rauði ON	river-mouth	árósinn OI, árósinn ON, árósinum OI, áróssins OI
Redbeard (name)	rauðskeggjaði ON		
red-bearded	rauðskeggjaði OI	Rjupa (name)	rjúpu ON
referred	veik OI, veik ON	Roaldsson (name)	hróaldssonar ON
reins	tauma OI, tauma ON	rock	bjarg OI, bjarg ON, sker OI, sker ON, skerið OI, skerinu OI, skerinu ON, skerit ON
released	leysti OI, leysti ON		
relieve	létta OI, létta ON		
religious	trúuð OI, trúuð ON		
remained	eftir OI, eftir ON	rocks	björg OI
remote	fásinni OI, fásinni ON	rode	réðst OI, réðst ON, reið OI, reið ON, riðr ON, ríður OI
repaired	bættu OI, bættu ON		
repay	launa OI, launa ON		
reproach	ámæli OI, ámæli ON	room	rúmi OI, rúmi ON, rúmið OI, rúmit ON, stofunni OI, stofunni ON
reproaching	átölur OI, átölur ON		
resistance	viðtöku OI, viðtöku ON		
resolved	ráðið OI, ráðit ON	rorqual	reyðr ON, reyður OI
		rose	reistist OI

266

English	Norse	English	Norse
Ross (place)	ross OI, ross ON	sailed	sigla OI, sigla ON, sigldi OI, sigldi ON, sigldu OI, sigldu ON, sigldum ON, siglir OI, siglir ON, siglt OI, siglt ON, sildu ON, silgdu ON
rough	hart OI, hart ON		
route	leiðar OI, leiðar ON		
routes	slóðir OI, slóðir ON		
row	róa OI, róa ON		
rowed	reru OI, réru OI, reru ON		
rowing	reri OI, reri ON	sailing	sigla OI, sigla ON, siglingu OI, siglingum ON
rule	ráða OI, ráða ON		
run	hlaupa OI, hlaupa ON, renna OI, renna ON, rennið OI, rennið ON	sailors	hásetar OI, hásetar ON, hásetum OI, hásetum ON
running	hlupu ON	sails	segl OI, segl ON, seglið OI
Runolf'S (name)	runólfs OI, runólfs ON	sake	sakar ON, sakir OI
Runolfsson (name)	runólfssonar OI	salmon	lax OI, lax ON
rushed	rásar OI, rásar ON	same	ein OI, ein ON, sama OI, sama ON, samir OI, samir ON, samt OI, senn OI, senn ON

S, s

English	Norse	English	Norse
		same-summer	samsumars OI
		sand-heaven's	sandhimins OI, sandhimins ON
sables	safali OI, safali ON	sands	sandar OI, sandar ON, sandinum OI, sandinum ON
sadness	fæð ON, ógleði OI, ógleði ON		
safe	höldnu OI, höldnu ON	sandy	sandar ON
saga	sögu OI, sögu ON	sank	sökk ON, sukku OI, sukku ON
said	frásögn OI, frásögn ON, kvað OI, kvað ON, kvaðst OI, kvaðst ON, kváðu OI, kváðu ON, kváðust OI, kváðust ON, kveðr ON, kveðst OI, kveðst ON, kveður OI, mælt OI, mælt ON, mælti OI, mælti ON, mál OI, mál ON, sagði OI, sagði ON, sagðir OI, sagðir ON, sagt OI, sagt ON, seggir OI, seggir ON, segir OI, segir ON, segja OI, segja ON, sögðu OI, sögðu ON, sögn OI, sögn ON	sat	sat OI, sat ON, sátu OI, sátu ON, setið OI, setit ON, settist OI, settist ON, settu OI, settu ON, settust OI, settust ON, sitr ON, situr OI
		saved	bjargaði OI, vistuðu ON
		saw	sá OI, sá ON, sáu OI, sjá OI, sjá ON
		Saxony (place)	saxlandi OI, saxlandi ON
		say	sagna OI, sagna ON, sé OI, segðu OI, segðu ON, segi OI, segi ON, segir OI, segir ON, segja OI, segja ON, táðit ON, tala ON
said-of	sögn OI	saying	kvað OI, kvað ON, kveðst OI, kveðst ON
sail	sigla OI, sigla ON	says	segir OI, segir ON
		scarcely	trautt OI, trautt ON
		scarcity	óárani OI, óárani ON

The Vinland Sagas   Word List (English to Norse)

English	Norse	English	Norse
scheming	undirförull OI	self-sowing	sjálfsáið OI, sjálfsáit ON, sjálfsána OI, sjálfsána ON, sjálfsánir OI, sjálfsánir ON
Scotland (place)	skotland OI, skotland ON		
Scots (name)	skotar ON	sell	selja OI, selja ON
Scots (place)	skotar OI	send	senda OI, senda ON, sendi OI
Scottish (place)	skoska OI, skosku OI, skozka ON, skozku ON		
scratched	klóraði OI	sent	sendi OI, sendi ON, sendr ON, sendur OI, sent OI, sent ON
Scull-Cleaver (name)	hausakljúfr ON, hausakljúfur OI		
sea	haf OI, haf ON, hafa OI, hafa ON, hafi OI, hafi ON, hafs OI, hafs ON, sjávar ON, sjó OI, sjó ON, sjóinn OI, sjóinn ON, sjónum OI, sjónum ON, sjór OI, sjór ON, sjórinn ON, sjóvar OI, sjóvar ON	separate	skilist ON, skilja OI, skilja ON, skiljast OI, skiljast ON, skiljist OI, skilnað OI, skilnað ON
		separated	fráskili OI, fráskili ON, skildu OI, skildum OI, skilðum ON, skilðust ON, skilja OI, skilja ON
		servants	karlmaðurinn OI
seal-fat	seltjöru OI, seltjöru ON, seltjörunni OI	set	setja OI, setja ON, sett OI, sett ON, settr ON, settu OI, settu ON, settur OI
sea-poem	hafgerðingadrápu OI, hafgerðingadrápu ON		
search	leita OI, leita ON	settle	byggja OI, byggja ON, byggva ON
sea-scattered	sæhafa OI, sæhafa ON	settled	biðuðu ON, bjó ON, bjuggu OI, bjuggu ON, bjuggust ON, búi OI, búi ON, byggðu ON, byggt OI, byggt ON, sætt OI, sætt ON
season	árferð OI, árferð ON		
seat	sætis OI, sætis ON		
seat-posts	setstokka OI, setstokka ON, setstokkana OI, setstokkana ON		
		settlement	bú OI, bú ON, búða OI, búða ON, búi OI, búi ON, búið OI, búit ON, bús OI, bús ON, byggð OI, byggð ON, byggðinni OI, byggðum OI, byggðum ON, óbyggð OI, óbyggð ON
sea-worms	sjómaðkr ON		
second	annað OI, annan OI, annan ON, önnur OI, önnur ON		
see	sé OI, sé ON, sjá OI, sjá ON, sjáið OI, sjáið ON		
seek	leita OI, leita ON, leitað OI, leitaðir ON, leitat ON, sækja ON	settles	bjuggu OI
		shadow	skugga OI, skugga ON
seem	þykja OI, þykkja ON	shall	mun OI, mun ON, muni OI, muni ON, munt OI, munt ON, muntu OI, muntu ON, munu OI, munu ON, munuð OI, munuð ON, skal OI, skal ON, skalt OI, skalt ON, skulum OI, skulum ON
seemed	sýn OI, sýn ON, sýndist OI, sýndist ON, sýnist OI, sýnist ON, þykir OI, þykkir ON, virðist OI		
seems	þætti OI, þætti ON, þykir OI, þykkir ON		
seen	sáit ON, séð OI, sét ON, sjá OI, sjá ON, sú OI		
seldom	sjaldan OI, sjaldan ON		

The Vinland Sagas   Word List (English to Norse)

English	Norse
shall-be	vera OI, vera ON
shallows	grunnsævi OI, grunnsævi ON
shall-you	skaltu OI, skaltu ON
shame	skammar OI, skammar ON, svívirða OI, svívirða ON
share	deila OI, deila ON
she	hana OI, hana ON, hann OI, hennar OI, hennar ON, henni OI, henni ON, hér ON, hon ON, hún OI, hún ON
sheathed-sword	skeið OI, skeið ON
shed	felldi OI, felldi ON
sheep's-stomach	sauðarvömb ON
shell-worms	skelmaðkurinn OI
shield	skjaldarins OI, skjaldarins ON, skjöld OI, skjöld ON
shields	skjöld ON, skjöldu OI, skjöldum OI, skjöldum ON
shine	skína OI, skína ON
ship	knarrar OI, knörr OI, knörr ON, skip OI, skip ON, skipi OI, skipi ON, skipið OI, skipinu OI, skipinu ON, skipit ON, skips OI, skips ON, skipsins OI, skipsins ON, skipum OI, skipum ON, skipunum OI, skipunum ON, þat ON
ships	skip OI, skip ON, skipa OI, skipa ON, skipi OI, skipi ON, skips OI, skips ON, skipum OI, skipum ON, skipunum OI, skipunum ON
ship's	skipsins OI, skipsins ON
ship's-berth	skipborðsins OI, skipborðsins ON
ship's-company	förunautur OI, skipverjum OI, skipverjum ON
ship's-cook	matsveinar OI, matsveinar ON
ships-his	skipsins ON
ships-ports	skipshöfnum ON, skipverjunum OI
ship-worms	maðksjá OI, maðksjó ON
shipwreck	skipflaki OI, skipflaki ON
shirt	serkinum OI
shoes	skóklæðin OI, skóklæðin ON, skúa OI, skúa ON
shore	strandar OI, strandar ON
short	skammt OI, skammt ON
shortage	skorti OI, skorti ON, skortir OI, skortir ON
shorten	svipta OI, svipta ON
shortly	skammt OI, skjótt OI, skjótt ON
short-stories	sagnaskemmtan OI
short-time-of-day	skammdegi OI, skammdegi ON
shot	skaut OI, skaut ON
should	lézt ON, mun OI, mun ON, mundi OI, mundu OI, muni OI, muni ON, muntu OI, muntu ON, munum OI, munum ON, mynda ON, myndi ON, skuluð OI, skuluð ON, skulum OI, skulum ON, skylda ON, skyldi OI, skyldi ON, skyldu OI, skyldu ON, skylt OI, skylt ON
should-be	skyldi OI, skyldi ON
shoulder	axlarliðnum ON, öxl OI
shout	kall OI, kall ON
shouted	æpðu ON, æptu OI
show	sýni OI, sýni ON
showed	sýndi OI, sýndi ON, sýni OI, sýnir ON
shown	auðsýnir OI, auðsýnir ON
sickness	sótt OI, sótt ON, sóttarfar OI, sóttarfar ON, sóttin OI, sóttin ON, sóttina OI, sóttina ON
side	megin OI, megin ON
sideboards	rekkjustokkinn OI, rekkjustokkinn ON

The Vinland Sagas   *Word List (English to Norse)*

English	Norse
sides	hliðum OI, hliðunum ON
Siglefjord (place)	siglufjörð ON
sign-herself	sig OI
Sigrid (name)	sigríðr ON, sigríður OI
Sigurd (name)	sigurði OI, sigurði ON
silence	þegði ON, þegðu OI
silent	fámálug OI, fámálug ON, þagði OI, þagði ON
silver	silfr ON, silfur OI
since	sem OI, sem ON, síðan OI, síðan ON, síðar OI, síðar ON, því OI, því ON
single	eitt ON
sister	systur OI, systur ON
sister-of	systur OI, systur ON
sisters	systr ON, systur OI
sit	sæti OI, sæti ON
sitting	setu OI, setu ON
six	sex OI, sex ON
Skagafjord (place)	skagafirði OI, skagafjörð OI, skagafjörð ON
Skeidsbrekkur (place)	skeiðsbrekkum OI, skeiðsbrekkum ON
skin-boats	húðkeipa OI, húðkeipa ON
skin-cots	húðföt OI, húðföt ON
skin-purse	skjóðupungr ON
skins	skinn ON
skin-sacks	skinnhjúpum OI, skinnhjúpum ON
skin-wares	skinnavöru OI, skinnavöru ON, skinnvöru ON
Skraeling	skrælingi OI, skrælingr ON
skraelings	skrælinga ON, skrælingar ON, skrælingja OI, skrælingjar OI
Skraelings (name)	skrælinga ON, skrælingar ON, skrælingaskipa ON, skrælingja OI, skrælingjar OI, skrælingjarnir OI, skrælingjum OI, skrælingum ON
Skraelings (place)	skrælingjalandi OI
Skraumuhlaupsa (place)	skraumuhlaupsár OI, skraumuhlaupsár ON
sky	loft OI, loft ON
slabs	hellur OI, hellur ON
slab-stone	hellusteinn ON
slapped	slettir OI, slettir ON
slayed	vegr ON, vegur OI
sleep	sofa OI, sofa ON
sleeping	sofnaða OI, sofnaða ON, soföndum ON, sofundum OI
sleeves	ermar OI, ermar ON
slept	sofið OI, sofit ON, sofna OI, sofna ON, sofnar OI, sváfu OI, sváfu ON
slew	vá ON, vó OI
slighting	sleitum OI
small	smáir OI, smár OI, smár ON, smátt ON
small-intestine	smáþarma OI, smáþarma ON
smoothly	greiðleg OI, greiðlig ON
Snaefell (place)	snæfells OI, snæfells ON
Snaefellsjokli (place)	snæfellsjökli OI, snæfellsjökli ON
Snaefellstrond (place)	snæfellsnesi OI, snæfellströnd ON
Snorrason (name)	snorrason OI, snorrason ON
Snorri (name)	snorra OI, snorra ON, snorri OI, snorri ON
Snorri'S (name)	snorra OI
snorting	gjalla OI, gjalla ON
snow	snjár OI, snjór ON
so	sá OI, sá ON, sé OI, sé ON, sem ON, séu OI, svá ON, svát ON, svo OI
sold	keyptu OI, keyptu ON, seldi OI, seldi ON, selr ON, selur OI
solitary	einþykkr ON, einþykkur OI
solution	bragð OI, bragð ON
Solvadal (place)	sölvadal OI, sölvadal ON
Sölvi (name)	sölvi OI, sölvi ON

The Vinland Sagas — Word List (English to Norse)

English	Norse
some	einhverju ON, eitthvert OI, nokkuð OI, nokkur OI, nökkur ON, nokkurar OI, nökkurar ON, nokkurir OI, nökkurir ON, nökkurn ON, nokkurra OI, nökkurra ON, nökkut ON, sum OI, sum ON, sumir OI, sumir ON, sumra OI, sumra ON, sumt ON
something	nokkuð OI, nokkur OI, nökkur ON, nokkurra OI, nökkurra ON, nökkut ON
sometime	nokkuru OI, nökkuru ON
sometimes	stundum OI, stundum ON
somewhat	nokkuru OI
son	son OI, son ON, sonar OI, sonar ON, sonr ON, sonur OI
son-of	son OI, sonr ON, sonur OI
Son-Of (name)	son OI, sonr ON, sonur OI, syni OI, syni ON
Son-of-Aslak (name)	áslákssonar ON
Son-of-Bard (name)	bárðarson OI, bárðarson ON
Son-Of-Bjorn (name)	bjarnarsonar OI, bjarnarsonar ON
Son-of-Erik (name)	eiríksson OI, eiríksson ON, eirikssonar OI, eirikssonar ON
Son-Of-Gudrod (name)	guðröðarsonar OI, guðröðarsonar ON
Son-Of-Halfdan (name)	hálfdanarsonar OI, hálfdanarsonar ON
Son-of-Helga (name)	helgasonar ON
Son-of-Herjolf	herjúlfsson OI, herjúlfssonar OI
Son-of-Herjolf (name)	herjólfsson ON, herjólfssonar ON
Son-of-Karlesfni (name)	karlsefnissonar OI, karlsefnissonar ON
Son-of-Karlsefni (name)	karlsefnissonar ON
Son-Of-Ketil (name)	ketilssonar OI, ketilssonar ON
Son-of-Kodran (name)	koðránsson OI, koðránsson ON
Son-Of-Olaf (name)	ólafssonar OI, óláfssonar ON
Son-of-Oxna-Thori (name)	öxna-þórissonar OI, öxna-þórissonar ON
Son-of-Ox-Thorir (name)	öxna-þórissonar ON, yxna-þórissonar OI
Son-of-Ragnar (name)	ragnarssonar ON
Son-of-Runolf (name)	runólfssonar ON
Son-Of-Sigmund (name)	sigmundarsonar OI, sigmundarsonar ON
Son-of-Snorri (name)	snorrasonar OI, snorrasonar ON
Son-of-Thorbrand (name)	þorbrandsson OI, þorbrandsson ON
Son-of-Thord (name)	þórðar OI, þórðar ON, þórðarsonar OI, þórðarsonar ON
Son-of-Thorgrim (name)	þorgrímsson OI, þorgrímsson ON
Son-of-Ulf (name)	úlfssonar OI, úlfssonar ON
Son-of-Vifil (name)	vífilsson OI, vífilsson ON
sons	sonu OI, sonu ON, synir OI, synir ON
son's-property	sonareignin OI, sonareignin ON
soon	brátt OI, brátt ON, fljótlega OI, fljótliga ON
sooner	bráðara OI, bráðara ON
sought	leitaði OI, leitaði ON, leitar OI, leitar ON, leituðu OI, leituðu ON, sækja OI, sækja ON, sóttu OI
south	suðr ON, suðri ON, suður OI, suðurátt OI, sunnan OI, sunnan ON, svo OI
south-east	landsuðr ON, landsuðrs ON, landsuður OI
southern	suðræn ON, syðra OI, syðra ON
southern-man	suðrmaðr ON, suðurmaður OI
southern-winds	sunnanveður OI

The Vinland Sagas — Word List (English to Norse)

English	Norse	English	Norse
south-islander	suðreyskr ON, suðureyskur OI	steered	stefndu OI, stefndu ON, stýrði OI, stýrði ON, stýrðu OI, stýrðu ON, styrkur OI
South-West (place)	útsynnings ON		
south-west-wind	útsynningsbyr OI	steering	stjórn OI, stjórn ON, stýri OI, stýri ON
sown	sáð OI		
space	bilstyggir OI, bilstyggvir ON	steersmen	stýrimenn OI, stýrimenn ON
spanning-long	spannarlangt OI	stern	skaut OI, skaut ON, stafn OI, stafn ON, stjórn ON
spared	unnit ON		
speak	mæla OI, mæla ON, máli OI, máli ON, máls OI, máls ON	steward	bryti ON
		still	enn OI, enn ON, kyrrt OI, kyrrt ON
spears	spjót OI, spjót ON	stirred	hrærðist OI, hrærðist ON
speck	flekk ON		
spectacular	þvílíka ON	stock	stokka OI, stokka ON
speech	máli OI, máli ON	Stokkanes (place)	stokkanesi OI, stokkanesi ON
speed	skjótleiks OI		
spell-platform	seiðhjallinum OI	stomachs	mögum OI, mögum ON
spirits	náttúrur OI, náttúrur ON	stone	stein OI, stein ON
spoke	er OI, mælti OI, mælti ON, mæltu OI, mæltu ON, töluðu OI	stones	grjótinu OI, grjótit ON, steinum OI, steinum ON
sports	hagleik OI, hagleik ON, leikar OI, leikar ON	stone-slab	hella OI, hella ON
		stood	stað ON, staðið OI, staðit ON, stóð OI, stóð ON, stóðst OI, stóðst ON
spread	bræddr ON, bræddur OI, brætt OI		
spring	vára ON, várar ON, vári ON, várit ON, vora OI, vorar OI, vori OI, vorið OI	stool	stóli OI, stóli ON, stólinn OI, stólinn ON, stólinum OI, stólinum ON
sprung	vár ON, vor OI	stop	hætti OI, hætti ON
staff	staf OI, staf ON	stopped	stopir OI, stopir ON
stand	stað OI, stað ON, standa OI, standa ON, standir OI, standir ON, stoða OI	stormy	hvasst OI, hvasst ON
		story	saga OI, saga ON, sögn OI, sögn ON
starboard	stjórnborða OI	straightaway	þegar OI, þegar ON
state	hagi OI, hagi ON	strait	sund OI, sund ON
stave	stef OI, stef ON	strange	undarlegi OI, undarlegum OI, undarligi ON, undarligum ON
stay	búast OI, búast ON, vistar OI, vistar ON		
stayed	var OI, var ON	strangers	ókunnugum OI, ókunnum ON
staying	haldið OI		
steady	stæði OI, stæði ON	Straumey (place)	straumey ON
steep-looking	brattleitr ON, brattleitur OI	Straumfjord (place)	straumfirði ON, straumfjörð ON, straumsfirði OI, straumsfjörð OI
steer	stýra OI, stýra ON, stýrir OI, stýrir ON		

The Vinland Sagas — Word List (English to Norse)

English	Norse
Straumsey (place)	straumsey OI
Straumsfjord (place)	straumsfjörð OI
straw-staves	hálmþúst ON, hálmþústum OI
stream	lækr ON, lækur OI, straumr ON
streams	straumar ON
strength	afli OI, afli ON, styrkr ON, styrkur OI
stretches	þokar OI, þokar ON
strike	höggva OI, höggva ON
striking	skörulegastur OI, sköruligastr ON
strong	rammlegan OI, rammligan ON, sköruleg OI, skörulig ON, sterk OI, sterk ON, sterkr ON, sterkur OI
strongly	sterklega OI
struck	hjó OI, hjó ON, sló OI, sló ON, slógu OI, slógu ON
Styrr (name)	styr OI, styrr OI, styrr ON
submerge	kaf ON
such	slík OI, slík ON, slíka OI, slíkan OI, slíkan ON, slíkra OI, slíkra ON, slíkt OI, slikt ON, slíkt ON, slíku ON, slíkum OI, svá ON, svo OI
Sudrey (place)	suðrey ON, suðurey OI
Sudreyar (place)	suðreyja ON, suðreyjar ON, suðreyjum ON, suðureyja OI, suðureyjar OI, suðureyjum OI
suggested	tillaga OI
suits	hentar OI, hentar ON
summer	sumar OI, sumar ON, sumarið OI, sumarit ON, sumars OI, sumars ON, sumra OI, sumra ON, sumri OI, sumri ON, sumrum OI, sumrum ON
sun	sól OI, sól ON
sung	kveðið OI, kveðit ON
sun-wise-motion	sólarsinnis OI, sólarsinnis ON
supplied	veita OI, veita ON, veittir OI, veittir ON
supplies	birgðir OI, föng ON, varðveita OI, varðveita ON, vistir ON
supply	veita OI, veita ON
supported	veitti OI, veitti ON, veittu OI, veittu ON
suppose	ætla OI, ætla ON
supposed	ætla OI, ætla ON, ætlaði OI, ætlaði ON, ætluðu OI, ætluðu ON
supposing	ætlan ON
suspect	grunar OI, grunar ON
Sutherland (place)	suðrland ON, suðurland OI
Sviney (place)	svíney OI, svíney ON
swiftly	tíðast OI, tíðast ON
sword	sverðið OI, sverðinu ON, sverðit ON
swords	sverð OI, sverð ON

T, t

English	Norse
table	borð OI, borð ON
table-games	töfl OI
tables	borð OI, borð ON
take	tæki OI, tæki ON, taka OI, taka ON, takast OI, takast ON, tekr ON, tekur OI, tökum OI, tökum ON
take-advantage	nýta OI
taken	færð OI, færð ON, fært OI, fært ON, höfð OI, höfð ON, nema OI, nema ON, numið OI, numit ON, taka OI, tekið OI, tekin OI, tekin ON, tekit ON, tók OI, tók ON, tóku ON, tókust ON, viðtaka OI
takes	tækist ON, tækjust OI, tekr ON
taking	nema OI, nema ON, tókust OI
talk	tala OI, tala ON, umræða OI, umræða ON

The Vinland Sagas   Word List (English to Norse)

English	Norse	English	Norse
talked	mælti OI, mælti ON, tal OI, talaði OI, talaði ON, taldi OI, taldi ON	the belly	ístruna OI
		the people	manna OI
		the-alternative	liggja ON
taught	kenndi OI, kenndi ON, kenndu OI, kenndu ON	the-arrow	örina OI
		the-axe	öxin OI, öxina OI
team	lið OI, lið ON, liði OI, liði ON, liðið OI, liðit ON, liðs ON	the-bishop	biskups OI, biskups ON, byskups ON
		the-Black	svarta ON, svartr ON
teams	liðin OI	the-Black (name)	svarta OI, svarti OI, svarti ON, svartur OI
tears	tár OI, tár ON		
temperamental	skapstór OI, skapstórr ON	the-Black's	svarta ON
ten	tigir OI, tigir ON, tigu ON, tíu OI, tíu ON	the-boat	bátinn OI, bátinn ON, bátum OI, báturinn OI
tens	tigi OI, tigir OI, tigir ON, tigu ON	the-bodies	líkinu ON, líkunum OI
		the-bottom-of	botn OI, botn ON
tent	tjaldi OI, tjaldi ON, tjaldinu OI, tjaldinu ON	the-breast	brjóstið OI
		the-church	kirkju ON
tester	reyni OI, reyni ON	the-company	liðit ON
than	en OI, en ON, það OI, þat ON	the-company-of	lið OI
		the-dead	dauða ON
thanked	þakkaði OI, þakkaði ON, þakkar OI, þakkar ON, þökkuðu ON	the-deep-minded	djúpúðgu ON
		The-Deep-Minded (name)	djúpúðgu OI
that	á OI, á ON, að OI, af OI, at ON, en OI, en ON, er OI, er ON, hana OI, hin OI, inn OI, inn ON, sá OI, sá ON, sem OI, sem ON, sú ON, það OI, þann OI, þann ON, þar OI, þat ON, þeim OI, þeim ON, þenna OI, þetta OI, þetta ON, því OI, því ON	the-door	durunum ON, dyrunum OI
		the-earth	jörð OI
		The-Easterner (name)	austmanns OI
		the-easternman	austmanns ON
		the-Farmer	bónda OI, bónda ON, bóndi OI, bóndi ON
		The-Farmer (name)	bóndi OI
		the-feast	veisla OI, veislunni OI, veizla ON, veizlan ON, veizlunni ON
that-might	mátti OI	the-foreman	verkstjórinn OI
that-to	það OI	the-Foul	saurs OI, saurs ON
the	á OI, á ON, að OI, at ON, er OI, hið OI, hin OI, hina OI, hina ON, hinn OI, hinni OI, hins OI, hinu OI, hinum OI, í OI, in ON, ina ON, inn OI, inn ON, inni ON, ins ON, inu ON, inum ON, it ON, sá OI, sá ON, sér OI, sér ON, sinn OI, sinn ON, sú OI, sú ON, þá ON, það OI, þann OI, þann ON, þat ON, þeir ON, þeira ON, þeirra OI	The-Foul (name)	saur OI, saur ON, saurr ON
		the-headland	nesið OI, nesinu OI
		the-house	húsunum OI, húsunum ON
		the-hunter	veiðimaðr ON, veiðimaður OI, veiðimanns OI, veiðimanns ON
		the-inlet	mynni OI, mynni ON

The Vinland Sagas *Word List (English to Norse)*

English	Norse	English	Norse
their	sér OI, sér ON, sinn OI, sinn ON, sinna OI, sins ON, síns ON, sínu OI, sínu ON, sitt OI, sitt ON, sú OI, sú ON, þar OI, þar ON, þeir OI, þeir ON, þeira ON, þeirar ON, þeirra OI, þeirrar OI	*then*	á OI, á ON, en OI, en ON, er OI, er ON, inn OI, inn ON, sem OI, sem ON, síðan OI, síðan ON, sinn OI, sinn ON, skip ON, þá OI, þá ON, þann OI, þann ON, þegar OI, þegar ON, þeir ON, þenna ON
the-Irish-Sea (place)	írlandshaf ON	*the-one-footer*	einfætingr ON
theirs	sér OI, sér ON, sín OI, sín ON, sína OI, sína ON, sínar OI, sínar ON, sinn OI, sinn ON, sinna OI, sinna ON, sinnar OI, sinnar ON, sinni OI, sinni ON, síns OI, síns ON, sínu OI, sínu ON, sínum OI, sínum ON, sitt OI, sitt ON, þeim OI, þeim ON, þeir OI, þeira ON, þeirra OI	*the-out-door*	útidurum ON, útidurunum ON
		the-people	manna OI
		the-platform	hjallinn ON
		there	þá OI, þá ON, þaðan OI, þaðan ON, þær OI, þær ON, þangað OI, þangat ON, þar OI, þar ON, þau OI, þau ON, þeir OI, þeir ON, þeira ON, þeirar ON, þeirra OI, þeirrar OI, þeirri OI
the-island	eyjar OI, eyjar ON, eyna OI	*the-Red*	rauða OI, rauða ON, rauði OI, rauði ON
the-king	konungr ON		
The-King (name)	konungs OI, konungs ON, konungur OI	*The-Red (name)*	rauða OI, rauða ON, rauði OI, rauði ON, rauðr ON, rauður OI
the-land	landið OI, landinu OI, landit ON	*The-Red'S (name)*	rauðs OI
them	sér OI, sér ON, sín OI, sín ON, þá OI, þá ON, þau OI, þau ON, þeim OI, þeim ON, þeir OI, þeir ON, þeira ON, þeirra OI	*The-Red'S (name)*	rauða OI, rauða ON, rauðs ON
		therefore	at ON, fyrir OI, þar OI, því OI, því ON
		the-river	ánni OI
the-matter	mál OI, máli OI, máli ON, málum OI, málum ON	*the-sad*	hryggs ON
		the-same	sama OI, sama ON
the-men	manna ON	*these*	sitt OI, sitt ON, þau OI, þau ON, þeim OI, þeim ON, þenna OI, þenna ON, þess OI, þess ON, þessa OI, þessa ON, þessar OI, þessar ON, þessara OI, þessi OI, þessi ON, þessir OI, þessir ON, þessum OI, þessum ON
the-middle	miðri ON		
the-mouth-of	mynni OI, mynni ON		
themselves	sér OI, sér ON, sig OI, sik ON, sjálfala OI, sjálfala ON		
		the-sea	sjó OI, sjónum OI, sjónum ON
		The-Sensible (name)	glóra ON

The Vinland Sagas — Word List (English to Norse)

English	Norse
the-ship	skipi ON, skipið OI, skipinu OI, skipinu ON, skipum OI
The-Skraelings (name)	skrælingjar OI
the-sun	sól OI, sól ON
the-sword	sverðið OI
the-team	lit OI, lit ON
the-way	háttað OI, háttat ON, háttr ON, háttur OI, leið OI
the-wedding	brúðkaupið OI
The-White (name)	hvíti OI, hvíti ON
the-woman	konan OI
the-woods	skóginn OI
the-worm-sea	maðksjónum ON
The-Worm-Sea (place)	maðkahafinu OI
they	af OI, hitt OI, sér OI, sér ON, sinn ON, sinni OI, síns OI, síns ON, sínu ON, þá OI, þá ON, það OI, þær OI, þær ON, þann OI, þann ON, þar OI, þar ON, þat ON, þau OI, þau ON, þeim OI, þeim ON, þeir OI, þeir ON, þeira ON, þeirs ON
they-saw	sjá OI
thick	gildir OI, gildir ON
things	hluti OI, hluti ON, hlutir OI, hlutir ON
think	hygg OI, hygg ON, þótti OI, þyki OI, þykir OI, þykist OI, þykki ON, þykkja ON, þykkjast ON
thinking	þykir OI
thinks	þótti OI, þótti ON
think-us	þykkjumst ON
third	þriðja OI, þriðja ON
thirty	þriði OI, þriði ON
thirty-and	þriði ON
this	í ON, sá OI, sá ON, sé OI, það OI, þann OI, þann ON, þat ON, þeir OI, þeira ON, þenna OI, þenna ON, þess OI, þess ON, þessa OI, þessa ON, þessi OI, þessi ON, þessu OI, þessu ON, þessum OI, þessum ON, þetta OI, þetta ON, þette ON
Thistilsfjord (place)	þistilsfjörð OI, þistilsfjörð ON
Thistle (name)	þistils OI, þistils ON
Thjodhild (name)	þjóðhildar OI, þjóðhildar ON, þjóðhildi ON, þjóðhildr ON, þjóðhildur OI
Thjodhildakirkja (place)	þjóðhildarkirkja ON
Thjodhildkirkja (place)	þjóðhildarkirkja OI
Thor (name)	þór OI, þór ON
Thorbjarnardottur (name)	þorbjarnardóttur OI, þorbjarnardóttur ON
thorbjorg	þorbjargar ON
Thorbjorg (name)	þorbjargar OI, þorbjargar ON, þorbjörg OI, þorbjörg ON, þorbjörgu OI, þorbjörgu ON
Thorbjorg's (name)	þorbjargar ON
Thorbjorn (name)	þorbirni OI, þorbirni ON, þorbjarnar OI, þorbjörn OI, þorbjörn ON
Thorbjornadottir (name)	þorbjarnardóttur OI
Thorbjorn's (name)	þorbjarnar ON
Thorbrand (name)	þorbrand OI, þorbrandr ON, þorbrands OI, þorbrands ON
Thorbrand'S (name)	þorbrands OI, þorbrands ON
Thorbrandson (name)	þorbrandsson OI, þorbrandsson ON
Thord (name)	þórðar OI, þórðar ON, þórðr ON
Thorfin (name)	þorfinnr ON, þorfinnur OI
Thorfin's (name)	þorfinns ON

The Vinland Sagas   Word List (English to Norse)

English	Norse
Thorgeir (name)	þorgeir OI, þorgeirr ON
Thorgeirsfell (place)	þorgeirsfelli OI, þorgeirsfelli ON
Thorgerd (name)	þorgerði ON, þorgerðr ON, þorgerður OI
Thorgest (name)	þorgesti OI, þorgesti ON, þorgestr ON, þorgestur OI
Thorgest'S (name)	þorgests OI, þorgests ON
Thorgest's-Sons (name)	þorgestlingum OI, þorgestlingum ON
Thorgils (name)	þorgils OI, þorgils ON
Thorgilson (name)	þorgilsson ON
Thorgun (name)	þórgunna OI, þórgunna ON
Thorhall (name)	þórhall OI, þórhallr ON, þórhalls OI, þórhalls ON, þórhallur OI
Thorhild (name)	þórhildi ON
Thori (name)	þóri OI, þóri ON, þóris OI, þóris ON
Thorid (name)	þuríðar OI, þuríðar ON
Thorir (name)	þórir OI, þórir ON
Thori's (name)	þóris ON
Thorjborn'S (name)	þorbjargar OI, þorbjarnar OI
Thorkell (name)	þorkel OI, þorkel ON, þorkell OI, þorkell ON
Thorlak (name)	þorláks OI, þorláks ON
Thorlak's (name)	þorláks ON
Thorsnes-Assembly (name)	þórsnessþingi OI, þórsnessþingi ON
Thorsnes-Thing (name)	þórsnessþingi ON
Thorsnes-Thing (place)	þórsnessþingi OI
Thorstein (name)	þorstein OI, þorstein ON, þorsteini OI, þorsteini ON, þorsteinn OI, þorsteinn ON, þorsteins OI, þorsteins ON
Thorstein's	þorsteins OI, þorsteins ON
Thorstein'S (name)	þorsteins OI, þorsteins ON
Thorun (name)	þórunn OI, þórunn ON, þórunnar OI, þórunnar ON

English	Norse
Thorvald (name)	þorvald OI, þorvald ON, þorvaldi OI, þorvaldi ON, þorvaldr ON, þorvaldur OI, þorvarðr ON
Thorvald's (name)	þorvalds OI, þorvalds ON
Thorvard (name)	þorvarði ON, þorvarðr ON, þorvarður OI
those	þær OI, þær ON, þau OI, þau ON, þeim OI, þeim ON, þeir OI, þeir ON
though	þó OI, þó ON, þótt OI, þótt ON, þóttú OI, þóttú ON
thought	hugðum OI, hugðum ON, hyggja OI, hyggja ON, íhuga OI, íhuga ON, þó OI, þótt OI, þótt ON, þótti OI, þótti ON, þóttist OI, þóttist ON, þóttu OI, þóttu ON, þóttust OI, þóttust ON, þykir OI, þykki ON
thoughts	alendu OI, hug OI, hug ON, þokka ON
thralls	þrælana OI, þrælana ON, þrælar OI, þrælar ON
thrall's-son	þrælssyni OI, þrælssyni ON
three	þrem OI, þremr ON, þrír OI, þrír ON, þrjá OI, þrjá ON, þrjár OI, þrjár ON, þrjú OI, þrjú ON
three-winters	þrévetr ON, þrívetur OI
threw	köstuðu ON, varp OI, varp ON
thriving	þrifum OI, þrifum ON
thus	þetta OI, þetta ON
tidal-pool	hópi OI, hópi ON
tide	fjöru OI, fjöru ON, flóðið OI, flóðit ON
tidings	tíðendi ON, tíðindi OI
tied	þvengi OI, þvengi ON
time	frá OI, frá ON, hríð OI, hríð ON, skipti OI, skipti ON, stund OI, stund ON, tíma OI, tíma ON
times	tíma OI, tíma ON

277

The Vinland Sagas   Word List (English to Norse)

English	Norse	English	Norse
tin-buttons	tinknappar ON	*to-speak*	mæla OI, tala ON
tip	oddrinn ON, oddurinn OI	*to-that*	hvað OI
		to-the-land	landinu OI
to	á OI, á ON, að OI, at OI, at ON, er OI, er ON, fyrir ON, í OI, i ON, í ON, it ON, signa OI, þeim ON, til OI, til ON, við OI, við ON, vit ON	*to-them*	þá ON, þeim OI, þeim ON
		to-travel	fara OI
		touch	spyrnast OI
		towards	á OI, á ON, að OI, at ON, mót OI, móti OI, móti ON, til OI, til ON
to-another	annars ON	*town*	bæ OI, bæ ON
to-be	vera OI, vera ON, verða OI, verða ON	*to-you*	þér OI, þér ON
to-bear	berja ON	*trading*	keipana OI, keipana ON
to-bear-to	berja OI	*trading-journeys*	kaupferðum OI, kaupferðum ON
to-follow	fylgja OI	*trading-men*	kaupmenn OI, kaupmenn ON, kaupmönnum OI, kaupmönnum ON
together	saman OI, saman ON, samfarir OI, samfarir ON, samflota OI, samflota ON, samt OI, samt ON		
to-go	fara OI	*trading-posts*	kaupstefna OI, kaupstefna ON, kaupstefnu OI, kaupstefnu ON
to-her	henni OI, henni ON		
to-him	hans ON, honum OI, honum ON	*Tradir (place)*	tröðum OI, tröðum ON
toil	vás ON, vos OI	*tradition*	sið OI, sið ON
told	sagði OI, sagði ON, sögðu ON, talat ON, taldi OI, taldi ON, talði ON, taldist OI, talðist ON, telgja OI, telgja ON, töluðu OI, töluðu ON	*transferred*	fluttr ON, fluttur OI
		travel	færi ON, færu OI, fara OI, fara ON, farar OI, farar ON, fari OI, fari ON, farið OI, farir OI, farit ON, fer OI, ferð OI, ferð ON, ferðar OI, ferðar ON, förum OI, förum ON
told-of	getið OI, getit ON		
to-lie	leggjast OI, leggjast ON		
to-me	mér OI, mér ON		
took	færði OI, færði ON, nam OI, nam ON, námu OI, námu ON, sótti OI, sótti ON, taka ON, tekr ON, tekst OI, tekst ON, tekur OI, tók OI, tók ON, tókst OI, tókst ON, tóku OI, tóku ON, tókust OI, tókust ON	*travelled*	færðu OI, færðu ON, fara OI, fara ON, farið OI, farit ON, fer OI, ferr ON, fór OI, fór ON, fórst OI, fórst ON, fóru OI, fóru ON, fóruð OI
		traveller-generous	fardreng OI, fardreng ON
		travelling	fara OI, fara ON, fór OI, förum OI, förum ON
took-to	tóku OI, tóku ON	*travelling-companion*	fardrengr ON, fardrengur OI
to-preach	boða OI		
tortured	píndi OI, píndi ON	*travelling-men*	förunautum OI, förunautum ON
to-sell	selja OI, selja ON		
to-sign	signa ON	*travel-we*	förum OI, förum ON

The Vinland Sagas

English	Norse
treasure	féið OI, féit ON, gersemi OI, gersimi ON
tree	tré OI, tré ON
trees	mörkina OI, mörkina ON, tré OI, tré ON, viðinn OI, viðinn ON
trenches	grafar ON, grafir OI, gröfunum OI, gröfunum ON
tried	reynt OI
true	
true	
true	
true	
trust	trausti OI, trausti ON
Tryggvason (name)	tryggvason ON, tryggvasyni OI, tryggvasyni ON
Tryggvason'S (name)	tryggvasonar OI
Tryggvason'S (name)	tryggvasonar OI, tryggvasonar ON
turn	horfa OI, horfa ON, snúast OI
turned	hverfr ON, hverfur OI, settu OI, settu ON, sneru OI, snúa OI, snúa ON
tusk-belt	tannbelti OI, tannbelti ON
twelve	tólf OI, tólf ON
twenty	tög ON, tögr ON, tug OI, tugur OI, tuttugu OI, tuttugu ON
two	tvá ON, tvær OI, tvær ON, tvau ON, tveim ON, tveir OI, tveir ON, tvennar OI, tvennar ON, tvennum OI, tvo OI, tvö OI
two-ringed	tvíhólkaðan OI, tvíhólkaðan ON
Tyrkir (name)	tyrkir OI, tyrkir ON

U, u

English	Norse
ulf	úlfs ON
Ulf (name)	úlfs OI, úlfs ON
Ulfson (name)	úlfssonar OI, úlfssonar ON

Word List (English to Norse)

English	Norse
unbroken-sea	ósæbratt OI, ósæbratt ON
unconsecrated	óvígðri OI, óvígðri ON
un-consecrated	óvígða OI, óvígða ON
uncovered	bert ON
under	undan ON, undir OI, undir ON
understanding	skyn OI
understood	skilði ON
uneasiness	óró ON
un-glad	óglaðari ON
unhappy	þungt OI, þungt ON
uninjured	óskatt OI, óskatt ON
uninviting	ógagnvænlegt OI, ógagnvænligt ON
unknown	ókunnu OI, ókunnu ON
unload	bera OI, bera ON
unmarried	kvonlausir OI, ókvæntir ON
unruly	ódæll OI
unsettled-land	óbyggðum OI, óbyggðum ON
until	áðr ON, áður OI, til OI, til ON, uns OI, unz ON
unwise	óvitrlig ON
unwisely	óhyggilega OI, óvarliga ON, óviturleg OI
un-worthy-men	auvirðismönnum OI, auvirðismönnum ON
up	upp OI, upp ON, uppi OI, uppi ON
upholstery	breiðabólstað OI, breiðabólstað ON
upped	upp OI, upp ON
up-to	undir OI, undir ON
urged	eggjaði ON, fýstu OI, fýstu ON
us	okkr ON, okkur OI, oss OI, oss ON
use	nýt OI, nýt ON, nytjum OI, nytjum ON
useful	nytjumaður OI

V, v

English	Norse
Valdidida (name)	avaldidida ON

The Vinland Sagas   Word List (English to Norse)

English	Norse
valiant	vaskasti OI, vaskasti ON
Vallthjof (place)	valþjófs OI, valþjófs ON
valued	þykja OI, þykkja ON
Vathjolfsstadr (place)	valþjófsstöðum OI, valþjófsstöðum ON
Vatnahverfi (place)	vatnahverfi OI, vatnahverfi ON
Vatnshorn (place)	vatnshorni OI, vatnshorni ON
vehemence	þjósti OI, þjósti ON
verse	kviðling OI, kviðling ON, vísu OI, vísu ON
very	ákafliga ON, mikið OI, mikill OI, mikill ON, mikit ON, mjög OI, mjök ON
vessel	farkost OI, farkost ON
Vestribyggd (place)	vestribyggð OI, vestribyggð ON, vestribyggðar OI, vestribyggðar ON
Vethild (name)	vethildi OI, vethildi ON
Vifil (name)	vífill OI, vífill ON
Vifilsdal (place)	vífilsdal OI, vífilsdal ON
Vifilson (name)	vífilsson OI, vífilsson ON
vines	vínvið OI, vínvið ON, vínviði OI, vínviði ON, vínviður OI
vine-trees	vínviðr ON, vínviður OI
Vinland (place)	vínland OI, vínland ON, vínlandi OI, vínlandi ON, vínlands OI, vínlands ON
Vinland-voyage	vínlandsferð OI, vínlandsferð ON, vínlandsför OI, vínlandsför ON
visit	fund OI, fund ON, vitja OI, vitja ON
Vog (place)	vágs ON
Vogs (place)	vogs OI
voice	raust OI, rödd ON
voyage	ferð OI, ferð ON, ferðar OI, ferðar ON, förinni OI, förinni ON, reiðfara OI, reiðfara ON
voyages	farar OI, farar ON, ferðum OI, ferðum ON

W, w

English	Norse
wait	bíða OI, bíða ON, vænti ON
waited	beið OI, beið ON
wake	vaki OI, vaki ON
walk	ganga ON
walked	gekk OI, gekk ON
walrus-tusk	tannskeftan OI, tannskeftan ON
wares	vara OI, vara ON, varnað OI, varnað ON, varning OI, varning ON, varningi ON, varninginn OI, varninginum OI, varninginum ON, varningr ON, varningurinn OI
warlike	ófriði OI, ófriði ON
warlock-songs	varðlokur OI, varðlokur ON
warrior-king	herkonungr ON
war-slings	valslöngur OI, valslöngur ON
war-taken	hertekinn OI, hertekinn ON, herteknir OI, herteknir ON
was	enn OI, enn ON, er OI, er ON, gerði OI, gerði ON, gerist OI, gert OI, gert ON, hét ON, stóð OI, sú OI, væri OI, væri ON, var OI, var ON, varð OI, varð ON, varstu OI, varstu ON, váru ON, vas ON, vera OI, vera ON, verða OI, voru OI
was-called	hét ON
was-carried	bar ON
was-done	gert ON
was-named	hét OI, hét ON, héti OI, héti ON
was-not	eigi OI, eigi ON
water	vatn OI, vatn ON, vatni OI, vatni ON
water-taken	vatnað OI, vatnat ON

The Vinland Sagas — Word List (English to Norse)

English	Norse
waved	veift ON
waving	veift OI, veift ON
way	hætti OI, hætti ON, háttr ON, háttur OI, leið OI, leið ON, leiðar OI, leiðar ON, veg OI, veg ON, vegir OI, vegir ON
ways	megin OI, megin ON, vega OI, vega ON, vegna OI, vegna ON
we	okkr ON, okkur OI, oss OI, oss ON, várum ON, vér OI, vér ON, við OI, vit ON
wealth	fé OI, fé ON, féið OI, féit ON, fjár OI, fjár ON
wealthy	auðigr ON, auðigur OI, stórauðigr ON, stórauðigur OI, vellauðigur OI
weapon	vápn ON, vopn OI
weapons	vápn ON, vápnin ON, vopn OI, vopnin OI
we-are	erum OI, erum ON, vér OI, vér ON
wearied	mæddir OI
weather	veðr ON, veðrátta OI, veðrátta ON, veðri OI, veðri ON, veður OI
weathered	veðrs OI, veðrs ON
wedding	brúðhlaup OI, brúðkaup ON, brúðlaup ON, brullaup OI, brullaup ON
week	vika OI, vika ON
weeks	vikur OI, vikur ON
welcomed	fagnað OI, fagnat ON
well	heil OI, heil ON, með ON, vel OI, vel ON
well-built	vexti OI, vexti ON
well-educated	menntr ON
wellspring	keldu OI, keldu ON
well-tempered	skapgott OI, skapgott ON
went	færðu OI, færðu ON, fara OI, fer OI, fór OI, fór ON, fórst OI, fórst ON, fóru OI, fóru ON, ganga OI, ganga ON, gekk OI, gekk ON, gengr ON, gengu OI, gengu ON, gengur OI, kómust ON, réðst OI, réðst ON
were	að OI, at ON, er OI, er ON, eru OI, eru ON, væri OI, væri ON, væru OI, var OI, var ON, varð OI, varð ON, váru ON, vera OI, vera ON, verða ON, verðr ON, voru OI, voruð OI
were-found	fundust ON
west	vestan OI, vestan ON, vestr ON, vestur OI
western	vestan OI, vestan ON, vestri OI, vestri ON
west-raiding	vestrvíking ON, vesturvíking OI
westward	vestarlega OI, vestarliga ON
westwards	vestrætt ON, vesturátt OI
west-wind	vestanveðr ON
wet	vát ON, vot OI
whale	hval OI, hval ON, hvala ON, hvalinn OI, hvalinn ON, hvalur OI
whales	hvalnum OI
what	að OI, hvað OI, hvað ON, hvat ON, hvert OI
what-was	vár ON, vor OI
wheat	hveiti OI, hveitiax ON
wheat-acres	hveitiakra OI, hveitiakra ON, hveitiakrar OI, hveitiakrar ON
when	en OI, en ON, er OI, er ON, hvenær OI, þá OI, þá ON, þegar OI, þegar ON
where	er OI, er ON, es ON, hvar OI, hvar ON, hvert OI, hvert ON, sem OI, sem ON, þar OI, þar ON

The Vinland Sagas — Word List (English to Norse)

English	Norse
wherever	sem OI, sem ON
whether	hvárt ON, hvort OI
which	að OI, at ON, en OI, er OI, er ON, es ON, hvert OI, hvert ON, sé ON, sem OI, sem ON
while	en OI, en ON, meðan OI, meðan ON, sem OI, sem ON, stund OI, stund ON
whip	svipu OI, svipu ON
white	hvít ON, hvítan OI, hvítan ON, hvítir OI, hvítir ON, hvítt OI, hvítum OI, hvítum ON
White-Leg (name)	hvítbeins OI, hvítbeins ON
White-Man-Land (place)	hvítramannaland OI, hvítramannaland ON
who	er OI, er ON, hver OI, hver ON, hverr ON, sem OI, sem ON
whole	heil OI, heil ON, heilu OI, heilu ON
who-was	er ON
why	hví OI, hví ON
wide	breiðu OI, breiðu ON, víðar ON
widely	víða OI, víða ON
wife	kona OI, kona ON, konu OI, konu ON
wild-animals	dýr OI, dýr ON, dýrin OI, dýrin ON, dýrum OI, dýrum ON
wild-birds	fugl OI
wilderness	öræfi OI
will	mun OI, mun ON, vár ON, velja OI, velja ON, vil OI, vil ON, vilda ON, vildi OI, vildi ON, vili ON, vilið ON, vilja OI, vilja ON, vilji OI, viljið OI, viljir OI, vill OI, vill ON, vilt OI, vor OI
will-be	hallist OI, verði OI, verði ON
willed	vildi OI, vildi ON, vildu OI, vildu ON, vilja OI, vilja ON, viljað OI, viljat ON, vill OI, vill ON
willing	fús OI, fúss ON, vildi ON, vildu OI, vildu ON, vilja OI, vilja ON
wills	vill OI, vill ON
will-you	vilir ON, villtu ON, viltu OI, viltu ON
wind	byr ON, veðr ON, veðrið OI, veðrit ON, vinda OI, vinda ON
winds	veðr ON, veður OI
wine	vín OI, vín ON
winter	vetr ON, vetra OI, vetra ON, vetrar OI, vetrar ON, vetri OI, vetri ON, vetrinn ON, vetrum OI, vetrum ON, vetrvist ON, vetur OI, veturinn OI, veturnætur OI, veturvist OI, veturvistar OI
wintered	vetr ON, vetur OI
winters	vetrum OI, vetrum ON
wisdom	fræði OI, fræði ON
wise	fróðir OI, fróðir ON, fróðr ON, fróður OI, víst OI, víst ON, vitr ON, vitur OI
wiser	fróðari OI
wise-woman	vísendakonunni ON, vísindakonunni OI
wish	annt OI, annt ON, vilda ON, vildi OI
wished	skyldi OI, vilda ON, vildi OI, vildi ON, vili ON, vilji OI, vill OI, vill ON
wishing	annt OI
with	á OI, með OI, með ON, við OI, við ON, vit ON
withdrawn	fálátari OI
within	innan OI, innan ON
without-gladness	óglaðari OI, óglaðari ON
without-mountains	ófjöllótt OI, ófjöllótt ON
without-peace	ófriðr ON, ófriður OI
without-quality	gæðalaust OI, gæðalaust ON
without-supplies	óbirgir OI, óbirgir ON
withstood	stóð OI, stóðst ON
woke	vakði ON, vakti OI

The Vinland Sagas — Word List (English to Norse)

English	Norse
woman	kona OI, kona ON, konan OI, konan ON, konu OI, konu ON, konum ON, kvenna OI, kvenna ON
women	konum OI, konum ON, konur OI, konur ON
won	unnu OI, unnu ON, vann OI, vann ON
wonder	undrast OI
wonderful	kynlegr OI, kynligr ON
wood	tré OI, tré ON, við OI, við ON, viði OI, viði ON, viðu OI, viðu ON
woods	skógi OI, skógi ON, skóginn OI, skóginn ON, viði OI, viði ON
word	orð OI, orð ON, orðið OI, orðit ON
words	orð OI, orð ON, orða OI, orða ON, orði OI, orði ON, orðum ON
work	verk OI, verk ON
working	unnið OI
worm-eaten	maðksmogið OI
worn	væstir ON
worse	verra OI, verra ON, verri OI, verri ON
worst	verra OI
worth	verðr ON, verður OI
worthiness	mannvirðingar OI, mannvirðingar ON, virðingar OI, virðingar ON, virðingarráð OI, virðingarráð ON, virðingu OI, virðingu ON
worthy	vert OI, vert ON
would	mun OI, mun ON, mundi OI, mundi ON, mundu OI, mundu ON, muni OI, myndi ON, myndu OI, skyldu OI, skyldu ON, væri OI, væri ON, vildu ON, vilja OI, vilja ON
would-be	mun OI, mun ON, mundi OI, mundu OI, mundu ON, væri OI, væri ON, værir OI, værir ON, væru OI, væru ON
wound	sár OI, sár ON, sári ON
wounded	sárir OI, sárir ON
woundingly	sárlega OI, sárliga ON
wounds	sár ON, sárir OI, sárir ON
wretched	vesæll OI, vesall ON
wrote	orta ON, orti OI, orti ON

Y, y

English	Norse
yet	á OI, á ON, enn OI, enn ON, þó OI, þó ON
Yngvild (name)	yngveldar OI, yngvildar ON
you	þeir OI, þér OI, þér ON, þið OI, þig OI, þik ON, þinn OI, þinn ON, þit ON, þú OI, þú ON, yðr ON, yður OI, yðvar OI, yðvar ON, ykkar OI, ykkr ON, ykkrar ON, ykkur OI, ykkur ON
young	ung OI, ung ON, unga OI, unga ON
younger	ungur OI
young-men	sveina ON, sveinana OI, sveinana ON, sveinanna OI
your	þín OI, þín ON, þínum OI, þínum ON, þitt OI, þitt ON, yðvar OI, yðvarr ON, ykkur OI
yours	þik ON, þín ON, þínir OI, þínir ON, þinn OI, þinn ON, þinnar OI, þinnar ON, þinni OI, þinni ON, þíns OI, þíns ON, þitt OI, þitt ON, yður OI, yður ON, yðvar OI, yðvar ON, yðvarr ON
you-two	þið OI, þit ON

The Vinland Sagas *Word List (English to Norse)*

English	Norse
Yule (name)	jól OI, jól ON, jólin OI, jólin ON, jólum OI, jólum ON
yule-feast	jólaveizlu ON
Yule-Feast (name)	jólaveislu OI